MARIANNE VAN DEN BOOMEN
TRANSCODING THE DIGITAL
HOW METAPHORS MATTER IN NEW MEDIA

Theory on Demand #14
Transcoding the Digital: How Metaphors Matter in New Media

Author: Marianne van den Boomen
Editorial support: Miriam Rasch
Design and DTP: Katja van Stiphout
Publisher: Institute of Network Cultures, Amsterdam 2014
Printer: 'Print on Demand'
First 200 copies printed at Drukkerij Steenman, Enkhuizen
ISBN: 978-90-818575-7-4

Earlier and different versions of Chapter 2 has been published in 2008 as 'Interfacing by Iconic Metaphors', in *Configurations* 16 (1): 33-55, and in 2009 as 'Interfacing by Material Metaphors: How Your Mailbox May Fool You', in *Digital Material: Tracing New Media in Everyday Life and Technology*, edited by Marianne van den Boomen, Sybille Lammes, Ann-Sophie Lehmann, Joost Raessens, and Mirko Tobias Schäfer. Amsterdam: Amsterdam University Press, p. 253-266.
An earlier and different version of Chapter 6 has been published in 2006 as 'Transcoding Metaphors after the Mediatic Turn', in *SPIEL* 25 (h.1): 47-58.

Contact
Institute of Network Cultures
Phone: +31 20 5951865
Email: info@networkcultures.org
Web: http://www.networkcultures.org

This publication is available through various print on demand services.
For more information, and a freely downloadable PDF:
http://networkcultures.org/publications

This publication is licensed under the Creative Commons
Attribution-NonCommercial-NoDerivatives 4.0 International (CC BY-NC-SA 4.0).

TRANSCODING THE DIGITAL
HOW METAPHORS MATTER IN NEW MEDIA

De transcodering van het digitale
Hoe metaforen ertoe doen in nieuwe media
(met een samenvatting in het Nederlands)

PROEFSCHRIFT

ter verkrijging van de graad van doctor aan de Universiteit Utrecht
op gezag van de rector magnificus, prof.dr. G.J. van der Zwaan, ingevolge
het besluit van het college voor promoties in het openbaar te verdedigen
op woensdag 12 februari 2014 des middags te 12.45 uur

door
Marianne Veronica Theresia van den Boomen
geboren op 28 november 1955 te Den Haag

Promotoren: Prof.dr. J.F.F. Raessens
Prof.dr. J. de Mul
Prof.dr. C.M. Slade

Copromotor: Dr. S. Lammes

CONTENTS

ACKNOWLEDGMENTS It takes a network	9
INTRODUCTION Metaphor, meaning, and code	12
1 — Where is my mail?	13
2 — The riddle of digital praxis	17
Transcoding the digital	
Translations in actor-networks	
Material semiotics	
3 — Metaphors we compute by	23
Overview of the chapters	
CHAPTER 1: INTERFACING BY INDEXICAL ICONS How your mailbox may fool you	27
1 — Interfaces, machines, and digits	28
A computer is not a coffee machine	
A computer is not a pianola	
The screen sucks	
Iconic condensation	
2 — Between iconicity and indexicality	37
Firstness, Secondness, and Thirdness	
Indexical symbols with virtual objects	
Tools ready-to-hand and present-at-hand	
3 — Conceptual metaphor	43
Sources, targets, and black boxes	
CHAPTER 2: MATERIAL METAPHORS How objects turn into social organizers	48
1 — Levels of materiality	48
2 — Material metaphor	50
Travels, roads, and maps	
Media-Specific Analysis	
Material-metaphorical networks	
Metaphor and indexicality revisited	
3 — Metaphorical objects in anthropology	58
Knives, pots, and villages	
Material metaphors as social organizers	
4 — Contemporary scripted objects	62
Doors, keys, and shavers	
Scripted objects versus material metaphors	
Disciplining artifacts and informational objects	
5 — Digital-material metaphors	67

Files, forums, and tweets
  Material metaphor analysis

CHAPTER 3: MEDIATION BY METONYMY AND METAPHOR   72
How media multiply and dissolve
1 – What do we call a medium?   73
  Media metonyms
  Discourse metaphors of media
2 – Metaphors of processing   79
  Media as membrane
  Media as master
  Spaces of media
  Media ecology
3 – Metaphors of transmission   89
  Media as channel
  The conduit discourse
  The toolmakers paradigm
4 – Metaphors of storage   96
  Media as container
  The inscription discourse

CHAPTER 4: IMMEDIACY BY METAPHOR   103
How mediation becomes invisible
1 – The desire for immediacy   103
  Closing the gap
  Transparent immediacy
2 – Windows, mirrors, and tools   108
  Virtual windows
  Multiple digital windows
  Windows and mirrors
  Mirrors or tools
3 – Remediating immediacy   115
  No remediation without demediation
  Aggressive remediation
4 – Remediation revisited   120
  Remediation produces media
  Transmediation beyond media
  Trajectories of digital transmediation

CHAPTER 5: CODE RULES   128
How software matters and metaphorizes
1 – The political history of software   128
  Commanding girls or computers
  Software as (forgotten) labor
  Software as ideology
  Software politics
2 – Coding digits, objects, and concepts   136
  Software as numbers
  Software as language

       Software as objects
       Software as prescription
       Software as battlefield
       Software as translator
3 — Digital-material coding and transcoding   150
       The materiality of software
       Inside the machine
       Outside the machine
4 — Repositioning materiality   154
       Software as material metaphor

CHAPTER 6: TRANSCODING THE SOCIAL INTO NETWORKS   158
How the digital gets socialized
1 — The virtual community metaphor   158
       Community as village
       Community discourse
2 — The Web 2.0 metaphor   162
       Web 2.0 as software upgrade
       Web 2.0 as sharing and linking
       Web 2.0 as harnessing and harvesting
3 — Recounting the web   165
       Web 1.1: Scripting the web
       Web 1.2: Extending the hyperlink
       Decentered spaces and socialities
4 — Network metaphors   170
       The telegraph and the nervous system
       Electronic highway
       Cyberspace imagery
       The network graph
5 — This is not a network   180
       Net-works, work-nets, and mobility
       Control by protocol

CONCLUSIONS: A MANIFESTO FOR HACKING METAPHORS   186
How metaphors matter in digital praxis
1 — What metaphors are not   187
       Metaphors are never just metaphorical
2 — Tracing digital-material metaphors   188
       Go beyond conceptual metaphors
       Material metaphors transfer, translate, and transform
3 — Hacking digital matters of fact   190
       Hack the icontology of interfacial immediacy
       Hack software ideology and its metaphors

References   195

Samenvatting   211

Curriculum Vitae   220

ACKNOWLEDGMENTS
IT TAKES A NETWORK

It takes a network to raise a PhD thesis, as everyone who ever did so, knows. During the years it took me to put this thing together, many people, from many different angles, clubs, and gatherings, on many different occasions, chipped in, sometimes without even knowing it.

Let me start with those who did know what this was supposed to be, even before I knew it myself. I am deeply indebted to the people at the Faculty of the Humanities, at the Institute for Cultural Inquiry (ICON), and at the Department for Media and Culture Studies (MCW) for creating the best job in the world. Thank you for hiring me as a so-called 50/50 teacher-researcher in the New Media and Digital Culture (NMDC) program, for your patience, and for your generous support that enabled me to visit several international conferences and to publish finally this book.

The best job in the world would be nothing without inspiring co-workers. In the NMDC staff I also found the best colleagues in the world. Thank you for being such a lovely, supporting, smart, critical, hard working, and life-enjoying bunch of people: Marinka Copier, Isabella van Elferen, Karin van Es, René Glas, Cris van der Hoek, Selene Kolman, Erna Kotkamp, Michiel de Lange, Ann-Sophie Lehmann, Johannes Paßmann, Thomas Poell, Joost Raessens, Indira Reynaert, Martina Roepke, and Tom van de Wetering. Special and warm kudos should go to my 50/50 fellows who soon became true friends, Mirko Tobias Schäfer and Imar de Vries. Our revels were fabulous and I deeply enjoyed our debates, drinks, dinners, seminars, travels, gossip, and jokes. You rock!

The MCW network is larger than new media studies. I learned a lot from my colleagues at gender studies, at seminars on posthumanism and new materialism, and while developing interdisciplinary courses: Cecilia Åsberg, Rosi Braidotti, Rosemarie Buikema, Sanne Koevoets, Kathrin Thiele, Iris van der Tuin, Berteke Waaldijk, and Doro Wiese. The same holds for the MCW media seminars, where I argued with inspiring colleagues from film and television studies about what a medium actually is and why the screen sucks: Rick Dolphijn, Chiel Kattenbelt, Frank Kessler, Eggo Müller, and Nanna Verhoeff.

The 50/50 position implied a lot of teaching, which has been a challenge as well as a great pleasure. I have met many great students that baffled me with their insights, ideas, and questions, of whom I can only mention a few: Koen Leurs, Elize de Mul, Shirley Niemans, Levien Nordeman, Tijmen Schep, and Tom van de Wetering.

At the Philosophy department in Rotterdam I found a hospitable academic home when I was still a nomadic PhD wannabee. At seminars and staff meetings there I had the honor to witness and partake in the wildest debates masterminded by this remarkable crowd of philosophers: Wim van Binsbergen, Bibi van den Berg, Ger Groot, Niels Helsloot, Jeroen van den Hoven, Jos de Mul, André Nusselder, Elke Müller, Henk Oosterling, and Awee Prins. There, I also found my supervisor Jos de Mul, who believed in me right from the start, and whose never ending warm support and wise comments kept me on the right track.

I am also much indebted to my supervisors in Utrecht. Christina Slade, with her amazing ability to pair the strictest analytical philosophy with wild creative thinking, guided me through the development of my argument. Joost Raessens, with his equally amazing ability to combine pragmatism with playfulness and Deleuzian philosophy, was extremely helpful in the last phase, and sharpened my thoughts on what my research was actually about. Sybille Lammes, my co-promotor, has been a generous sparring partner during all those years and taught me a lot about the finesses of actor-network theory and digital cartography.

My gratitude also goes to the people who put together the last pieces into a book published by the Institute of Network Cultures. Thank you Geert Lovink, Miriam Rasch, and Katja van Stiphout for your enthusiasm and careful handling of my stuff.

There are many people who commented on various proposals, drafts, random ideas, bold claims, articles, and presentations, in various phases of my PhD trajectory. I especially want to pay tribute to Marijke Ekelschot, Theo Hug, Frank Kessler, Bernhard Rieder, Anneke Smelik, and William Uricchio for their valuable comments on very early try-outs.

I also want to thank the smart and kind people of the informal clubs of which I am proud to be a member. It is hard to say whether these clubs are communities or social networks, but luckily they have names. First of all, the Media Ladies: Irene Costera Meijer, Joke Hermes, and Garjan Sterk. Thank you Ladies, for your great insights in media trends, for the fun we have at our dinner meetings, and for your friendship and support.

Then there is the Internet Club: Justine Pardoen, Henk Boeke, Niels Helsloot, Peter Olsthoorn, and Louis Stiller. And the Metaphor Club: Charles Forceville, Ilna Hellsten, Jozef Keulartz, Chung-lin Kwa, and Cor van der Weele. Thank you all for your spicy comments on raw and cooked ideas and for sharing your knowledge with me.

I am also indebted to the inspiring people I met in the early years of the Digital City. This is where my thinking about digital-material metaphors all started, thanks to you: Rop Gonggrijp, Christine Karman, Steven Lenos, Geert Lovink, Erik van den Muijzenberg, Caroline Nevejan, Felipe Rodriquez, Karin Spaink, and Marleen Stikker.

The strongest networks are often also the oldest. After more than 35 years I still have my psychology mates around. As 'Eating Women' (evolved from the feminist Reading Group, years before Women's Studies emerged) we gather every six weeks in order to eat, talk, drink, and discuss life's issues. I am happy to have such a bunch of faithful girlfriends, thank you for being there, in good times and bad times: Dymf van Berkel, Erica de Bruïne, Inge Meyer, Leonore Nicolai, Liesbeth Niessen, Ellen Snel, and Elly Vos. I especiallly want to thank Dymf van Berkel, once my psychology teacher, now a dear friend, for opening up her house so hospitably not only for the famous Utrecht Ladies Salon de Bonbon, but also for my PhD reception.

Kudos should also go to the flamboyant feminist activists of the UVEZ (Utrechtse Vrouwen voor Economische Zelfstandigheid), also known as the Society for the Preservation of the Fruit Hat. Always ready to take action, with or without fedoras or fruit hats. You keep me going and make me laugh: Nelleke Altena, Ingrid Baart, Dymf van Berkel, Agaath Beuk, Wil Bom, Els Diekerhof, Marjet Douze, Corrie van Eijl, Marian de Groot, and Trees Limburg.

Sometimes powerful networks do not look like a network at all. Sometimes they take the form of a person, embodying a material metaphor that articulates an assemblage of wisdom, good food, experience, practical advise, fun, long walks and long talks. Usually such people are called friends. I want to express my special gratitude to dear old friends who nurtured my intellectual unfolding during the last three to four decades: Jos van der Lans, Peter van Lieshout, Annemarie Mol, and Ben Smit.

Many other friends were also part of the network that raised me and my thesis. Thank you for your good company, support, and friendship: Marja Bosma, Lidi Bosman, Els Bransen, Mirjam de Klerk, Anet Klinkert, Daan Landsmeer, Hans Landsmeer, Marja de Lint, Marja Metten, Antoine Verbij, and Stella Werner.

Networks that raise a PhD thesis do not only consist of people. They also consist of things: books, articles, libraries, laptops, and note books of course, and in my case also numerous packets of Samson and bottles of Campari. Credits should also go to the open-source software that collected my thoughts (KeyNote), my writing (LibreOffice), my mail (Thunderbird), my browsing (Firefox), and my resources (Zotero), plus other digital-material entities: the Nettime mailing list, the Usenet groups dds.technopolis and xs4all.mediacul, and several blogs and repositories.

Since the summer of 2011 my support network had to be enlarged with doctors, nurses, physiotherapists, nurse practitioners, pills, chemos, and CT scans – thank you for keeping me alive and kicking thus far.

No network can do without a home base. My home is a special home, a network in itself, built, inhabited, and sustained by about forty adults and children. A true community, including all the hassle that comes with maintaining the building, the garden, and general consensus. Dear housemates, thank you all for your collective and personal efforts that make this into a home.

The three that tack together a household with me of course stand out. They endured my hasty meals and my complaints about written words that do not behave in accordance with my thoughts. Neighbor and friend Nelleke Altena, better in taking care of others than of herself, thank you for your diligence and pertinent insights. And last but not least, Piet Zweers, love of my life, personal musical and philosophical master, and best friend forever, and Masja Zweers, our smart, strong, kind, and beautiful daughter. My dears, I dedicate this one to you.

Utrecht, 26 January 2014

INTRODUCTION
METAPHOR, MEANING, AND CODE

Perhaps more than any other communication medium, the coherence of the Internet relies on a set of imaginary beliefs held together by neologisms, metaphors, and other tropes of language.
(David Trend, 2001)

Metaphors are heuristic tools.
(Douwe Draaisma, 2000)

For more than a decade, new media have not been considered brand-new anymore. And perhaps they are not even seen as media anymore. Although new media scholars continue to use these terms to refer to their academic discipline, it is widely acknowledged that the Internet, once considered a new separate world called cyberspace, has been 'slouching towards the ordinary' (Herring 2004). Internet activities are nowadays so deeply embedded in daily practices that we barely realize we interact with media and operate machines. We just do our thing. We mail, we chat, we tweet, we search, we browse.

We also barely realize that all the above terms are metaphorical. Verbs such as 'mailing', 'chatting' and even 'searching' are taken for granted but when we look at these terms more closely, we see that they are metaphors for particular things we do online. Or better, for particular things we let our computers do online. These things or acts have no proper names to differentiate and identify them, as they consist of changing and exchanging digital code, that is, patterns of zeros and ones inside machines. In fact, even the very notion of 'zeros' and 'ones' is metaphorical, since computers do not recognize numbers, but just different voltage states.

We only have to consider our daily encounters with our computer to observe the use of metaphors everywhere: mailbox, file drawer, photo album, media player, buttons, menus, and so on. While digital code often confronts us with all kinds of problems and riddles regarding its articulations and effects, the assigned metaphors are usually considered unproblematic, or at least of a secondary order. We rarely have any second thoughts about a smart phone with a separate telephone icon, or about metaphorical constructions such as 'voice mail' and 'electronic ink', let alone about the simple notion of email. After all, if your mail is not working properly, you do not ask yourself whether the metaphor of email as derived from postal mail is appropriate or not. You just want your problem to be fixed.

The important point to note here is that the very way of defining problems and imagining possible solutions is channeled by the manner in which digital code is represented to us. This is the case not only at the level of the user interface, but also in social discourse. At both levels it seems that the practice of digital code exchange can only be articulated, perceived, and conceived when it is translated into metaphors. That is, translated into terms imported and transferred from elsewhere, as in the classic Aristotelian definition of metaphor.[1] If metaphors structurally encapsulate digital practices, we may wonder what they exactly do to our understanding of digital code, and what this means for digital code's far reaching implications for culture and society. This study probes this hypothesis by tracking down metaphors in digital practices. It investigates how they shape and transform digital practices and social ordering, and vice versa.

It should be clear that tracing metaphors in digital practices will lead us to and through various levels, themes, and issues. To show in a preliminary, very condensed form the issues that are at stake, I will start with a short story, an anecdote that contains pointers to practically all the themes we will encounter in this study. This small narrative is more than just an example of ordinary digital practice that involves metaphors; it serves as an allegory for the entire study.

1 — WHERE IS MY MAIL?

Sometime in 1997, a friend of mine was having problems with her brand new cable connection. It has just been installed. Knowing that I was one of those people who take great pleasure in fooling around with computers, she asked me if I could have a look. Her computer was already on, and when she clicked on her email icon an empty inbox showed up. She said, "You see, no mail. And I'm sure I have mail; I forwarded some from my office. The mechanic who did the installation yesterday said everything was working – 'just click and go, ma'am'. But where is my mail? It should be in the inbox, right? Or may be elsewhere on my computer, but where?"

"Okay," I said, "First, are you sure you are online?"

She motioned to the wires. They were hanging chaotically all over the place. The tangled wires snaked down the hallway up the wall to the ceiling where they dangled down to her desk and her computer. Looking overhead, I prayed these wires were okay. In any case, I was not referring to the hardware and cables, I was referring to the software configuration. There was a network icon on her desktop, represented by the image of a telephone connecting

---

1. The most commonly used definition of metaphor is stating one thing in terms of another. In his *Poetics*, Aristotle wrote that 'a metaphor is a carrying over of a word belonging to something else, from genus to species, from species to genus, from species to species, or by analogy' (Aristotle 1996 [328 BC], 52). It should be noted that in the present study, the take on metaphor departs from the usual distinction between metaphor (as based on resemblance, similarity, or comparison) and metonymy (as based on proximity, contiguity). In order to trace the mechanisms of any kind of metaphorical transference, the working definition used in this study also subsumes analogy, metonymy, synecdoche, and compressed simile, thus including any trope that evokes condensation, displacement, or replacement. See also Goossens (1990) who proposes the hybrid tropical concept of 'metaphtonymy.'

In metaphor theory, spawn from rhetorics, poetics, and linguistics, several definitions of metaphor circulate. Metaphor is usually described as a directed relation between two semantic domains, dubbed by different terms: principal and subsidiary subject, focus and frame, tenor and vehicle, lexicon and predicate, source and target. Various foundational relations has been proposed as the heart of metaphor: substitution (Aristotle 328 BC), comparison, interaction (Richards 1936, Black 1962), and tension (Ricoeur 1975). More recent is the so called Conceptual Theory of Metaphor based on mapping (Lakoff and Johnson 1980, Lakoff 1993) and blending (Fauconnier and Turner 2003).

two computers.² Fortunately, her network connection turned out to be correctly configured with the right network protocols, the right IP address for her provider, the right login name, and the right password. Only a double-click was necessary to establish her connection. After she clicked the 'get mail' button in her mail program, a stream of mail flowed into her inbox. "That's it," I said. "You first have to connect to the Internet with that icon."
My friend was puzzled. "That telephone icon? I used that before, to dial up my provider, but now I have a permanent connection. Just like I have at work, and there, I always see my mail immediately in my inbox without having to click on anything. I don't even have a telephone icon."
I was able to explain that. "Apparently your computer at work is configured that way. That telephone icon stands for any kind of connection whether it is a dial-up telephone line or a cable connection. But you can bypass it. It is possible to connect automatically to your provider as soon as you start your computer or your mail program. It is also possible to get your mail as soon as you start your mail program. We can arrange that, if you want."
And so we did.

That was all. While computer problems often cost hours of trial and error to solve them, here we had a clear and explicable problem. Just one small conceptual error, the overlooking of a small hidden step between actually connecting to the Internet Service Provider and bringing in the mail from the mail server. Yet, the story is typical for how human-computer interaction works, how it often fails to work, and how all this is intertwined with the ambivalent but stable instability of digital-symbolical objects, material configurations, and, most of all, hidden steps in between. This story also shows how these hidden steps that lie in between can be brought to the fore by focusing on the metaphors, and tracing their various connections – to human interpreters and digital-material networks, and to the social and discursive machinery in which both are implicated. We can preliminary identify several issues in this short narrative that we encounter when we follow the trail of metaphors.

Reification by metaphor
The two digital-symbolical objects at stake here ('mailbox' and 'connection button') are formatted as metaphors. Email is derived from postal mail. It is delivered like regular mail in a mailbox, as if there is a physical container where email messages are stored. The act of connecting to an ISP is metaphorized into an icon depicting a telephone device. Reading and using these interface metaphors requires a precarious balance between, on the one hand, being able to recognize their compressed metaphoricity that stands in for a complex dynamic machinery, and on the other

---

2. Over the years the Windows display of the network connection icon has transformed, until it 'vanished into everywhere' (Stoter 2009). While it started with the image of a plain *telephone device* in Windows 3.11, it evolved in Windows 95 into a more appropriate *telephone modem*, and finally with Windows XP into an abstract device, standing for any kind of connection whether by a telephone modem, a cable modem or a wireless connection. After the advent of broadband and always-on configurations (Windows 2000, Windows Vista), the icon vanished completely from the desktop. The average current Internet user would most likely be unable to interpret the telephone icon as a network connection since most users are unfamiliar today with the older more cumbersome dial up accounts. Telephone icons are currently used for other applications, such as voice over IP, or it can also be used to indicate the plain voice telephone function on a smart phone.

hand, being able to forget this, that is, reify the metaphor and take it as a thing in itself.
My friend was stuck in the latter mode, and confused the icons with a thing-like ontology. She took the mailbox for the mail itself and the telephone icon for using the telephone itself, thereby ignoring the machinery in between that has to be set in motion. In fact, she seemed to assume that having a permanent Internet connection meant that you could teleport mail directly from PC to PC.
It is tempting to say that my friend took the icons too literally, but we could just as well say that she did not take them literally enough. After all, she had no mail because no postman was instructed to deliver it. However, parsing the metaphor in a supposed literal versus a figural meaning is of limited help when meaning is entangled with digital code.[3]

The shining and blinding screen
The metaphorical and symbolical representations on the screen provide the user with an interface that enables operating the machine, yet at the same time it channels attention away from the machinery. The expression 'See, no mail', alludes to the dominance of vision and pictorial visualization in contemporary computing. What you see, is what you get, which suggests that, that is all there is to get. The machinery gets reduced to the screen, or better, to the representations on the screen. No screen representation, then no reminder and no inducement to act. No telephone icon, then no urge to establish a network connection. In the name of user-friendliness, the user is actually deterred from knowledge and access to the inner workings of the machine and its software. The screen shows but also blinds.
Moreover, since offline as well as online practices are represented on the same local screen, the difference between being offline and being online easily gets lost. 'Where is my mail?' asked my friend, convinced that it was in any case somewhere on her computer. That was the case during the 1990s, when pop mail was common. Pop mail was a mail transfer protocol that physically transferred mail to your own computer. Nowadays, after the silent switch from pop mail to cloud mail – where the mail remains on a server somewhere 'in the cloud', although it shows on the screen as if it resides locally on your computer – the question 'where is my mail?' is even more urgent. Unfortunately, this question only tends to pop up in cases of network breakdown, and is by far asked too infrequently when everything is working properly.

Meaning that matters
The icons not only represent a conceptual metaphor, they also refer materially to performing code. This code is, in the last instance, unambiguous, insensitive to human meaning and interpre-

---

3. Of course, the distinction between the literal and figural can be useful in specific practical contexts. Sometimes possible misinterpretations of metaphors can be corrected by an explicit demarcation between the literal and the figural meaning: 'And I mean this literally', or, conversely, 'This is of course figuratively spoken, a metaphor.' Helpful as this maybe in avoiding confusion, the distinction is contested in metaphor theory. While interactionist metaphor theoretician Max Black (1962) posits that metaphors acquire their meaning from the distinction and interaction between the literal and figural, Donald Davidson (1978) insists that there is no such thing as an 'other' extra figurative meaning – mobilizing the literal suffices to explain the metaphorical. For Davidson, metaphors are not cognitive linguistic entities but rather speech acts: 'What distinguishes metaphor is not meaning but use – in this it is like assertion, hinting, lying, promising, or criticizing' (Davidson 1978, 43).

tation – it just runs, or not. Without the right computational command there will be no mail. One can delegate such a command to the machine by configuring it ('connect to my provider as soon as the computer starts'), but in any case an explicit command is required in order to accomplish a meaningful act.

This shows that the meaning of a digital-metaphorical object is not only a cognitive, conceptual issue that resides in the mind of the human actor, but that its meaning also has non-human components. For the machinery, meaning is something that *matters* – literally, in the form of material enactments that set in motion specific strings of code, translating and inscribing them into machine states. Mail is not teleported from PC to PC, from an outbox here to an inbox there; it first has to be materially transferred and translated before it emerges as a meaningful object in someone's mailbox. Multiple instances of processing, transferring, and storing go on inside the machine and the network we call the Internet in order to finally deliver a specific product or effect that is represented on the screen.

The desire for immediacy

The fourth theme that can be identified in this little story concerns the withdrawal of mediation as articulated in the discourse of immediacy: the desire for an instant result, as effortlessly as possible. Sent mail is supposed to arrive immediately in the inbox, without any fuss. Always-on means 'just click and go, ma'am', nowadays extended to 'just swipe and tap.'

Taking into consideration the issues regarding computational referencing and the machinery of transferences, this discourse of immediacy is necessarily a matter of ideology, aimed at making invisible what counts, what computes, what mediates, and what materializes behind the screens. While the productivity of the shiny screen of representation and reification pushes itself to the fore, an unacknowledged black box is working hard in the background to accomplish numerous invisible transferences.

Forgetting software

The productivity of interface metaphors does not only reside in what they show, it also resides in what they hide. They enable human beings to operate the machine, precisely by obscuring its inner workings as driven by software. Interface metaphors such as 'mailbox' or 'document' let us forget the software that is operating behind the screen, and this may affect our ability to operate the machine.

The tendency to forget software can also be found in another, more hidden, metaphor that plays a role in this small story. This concerns the notion of 'being online'. My friend's first association with 'being online' was with the cable stuff in her room, and no wonder. Although barely recognized as a metaphor, 'being online' imports an image of lines and cables as network connections – that is, a matter of hardware, not software. Paradoxically, the recognition of hardware does not initiate a more material perspective, since by the same movement hardware gets black-boxed, and hence can be dismissed easily. After all, 'that man said everything is working fine.' While metaphors let us forget software, software lets us forget hardware and physical networks.

Social transference and delegation

Finally, the story also tells us something about social transference. That is, transference as an act of delegation, the outsourcing of particular acts or specific labor. My friend delegated the technical hardware installation to a professional and asked me to have a look at her computer. In principle, delegation saves time and effort, but it usually comes with a price, such as money, the loss of direct control and autonomy, and the preclusion of knowledge. Delegation and the division of labor — either between humans or between humans and machines — obviously has significant implications for social ordering. It was no coincidence, in my friend's case, that the technician who installed her computer was male. The classical labor division based on gender is still persistent and even increasing in computing and software (Valenduc et al. 2004).

Overall there are several levels on which transferences are at work: cognitive, semantic-metaphorical, mechanical, digital, and social. And probably also between those levels. The hidden machinery of human-computer interaction turns out to be an intricate chain of layers and nests of heterogeneous transferences.

These are the main themes that can be distilled from the story of my friend. These themes will be examined more closely and will be further elaborated on in this study. While this particular anecdote seems to be rather time-bound to the state of affairs in the late 1990s, the themes are certainly not outdated. On the contrary, these issues are currently even more urgent with the advent of 'the cloud' and always-on devices such as smart phones and tablet computers. These developments reinforce all the more the discourse of immediacy, the forgetting of software, and the beclouding of digital-material and other transferences.

All that is solid seems to melt in the cloud. It is time we get a grip on the practices that so deeply configure the way we live, think, and act. In the next section, I will address how this study will deal with this challenge.

2 — THE RIDDLE OF DIGITAL PRAXIS

Undoubtedly, the study of the role of metaphors in computing practices should begin with the user interface, that permeable membrane that exists between the human user and the machine. This is, indeed, where a lot of metaphors can be captured. Yet there are more strings attached to computing metaphors than merely interface topics. And while metaphors may have implications for issues such as usability and design, these matters are not the main focus of the present study.[4] This study aims to go beyond the interface. It seeks to solve the riddle of what I call *digital praxis*. Praxis is more than just practice; with its slight tinge of heterodox Marxism it explicitly takes social and political structuring into account. In this study, digital praxis refers to a more or less coherent set of everyday practices — acts, habits, routines, rituals — that involve the manipulation, modification, and construction of *digital-symbolical objects* that somehow matter socially. Examples of these digital-symbolical objects are mundane things such as mailbox, blog, tweet, and file, but also more complicated assemblages such as Windows, Facebook, search engines and online communities.

There is a rich history of new media research that aims to map digital practices. These studies range from surveys on media use and case studies of communication strategies to qualitative and

---

4. Yet it should be noted that software development, in particular interface design, is, one of the few professional fields which explicitly has taken up the application of metaphors in its body of knowledge and education (see Chisholm 1985, Madsen 1994, Neale and Carroll 1997, Barboza and Souza 2000, Saffer 2005). A few other disciplines, such as psychotherapy (Lawley and Tompkins 2000) and education (Wormeli 2009), have marginally developed methods based on the deployment of metaphors.

ethnographic analyses in the fields of game studies, Internet studies, and software studies. While the latter traditions have a respectable track record of investigating digital-symbolical objects in specific practices, still the majority of new media investigations consists of communication research that presupposes digital objects without problematizing their existence. In general, new media research tends to run from case to case, desperately trying to keep up with the increasing pace in which ever 'new new media' (Levinson 2009) and new digital practices emerge. The problematization of digital objects tends only to happen during the brief period in which the new media are sparkling fresh. In the early nineties this concerned plain text appliances: IRC (Reid 1991), Usenet (Hauben 1993), mail (Van den Boomen 1994), and MUDs (Bruckman and Resnick 1995). When the World Wide Web took off – still in its early days, later recursively called version Web 1.0 – research focused on web sites (Catledge and Pitkow 1995), personal homepages (Wynn and Katz 1997) and web portals (Gallaugher and Downing 2000). After that the focus moved to mobile phones (Katz and Aakhus 2002) and computer games (Cassell and Jenkins 1998, Eskelinen 2001), while on the web attention shifted to blogs (Blood 2000, Herring et al. 2004) and wiki's (Leuf and Cunningham 2001). In the last couple of years, the new kids on the block are Facebook (Boyd and Ellison 2007), mobile apps (Goggin 2010) and Twitter (Murthy 2013). Unquestionably, this kind of perpetual updating work has to be done, but there is definitely room for fundamental research that takes a step back from the newest platform or app and delves into the basic conditions of digital praxis. My inquiry aims to contribute to this kind of research.

This study digs into the riddle of how digital-symbolical objects come into being as socially meaningful objects. That is, as objects that matter in the daily life of ordinary users, and therefore for society at large – not just as commodities, tools, or entertainment, but as crucial mediators or generators of social, cultural and political imperatives. I consider digital-symbolical objects as an onto-epistemological[5] riddle because they are neither pure objects, nor pure symbolic forms, nor pure digital patterns. They are hybrids of computation, algorithms, and language – artifacts cut out of arbitrarily assigned numbers, processed by machines and humans, represented, symbolized, ontologized, and incorporated in the social texture. The riddle then is: how do such composites of numbers and language, of algorithms and discourse, of computer code and cultural code, come about and get stabilized? And how do metaphors contribute to (or perhaps hinder) these processes?

Transcoding the digital

In order to flesh out the methodology of this study, let me first say a few things about the vocabulary in which this endeavor will primarily be framed. What I initially called the machinery of transferences in the discussion of my friend's story can be further fleshed out in terms of transcoding (this section) and translation (next section).

In his foundational work *The Language of New Media* (2001), Lev Manovich coined the notion of *transcoding* as a general term to indicate the exchange between what he calls the computer layer and the cultural layer (Manovich 2001, 45-47). Manovich considers transcoding as one of the basic principles of digital media. The concept indicates the 'computerization of culture' through a

---

5. I borrow this term from Barad (2003) in order to stress that there is no ontology that is not at the same time an epistemology.

'process of "conceptual transfer" from the computer world to culture at large' (ibid., 47).
The term transcoding is in itself a metaphor, not coincidentally taken from the domain of computing practice. In this field it refers to digital-to-digital data conversion of one format into another, for example the conversion of a Word document into a PDF file. In contrast to plain conversion, which can also refer to upgrading or downgrading a format (e.g. converting a Word 2000 document into Word 2010), the prefix 'trans' emphasizes a conversion from a source to a completely different destination, namely, another hardware device, another operating system, another database, or another application program. Manovich's metaphor covers a similar process. He is concerned with digital-to-cultural conversions that yield to new composites of the digital and the cultural, 'a blend of human and computer meanings, of traditional ways in which human culture modeled the world and the computer's own means of representing it' (ibid., 46). Manovich's most prominent example of digital-to-cultural transcoding is the database, which, he claims, is superseding the formerly dominant cultural format of the narrative. Hence, transcoding refers to the translation of computer forms into cultural forms, but also, I would add, vice versa, the translation of cultural forms into computer forms.

I take the metaphor of transcoding as the leading heuristic of this study, since it enables us to zoom in on the exchanges between the digital and the cultural. And again, vice versa. In identifying and unraveling instances of transcoding in the formation of digital-symbolical objects, we have to be agnostic about the transversal direction. It can just as well be digital-to-cultural as cultural-to-digital, and, not to forget, digital-to-digital, as a mediating step in-between.

Transcoding is a useful heuristic metaphor for the current study for three reasons.

First of all, the notion of transcoding takes *code* as such on board. It reminds us that what we currently refer to as new media are media that run on code – that is, computer code, programs, software. Oddly enough, software is not by definition a focal object in new media research. Often it is taken for granted, as a black box in the form of a product, interface or functionality. Yet there is a growing body of work that investigates software as something that produces meaning, value, and ideology already at the level of digital code. Manovich's book *The Language of New Media* is a case in point. This work explicitly draws on the fine-grained analysis of software, and includes a passionate plea for the development of software theory and software studies (Manovich 2001, 48). But also prior to Manovich's call, several humanities scholars pioneered in this field by taking software as their primary object of study.[6] The recent establishment of software studies as a distinguished branch of knowledge seeks to develop the field further (Fuller 2008). I consider this an important extension of the field of new media studies, which, as critical network theoretician Geert Lovink claims, should get rid of the representational frames of film and television studies (Lovink 2012). Because human and institutional tasks are increasingly being delegated to software, the study of computer code becomes an imperative, not just for software engineers, but also for media and culture scholars.[7]

Moreover, code also refers to other kinds of code: linguistic, semiotic, cultural, moral, political, and social code. These all pertain to domain-specific protocols: rules of conduct, alignment, norms,

---

6. For example earlier and recent work by Katherine Hayles (1993, 1999, 2001, 2002, 2004, 2005), Lucy Suchman (1987, 2006), Wendy Hui Kyong Chun (2004, 2006, 2011), Florian Cramer (2003, 2005), Adrian Mackenzie (2005, 2006), and Alexander Galloway (2004, 2007).

7. This does not necessarily imply that media and cultural scholars should learn to program and develop software, though basic hands-on knowledge is of course crucial.

and standards for legitimate behavior. It is telling that the notion of code is inherently polysemous, and we should keep this in mind. The assemblage and the mutual embedding of those meanings is precisely what this study aims to trace: how digital code translates into social and cultural code, and vice versa.

Secondly, there is the prefix 'trans' that implies movement, transport, transference. Most of our daily computing activities consists of acts of transference: transferences between different computers (sending mail, replying on a blog, P2P file sharing), between different applications and formats (Word to PDF, wav into mp3) and between different media forms and modalities (speech to text, scanning a picture, streaming of television broadcasts). All transferences are in their turn mediated and conducted by several nested layers of digital translations, piled up in a sort of Tower of Babel. Although in 1949 Warren Weaver optimistically claimed that machine translation would be 'the New Tower of Anti-Babel', that would enable free and unrestrained communication (Weaver 1955), digital praxis is still and probably forever will be held captive in the old tower of puzzling translations.

Sometimes these translations are manually evoked, but most often they are enacted by hidden software processes. They usually pass smoothly, but sometimes ruptures can occur. If we consider the number of mutual interactions and interferences that exist between different computers, different configurations, different applications, and different formats, it is actually amazing how often computerized transferences succeed without failure. It was quite a little miracle that the problem my friend was having with her computer required only one step to make the transference from work to home complete. Think of the thousands of things that could have been different: the technician could have done a bad job with the wires or the configuration of the cable modem; her network connection at home could have not been configured yet with the right IP numbers of her provider; a network protocol could have been missing; her mail program at home could have not properly been configured for the mail server; her password could have been expired, and so on. Digital transferences seem to be both precarious and robust.

Thirdly, transcoding implies that technically no conversion or translation is ever lossless. By transcoding a digital format into an other digital format some information and thus functionality is lost, while other functionality is gained. Obviously, this applies even more to digital-to-cultural transcoding, since the source and target domain are so profoundly different that any one-to-one translation is impossible. Recalling this technical premise of inherent data loss in any practice of transcoding, should keep us sharp when encountering popular common beliefs in digital seamlessness and the discourse of one-click immediacy. There is simply no transcoding and transference without transformation.

Translations in actor-networks

In that regard, the notion of transcoding is very akin to what in actor-network theory (ANT) is called *translation*. However, the ANT focus is different. It is at the same time more broad and more narrow than Manovich's transcoding. ANT translations are also processes of conversion and transformation, but not between presupposed separate domains, such as the digital and the cultural, or the social and the technological. Nor is it about translations between different discourses or languages, at least not in the classic linguistic sense. And, although actor-network theory is also known as 'the sociology of translations' (Law 1992), it is not about the relations between social groups and social structures. Translations between what then? Briefly put, between the heterogeneous bits and pieces that hold society together. We can also say, between actors and networks – but again, not in the classical sociological sense of actors-as-agents and networks-as-structure (Law 1992; Latour 1996, 1999, 2005). ANT actors can be human beings, but also things, technological innovations, institutions, laws, patents, documents, money, and other small or large artifacts. Networks, in their turn, can be recognizable infrastructural networks, such as roads, electricity grids, or computer networks, but also entities that, at first sight, do not resemble a network at all: a laboratory, a software program, a remote control, or a brand. Actor-network translations can be defined as strategies and procedures that aim to interest, enroll and mobilize actors in order to accomplish a stable matter of fact (Callon 1986).

To use a metaphor, such translations are the metabolism of society. They produce and reproduce the heterogeneous stuff that feeds society and that holds things together. Yet, this metabolism is not a fixed structure or infrastructure; translations can change, fail, collapse, or otherwise lose their cohesive forces. Most significantly, they are not abstract. They consist of phenomena that can be investigated empirically and locally. As ANT scholar John Law puts it, translations are 'local processes of patterning, social orchestration, ordering, and resistance' that generate 'ordering effects such as devices, agents, institutions, or organizations. So "translation" is a verb which implies transformation and the possibility of equivalence, the possibility that one thing (for example, an actor) may stand for another (for instance a network)' (Law 1992, 386). Elsewhere Law added,

> To translate is to make two words equivalent. But since no two words are equivalent, translation also implies betrayal: *traduction, trahison*. So translation is both about making equivalent, and about shifting. It is about moving terms around, about linking and changing them. (Law 2009, 144)

In other words, ANT or the sociology of translations investigates empirically how heterogeneous bits and pieces are accommodated and calibrated, negotiated and modified, shifted and betrayed in order to get aligned in a network of linked and nested translations. When such an actor-network succeeds to acquire a durable form, it emerges as an actor in itself, concealing and betraying its assembled network construction.

Again, it should be stressed that actors can be of any form, human or non-human, network-like or thing-like, natural or cultural, digital or analog, simple or complex. As long as an entity is empirically and materially traceable, it can be an actor, a mediator. When the alignment of translations between mediating actors succeeds, it manifests itself as an irrefutable naturalized fact or artifact. It has then turned into a black box, so taken for granted that we do not see the translation labor anymore. According to ANT, that is the stuff the social is made of, enacted into being. Society is an effect, not a cause. As Bruno Latour states boldly, 'there is no society, no social realm, and no social ties, but there exist translations between mediators that may generate traceable associations' (Latour 2005b, 108).

I use the ANT notion of translation as a second heuristic tool for my inquiry into digital praxis. Or better, I calibrate Manovich's concept of transcoding by seeing it through the ANT lens of translation, including the onto-epistemological implications. This adds two important features to the guiding principle of transcoding in this study.

First, it imports ANT's agnostic principles regarding what may count as a relevant actor and what can be a legitimate starting point for an analysis. This study seeks to flesh out traceable translations in digital praxis with metaphors – in themselves already translations – as a starting point. As we will see throughout this study, they will lead us to various other translations and transcodings that may fail or succeed in keeping up appearances.

Second, there is the emphasis on empirical, material traces. This implies that the translations we are after are more than just the 'conceptual transfer' Manovich mentions (Manovich 2001, 47). It is more than just a mental shift. If such transferences leave no material trace that nails them down, then no translation can take place; at least, not a durable translation that matters.

In new media studies such a materialist epistemology is, though not predominant, not uncommon. Manovich already called for 'digital materialism' (ibid., 10), and I consider myself a faithful member of the Utrecht School of New Media Studies, that aims to develop a principally material perspective on new media and digital culture by investigating digital material (Van den Boomen et al. 2009). Consequently this study aspires to contribute to the further development of a digital-material approach, in particular of the underexplored borderlines of new media studies and metaphor research.

Material semiotics

Admittedly, a materialist approach is not common in the field of metaphor research, to put it mildly. Metaphors are traditionally investigated in the disciplinary frames of linguistics, literary studies, and rhetoric. Only now and then metaphor researchers dip a toe into the adjacent waters of philosophy, anthropology, cognitive psychology, or media studies. But in practically all cases metaphors are studied primarily as conceptual transferences of meaning, not as material translations embedded in wider material networks, let alone as digital-material transcodings.

As the present research roams the underexplored wilderness situated in the disciplinary no man's land between new media studies, actor-network theory, and metaphor studies, its methodology had to be assembled and invented underway. The object of this study – digital-material transcodings by metaphors – requires the selective tapping of these three resources. This implies that the methodology is eclectic by necessity, but certainly not noncommittal. It also implies that it will be sometimes unfaithful to its origins. Hence, this study is not an elaborated ANT case study, and also not classic metaphor research in the sense of a systematic mapping of the corpus of circulating metaphors in new media discourse. However, it does utilize tools and mobilize concepts from these methodologies – sometimes affirmative, sometimes critical, and sometimes extending and modifying them.

The same applies for other vocabularies and perspectives this study draws upon. Two of them stand out. First, there is Charles Sanders Peirce's pragmatic semiotics, in particular his notion of *indexicality*, since this concept provides a first link from the domain of signs and signification to the material physical world (Peirce 1931b). The second one is Katherine Hayles' so called 'medium-specific analysis', in particular her notion of *material metaphor* (Hayles 2001b, 2002, 2004). This concept enables a similar shift from semiosis to material praxis like Peirce's indexicality, but it takes it a step further. It foregrounds metaphorical translations that are inextricably inscribed in specific media-technological artifacts – be it books, computers, or software constructs. As we will see, material metaphors not only organize ways of reading, referring, and interpreting, but they also configure social and cultural praxis.

If this variety of methodologies, terms and tools needs a label, it could best be described as social semiotics (Hodge and Kress 1988; Kress 2013), or better, what ANT scholars call material semiotics (Law and Mol 1995; Law 2009).[8] Here signifiers and signifieds, texts, codes, and discourse are not studied as pure linguistic or semiotic entities, but as material objects and translations embedded in and generating specific practices – social, cultural, professional, domestic, political, and economic. In other words, material semiotics traces semiotic relations beyond the domain of language, catching it at work in heterogeneous practices of enactments (Law 2009). As John Law and Annemarie Mol explain,

> Linguistic semiotics teaches that words give each other meaning. Material semiotics extends this insight beyond the linguistic and claims that entities give each other being: that they enact each other. [...] In the stories that material semiotics makes possible, an actor does not act alone. It acts in relation to other actors, linked up with them. This means that it is also always being acted upon. Acting and being enacted go together. (Law and Mol 2008, 58)

Hence, material semiotics investigates how meaning matters beyond language, how it matters and materializes in a linked-up network of translations. This study aims to tell such material-semiotic stories of enacting, acting, and being acted upon, stories in which metaphors are followed through various digital-material transcodings and their further translations.

Armed with the above vocabulary we can refine the initial research question about the channeling role of metaphors in digital praxis. The main question of this study is still: how do metaphors channel (format, constitute, configure) digital praxis? This question implicates the following subquestions:

1. Which digital-material transcodings and material-semiotic translations can be traced when we follow metaphors as actors?
2. How do such transcodings and translations get fixated into stable taken-for-granted entities and naturalized matters of facts?
3. Which further translations are attached to the transcoding labor of metaphors; which ideologies, narratives and discourses are enabled and sustained and which are suppressed and excluded?

3 — METAPHORS WE COMPUTE BY

As we will see in this study, following the trail of metaphors in digital praxis will lead us to and through various levels in which metaphors perform their translation labor. To start this endeavor the user interface seems an obvious point of departure, as metaphors are abundant here: windows, buttons, mailbox, documents, desktop, browser. Zooming in on these interface metaphors reveals already interesting differentiations. Some of them refer to interfacial operations or tools (button, browser), some refer to objects (document, mailbox), and others refer to general representational frames (windows, desktop). Moreover, interface metaphors are embedded in wider configurations and discourses which are in turn organized by their own discourse metaphors. These tropes format discourses on, for example, *media* (with discourse metaphors such as win-

---

8. Yet, material semiotics is not invented in ANT; earlier traces can be found in Michel Foucault's extended notion of discourse as material assemblage of the linguistic as well as the non-linguistic that organizes power, knowledge, truth, and subject positions (Foucault 1966, 1971, 1972), and in Donna Haraway's evocations of situated knowledge and nature-culture hybrids (Haraway 1988, 1991).

dow on the world, container, and channel), *software* (as labor, as thing, as language), *networks* (electronic highway, cyberspace), and *sociality* (village, community, social network).

Of course, the list of metaphors we compute by cannot be exhaustively addressed in one thesis. The above-mentioned interface and discourse metaphors will be investigated in this study (among others), but I am aware of the fact that there are many more tropes circulating in the wider discourse of new media. I have restricted my metaphor corpus to the most common metaphors in two discursive fields: firstly, those that format the mundane digital practices of ordinary users, and secondly, those that inform popular and academic discourse on media in general, and new media in particular.

Accordingly, this study is divided into six chapters that trace those metaphors in their translation praxis, arranged by the following themes: 1) interfacial representation on the screen, 2) digital objects as performative material metaphors, 3) media and mediation metaphors, 4) tropes of immediacy and transparency, 5) software as mediator and metaphor, and 6) metaphors of sociality. The order of the chapters is organized along the lines of increasing scale – zooming out from user interface to the attached technological machinery to media discourse to social organization – but in fact each chapter investigates the same issue from a different angle, namely, the metaphorical translations and transcodings of digital sign-tool-objects.

Overview of the chapters

1. Interfacing by indexical icons

The first chapter takes the most mundane level of our encounter with digital entities as a starting point: the user interface. The interface is the plane where human-readable sign-tools are metaphorically represented as 'ready-to-hand' objects. These representations are problematic since its buttons, products, and programs are all made of the same stuff, namely digital code which consists of patterns of digits (numbers) in the last instance. Differentiations in access levels are arbitrarily assigned, but non-arbitrarily signified by interface metaphors.

The chapter shows how these metaphors tend to 'icontologize': they deliver ontologized iconic screen representations while depresenting the indexical relations to executable code. It will be argued that the classic conceptual theory of metaphor is of limited use here, since it leaves no room for theorizing beyond the interfacial screen and human cognition. The argument will be made that indexicality, situated in Peirce's triad of Firstness, Secondness and Thirdness, is crucial to understand digital sign-tool-objects.

2. Material metaphors

In this chapter the notion of material metaphor is introduced as a concept that is able to account for the extra-linguistic and extra-conceptual object-like properties of metaphorical sign-tool-objects. The concept of material metaphor is imported from two different fields, respectively media research and anthropology. Katherine Hayles (2002) has used the term for her material-semiotic inquiries into new media art, while in post-structuralist anthropology the term material metaphor is used for investigations in the social organizing power of particular material objects. These are distinct objects that embody a specific metaphor which activates and enforces specific social norms and rules of conduct.

I will argue that the two perspectives should be merged for the study of digital sign-tool-objects, since digital-material metaphors function both as media-specific interfaces and as disciplinary social-organizing artifacts. Digital-material metaphors thus enable translations between the digital, the material, and the semiotic, that is, between the non-arbitrary and the arbitrary, thereby evoking and constituting conventions and ideologies.

3. Mediation by metonymy and metaphor
If we consider that any display and representation tends to icontologize, then the question of the representation of the medium itself becomes urgent. This chapter deals with the metaphors and metonymies of what we call media. While media – old as well as new, digital as well as non-digital – can formally be conceived as heterogeneous apparatuses of processing, storage, display, and transference, that is, as material machineries of mediation, their materiality tends to withdraw behind the representations and products they proffer. Media predominantly tend to serve the experience of immediacy and demediation, not that of mediation and translation.
In order to find out how this is achieved, several metaphors of media will be investigated. These metaphors include media as membrane, as master, as space, as channel, as tool, and as container. It will be argued that, although some of these discourse metaphors enable a more material perspective on media, the most dominant metaphors obfuscate the material machinery involved.

4. Immediacy by metaphor
While immediacy seems to be the flip side of mediation, it is in fact the goal of any medium or mediation mechanism. The most successful media are those that make themselves invisible, usually by mobilizing tropes of transparency and reflection such as windows (looking through) and mirrors (looking at). But, as will be shown in this chapter, when taken seriously as material metaphors, windows and mirrors may also facilitate looking inside the material apparatus.
Bolter and Grusin's (2000) classic influential theory of remediation also aims to account for the principle of concurrent mediation and demediation. The remediation thesis explains the logic of successive new media as a perpetual refashioning of previous media forms, sustained by the simultaneous dynamic of immediacy and hypermediacy. However, a close reading of this theory shows that the main hypotheses also are marked by obfuscating windows and mirrors metaphors, without accounting for their productive and icontologizing labor. It will be argued that material metaphors provide the missing link in the theory of remediation which thereby turns into a theory of transmediation. This is remediation that goes beyond mirroring media forms as it taps from a far larger reservoir of social and cultural resources.

5. Code rules
Digital transmediation is per definition also transcoding, that is, the translation of digital code into media and cultural objects, and vice versa. Programmed code, the primal marker of digital media, is in itself only intelligible by metaphor. As such, software is always a hybrid of the digital and the analog. This chapter explores the onto-epistemology of software by following its political history (marked by the demolition of specific women's labor), its formal and material affordances, and its metaphors, among others software as labor, as numbers, and as language. It will be shown that each software metaphor entails and mobilizes different discourses, ideologies, and material implications (for subject positions, business models, juridical status). Software then, tipped as the ultimate immaterial stuff that nevertheless rules the world, turns out to be the ultimate material metaphor.

6. Transcoding the social into networks

This chapter explores how the social gets transmediated and transcoded into digital dynamics (and vice versa) by tracing how the discourse metaphor of the virtual community shifted to Web 2.0 and social network metaphors. Analyzing these tropes as digital-material metaphors reveals the mechanisms of digital-social transcoding as sustained by software-driven icontologies and indexical connections.

Tracking down these digital-material transferences and translations leads us to the black boxes of networks. The notion of network will also turn out to be deeply informed by metaphors. Three root metaphors will be identified: network as infrastructure, as organism, and as graph. Classic Internet metaphors, such as the electronic highway and cyberspace, but also current metaphors of social networks, tap selectively from these root metaphors, translating them into different material configurations which have various political-ideological implications.

Manifesto for hacking metaphors

The concluding chapter seeks to gather the findings of this study in the format of a manifesto. This manifesto proposes a research methodology for the study of metaphors in digital-material praxis. Building on the results of this study, I assert that digital-material praxis is constituted by transference acts, icontologized metaphors, and other black boxes. However, these black boxes can be hacked, that is opened up by reverse engineering: decomposing its constituting elements and following the trails back in order to unravel the connections and translations that hold the device together. Whereas metaphors in action usually close and lock black boxes by their icontological mechanisms, an analysis in terms of digital-material metaphors might reverse this process into opening and unlocking the black box. To use a metaphor for a metaphor: metaphors are keys, able to lock, but also able to unlock.

CHAPTER 1
INTERFACING BY INDEXICAL ICONS
HOW YOUR MAILBOX MAY FOOL YOU

> *For a metaphor says only what shows on its face –*
> *usually a patent falsehood or an absurd truth.*
> (Donald Davidson, 1987)

> *What, then, is truth? A mobile army of metaphors, metonyms, and*
> *anthropomorphisms – in short, a sum of human relations which have*
> *been enhanced, transposed, and embellished poetically and rhetorically,*
> *and which after long use seem firm, canonical, and obligatory.*
> (Friedrich Nietzsche, 1873)

Operating a computer seems to be quite easy nowadays. We can easily navigate our way around our desktops. We know how to open our mail, how to choose from a menu, and how to save files in folders. This kind of work with computers has become such common practice that we barely realize how these operational actions are framed by metaphors. Our first association with 'cleaning a desktop' probably has more to do with deleting unused icons and files than with polishing a work table surface. Behind our personal computers, we are all disciplined office workers (Kaptelinin and Czerwinski 2007). Many operating metaphors are drawn from an office setting but we have no problem when they blend with metaphors from other settings, such as home, play, portal, or dashboard.

Reading these metaphorical signs – no matter whether they are words or pictures – and using them as tools usually goes on effortlessly. What you see is what you get, or better, what you metaphorically see is what you get. A menu presents its options, a window opens, and the inbox shows your mail. But, as we all know, sometimes things go wrong. Sometimes the use of the sign-tools on our screen does not render the expected results. You do not get what you want, and you do not understand what you see. Then the machine closes itself for us as users. It suddenly exposes its status as a black box: an opaque machine with unknown cogs and puzzling signs.

In this chapter, I aim to track down what exactly happens when we are 'reading' and operating a computer, and how metaphors enable or disable our access to this black box. First, I introduce the basics of user interfaces and the way they organize and sometimes disorganize our access to the machine. Second, I undertake a close reading of interfacial icons as signs, using C.S. Peirce's semiotic vocabulary, and relate this to the icons' functioning as tools. As might be expected this leads to contradictions, induced by the indeterminate ontology of compressed sign-tools that seem to be indexical but also iconic and metaphorical. Third, I will try to disentangle this sign-tool-metaphor entity with a metaphor analysis based on the conceptual theory of metaphor, also known as the contemporary or cognitive theory of metaphor (Lakoff and Johnson 1980, 1999;

Lakoff 1987, 1993). Finally, I conclude that this approach may proffer an account of the transference between the cognitive level and the interface level, but that it leaves the crucial transferences unexplored and unexplained.

1 — INTERFACES, MACHINES, AND DIGITS

In order to flesh out the specific qualities of computer interfaces it is first of all important to note that what is called an interface is not restricted to digital devices. The term, indicating a common boundary where mediating traffic occurs between two or more different systems, is also used in biology, chemistry, and sociology (Johnson 1997). In the field of computing the notion of interface can refer to five different interaction boundaries (Cramer 2008). These include boundaries between hardware and users (interfaced by the screen, keyboard, and mouse), between hardware and other hardware (interfaced by slots and connectors), between hardware and software (by operating systems and device drivers), between software and software (by APIs, application programming interfaces), and between symbols, software, and users (by icons and textual commands). The last one is commonly referred to as the human-computer interface, or the user interface.

However, not only computers have a user interface. Any machine that can be operated by humans in variable modes comes with its own user interface: a specific arrangement of switches, buttons, levers, signals, and other operating tools. Such a switchboard allows operational access to any machine. It can consist of a dashboard, steering wheel, speed indicator, and pedals in the case of a car, it may be the buttons for cappuccino or espresso on a coffee machine, or the screen, the keyboard and mouse which we use to operate our personal computer.

All machines execute their task by physically transforming input (energy, raw material) into some output (a product, an effect, an event). A coffee machine delivers cappuccino, a car produces movement, a pianola generates music. While physical transformations are also produced by the computer, as a machine it does more. In addition to its physical transformations (changes in the states of the electronic circuits inside) it stores machine-readable representations of these states in computer memory, and translates parts of them into human-readable symbols (usually visual, sometimes auditory). This double processing is what makes the computer a special machine; it is both a *physical* processing machine and a *symbol*-processing machine. These processes run parallel and mutually feed into each other: symbols may function as commands and input for the physical machine, and physical changes of state produce new arrangements of symbols as output that in turn can be reprocessed as new input.

This traffic between the physical and the symbolic is accomplished by the mediating language of digitality. This is an artificial language of digits, that is, numbers — real numbers, integers. Digitality or digitization is essentially the assignment of numbers to discrete entities, thus enabling the manipulation of these entities by means of computation.[9] Our contemporary electronic computer systems work with binary numbers. Binary digits (bits) are numbers represented by using only two symbols, 0 and 1, in order to compute, instead of the usual ten symbols of the decimal system. While numbers seem to be of a completely different order than human language, the computing trick is that numbers can be arbitrarily (yet systematically) assigned to electronic circuit states

---

9. Computation can be defined as machine operations on numbers according to specific algorithms, that is, finite sets of elementary instructions.

as well as to human-readable symbols (or parts of them). Hence, both physical machine states and human symbols can be translated into digital code. This pattern of binary digital code is in fact an analogical mapping of the machine state as expressed by the levels of the numerous tiny voltage circuits on the microprocessors (chips) inside the machine. Usually a lower voltage level is represented as 0 (0 to 1 volts) and a higher voltage level as 1 (2 to 5 volts). In order to achieve a particular state the machine has to change itself reiteratively by computing: reading incoming numbers, executing specific instructions (algorithms) on them, erasing previously stored numbers no longer necessary, and writing the resulting new number patterns in its random access memory or its hard disk. The instructions, including the basic general instructions of the operating system, have also been fed to the machine, as executable programs, again in the form of digits and digital code referring to electronic circuit states.[10]

All in all, inside the computing machine nothing expect electronic inscriptions and erasures happen, representing assigned and computed numbers. In contemporary digital praxis we tend to forget the hardware embodiment of digital processing just as we tend to forget the numerical base of digitality, but digital processing is, in the last instance, a purely formal, electromechanical procedure, consisting of the formal reading and writing of binary digits and adjusting the internal states of the electronic circuits accordingly. As my father used to tell me as a child: 'A computer can do nothing but discriminate between a 0 and a 1, in fact a hole and a non-hole, just like a barrel organ or a pianola.' He was absolutely right, but did not live long enough to see what could be done with this principle by attaching it to sophisticated human-readable and controllable input and output. In short, to a sophisticated interface.

A computer is not a coffee machine

In order to deliver such human-readable output – a representation of the specific parts of what is inscribed in the circuits – contemporary computers use a convoluted device, namely, a screen that shows in human-readable form both the output and possible entry points for input. The screen of an ordinary PC or mobile device displays visual representations of the inner state of the machine, ordered by pictorial icons, textual menus and sub-screens (the planes we have come to call windows). This is the so called graphical user interface (GUI).[11]

The graphics displayed on the graphical interface can have various functions. First, they can function as buttons to give instructions to the machine, comparable with the pedals in a car, such as the icon for starting your mail program,or menu items such as save or print. Secondly, they may

---

10. In order to program the machine to perform the tasks as envisioned by humans the formulation of these instructions has to go through a 'tower of Babel' of subsequent translations (Hayles 2005, 110), several hierarchical levels of different computer control languages: the high-level programming language that is used by software developers to create the human-readable – or better, expert-readable – source code; the lower-level of compiler or interpreter languages that translate these instructions into executable code, which finally gets translated into lowest-level machine-readable strings of binary digits. Off-the-shelf software consists of executable code in low-level language, easily processable by the machine, and easily operable for the human, but hardly readable or modifiable by the human, expert or not.
11. While the graphical user interface, with its easy access to executing code, is typically conceived as the most user-friendly level of the computer, it is, from the perspective of possible intervention in the source code, the most user-unfriendly level. As Florian Cramer (2008) argues, it is arbitrary at which level we situate the user interface, since at every level humans may be granted access. The choice of level is a matter of design politics.

be feedback signs, indicators of how the machine is working, comparable with the speed display in a car, as with an icon in the task bar indicating your computer is online or that your virus scanner is outdated. Thirdly, they can display a product, that is, a data object composed of signs, such as a digital photo or a text document, comparable to a cup of cappuccino delivered by a coffee machine. Although these data objects can be saved and stored in memory, the output does not necessarily need to be an end product, as was the case with the cappuccino. Since its digital construction enables further computing, the output may function as input for yet another product, by the use of commands such as edit, cut, or copy. Notably, these reiterative functions have no equivalent in the user interface of a car, a coffee machine, or a pianola. Moreover, the digital output object can even be not merely a data product, but rather a tool for manipulating other data products, as is the case with application programs, scripts, plug-ins, or complete operating systems. Needless to say, these reiterative functions also have no equivalent in other physical machines. The coffee machine just delivers espresso or cappuccino, not another coffee machine. The onto-epistemology of the computer is thus marked by reiteration in two ways: the machine reinserts the physical into the symbolic and vice versa, and it embodies a set of tools for the (re)production of data objects and tools that can be fed back into the machine. In that regard, a computer is not just complicated but complex, that is, an open-ended system with nested layers of reiteration and feedback loops that actualizes potentialities by interaction between its components and external input (Cilliers 1998, 4-5).

As a further complicating factor the tools and products of this complex machine exist in various forms, depending on their function. They can be mutable data objects (files [12]), executable sets of instructions (programs), or interfacial signs (icons and buttons, menus, audio signals, moving bars, among others). This complex assemblage of interface, programs, and data objects becomes even more complex when hooked up in a network with other computers, thereby further enabling the transference of files, commands, and programs to other machines in the network, setting in motion inimitable transformations in physical and symbolic systems elsewhere.

Yet, as different as the various digital entities may seem to be, the distinctions are in fact arbitrary, and not functionally or ontologically determined. The way digital entities are represented is informed and channeled by the design politics of user interfaces and operating systems. Executable programs can be made visible and accessible as sets of files ordered in directories and subdirectories [13], but also as shortcuts on the desktop or embedded in the menu of another program. Even the operating system itself can be represented as sets of files. Shortcuts and other interfacial entities are representations of executable commands in a program, and thus they eventually also refer to particular program files, including particular operating-system files. A data object is also a file, but it can be translated into a shortcut pointing to the data file, and also, by its extension that links it to a specific program, to the execution of specific program files and operating system files. For instance, when you click on a .doc file, it opens in your default word processor. In other words, there is no ontological difference between a data file, a program file, an operating-

---

12. The notion of a file is of course already a concept formatted for human understanding, a metaphor taken from the world of print. And even the concept of data object is a metaphor, taken from the world of physical things.
13. However, the interface design may deliberately foreclose specific representations. In the iPad for example there is no user interface anymore that shows directories and files that represent the operating system or installed apps.

system file, or an interfacial shortcut. At the end of the day, all elements are files. Or better, they are represented as files, as a temporary freeze of the endless chain of nested representations in representations. Indeed, files are representations of delineated patterns of numbers, and numbers are in their turn representations of electronic states. A computer is a representation multiplier, increasing its complexity with every level of interfacial legibility.

In order to reduce the interfacial complexity, it is tempting to divide the screen representations into interfacial operational entities on the one hand, and content entities on the other hand. After all, means and ends, tools and products, are ontologically quite different. Like with the coffee machine, with its clear difference between the button for cappuccino and the cappuccino itself. We never mistake the button for the coffee itself. But a computer is not a coffee machine. And in fact it is quite common in computing praxis to take the button for the coffee itself.

This problem is caused by the fact that the interface tools are made of the very same digital material as the output products, and that both are displayed as signs and symbols on the same plane, the screen. How can we tell the difference? In fact, we have no means of separating digital content from the interface and the operating system that encapsulates and informs it. We may be able to see an empty interface, for example, when we start our web browser with a blank page, but we cannot perceive digital content without an adequate interface. We cannot read a text document without a word processor; we have no access to mail without the specific interface of a mail program. Only at a formal level are data digits separated from instruction digits.

A computer is not a pianola

It might be argued that the same holds for a pianola or a gramophone. You cannot hear the encoded pattern as music unless you use the proper apparatus or interface to decode it. The same could be said of a book: you cannot read the text without having the book. So, what is so special about the computer? Unlike a pianola, the 'piano rolls' of a computer, that is, its programs, are of the same order as its interface and data objects. Again, a computer is not a pianola. It is a set of piano rolls that can in principle be turned into new piano rolls, into a piano roll factory, into a pianola and into a pianola factory.

This is because digital encoding and digital decoding works according to the same principles as numerical translation, and can be performed by the very same apparatus. The shared language of digital code allows in principle any reiteration, mutation, and fusion between program, interface, and object – regardless of its initial function. [14] An mp3 file can be played, like a piano roll, but nothing prevents other interfacial formatting. Its digital code can just as well be translated into hexadecimal numbers as in colored moving patterns or in graphically displayed frequency spikes. The file can be edited with dedicated sound editor software, but you can also treat it as text and mutate/mutilate it with a simple text editor by performing random copy, cut, and paste operations. You can even take the hexadecimal numerical representation of a file and add or subtract some numbers with a random value. This could result in the creation of a moving piece of music, or it may not be so interesting.

---

14. Provided the computer device comes with a user interface that enables the intervention and manipulation of digital code, such as the PC. Yet, even digital code that is packaged without a user interface or with a restricted user interface, such as embedded chips regulating a system, or digital data carriers such as DVDs, can in principal be accessed and hacked by using a computer with the proper interface and software – just because the code is digital. In principle, all digital code is accessible, that is, hackable.

Indeed, a computer is not a pianola. It is not a machine that can just perform preprogrammed steps of algorithms that are designed and encoded elsewhere. The computer may be dystopianly depicted as an uncanny pianola with a spooky self-moving keyboard, but actually it could not be more different. Its keyboard does not move 'automagically', entirely controlled by piano roll programs. A computer keyboard or a touch screen is at least partially controlled by human fingers. Etymologically it is no coincidence that digit, *digitus* in Latin, means number as well as finger. Indeed, the digital can be conceived as an extension of human fingers. It is an extension of the ability to point at, touch, tap and push on things, as well as the ability to count discrete entities, to assign numbers to things and to remember them. All in all, this constitutes the basic ability to represent things by embodied symbols, and to do things with symbols and with machines.

In other words, human acts – acts of manipulation as well as acts of attribution and interpretation, performed by designers and users – are indispensable for the operation of a computer, no matter how sophisticated its machinery. This is no trivial statement; as I will argue throughout this study, it has profound epistemological and political implications if we acknowledge the human attribution labor that is incorporated in digital praxis, along with the digital-material configurations that enable and disable particular practices.

This premise indicates a possible answer to the riddle of digital material: the riddle of how can we make sense of the various nested layers of numerical representations and its translations. How do we freeze-frame the shifting digits and make them accessible as functional interfaces, programs, and data objects? I argue that this can be achieved by metaphors – not just as convenient helper accessories, but as foundational organizing and informing mechanisms. Interfaces, programs, data objects, and files are not first there and then we make them comprehensible by importing metaphors from elsewhere – these very differentiations only exist *through* metaphor. Metaphor is what makes them legible, articulated, delineated, operative, and operable.

Of course, I am not the first to point out the relevance of metaphors. Especially in the field of human-computer interface design, the notion of metaphor is part of the professional vocabulary. The organizing power of metaphor is also widely acknowledged in the broader field of new media studies. For instance, in *The Language of New Media*, Lev Manovich observed that computer interfaces, programs, and content are articulated by employing concepts taken from three main reservoirs of metaphors. These include three different media domains: print, cinema, and HCI, human-computer interaction (Manovich 2001, 72). And indeed, we can easily recognize these articulations. Notions of documents, files, pages, and browsing come from the domain of print and paper, just like the standard graphic icons for edit (pencil), cut (scissors), and paste (glue brush) and – not to forget – the alphanumerical keyboard as such. Representations of cinema can be found in notions of windows, frames, moving images, zooming, and the screen display in general. Even notions of play and record bear echoes of cinematic apparatuses (projector, camera) though these concepts are also associated with the gramophone apparatus, or with the cassette deck, including its forward and backward buttons. According to Manovich, HCI representations concern all representations that cannot be traced back to other media, such as cursor movements, clicking, saving, and reloading. In that regard, HCI representations can be typified as metonymical rather than metaphorical, since it explains itself by borrowing from the HCI domain itself.

While these observations seems to be a prelude to an elaborate theory of metaphor in digital praxis, Manovich's theory of new media language takes another direction. He proposes the idea of a universal media machine explicitly framed by the screen and the cinematic apparatus. As I will argue in the next section, this dominant cinematographic metaphor impairs rather than illuminates our understanding of semiosis in digital praxis.

The screen sucks

Manovich starts his book with a prologue dedicated to Dziga Vertov's avant-garde film *Man with a Movie Camera* (1929). The prologue consists of screen shots from the movie plus Manovich's comments and associations that relate the cinematographic experiments to the principles of digital media: visual Esperanto, montage within a shot, mobile cameras, mobile signs, databased narrativity, metatexts, loops, multiple windows – all arranged in rectangular frames. The idea is that *Man with a Movie Camera* 'will serve as a guide to the language of new media' (Manovich 2001, xiv). It turns out to be more than merely a guide. The movie *Man with a Movie Camera* as well as its programmatic title can be considered the organizing metaphor of Manovich's project: here we have a man with a movie camera who is trying to capture digital praxis.

According to Manovich, the computer screen is 'the key element of the modern interface' (ibid., 68). Admittedly, the screen assembles and unifies representations of print, cinema, and HCI on its visual plane, but Manovich reduces the screen further to the cinematic paradigm, as he claims: 'Rather than being merely one cultural language among others, cinema is now becoming *the* cultural interface, a toolbox for all cultural communication, overtaking the printed word' (ibid., 86). To put it bluntly, the key to a computer is a screen and the key to screens is cinema.

While such cinematographic overdetermination might be a valid perspective concerning new media culture at large, marked as this is by the proliferation of more and more screens, such as digital billboards, information pillars, mobile phone screens, and navigation screens (see Verhoeff 2012), it certainly does not cover an ordinary PC. After all, its HCI interface not only consists of a screen, but also a keyboard and a mouse. These mediating devices even correspond neatly to Manovich's triad of metaphorical domains: the keyboard comes from print, the mouse from HCI, and the screen from cinematographic and graphic representations. Yet, while the screen simulates cinematographic operations (framing, projecting, zooming), it just as much simulates print (in the form of files, letters, documents, type fonts) and clickable HCI (cursor movements, selecting, clicking). These three interfacial devices – screen, keyboard, pointer – are indispensable [15] for contemporary PC operations, and there is no reason to privilege one above the other. The screen just reassembles various interfacial processes, translating and returning them as visual representations on a flat visual plane. The screen, then, is just a specific sub-interface *within* a broader human-computer interface.

Manovich's overemphasis of the screen is all the more puzzling considering the significant personal anecdote he reveals in the introduction of his book. The story stems from his early years in education as a computer programmer. At that time, in 1975, the students had no access to a physical computer, so they had to write their programs with paper and pencil. At the end of the

---

15. Of course, one may get rid of the mouse by using keyboard combinations to navigate the cursor. And in case of RSI one can use a voice recognition software interface in order to circumvent or at least minimize the use of the mouse and the keyboard. But dropping any interface for manipulating and entering text would make a computer inoperable for human beings. Even tablets and smart phones, celebrating the magic disappearance of the physical keyboard, need to represent the keyboard metaphorically on the screen.

two-year course they were taken once to a data-processing center to have their programs executed. Saliently, Manovich's own program failed: 'Because I had never seen a computer keyboard before, I used the letter O whenever I need to input a zero' (ibid., 3). What this story reveals is how relevant print culture with its alpha-numerical keyboard is for the deepest layers of computation. A human being can confuse the letter 'O' with a zero, but a computer will not compute, not in 1975, neither today. Manovich eventually changed his academic discipline to the visual arts, and this may explain his inclination to overrate and reify the screen. [16] Yet, this is not a minor theoretical issue, it has serious implications. By neglecting the keyboard and pointing device [17] as tools in the hands of human users, that is, as devices which they use to interact with the formal machinery, any human contribution and attribution to computational praxis is ignored and obliterated. A computer is not a television.

Meanwhile, the tendency to conceive the screen as *pars pro toto* for computers, contemporary media, and contemporary culture is not limited to visual arts scholars. [18] The screen is widely used as metaphor, or better metonym, for computing, not only in ordinary speech, but also in new media studies. New media studies is not so much dominated by technological determinism, but rather by screenic overdetermination: what you see is what is to be studied. This tendency could be explained by the ability of the GUI to swallow up all other components in its visual representations, thus rendering irrelevant what remains invisible. The screen sucks. What you see is what you get, and that is all there is to get. At least, that is what the GUI suggests. [19]

Iconic condensation

Hence, the GUI is an interface within an interface, a nested interface, with a strong tendency to absorb and obfuscate the other components. And this tendency does not stop here, since the GUI is in itself a nested compound, consisting of relatively autonomous smaller user interfaces.

---

16. Despite Manovich's penchant for the screen metaphor, I consider his book *The Language of New Media* as foundational for critical new media studies, not in the least because of his simultaneous insistence on the importance of software. He writes: 'To understand the logic of new media we need to turn to computer science. It is there that we may expect to find the new terms, categories and operations that characterize media that became programmable. *From media studies, we move to something which can be called software studies; from media theory – to software theory'* (Manovich 2001, 48, italics in original). In 2013, Manovich made software the main subject of a subsequent book entitled *Software Takes Command*. He warns, 'if we don't address software itself, we are in danger of always dealing only with its effects rather than the causes: the output that appears on a computer screen rather than the programs and social cultures that produce these outputs' (Manovich 2013, 9).
17. Although I have to admit, that when I saw a mouse (and the accompanying graphical user interface) for the first time in my life, sometime in 1986, I thought that this would be the end of user control.
18. Cf. Sherry Turkle's metaphorical book title *Life on the Screen: Identity in the Age of the Internet* (1995). In Steven Johnson's *Interface Culture: How New Technology Transforms the Way We Create and Communicate* (1997), the human-computer interface equals the screen with its visual metaphors. Even in Bolter and Grusin's *Remediation: Understanding New Media*, the basic principles of (re)mediation immediacy and hypermediacy are both defined as 'styles of visual representation' (Bolter and Grusin 1999, 272).
19. Contrary to a so called command-line interface (MS-DOS, Unix), where the keyboard is the dominant interface device and the dominant metaphor/metonymy. This interface is waiting for the user to type specific commands in order to let the machine do something. You do not see a visual approximation of what you will get – you see an empty space which has to be filled with your knowledge of commands. Here what you write is what you get.

These include operating system interfaces, application interfaces, and helper interfaces which all have their own buttons, icons, and other displays. Since these tools are all visually represented, they are all subject to the absorbing mechanism of any visual representation. In other words, they devour all other components and modes during the very act of translating them into visuals; by showing they hide, by translating they substitute, and by representing they reify.

This is especially the case with computer icons. These small pictures are nothing but shortcuts to specific software commands in order to yield some desired result. However, in our daily computing praxis this is rendered invisible wherever possible. Instead of explicitly referring to specific software commands they cloak this, by pretending to refer to places on a computer (My Documents, My Pictures, mailbox, folders, Google Drive, the Internet) or to things (data objects, files, mails, documents).

Sometimes it is not quit clear whether an icon refers to a place, a data object, or a program. For example, consider the mailbox icon. What does it stand for? 'Well, my email of course.' But what exactly is implied in the conceptual shortcut 'my email', does it refer to a specific program running? Or to a place on your computer, the mailbox, where your mail resides? Or to specific files, sent to you formatted and protocolized as email messages? Or perhaps to all these notions in one?

Usually, when your mail just works as expected, these questions are irrelevant. Who cares? But sometimes these questions pop up, as we have seen in story of my friend, who wondered where her email was after setting up her broadband connection. She assumed her mail would be in her inbox immediately, just as it was with the computer at her office. The mail icon for her just referred to a place on her computer, her inbox, with her mail messages in it. She did not realize that in order to receive her messages there it required a set of instructions be executed.

The story of my friend's email puzzle might easily be read as a classic example of computer illiteracy, but that would be missing the point. This is a story about literacy. My friend was acquainted with email at work and at home, she knew the difference between dialing up and a broadband connection, she was able to forward mail. We may even say that she was rather too literate, or more accurate, too literal, especially regarding icon reading. She took the icons literally, thereby confusing referrer and referent. She took the mailbox icon for the mail itself, and the telephone icon for using the phone itself. For her, the mailbox icon was not referring to a process, a string of commands and programs set in action in order to obtain a computed result; for her it functioned as a key to a specific place, her inbox, where she expected her mail to be, immediately. The icon was not read as reference, but as immediate access to the referent itself. The icon seemed to have absorbed all references, transferences, and network labor involved. Indeed, a shortcut.

This way of icon reading is not idiosyncratic of my friend – such a reading is quite common, and it is induced by the very iconicity of the icon. Computer icons embody and enact iconic condensation, that is, a condensation of reference, in which reference and meaning are presented in one visual sign. Therefore, the inclination to take the icon for a specific *state* (result, place, thing), instead of a referential button able to invoke a material *process*, is very strong.[20] It is part and parcel of the very function of icons, since desktop icons are shorthand for complex machine

---

20. The analytical distinction between *process* and *state* is elementary for programmers and software designers (I must thank Bernard Rieder who taught me this), but less so for semioticians, media scholars, and social scientists. Structuralists distinguish between diachronic and synchronic analyses, but these analyses tend to generate different studies with different methodologies. The distinction of state and process *within* structures or transformations seems to be underexplored.

processes. They embody the condensations of the core business of graphical user interfaces: translating machine states and processes into human-readable stable signs, and translating user action into machine-readable processes and states. Icons can only carry out their signifying *and* executing job by concealing the involved complexities, and representing stable entities instead.

Hence, the mail icon necessarily hides the complex nested processes that it refers to: executing the mail program, including its configurations for a particular Internet connection and log-in procedure at a particular Internet provider, a particular mail account, with its own log-in procedures, and configurations for particular incoming and outgoing mail servers located at the service provider.[21] Instead, the mail icon represents a specific result of the process (received mail) located at a specific place (the mail box). The same holds for the telephone icon my friend thought she could ignore – that icon conceals that it is referring to the execution of the Internet connection script, including its configurations; instead, it represents the contiguous telephone device.[22]

In short, both icons refer to machine processes to be executed, and not to a specific stable state, place, or thing. At the same time they have to conceal this, and represent stable, ontologized entities in order to function as a human-readable sign. This concealment goes further than just 'non-representing' which is an omission that can be corrected just by adding or showing the absent entities. In the case of computer icons such a disclosure of the hidden processes would kill the principle of the shortcut, making it illegible by the obfuscating stream of messages about ongoing (or halted) machine processes. The concealment of processes is not contingent, it is a purposive construction to withhold particular representations, built in by interfacial design. I propose to call this built-in principle *depresentation,* in order to distinguish it from contingent non-representation.[23] We can then say, the icons on our desktops do their work by representing an ontologized entity, while depresenting the processual and material complexity involved. This is the way icons manage computer complexity, this is the task we as users (in tacit conjunction with designers) have delegated to them. And this is why we are seduced, indeed compelled, to take icons literally, at interface value.

The process of ontologizing is constitutive for interfacial computer icons, and probably for any human-computer interaction. Some scholars would call such a mechanism essentializing or substantializing (Rammert 1999). However, I consider substantializing (to treat as if a substance) essentializing (to treat as if predetermined by an immanent essence), naturalizing (to treat as if inevitable and natural), reifying (to treat as if a thing), and anthropomorphizing (to treat as if a

---

21. At least, in the case of so called pop mail, which transfers or copies the mail from its location at the mail server to the PC of the user. In the case of web mail 'in the cloud', the mail remains located at the server of a service provider, and the configuration of incoming and outgoing mail servers is taken care of by the back office of the service provider. However, even then the icons and the mailbox are displayed as if they are things or places on the local PC. 'In the cloud', the difference between the local and global, your own PC and the machines of your provider, is wiped out, along with your personal control.
22. The telephone icon in fact embodies an already forgotten displacement: it stands for using the telephone modem and not the telephone device itself. In that regard the telephone icon is not a metaphor in the strict classical sense (based on similarity or comparison) but a metonymy (based on contiguity).
23. In the same vein issues about the non-representation of women, whether in politics, higher management functions, or in scholarly theory, may be more a matter of built-in depresentation (only reparable by a profound reconfiguration of the constitutive and enabling principles) than of a merely forgotten representation (reparable by just adding them or making them more visible).

human being) all as particular instances of ontologizing. In other words, ontologizing means: to treat as if stable, as if a matter of fact, in whatever metaphorical form.[24]

Although ontologizing implies per definition depresentation, reduction, and fixation, it should be noted that as such it is a productive epistemological move, a classifying act, with the ability to create objects of knowledge and intervention. In the act of ontologizing dynamic processes get substituted with their results (for instance, the price of a commodity, behavior of people, or the output of a computer), with selected properties that are represented as something stable (as fact, thing, human being, state, or place). These ontologized entities need not necessarily emerge as isolated; they may imply or evoke their own external connections. When taken up in a broader discursive formation this may result in the historical creation of new concepts, new objects of knowledge, intervention, and power (Foucault 1972; Hacking 2002). In any case, ontologizing is not a harmless categorical mistake or just an analytical theoretical flaw in an isolated domain where only philosophers squabble; it creates ontologies in social and political praxis, and thus it creates realities that matter.

2 — BETWEEN ICONICITY AND INDEXICALITY

We have seen in the previous section that, by the simultaneous enactment of representation and depresentation, the computer icon tends to ontologize its dynamic properties. Its ontology turns into what I will call *icontology:* the icon is collapsed into a single sign, condensing reference, referent, and meaning. This begs the question what kind of signs computer icons actually are. Would a theory of the sign be able to explain that strange icontologizing capacity of icons? To further disentangle the affordances of icons, I will briefly introduce Charles Sanders Peirce's theory of the sign in the following section. Peirce's semiotics seems typically apt to solve the riddle of the icon, not only because it addresses explicitly iconicity, but also because his triadic notion of the sign enables a dynamic and performative perspective on semiosis, and most of all, it enables a connection to the world outside language.[25] The specific vocabulary of Peirce's framework will prove to be of great value for a proper analysis of digital signs, and it will keep popping up during this study. Especially Peirce's notion of indexicality, which I will extend further, will turn out to be key to interfacial digital semiotics.

What I above loosely called a collapse of reference, referent, and meaning, echoes faintly the three factors which constitute a sign according to Peirce. A sign is an entity that is characterized

---

24. Although ontology pertains to the philosophical inquiry into the modes of existence of *being,* including its *becoming,* implying that both states and processes, fixed entities and transformations, are matters of ontology, it is predominantly preoccupied with states of being rather than processes. For that reason I use the term 'ontologizing' for any articulation that freezes and reifies processes into fixed entities (states, places, human beings, or things).
25. Peirce's triadic semiotics differs fundamentally from Saussure's structuralist semiology (Saussure [1916], 1983). Saussure only distinguished between two constituting factors of the sign: the signifier (material embodiment of the sign) and the signified (mental concept, produced by the differences in the chain of signifiers, arbitrarily/conventionally connected to a signifier). In this linguistic conception of the sign, any notion of referring to something outside language is disabled. While this precludes the pitfalls of claiming natural correspondence between words and things, between language and reality, it also tends to exclude any conceptualization of social relations and meaning production outside plain language.

by having 1) a perceivable quality enabling reference to 2) something else, the referent, thus producing 3) meaning, signification for a human being. As one of Peirce's shortest definitions of the sign reads: 'A sign is something which stands for another thing to a mind' (Peirce 1981; cf. Marty 1997). Peirce used several terms to indicate the three building blocks of the sign, but he mostly used the terms *representamen* (pertaining to the detectable quality of the sign, more or less corresponding to the Saussurean notion of signifier), *object* (the thing or phenomenon referred to, the referent) and *interpretant* (mental effect, idea, thought, more or less corresponding to the Saussurean signified).

According to Peirce, a sign can only function as a sign in the full dynamic trinity of representamen, object, and interpretant. These three co-determine each other in a recursive manner: the third element (interpretant) always implies the two others, and the second element (object) always implies a relation with the first (representamen). For example, the sign triad of a red traffic light is made up by the representamen of redness (while also qualities such as 'light' and the particular 'thingness' of the traffic light could be counted in, as signs may be compounds of several representamen), by the object of a busy crossroad, and by the interpretant 'you are supposed to stop here in order to let the other traffic pass.'

Firstness, Secondness, and Thirdness

That the Peircian sign comes as a triad is no coincidence. The idea of a first, second and third level is ubiquitous in Peirce's work, as he analyzed all kinds of phenomena (signs, logic, science) in terms of nested triads. This resulted in a general classification scheme of three basic ontological categories which he dubbed Firstness, Secondness and Thirdness. Peirce was aware of his strange penchant for this numbered trinity. He wrote in a letter:

> This sort of notion is as distasteful to me as to anybody; and for years, I endeavored to pooh-pooh and refute it; but it long ago conquered me completely. Disagreeable as it is to attribute such meaning to numbers, and to a triad above all, it is as true as it is disagreeable. The ideas of Firstness, Secondness, and Thirdness are simple enough. [...] Firstness is the mode of being of that which is such as it is, positively and without reference to anything else. Secondness is the mode of being of that which is such as it is, with respect to a second but regardless of any third. Thirdness is the mode of being of that which is such as it is, in bringing a second and third into relation to each other. (Peirce 1958 [1904])

Firstness can thus be described as the level of qualities as such, Secondness as the level of relations, and Thirdness as the level of relations of relations, in a systematic arrangement. We should keep in mind that Firstness, Secondness, and Thirdness are analytical categories – they cannot be found separately in the real world. Any existing and functioning sign always already embodies Firstness, Secondness, and Thirdness. It should also be noted that Secondness, as implying a relation, is not confined to a relation with a physical-material object or referent; it may also refer to a relation with another representamen or interpretant.

The beauty of this analytical triad is that the categories can be reiterated at any level. Thus, while a sign consists of instances of Firstness (signifier), Secondness (relation to an object) and Thirdness (signified), its Secondness – as possible ways of relating to an object – can in its turn also be analyzed as a threefold of Firstness, Secondness, and Thirdness. This is Peirce's most well known triad, based on the three basic relations a sign can have to its object: iconic, indexical, or symbolic. The icon (Firstness, affordance of qualities) refers to its object by resemblance or analogy, for example, the portrait of a person, a traffic sign with a picture of a dangerous dip in the road, or the street map of a city. The index (Secondness, of external relations) refers to its object by an existential or causal connection, for example, smoke indicating fire, a fingerprint identifying a person, or a sundial indicating time. The symbol (Thirdness, a system of relations) refers to its object arbitrarily, by habit or convention, for example, the flag of a country, the logo of a company, or the letters of the alphabet for phonemes.

In the same vein, the triad can also be reiterated on the level of Thirdness: the interpretants can take on the mode of (First, quality) a possibility, (Second, relation) a fact, or (Third, systematic arrangement) a rule or a reason. Applied to the interpretants of traffic signs, the sign for a parking lot signifies a possibility, the sign for a dangerous dip in the road signifies a fact, and a sign for one-way traffic signifies a rule. For all nested instances of First, Second, and Third, the principle of recursiveness holds: a Third always implies a Second and a First, and a Second always implies two Firsts. In fact, just like counting integers: $3 = 2 + 1, 2 = 1 + 1, 1 = 1.$ [26]

Peirce's triadic recursive classification scheme provides a vocabulary to help dissect and understand the working of signs at several intertwined levels, since it is scalable and dynamic. It gives an account of how a sign may be a composite of more signs; how it may refer to a single object or to a compound of objects or signifiers, and how it may do so in various ways, by various relations and embedded in various rule systems. Its strongest feature is the principle of nestedness, that is the principle that in every instantiated Third there is also something Second and something First. For example, a traffic sign is always a symbol, as it is taken up in a system of rules and conventions about forms, colors, and meaning, but it may be indexically referring to a dip in the road, and it may do so by an iconic image resembling a dip.

Peirce's triad also gives an account of how signs may change during their circulation in social semiotic praxis. An icon can become a symbol. For example, the iconic picture of Che Guevara becomes a symbol when printed on a T-shirt, signifying not so much the person Guevara but radical left sympathies (or just fashion). Likewise, a symbol can be reiterated as an index. For instance, a yellow letter M is a symbol representing the brand name for McDonald's, but as a sign on a pole it is indexical for a McDonald's outlet nearby. In short, the scheme accounts for social-semiotic transformations and slidings; interpretants may break loose and become new representamen, invoking new objects and interpretants, new signs, with other relations and rules.

Indexical symbols with virtual objects

Peirce's dynamic triad may be fruitful for fleshing out the social-semiotic interactions at work in computing praxis, especially when it comes to computer icons. At first sight, these icons seem to be no Peircian icons at all; rather, they are Peircian symbols. After all, they are arbitrarily assigned to computational processes; what a specific icon stands for – a file, a program – we have to learn and find out by experience. But other Peircian readings are also possible. The icons display small graphics which refer to their object, and drawing on Peirce, this can be done in three ways: by resemblance (iconic), by an existential relation (indexical), or by convention (symbolic). The mailbox icon would then be a Peircian icon, since its relation to its depicted object is based on a particular

---

26. And since 4 or more can always be parsed in combinations of 3, 2 and 1, a trinity suffices, as Peirce asserts in 'A guess at the riddle' (Peirce 1931a [1888]).

resemblance, an assumed similarity between postal mail and email. But the Internet connection icon, which depicts a telephone device connected to a computer, would be considered more an indexical sign rather than an icon, since its representation is not based on resemblance, but on an existential relation. The desktop icon for Microsoft's Internet Explorer, the branded stylized 'e', (or the icon for Mozilla's Firefox browser, displaying a fox curled around a globe) would then be considered a Peircian symbol, since the image is arbitrary and conventional.

Hence, from one perspective all computer icons can be seen as symbolic signs, and from another perspective they appear as either icons, indices, or symbols. The latter reasoning is based on how the sign represents its object, the former locates the object elsewhere, outside the sign. In fact, these two kinds of objects are of a completely different kind, as Peirce also noticed. He called the first one the *immediate object* – the object as represented by the sign – and the second one the *dynamical object* – the object in the world, existing or assumed to exist, as an interpreted instance or phenomenon. Peirce notes that we have to distinguish between the immediate object and the dynamical object, 'which, from the nature of things, the Sign *cannot* express, which it can only *indicate* and leave the interpreter to find out by *collateral experience*' (Peirce 1998 [1909], 498).

This differentiation between kinds of objects enables us to track down how computer icons work. As we have seen, desktop icons materially refer to an act of executing machine code. From this perspective, all desktop icons are indexical signs. They refer to existential, physical chains of causation, to machine processes to be executed in order to yield a specific result. Their dynamical object is thus code, software instructions. However, there are two kinds of code involved: machine-readable digital code, to which the icon refers indexically, and human-readable code, to which the icon refers symbolically, for example, as mail, file, or program. We can thus say: computer icons are Peircian indices (referring to the dynamical object of machine code), wrapped in Peircian symbols (referring to the dynamical object constituted by human code). In that regard, computer icons are only contingently iconic, that is, only when they represent the symbol by means of visual resemblance. However, in their signifying practice, the icons completely reverse this; they appear as primarily iconic. In other words, while computer icons are almost never genuine Peircian icons, they all exhibit what I have called icontology – reified iconicity. They do so by equating and substituting the sign with its immediate object of reference as displayed by the sign, thus nullifying its indexical reference to the (twofold) dynamical object of digital and human code. In short, they enact their iconicity by hiding, or better, de*presenting* their indexicality.

Again, we can see a Peircian triad shimmering through: the immediate object as internal Firstness and the dynamical object as relational Secondness. Could there also be an object-bound Thirdness? Peirce himself never did propose a third kind of object, but we could infer such an object from the double dynamics of computer icons, referring to machine code *and* to human code. I propose – following Peircian triads – to call the reference to symbolic human code a Third kind of object, that is, a future object, a not yet actualized object, an object to become, in short, a *virtual object*.[27] This virtual object is not represented in the sign, neither is it completely

---

27. This notion of virtuality does not by definition refer to modeling through the use of a computer (though here it does, contingently), neither does it refer to the opposite of the real. Here, the concept is compliant with the way Deleuze and Guattari (1987) and Massumi (1998) conceive the virtual: as opposed to the actual, referring not just to what may be actualized as derivation from a predetermined potential, but rather to the emergence of new potentials.

captured by the indexically executed machine code. The virtual object is what *may* be actualized by this code, what *may* be done with it, by user action combined with machine action – which, as we all know, can yield expected as well as unexpected results. It is not just executing your mail program, it is that you may have mail and get it. It is more than just running your browser, it is the World Wide Web, opened up for you. The virtual object is where immediate object, dynamical object, interpretant, and action get together, embedded in a cultural system of design, attribution, and rules. Virtual objects are Peircian Thirds, as they are organized by systematic rules (human code and interpretation), in conjunction with nested Firstness (immediate objects, qualities) and Secondness (dynamical objects, relations). They refer to a possible configuration of actualized relations in a complex system, which may set in motion new significations.

Tools ready-to-hand and present-at-hand

In our attempts to extricate the relations of the computer icon with its object and its implications for how we handle these signs as tools to accomplish a task, we now have the contours of a analytical framework in terms of object references: an immediate object, a dynamical object, and a virtual object. Though Peirce is widely considered the founding father of the American branch of philosophy called pragmatism – or, as Peirce himself preferred to call it, 'pragmaticism', as a method of thinking (Preucel 2006, 52) – the pragmatic implications of actually handling dynamical objects has not been addressed elaborately in his theory of signs. Let alone the implications for what I have called the virtual object, which seems to be crucial in computing and networking praxis. The problematics of virtual objects is related to the moment that the sign becomes a *tool*: not something to be read and interpreted by a cognitive human being, but a thing in the hands of a tool-using human being, a thing by which things can be done, things not yet present, things partly unknown or never seen before, but somehow prefigured – in short, virtual things.

Heidegger, like Peirce also not quite computer-inspired in his thinking, made some useful observations regarding the daily use of tools. His distinction between tools ready-to-hand (*Zuhanden*), and present-at-hand (*Vorhanden*) (Heidegger 1979 [1927], 66-83) has been appropriated in the field of cognition and computer design (Winograd and Flores 1985). These notions can be used to shed more light on the dynamical and virtual objects at stake in digital signification.

Heidegger pointed out how tools exist in a mode of being *Um-zu* (in order to), that is, their being refers to a work to be done, in a system of other equipment and labor. A tool we just use is called *ready-to-hand*; the object (hammer, pencil, pointing device) aligns with the activity in our hands and the goal in our minds. The object blends seamlessly with its implicit reference, its *Um-zu,* and does not call for further reflection. We do not think consciously about a hammer when we need it; we just reach for it and use it. But when a tool does not function according to its *Um-zu*, for example, when it breaks, it becomes estranged and detached, and turns into a puzzling isolated object. It is not ready-to-hand anymore, but *present-at-hand,* open to questions and inquiries about what is the matter with it. We then have to reconsider our engagement with the tool as object, repair it, replace it, or change our goal altogether.

Desktop icons cannot break like an object, such as a hammer, but the modes of being as ready-to-hand versus present-at-hand seem to be appropriate here. Icons are ready-to-hand when they yield the result we expect from them. We then routinely take the icons for granted, we neither have to think about them as tools, nor as signs. Rather they appear as compressed sign-tools [28] in their iconic ready-to-handiness. Our unconscious eye-hand coordination makes us even forget the sign-tools are connected to our hands and our clicking actions; the screen seems to be working on its own, by its own icontology. However, when the icon does not yield the expected result, it is no longer ready-to-hand. The icon decomposes into a tool and a sign part, now both present-at-hand, raising questions about whether the tool-equipment chain is broken somewhere, or whether we just misinterpreted the sign.

In Peircian terms, we could say that such a break down raises questions about the relation of the sign to its object. This relation seemed to be unproblematically iconic with an immediate object when the sign-tool was ready-to-hand, but the sign exposes its indexical relation to other kinds of objects (dynamical and virtual) when suddenly turned into a thing present-at-hand.

From this perspective, the change of the desktop icon from an integrated ready-to-hand sign-tool into a decomposed present-at-hand object or sign is not a disturbing inconvenience, but an opportunity. An opportunity to investigate actions and notions taken for granted, an opportunity to raise questions and learn something about the way digital tools and equipment works, how it refers to other equipment and code, how it represents and ontologizes in iconicity, how it conceals its indexicality, how it can fool you, and how you can counter this. As Winograd and Flores put it:

> Breakdowns serve an extremely important cognitive function, revealing to us the nature of our practices and equipment, making them present-to-hand to us, perhaps for the first time. In this sense they function in a positive rather than negative way. (Winograd and Flores 1985, 77-78)

Bill Brown (2001) pursues the same line of argument in his proposal for a 'thing theory' as opposed to a theory of objects. For Brown, the object becomes a thing when it breaks down, and only then it becomes epistemologically illuminating. He writes:

> We look through objects because there are codes by which our interpretive attention makes them meaningful, because there is a discourse of objectivity that allows us to use them as facts. A thing, in contrast, can hardly function as a window. We begin to confront the thingness of objects when they stop working for us: when the drill breaks, when the car stalls, when the windows get filthy, when their flow within the circuits of production and distribution, consumption and exhibition, has been arrested, however momentarily. (Brown 2001, 4)

---

28. In §17 of *Sein und Zeit*, Heidegger uses a similar term, *Zeig-Zeug*, to indicate that the sign in general is 'equipment for showing' (Heidegger 1979 [1927], 79). According to Heidegger, contrary to other tools the sign-tool does not recede into the background, but serves conspicuously as an orientation device. The sign is 'a piece of equipment that explicitly raises a totality of equipment into circumspection, so that together with it the worldly character of the available announces itself' (Heidegger 1979 [1927], 79-80). Signs are therefore considered special tools, they are cognitive orientation tools. In Heideggerian terms, digital sign-tools would then be sign-tool-tools; every sign is a cognitive tool, but digital signs are in addition to that also material tools.

3 — CONCEPTUAL METAPHOR

Heidegger's concepts of ready-to-hand and present-at-hand (or Brown's distinction between objects and things) combined with Peirce's notions of immediate, dynamical, and virtual objects, enables us to see computer icons as semiotically and materially integrated in an operational system where a perpetual sign-tool-machine processing is at work. However, neither Peirce nor Heidegger gave a satisfactory account of how signs can become material tools or vice versa, let alone how the digital sign-tool dynamic comes about. How can something be sign and tool in one? Signs belong to the order of language, they function in the domain of naming, referring, predicating and signifying, while tools belong to the order of being, they function in the domain of doing and transforming. How can such an ontological gap be bridged? I would argue that such a jump can only be accomplished by the bridging and mediating labor of metaphors.[29]

How does this come about? Metaphors are specific compound signs: they assemble two (or more) references, by equating or substituting terms from different domains. Think of 'love is a battlefield', 'DNA is the book of life' or 'the beating heart of a computer'. We are able to create one thing out of two — the love battlefield, the DNA book, the computer heart — and we are able to reveal two things in one; indeed, metaphors play an intricate game with sameness and difference. Moreover, they evade logic and verification, as they paradoxically declare that something *is* and *is not* equal to something else. While this all sounds rather grandiose, metaphors are ubiquitous, they pervade every day language, and 'we cannot get through three sentences of ordinary fluid discourse without it' (Richards 1936, 92). Indeed, 'fluid' discourse — a metaphor.

Their mechanism can be defined quite simply: metaphors compress two (or more) references or associations by transferring and incorporating qualities from the one into the other. As a result, they do not just refer or represent something which can not be expressed otherwise, they also differentiate, predicate, and qualify by transferring specific qualities from one domain to another.[30] This transference of qualities can be done with words, but equally so with other forms of media or modes, such as images, sounds, or gestures. For instance, Charles Forceville (2008) analyzed advertisements and found articulations of pictorial metaphors such as a mobile phone fused with a diamond necklace as precious jewelry, and music scores signifying computer networks in need of a Maestro conductor to 'make it all come together.'[31] Even material-physical objects may stand for and predicate something else, by infusing some of their qualities into the signified (Tilley 1999; Gutenplan 2005). For example, Samuel Gutenplan (2005) points out how a saltshaker and a tablespoon can be used as metaphors for cars, in order to describe a traffic accident. Another example he provides is how a tree in the park, bending and weaving

---

29. As argued elsewhere, metaphors can perform different functions, in different domains: bridging, mediating, framing, distributing, managing, and agenda-setting (Van der Weele and Van den Boomen 2008). For more elaborate accounts of these functions, see the special issue of *Configurations* dedicated to the theme 'How to do things with metaphor?' (Vol. 16, Autumn 2008).
30. Samuel Gutenplan, in his work *Objects of Metaphor* (2005), contends that most metaphor theories are only focusing on the function of reference, ignoring processes of predication and qualification. Gutenplan pleas for a symmetric assessment of both reference and predication/qualification, and calls for a 'predicate liberation' (Gutenplan 2005, 6).
31. See for a more elaborate account of some of Forceville's pictural hybrid metaphors 'Metaphors in computer advertising' (10 October 2006) on my blog *Metamapping*, http://metamapping.net/blog/?p=83.

wildly in a storm but not cracking, may be conceived as adequate metaphor for a troubled mind. Hence, metaphors are vehicles of transference, notably transference between conceptually-semantically different domains, but also between ontologically different domains or modes: between words and objects, words and images, images and objects, gestures and words – and thus, maybe, also between signs and tools, digits and symbols.

In order to develop this idea further, the next section will focus on the so-called Conceptual Theory of Metaphor developed by Lakoff and Johnson (1980, Lakoff 1993). This theory, also known as the Cognitive Theory of Metaphor and the Contemporary Theory of Metaphor (in any case: CTM), is widely considered the dominant paradigm in metaphor analysis. The theory not only addresses poetic, linguistic, or instructive metaphors; it also claims to cover the very fundamentals of all human language, thought, and action. We will see whether this also includes the dynamics of digital sign-tools and icontology.

Sources, targets, and black boxes

Lakoff and Johnson's theory of metaphor is founded on an elaborate notion of conceptual transference. Metaphor is conceived as the transference of concept x taken from source domain X and transported to target domain Y, with the result that concept y is understood in terms of x (Lakoff and Johnson 1980, 5). Metaphors are thus defined as cross-domain mappings, sets of conceptual correspondences [32] across conceptual domains, though not all elements from the source and the target are used in the metaphor, a selection suffices, and non-used aspects are downplayed. Any metaphorical articulation can be analyzed as derived from a basic underlying conceptual metaphor (or metaphorical concept), which in the CTM is conventionally written in the small caps formula: Y IS X, or TARGET IS SOURCE (Lakoff 1993, 207).

Lakoff and Johnson claim that metaphors are ubiquitous and constitutive for mundane speech, thought, and action, as well as for science and philosophy (Johnson 2008). Metaphors do so by providing the means for expressing abstract concepts (nouns as time, life, energy, and causality; verbs as communicating, caring, and belonging; adverbs as happy, more, good, and conscious) into more concrete familiar forms.[33] For example, the expression 'That will cost a lot of time' is based on the metaphorical concept TIME IS MONEY, and all other expressions in terms of saving, spending, investing, borrowing, losing, and wasting time are derived from that basic concept. Other classic examples of basic conceptual metaphors are: ARGUMENT IS WAR, LIFE IS A JOURNEY, COMMUNICATING IS SENDING, and MORE IS UP.

---

32. These correspondences are not confined to resemblance or similarity. While most other theories of metaphor hold that metaphor is a trope of resemblance, Lakoff and Johnson (1980, 151) argue that the perception of similarity can actually be produced by conceptual metaphor. Moreover, they conceive metonymy, synecdoche, and symbols as special instances of metaphorical concepts. I will follow them in this categorization.
33. The most concrete and familiar forms residing in the source domains are, according to the CTM, in the last instance based on bodily experiences (with corresponding basic conceptual metaphors as SICK IS DOWN, HAPPY IS UP, ANGER IS HEATH). These embodied prelinguistic experiences are stored in mind as so called image schemas, basic models which preconfigure patterns of understanding, categorization, and metaphorical mapping (Lakoff 1987). Image schemas typically concern inferences regarding space, motion, force, and transformation, with as the most prominent schemas those build around notions of container, path, and blockage.

We can apply this model of mapping for example to the email icon. The underlying regulating conceptual metaphor is then EMAIL IS POSTAL MAIL, and the cross-domain mapping looks like this:

source domain: postal mail	target domain: email
mailbox	inbox of mail program
postbox	outbox with sent mails
letters, packets	messages, attachments
sending and receiving	send or get mail button
sorting, disposing	distribution to folders, deleting
[postal distribution system]	[mail-server network at ISPs]
[delivery by postman]	[connecting to mail-server; deliver mail]

Here, the source domain consists of a familiar socio-cultural practice, and the target domain emerges as a more or less coherent semantic or conceptual field. The distribution over the source and target looks quite obvious and recognizable, but in fact the list contains some anomalies. The last two correspondences – indicating a postal or email distribution system, and a delivery act – should be part of the metaphor mapping as they are necessary for the successful transference, but these aspects are also exactly what is hidden in the iconic metaphor of email. They *are* and *are not* part of the conceptual mapping; they are what I have called depresented, while the other correspondences are represented as such on the interface, in the form of buttons, menu options, listed messages, and so on.

It is important to note that depresentation is not equivalent with Lakoff and Johnson's notion of downplayed or hidden parts of the domains. Examples of non-represented unused parts in the metaphor EMAIL IS POSTAL MAIL would be stamps [34] in the source domain, and viruses in the target domain. These aspects have no cross-domain correspondence in the metaphor, and they are not necessary to establish the metaphorical concept of email. On the contrary, the aspects 'postal distribution system' and 'delivery by postman' in the source domain do have an aligning correspondence in the target domain. These correspondences are even indispensable for a successful transference – literally and figuratively: without delivery no mail and no email. However, as such they are not represented in the iconic concept mediating between the source and the target domain. Their operation is depresented, purposely made invisible, delegated to hidden processes in a black box of software and machinery.

This implies that the contribution of CTM to the understanding of computer icons remains at the surface of the graphical user interface; it does not provide an entry into the black box. The conceptual mapping model accounts for how the mailbox icon connects the source domain of postal mail with the target domain of email, but the model has no room for the material, indexical operations also implied in the transference: a network connection with an Internet provider, a mail client consulting a mail server, and the subsequent transport of new mail messages to the user's machine.

This can be illustrated by a schematic image (Figure 1). It shows how an input-output mechanism is represented on the screen interface as a visual-conceptual loop (thick black arrows), mediated

---

34. However, the idea of a digital stamp may easily emerge and be connected to the established mail metaphor, as now and then happens with proposals for a 'bit-tax' or for a mechanism for spam-prevention by means of paying a micro fee for each sent mail.

by the metaphorical mailbox icon and the (unconscious) conceptual mapping across the source and target domain. The implicated indexical references (dotted lines) towards the black box of software, configurations, and machinery, remain hidden, therefore, depresented.

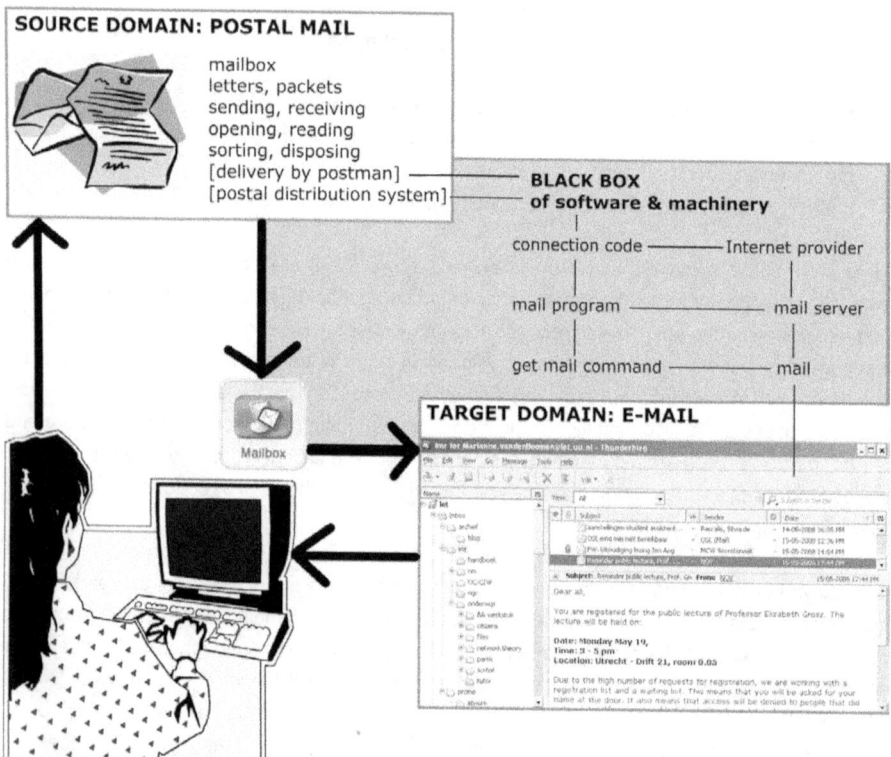

Figure 1. Input-output mechanism of the conceptual metaphor email is postal mail.

Usually, when everything works smoothly, this situation is not problematic. In that case, the iconic sign-tools are so ready-to-hand we can afford to forget them as indexical tools and equipment, and read them as ontologized signs, even forgetting that they are conceptual metaphors. The user can take them at interface value because the sign coincides with the object. However, reading and understanding the icon conceptually is not enough to let it do its job. While this usually suffices for linguistic or visual metaphors, it will not do for this sign-tool. The desktop icon needs *action* to complete its signifying task successfully: not only tool-handling by the user, who should at least click on the icon, but also a chain of actions inside the machine. In that sense, the icon is a two-faced Janus: one side is directed towards the user, who must be able to read, understand, and operate it, and the other side is directed towards software and machine processes. The user is able to read the icon precisely because the other side is concealed and depresented, blackboxed. And that is exactly what the icon does by its icontology: equating the sign with its immediate object, effacing its indexical relations with its dynamical object (code executions) and its virtual object (my mail).

In other words, the conceptual theory of metaphor only covers the situation partially. It focuses on the cognitive and conceptual reading of the icon, on its relation with the immediate object. It gives an account of the conceptual condensation of source and target, of the blending of reading and meaning in the mind of the user. But, as pointed out before, this only works for sign-tools ready-to-hand which render their output seamlessly. The ready-to-hand tool then functions as a 'ready-to-eye' sign, concealing its tool-being and its object-being. But when a sign-tool becomes present-at-hand due to a break down of whatever origin – a quite common mode of being in computing praxis – we can no longer ignore its relations to its dynamical and virtual objects, the material indexicality which enables the completion of the digital-material performance. When the tool becomes present-at-hand we have to open the black box, investigate the depresented chain of equipment, and check if and where a link is broken.

We may conclude that the CTM needs to be extended in order to give a full account of metaphorical sign-tools that blends machine-readable and human-readable code. Interface metaphors, such as icons, menu options, and hyperlinks, function that way, but also the digital objects we create, such as mails, documents, blog posts, comments, status updates, tweets, and the like, are such digital sign-tool-metaphors. While all these concepts are borrowed from other semantic domains, in line with the CTM, they branch out far beyond the cognitive and the semantic realm. They enable traffic and material-semiotic transference between various practices: between and among media forms, cultural discourses and resources, machine-readable code and human-readable code.

However, this machinery remains hidden in the black box produced by the graphical user interface. It does so by translating the machinery into nested metaphorical signs, translating what you get into what you see, thereby depresenting the indexical transferences. In short, they function by means of metaphorical icontology. As long as we conceive these metaphorical signs as plain iconic signs or conceptual metaphors, we get fooled by this icontology. And no matter how convenient and user friendly this may be in daily praxis, we need epistemological access to this black box. As Katherine Hayles puts it:

> Why *should* the user know what is going on in the guts of the machine? Or to put it another way, what is wrong with the user staying at the surface, as long as the interface is robust and functional? One problem is that the interface may not really be that robust [...] [And second, those] who fail to understand the technology will inevitably be at the mercy of those who do. (Hayles 2005, 125-126)

In other words, we need to grasp digital technology, otherwise it grasps us. If we don't, we are not only left at the mercy and politics of those who do (or think they do) understand the indexical black boxes, but we will also be at the mercy of the defaults and built-in politics of the machinery – carried out precisely when it is working robustly without failure.

How should these depresented qualities be incorporated in metaphor analysis and theory? What we need is a conception of metaphor that accounts for indexicality, materiality, and performativity. Katherine Hayles (2002) proposed the concept of *material metaphor* as an analytical term that covers the fact that digital symbols – contrary to other symbolic sign systems – are able to actually *do* things in the world, inside and outside machines. In the next chapter, I will explore this concept and examine how it can be used as a building block for a theory of metaphor that accounts for the digitally enabled tricks of icontology and depresented indexicality.

CHAPTER 2
MATERIAL METAPHORS
HOW OBJECTS TURN INTO SOCIAL ORGANIZERS

> *To be materialist now implies that one enters a labyrinth more intricate than that built by Daedalus.*
> (Bruno Latour, 2005)

As we have seen, digital entities do not expose their secrets easily. They play hide and seek by oscillating between tools, signs, and conceptual metaphors, inimitably switching between iconicity, indexicality, and materiality. As the conceptual theory of metaphor appeared to be unable to account for the material and indexical features of digital metaphors, we have to look elsewhere. This chapter explores the notion of material metaphor, in order to investigate if and how it is usable for the analysis of digital sign-tool-metaphors.

Since the idea of materiality is by itself far from clear, the chapter starts with an analysis of the different levels or instances of materiality. Subsequently, the concept of material metaphor will be fleshed out from two perspectives, respectively as mediating interface and as physical object. The perspective of interface is based on Katherine Hayles' appropriation of material metaphor in her so called Media-Specific Analysis, while the perspective of objects is drawn from the field of anthropology, where the term pertains to physical objects that metaphorize and organize social relations. The last section of the chapter proposes a combination of the two perspectives in order to analyze digital-material entities.

1 — LEVELS OF MATERIALITY

Before zooming in on the notion of material metaphor, let me briefly address the different levels of materiality we have encountered already. The problem is of course that materiality is manifold. The materiality of a subatomic particle is different from the materiality of DNA, an illness, or a database. The materiality of a stone is different from the materiality of a sign, or that of a tool, let alone the various kinds of materiality we encounter in sign-tool-objects we take for granted as digital entities. When it comes to these entities, three different levels can be distinguished.

First, digital entities as human-readable forms, rendered on the interface, have a specific materiality *as signs,* or better signifiers, being the material substrate of signs. In this sense, all signs are material, physically embodied, inscribed.[35] They can come in the form of words, images, graphic symbols, sounds, movements, and various combinations of these sign types, assemblages we have come to call separate media or genres: movies, pdf files, mails, web sites. Virtually any collection, selection, or composite of material sign qualities can be incorporated in a digital entity.

Second, digital entities also have a materiality *as tools,* an indexical materiality, referring to software instructions and executable machine code. This not only holds for clickable hyperlinks and icons, but also for data objects such as Word documents, jpg images, and mp3 files, since such objects are implicitly clickable. The specific format and internal configuration of these data objects implicate specific indexical references to specific application programs which are able to process the data files. We have seen in Chapter 1 how this indexical materiality refers to the dynamic objects of software and machinery, and that this materiality is usually depresented in conceptual metaphors, since these only represent the immediate object of the sign.

The third kind of materiality is the most complicated. It is the materiality of the *virtual symbolic object*. This refers to what is evoked by the metaphorical condensation of the immediate objects and the dynamical object into a virtual object – an object to become, but nevertheless material. This level of material signification has to be distinguished from the material qualities of the signifiers and from the material indexicality of the tool. We may consider this a specific materiality *as metaphorical objects*.

Admittedly, the materiality of this level is not self-evident, as metaphors seem to be primarily conceptual and cognitive, belonging to the order of mind, thought, language, and representation, distinct from the order of material physical dynamics. Yet, it must be acknowledged that these digital object metaphors are not just cognitive. We do not just *think* that a particular set of assembled digital code looks like a document or a mail; it *is* also a bounded, delineated document or a mail message, and we handle them accordingly, as a tool-object, as a metaphorical tool. Such a metaphorical tool connects the immediate object (the object as displayed by the sign), via the depresented dynamical object (the object referred to, inside the black box of machinery) to the virtual object (the object to become). In other words, these metaphorical tools do not just refer and represent; they embody specific semiotic-material objects, objects that can be acted upon.[36] The mail metaphor enables the writing and sending of mail messages, the windows metaphor enables shifting between multiple screens – not just because we attribute mail-like or windows-like behavior to these acts, but because they are materially and formally designed to act this way.

---

35. While popular discourse usually assumes some kinds of signs to be non-material (such as spoken words, the 'text behind the text' in literature, and digital constructs), this premise is not prevalent in media studies and cultural studies. Yet, the tendency to believe in a transcendental signified, a signified so self-evident and self-present that it needs no material instantiation in a signifier, in hard to exorcise. Even the concept of 'floating signifier' (Lévi-Strauss 1950; Barthes 1977; Lacan 1977; Derrida 1978), indicating signifiers that have a variable, deferred, or non-existent referent, has a tendency to slip into non-material non-media-specific transcendence. For example, when a particular word is loosely called a floating signifier, as if it does not make a difference whether this word is spoken, written, painted, or digitally represented, let alone by whom it is spoken and by what authority.

36. In his splendid work on the materiality of new media objects entitled *Mechanisms: New Media and the Forensic Imagination*, Matthew Kirschenbaum, (2008) employs a similar tripartite model by defining digital objects as compounds of physical objects (signs inscribed in a medium), logical objects (formal data structures enabling specific software recognition and interpretation) and conceptual objects (Kirschenbaum 2008, 3). In criticizing new media studies' predominant focus on the third, conceptual level induced by 'screen essentialism' (ibid., 31) and 'medial ideology' (ibid., 36-45), Kirschenbaum proposes a reformulation of the levels in terms of *formal materiality* (processual transmission) and *forensic materiality* (inscription of traces). Yet, by reducing digital signification to formal and physical traces, the author seems to ignore media-specific interfaces and the conceptual metaphorical level, which would enable connecting his notions of materiality to a material semiotics that also accounts for how medial ideology and conceptual icontology is produced.

At this third level of materiality the digital entity tends to emerge as a unity: the sign, the tool and the metaphor are blended and ontologized into one signified.[37] This unified digital object is intertwined with the immediate object of the conceptual metaphor, but also with the medium-specific signifier modality and the indexical reference to machinic inscription and execution. These digital objects exist for us users as delineated manipulable objects on several nested levels; they may be recognized and delineated as icons, files, documents, mail messages, or pictures, but also as programs, scripts, or operating systems. As objects they consist of reified and ontologized assemblages of immediate, dynamical, and virtual objects.

In other words, they cannot be reduced to plain material signifiers or to symbolic signifieds, nor can they be reduced to indexical references to machine processes. Even our preliminary notion of sign-tools does not completely cover these unified objects, these icontologized sign-tool-metaphor-things. While they are both indeed symbolic signs and material tools, digital objects are also more than that. They can acquire a relatively autonomous material existence of their own provided there is a material infrastructure by which they can travel. They can be copied, multiplied, inscribed on a carrier, packaged, transferred, and exchanged. They can be sold or shared as software packages and files, or just set loose in a network, as a virus or a meme. And, by circulating as relatively autonomous objects in social, cultural, political, and economic settings, they affect things in the world. We work with them as sign-tools and data objects, but they also backfire on us, rearranging social relations, signification, and communication patterns.

To resume, we can distinguish three levels of materiality in digital entities: as medium-specific signs, as indexical tools, and as icontologized sign-tool-metaphor-things. In order to unravel these interpenetrating layers of materiality while retaining a perspective on signification and metaphorization, a material-semiotic perspective on metaphor is needed. That is, a perspective on metaphor that not only tracks down transferences and translations from concept to concept, but also between different ontological domains: from concepts to objects, from objects to machine execution, from software instructions to representations, from one medium to another, from metaphor to object, from signs to tools, and vice versa. In short, what we need is a theory, of what Katherine Hayles (2002) has dubbed, *material metaphor*.

2 — MATERIAL METAPHOR

Hayles (2002) defined material metaphor as those instances of metaphor in which transference does not take place between different words or concepts, but between words or symbols and physical artifacts. She observed that in some instances of metaphor,

> the transfer takes place not between one word to another but rather between a symbol (more properly, a network of symbols) and material apparatus. This kind of traffic, as old as the human species, is becoming increasingly important as the symbol-processing machines we call computers are hooked into networks in which they are seamlessly integrated with apparatus that can actually do things in the world, from the sensors and actuators of mobile robots to

---

37. These three levels of materiality are conform a Peircian triad, connecting a quality of Firstness (media-specific format) to a relation of Secondness (indexical connection to machine code and processes), and finally a systematic signified of Thirdness (the materially and metaphorically unified digital object).

the semiotic-material machinery that changes numbers in bank accounts. To account for this traffic I propose *material metaphor*, a term that foregrounds the traffic between words and physical artifacts. (Hayles 2002, 22)

In these instances of metaphor the transference is not between linguistic concepts or semantic domains, but between words or other symbols and a material-physical system that affects a state of affairs in the world. Important here is that Hayles explicitly considers material metaphor a matter of traffic, that is, of movement, displacement or travel. As she explained elsewhere: 'I think of [material metaphor] as a physical object that, through its construction and functioning, acts as a crossroad or a juncture point for the traffic between the physical and the verbal' (Hayles 2004). While most theories of metaphor speak of transference and take the *aftereffect* of metaphorical movement (substitution, condensation, blending, or whatever is considered basic to metaphor) as their primary object of study, Hayles' notion of material metaphor does not consider so much the aftereffect but the *act*, the process, the traffic, as primary.

This reminds us that metaphor is by definition transference, already traceable in the etymology of the word. The Greek prefix *meta*, means 'after, over, across', but also 'changed', whereas *pherein* in Greek means 'to bear, to carry'. Metaphors are thus matters of transference in the broadest sense: a blend of transport, translation, and transformation.[38] This is not just etymological wordplay. Using a metaphor is mobilizing a metaphor: moving something across space, thereby transforming not just the stuff moved, but also the spatial plane and ordering as such.

Travels, roads, and maps
In that regard, Hayles' notion of material metaphor is close to Michel de Certeau's stance on metaphor as vehicles for narratives (Certeau 1984).[39] As he puts it:

In modern Athens, the vehicles of mass transportation are called *metaphorai*. To go to work or come home, one takes a 'metaphor' – a bus or a train. Stories could also take this noble name: every day, they traverse and organize places; they select and link them together; they make sentences and itineraries out of them. They are spatial trajectories. (De Certeau 1984, 115)

The notion of material metaphors as spatial trajectories, setting in motion traffic and narratives – including the traffic of narrative and the narrative of traffic – may be able to open up some of the

---

38. I am aware of the fact that by defining metaphor in terms of generalized transference, the notion of metaphor tends to loose its distinction from concepts such as interface, medium, mediation, communication, representation, translation, exchange, and network. Indeed, these concepts all imply transference, yet all different in kind. Moreover, these concepts in their turn also draw upon metaphors in different ways. This raises important onto-epistemological questions regarding difference and sameness, differentiation and equalization – and that is precisely what a perspective in terms of metaphorical transference should enforce: a more fine-tuned and differentiated notion of how transferences work.
39. Note that Richards (1936) also used the notion of vehicle in his theory of metaphor. According to Richards, metaphor is comprised of two elements: the *tenor*, that is, the referent, the object referred to (in Lakoff's terms: the target), and the *vehicle*, the metaphorical expression. Richards argues that the tenor and the vehicle interact in the mind of an interpreter, but, to stay within the metaphor, the vehicle halts there. It is not a vehicle for further narratives.

black boxes in the digital sign-tool-machine network, as it focuses on material and semiotic traffic that implies more than just the figural transference of conceptual meaning from one semantic domain to another. Material metaphors organize stories, spaces, and travelers, they indicate and facilitate (but also block) specific routes and perspectives on the environment.

If we take this traffic metaphor as a metaphor of metaphor itself, then we can say that material metaphors function as travel guides and policemen, but also as the roads, crossroads, and vehicles themselves. In that sense material metaphors as indicated by Hayles and De Certeau are not seen as maps or mirrors (which seem to be the primary metaphors of metaphor in most theories of metaphor), they are active *mediators* (Van der Weele and Van den Boomen 2008). In this way, they enable, produce, and organize traffic, thereby creating the territories, roads, and road blocks, rather than mapping pre-existing regions and trajectories.

The connection with stories as organizing principles is not coincidental in Hayles' work. As a literary scholar (in addition to being trained as a chemist), she proposed the concept of material metaphor in her book *Writing Machines* (2002) as an intervention in literary theory, with important implications for media theory. In this book, she explores what difference it makes when works of literature are not materialized as flat durable marks on printed paper, but as digitally produced 'technotexts': texts constituted by dynamic unstable symbols on screens, *flickering signifiers*, as she has called them elsewhere (Hayles 1993b, 1999). Hayles argues that digitally produced signifiers – be it in the form of words, graphics, or images – are problematic as representations because they are also simulations. Where representations suggest the replication of an *a priori* original, of something that has been present before, simulations go beyond plain mimesis: they evoke emergence. Therefore, the compound simulated representations that materialize in digital technotexts not only refer to (conventionally established or artistically created) signifieds, but they also function dynamically and productively as movable and moving objects, acquiring a life of their own. In order to investigate the dynamic boundaries between representations, simulations, and the technologies that produce them Hayles incites literary scholars to stop focusing on the ideational and representational 'text behind the text', and turn instead to the material texture, the materiality of the text itself, as it 'offers a robust conceptual framework in which to talk about *both* representation and simulation as well as the constraints and enablings they entail' (Hayles 2002, 6).

It should be noted that the idea of materiality in Hayles' view does not completely coincide with physical materiality, consisting of an infinite array of physical attributes. At issue is that technotexts (and any digital entity, I would add) select and mobilize a few of these attributes in order to put specific concerns in the foreground. This kind of materiality is by no means stable, it is profoundly dynamic and performative. As Hayles puts it, this notion of materiality,

> cannot be specified in advance, as if it pre-existed the specificity of the work. An emergent property, materiality depends on how the work mobilizes its resources as a physical artifact as well as the user's interactions with the work and the interpretative strategies she develops – strategies that include physical manipulations as well as conceptual frameworks. In the broadest sense, materiality emerges from the dynamic interplay between the richness of a physically robust world and human intelligence as it crafts this physicality to create meaning. (Hayles 2002, 32-33)

Put differently, materiality is that what *matters* in the double sense of the word: as that which is both physical *and* charged with socio-cultural meaning and significance. Materiality *matters* – as a verb and as a noun. [40] The materialist framework she proposes should enable the investigation of how such 'mattering' and 'matter' comes about, how it is enacted in the interaction between the materiality of inscription technologies and the inscriptions they produce as readable signs.

Media-Specific Analysis

Hayles dubs this kind of investigation 'Media-Specific Analysis, a mode of interrogation alert to the ways in which the medium constructs the work and the work constructs the medium' (Hayles 2002, 6). This perspective has profound implications for literary studies and media studies, since these disciplines have their roots in the very labor division between the study of the work or the message and the study of the medium respectively, leaving little room for the analysis of the mutual interaction and co-construction of message and medium. [41] Hayles' proposal for Media-Specific Analysis is closely attached to her notion of material metaphor, as both concepts try to capture the material and the symbolic as mutually interpenetrated. [42] A Media-Specific Analysis tries to read media texts in terms of the material metaphors set in motion, by fleshing out the specific conjunctions of symbolic meaning and material construction they mobilize.

The question is on what level such a conjunction can be located. What is considered a medium in Media-Specific Analysis, and what counts as material metaphor? When Hayles addresses the way classic literary scholars treat (or better, ignore) the materiality of their object of study, she starts with a rather broad gesture. In order to show that the mutual co-construction of medium and message is not confined to the field of electronic literature, and that it also applies for printed book-bound literature, her first example of a material metaphor is the book as such:

> We are not generally accustomed to think of a book as a material metaphor, but in fact it is an artifact whose physical properties and historical usages structure our interactions with it in ways obvious and subtle. In addition to defining the page as a unit of reading, and binding pages sequentially to indicate an order of reading, are less obvious conventions such [as] the

---

40. Other scholars, especially feminist scholars, have made similar claims on the inseparability of the discursive and the material, as for example, Coward and Ellis (1977), Haraway (1991), Barad (2003), and Braidotti (2012).
41. Media theory in itself can be said to suffer from the same dichotomy of medium and message. The tradition of 'media apriori' focuses primarily on the materiality or technology of media (media archaeology, media ecology, with McLuhan and Kittler as the most prominent exponents) while the tradition of the 'message apriori' primarily focuses on the hermeneutics of representations (visual culture studies, cultural studies, film and television studies). Although both perspectives have their own merits, and while both may incorporate the other pole as secondary focus, they are still both prone to the inherent danger of determinism, that is technological determinism and representationalism respectively. A symmetrical focus on the medium and the message, including the interrelations of medium as message and message as medium, is rare. In that regard, science and technology studies and the emerging field of software studies (Fuller 2008) have more promising records.
42. In the 'Lexicon linkmap' (the 'index cloud' of *Writing Machines*, a technotextual representation c.q. simulation of the classical index — in itself a great exemplification of material metaphor — to be found at the books web supplement (http://mitpress.mit.edu/sites/default/files/titles/content/mediawork/titles/writing/sup/sup_index.html) the terms 'media-specific analysis', 'material metaphor' and 'technotexts' are the largest words in the index cloud, and positioned layered over each other, on the verge of illegibility (until you move your cursor).

opacity of paper, a physical property that defines the page as having two sides whose relationship is linear and sequential rather than interpenetrating and simultaneous. To change the physical form of the artifact is not merely to change the act of reading [...] but profoundly to transform the metaphoric network structuring the relation from word to world. (ibid., 22-23)

This seems to imply that material metaphors indicate a general way of mediating and organizing a network of traffic between words and world. [43] Defined that way they seem to coincide almost with commonly recognized medial carriers or interfaces such as books, film, television, and computers perhaps. And indeed, Hayles also considers the computer a material metaphor. She argues, 'in its flexibility, range, and functionality the computer is perhaps the most important material metaphor at work in the contemporary medial ecology' (Hayles 2004b).

Therefore, Hayles' notion of material metaphor seems at first sight concerned with broad classes of media technology – The Book, The Computer – framing them as general material-semiotic assemblages of physical materiality and symbolic messaging. However, her employment of the term does not stop with these broad categories, as her numerous case studies show. For example, Hayles also detects material metaphors at the level of dedicated hardware and software construction in works of art such as the text-to-speech device called *Reading Eye Dog* (Hayles 2002, 23) or the performative installation called ~~database~~ (ibid., 101). She also locates them in the page formatting of the printed book *House of Leaves* (Danielewski 2000) and in science-fiction novels describing specific interfaces – as in *Permutation City* (Egan 1994) where instances of disembodied human consciousness create specific material interfaces for themselves in order to interact with and interfere in the material world.

Hayles' material metaphor is thus a scalable concept that can be traced on various levels. Books in general can function as material metaphors, but also a specific book, a specific literary technique, a specific protagonist, object, or word in a story, a specific graphic arrangement on the pages, or a specific arrangement of the pages themselves, for example as codex or as scroll. [44]

In the same way, cinema in general can be analyzed as a material metaphor (cf. Manovich's cinematic frame in *The Language of New Media*), but also a specific movie (cf. Manovich's take on *Man with a Movie Camera*), or specific phenomena represented or simulated in a specific movie. For example, in the movie *Minority Report*, the ubiquitousness of invisible interfaces to personal information stored in numerous databases can be considered a material metaphor. These specific interfaces not only organize and internally direct the narrative, the characters, and their behavior, but they also send a message to the public watching the movie. The material metaphor – a condensation of technology,

---

43. While the importance of media specificity may be clear here, one may wonder, in what sense could books be conceived as metaphors? Metaphors for what? Books can be seen as specific material codifications of knowledge, and thus of a particular metaphorization of power and authority. Adhering to the classical Aristotelian idea of metaphor as substitution, books have been analyzed as replacing the cathedral since Victor Hugo used this image in *The Hunchback of Notre-Dame* (1831): 'Alas, this will destroy that,' archdeacon Frollo sighed, looking up from a printed book to the impressive cathedral visible through his window (quoted in Gunkel 2003, 278). In that sense, books can be seen as a metaphor for secularization, dispersion, emancipation, education, Enlightenment, and humanism – or better, they embody, assemble, and configure this metaphorical network of various cultural and social transformations. However, it is important to note that these metaphorical-indexical connections are not represented in the sign (as would be the case with a conceptual metaphor).

TRANSCODING THE DIGITAL

imagined technology, narrative, and the political desire to eradicate crime by preventing it before it is even committed – warns us about the new horrors such condensations can invoke when implemented in society.

Material-metaphorical networks

In short, as Hayles defined them, material metaphors are metaphorical interfaces that can be found at any level of what we may call a medium, and can take any form: an object, an arrangement, a technique, a narrator, a protagonist, a technology, a symbol, a concept, a word. Decisive is the traffic they enable, conduct, or invoke between the symbolic and the material, thereby constituting what can be known, imagined, and narrated, and how it can be addressed, appropriated, and enacted. These material metaphors do not just signify and represent – as all metaphors do – they are also able to evoke acts in the material world with their mobilization of particular physical-material attributes. While conceptual metaphors primarily map correspondences between conceptual source and target domains, material metaphors mobilize other kinds of transference: not only between conceptual domains, but also between symbolic and material domains, thereby reaching out toward wider discourse networks.

Material metaphors can presuppose and exploit recognizable conceptual metaphors, but this is not necessarily the case as Hayles' case studies show. For example, we are not used to thinking of codex books, graphical user interfaces, or databases in terms of metaphors. On the other hand, when medial interfaces do get recognized as metaphors, they tend to get reduced to their respective conceptual metaphors, such as EMAIL IS POSTAL MAIL and other mundane interface notions as browsing (THE WEB IS A BOOK), drag and drop (A FILE IS A THING), wizard (SOFTWARE IS MAGIC) or exit (A PROGRAM IS A BUILDING). In other words, we tend to see either too little metaphor in media praxis, or we see only metaphor, that is, conceptual metaphor.

However, the sole focus of iconic appearance as conceptual metaphor entails the danger of an uncritical absorption in condensed icontology. This icontology should be taken seriously, but it should be explained instead of taken as an explanation. Conceptual metaphors are only half the story. While conceptual metaphors such as mail, wizard and exit may explain what happens inside the head of the sign interpreter, they remain inside the cognitive order of semantics and language. Extending the cognitive theory of metaphor with Haylesian material metaphors reveals the implicated but depressented indexical and material-symbolical traffic to other domains. Analyzing them as material metaphors – that is, as the material-metaphorical network invoked by the

---

44. The German media historian Friedrich Kittler (1990, 1997) considers the historical transition from scroll to codex, that is, from rolls of papyrus to bounded browsable books, as a crucial turning point that enabled fundamental rearrangements of knowledge and power. Contrary to the scroll, the codex allowed by its material arrangement random and hands-free reading, comparison of text parts, page numbering, and indexing. Kittler's notion of media as inscription devices that allow storage, transmission, and processing of data by their specific arrangements of material addressability can be seen as articulations of material metaphor similar to Hayles' notion. In terms of Kittlerian addressability, web pages are particularly interesting material metaphors. The material-metaphorical transposition of the limited page of the codex to the scrollable web page with its own URL, in its turn divided in separately addressable parts of, for instance, blog entries, each with its own permalink, entails new material-semiotic configurations that may be comparable with the transition from scroll to codex in the Middle Ages. For a funny exploration of this idea, see *The Medieval Helpdesk* on YouTube http://www.youtube.com/watch?v=pQHX-SjgQvQ).

seemingly simple concepts such as mail, browse, or exit – forces us to trace other routes and other traffic, indexical traffic. There is indexical traffic from the head of the sign interpreter to the hands of the tool user, and from there through and behind the screen interface, inside the black box of software and machinery, and further to the larger mediating networks involved: cultural and institutional configurations of users, narratives, artifacts, and interfaces.

Material metaphors are by definition attached to a broader discourse. Think for instance of the notion of computer memory, a blend of a metaphorical concept (A COMPUTER IS A BRAIN) and a physical-material artifact that is associated with the long standing philosophical discourse of MIND AS MACHINE and MACHINE AS MIND (Minsky 1986, Coyne 1995, Draaisma 2000). In the same vein, the button marked *home* in our browser can be seen as a metaphorical residue of the nineties discourse of the electronic highway, while brand names as Explorer and Navigator for web browsers are inscribed in the discourse of adventurous cyberspace (see Chapter 6 for a further analysis of the metaphors of electronic highway and cyberspace).

Common digital-material metaphors are often derived from other media practices and formats (think of: page, scroll, library, index, zoom, tab, chat, channel, send, paste, write, e-ink, Facebook), but they also borrow from architecture (portal, site, home, window, room, enter, exit, MySpace), objects (shopping cart, menu, button, mailbox, file, map, packet), human roles and occupations (server, client, host, wizard, avatar), or public space (forum, community, Digital City). The intriguing observation can be made that, while these metaphors are imported from quite different and heterogeneous semantic-conceptual domains, they seem to be mixable and nestable without posing any conceptual problems for common use. On the Internet a *portal* consisting of *pages, buttons, boxes, archives, movies* and *rooms* is quite common, one rarely gets confused by such a heterogeneous and internally conflicting assemblage of metaphors. Yet, confusion can occur when it comes to performative acts by material metaphors. Can you safely *cancel* a *document* (in the print dialog box) without deleting it completely? Would dropping a disk in the trashcan (of a Mac) indeed lead to the ejection of the hardware object, or will the information on it be erased? In these practical questions, we can recognize something of the depresented material indexicality of conceptual metaphors that are in fact material metaphors.

Metaphor and indexicality revisited

Though Hayles does not use the notion of indexicality in this context, her idea of material metaphor can also be seen as an intervention in the debate on indexicality in film and media studies. In this debate, mainly concerning photography and documentary film, indexicality is considered as a reference to the real, as a truth claim, and even proof of the real (Gunning 2007, Doane 2007, Kessler 2009). In Peirce's terminology photography is both iconic (based on analogy and similarity with the object represented) and indexical (based on a physical, causal relation with the object). This combination seems to secure an equivalence and verisimilitude between what 'has been there' and what is represented, based as it is on the causal physicality of a technological apparatus that is able to capture physical traces of light reflected from an object and translate these to analog inscriptions on an artifact. The apparent objective causality of photographic technology yielded to an all too easy equation between indexicality and truth for photography and documentary film. While the claims regarding truth, authenticity, and the precision of these media-specific artifacts have always been fragile and contested, the debate got a renewed impulse with the advent of digital imagery. Due to digital-numerical storage and their algorithmic reconstruction process, digital images were supposed to definitely cut off any physical-analog connection with the real, dissolving any indexical trust attributed to photographic images. The criterion of indexicality thus moved from a supposedly inherent quality of the image towards the ease of tampering and manipulation, in fact, a move from indexicality as a feature of the sign (the photograph, the image) to a feature of the tool, the production apparatus.

Notwithstanding these media-theoretical worries, the praxis of digital imaging did not eliminate indexical truth attribution. Quite on the contrary, considering the unproblematic use of digital photographs on passports, and the proliferation of forensic indexical material as fingerprints or DNA traces. Fingerprints and DNA traces are, after all, only indexical tokens for authenticity and proof when authenticated by a matching record in a database. In that sense, indexicality becomes more and more a matter of digital storage, indexing, and retrieval. Admittedly, the securing of digital indexicality is only achieved with a proliferation of authentication, warranty, and security measures, but in any case indexicality is far from dissolved by digitality. I would even argue that digital indexicality has become predominant in any digital praxis, ranging from forensics to governance to daily computing. The ubiquitousness of databases, IDs, passwords and login names established a regime of indexicality, driven by the logic of assigning privileges and legitimate positions to indexable, addressable subjects as users, customers, and citizens.

Though Hayles does not address these social-political ramifications in terms of indexicality, the concept of material metaphor does allow for such a perspective. Her work incites a return to Peirce's indexicality, that is, indexicality as an existential or causal relation, not in terms of icontologized truth claims, but as the indexical traffic between the symbolic and the material. Hayles' Media-Specific Analysis tracks down any traceable traffic a medial interface mobilizes. That is, any indexical relation, on any scale, articulated by any sign or assemblage of signs, regardless of whether it is icontologized as metaphor, as object, as computer code, or as the index in a book. This implies that indexicality does not just reside in the image (what you see) or in the production apparatus (what you get), but that it reaches much further.[45] Indexicality, understood in terms of material metaphor, concerns the media-specific metaphorical condensations and the traffic in its slip stream that aligns and sustains broader material-semiotic networks – networks of machinery and black boxes, including their attachments to social-cultural networks of practice, of discourse, of control, of ideology, of taken-for-grantedness.

Again, Hayles does not explicitly address these ramifications. Her work mainly concerns artistic technotexts, installations, and interfaces. But there is no reason to confine the notion of material metaphor to the artistic critical fringes of digital culture. It can be extremely useful for the critical analysis of more mundane digital practices as sending an email, logging in, clicking on hyperlinks, adding a friend to Facebook, or gazing at your mobile phone. These practices all involve assemblages of sign-tool-metaphor-things, but we are rarely aware of this compound constitution.

---

45. Frank Kessler (2009) makes a similar move by differentiating three conceptions of indexicality: 1) indexicality as *what you see,* a supposed correspondence between the represented image and what 'has been there' or at least what has been seen there for the image taker, 2) indexicality as *what you get*, produced by the interplay of the physical affordances of the interface, the technological production apparatus, and the interventions of the producer (whether produced analogically by physics and mechanic translation, or produced digitally by causal physics, numerical conversions, and algorithmic processing), and 3) indexicality as *what you get to see,* induced by a specific discourse or dispositif that positions specific artifacts as negotiable candidates for truth or falsehood in specific practices and uses. Again, we can recognize a Peircian triad in Kessler's analysis.

And, as if the oscillation between sign and tool does not give us enough trouble, there is also a complicated hide-and-seek game going on between objects and the metaphors at stake. Sometimes we see the object (the screen, the software package, the computer, the mobile phone), but not the metaphorical assemblage this object embodies. Sometimes we sense something of metaphor (mail, browsing, portal), but we are then blind for the object properties of these metaphors. And sometimes digital sign-tools are so abstract we neither see objects nor metaphors. This is the case, for instance, with hyperlinks, log in names, and social network profiles.

While seeing the metaphor *or* the object is already hard enough, thinking the two together and entangled into each other is even more difficult. It is like seeing either the rabbit or the duck in the famous ambiguous picture. Can we see the rabbit and the duck simultaneously? Such a double perspective is required when we want to track down the traffic invoked by digital objects as indexical organizers of people, places, and privileges. Hayles opened the way for doing this by analyzing various interfaces as material metaphors, foregrounding their media-specificity. While the notion of interface is a main conceptual asset in new media studies and computer science, the role of metaphor is only acknowledged in the field of interface design and usability, rarely in new media studies. But even then the study of metaphor usually remains restricted to conceptual metaphor. Hayles goes a step further and points at the indexical and material implications of interfaces by conceiving them as material metaphors.

Her analysis starts with a recognized medial interface – book, computer, screen, text, image – and then follows the traffic enabled by both the object and the metaphor. But what about objects that are not immediately recognized as medial interfaces, but that do function as material-symbolical organizers, say, as a kind of social interfaces? Think for instance of passports, money, uniforms, or wedding rings. Should such objects also be considered material metaphors? Hayles does not address this question, but just in passing, she mentions she has borrowed the idea of material metaphor from the field of anthropology (Hayles 2002, 42). In this field, the notion of material metaphor is broader than what media scholars consider medial interfaces; it pertains to any object that can function as a social interface, by its specific affordances, attributions, and usages. Media studies may benefit from the insights developed here, especially since the advent of embedded digitality seems to blur the boundaries between medial interfaces and ordinary objects. In order to excavate the relation between medial and social interfaces, I will first address the anthropological notion of material metaphor, and then turn to the implications for contemporary technological objects of inscription.

3 — METAPHORICAL OBJECTS IN ANTHROPOLOGY

The interpretation of objects has of course always been the main research question for anthropology and archaeology. But especially since the structuralist-linguistic turn, inspired by the work of Ferdinand de Saussure (1916) and Claude Lévi-Strauss (1958), these fields have been struggling with the relation between words and things, language and materiality, interpretation and social practice. In classical structuralist anthropology, cultures are 'read' as languages. In other words, cultures are conceived as coherent systems of myths and rituals that are structured as a language and subjugated to the same structuring rules as language. One of the crown jewels of structuralist linguistics, as formulated by Saussure (1916) is the arbitrariness of the sign, that is, the arbitrary relation between signifier and signified. Yet, as several anthropologists and archaeologists have pointed out, this foundational ground rule does not seem to hold when physical objects function as symbols. Ethnographic research encounters a multitude of such objects – pots, canoes, houses, villages – that embody symbolic signifieds that cannot be discovered by structuralist analysis for two reasons. First, objects have, contrary to words and concepts, a material existence in the world that generates its own constraints and affordances. And second, the functioning of objects as symbols or signs can differ from the way linguistic symbols work. To put it bluntly: an object is not a word, and a word is not an object.

Knives, pots, and villages

Archaeologists as Hodder (1987) and Tilley (1991) have criticized the structuralist inability to explain particular historical contexts, material formations, and the contributions made by meaningful actions of individuals. They argue that, if myths and material objects can indeed be structurally 'read' as a language, then it should at least be acknowledged that humans and material forms also contribute to it with a kind of 'writing', thereby co-constituting rather than just reflecting social realities and structures. Moreover, they point out that, although material objects may work (and thus be read) as symbols, they are however not as arbitrary as words are. Their form and affordances affect the structure and possibilities of their use, both as symbols and as tangible manipulable material objects – putting it in my terms, both as signs and as tools. Hodder suggests that semiotic-structuralist approaches are thus incapable of dealing with contextual meaning that is evoked by objects that refer. As he puts it,

> Thus a pot may be a signifier of a concept, such as 'young man', which is the signified. It is important to recognize that in most semiotic analyses the relation between the signifier and signified is seen as arbitrary. The concern is with the organization of signifier and signified, rather than with the particular concept 'young man' and how it might appropriately be referred to by the pot and its associated meanings. As a whole the analysis remains abstracted from the reality of a 'young man'. (Hodder 1987, 2)

Hodder here suggests that a semiotic-structuralist analysis ignores how the young man (and thus his others: the young women, the old man, the old woman) may be affected or even constituted as a subject by the use of the pot and the attributed meaning of the pot. To put it differently, the indexical reference to the real existing young men, that is, the traffic between the pot and the young man (and his others), is ignored. Such an analysis is not able to give an account of the contextual and cultural functioning of material objects, and how they may function as material-symbolic hybrids that assemble and organize signification, material practice, and social categories in what has come to be called material culture.[46]

---

46. The criticism on the structuralist frame in archaeology and anthropology developed into a new field of study that came to be called material culture: the field concerning the interconnections between material artifacts and social relations. While the term material culture is mentioned in classic functionalist anthropology (even as early as 1910), the term only became prominent in post-structuralist inspired archaeology in the late 1980s through the works of archaeologists and anthropologists, like Hodder and Tilley. The idea was taken up later in other fields, such as cultural studies and science and technology studies (Buchi 2004, Dourish 2004, Dant 2005, Tilley et al., 2006). Latour's actor-network theory (1987, 2005) can also be seen as being part of this 'material turn', just as the recent interest in 'thing theory' (Brown 2001, Harman 2002, 2005, Turkle 2007).

As mentioned before, there is a big difference between objects and language. On the one hand, objects seem to be more static than language. They are after all solid material things, rather than floating signifiers. But on the other hand, they are also more dynamic since they imply the transformation of matter by means of social labor (Preucel 2006, 138). Material cultural objects have to be produced, reproduced, and maintained by organized labor in order to counter the deterioration and wear inherent to materiality and usage. This principle of social labor – that is, the organized transformation of activities as performed by humans and distributed over different social categories – implicates that the objects and objectification processes are part of a dynamic social system, involving an interpenetration of materiality, praxis, labor, communication, and signification. Material culture thus not only consists of the use of things, but also of the use of language, and most of all of the intertwining of these uses, where 'neither language or the production, reception and use of material forms can be claimed to have any ontological primacy' (Tilley 2002, 24).

A special instance of objects in material culture consists of 'objectified' metaphors: metaphors that are not expressed verbally or written, but that are articulated by material objects. For example, when a village is laid out and built as a human body, including a more or less recognizable head, heart, legs, and so on, with strict implications regarding what social categories or activities are allowed at which places. Or a knife or a pot signifying a young man, with implications about what social groups can use this pot to cook. These signifying objects are clearly not arbitrary signs. Their significance is derived from a specific analogy – perceived, assumed, inferred, or retrospectively produced, but anyway enforced and reinforced by the material affordances, construction, and practical use of the object. And most importantly, as Tilley remarks, 'The analogies so construed may then also act back recursively on the more familiar elements of the metaphorical relationship' (Tilley 1999, 28). In other words, such objectified metaphors can backfire on certain social categories, including the head of the clan, young men, young women, virgins, and so on, disciplining and positioning them by the use of the objects at stake in daily practices and rituals.

Material metaphors as social organizers

Keith Ray dubbed these 'objectified' analogies material metaphors in 1987, long before Hayles appropriated the term. According to Ray, the term pertains to material objects that act as metaphors, that is, objects that have an extra signifying function on top of, or better, blended with their plain use function (Ray 1987). This signification may or may not be clearly expressed by the specific form, material, color or ornaments of the object, but in any case the articulation of meaning, and thus the assignment of subject positions, resides primarily in the way the objects are used in daily life and rituals.

Ray employed the concept of material metaphor to elucidate the patterning of motifs on various metal works, pottery, textiles, walls, and doors he found at archaeological sites of the Igbo clan in Nigeria. However, the classical analysis of making a list of the motifs and tabulating their occurrences on different classes of objects did not reveal any significant meaning. Only when the form of the objects and their situatedness in specific cultural practices were taken into account did a pattern of 'focal material symbols' emerge (Ray 1987, 68). Ray derived his notion of material metaphor from this case study, defining it as,

> a representation or group of representations that encapsulates in material form certain kinds of moral or social or ritual relationships, or certain kinds of interaction, by means of either a simple metaphorical or complex proverbial portrayal of objects or creatures. (Ray 1987, 67)

To put it more simply, a material metaphor is a metaphorical representation of social relations embodied in a material object. Material metaphors thus assemble and condensate significations that go beyond the functional properties of objects, and beyond an arbitrary symbolic attribution; they assemble and (re)produce specific social relations.

At first glance the formula for conceptual metaphor TARGET IS SOURCE seems to be quite capable of analyzing such material metaphors.[47] Just find the basic conceptual metaphor – POT IS YOUNG MAN; VILLAGE IS HUMAN BODY – map the correspondences between the source and target, and infer the implications and the broader conceptual scheme.

However, there are some problems with this procedure. Firstly, the formula TARGET IS SOURCE is too abstract. At issue is not the conceptual metaphor POT IS YOUNG MAN or VILLAGE IS HUMAN BODY, but *THIS* POT IS A YOUNG MAN and *THIS* VILLAGE IS A HUMAN BODY. The metaphor is indexical rather than conceptual as it points directly to a specific target: *this* specific pot, and *this* specific village. One has to go back to the specific material construction and situated use of the target (the pot, the village) in order to be able to perceive and conceive any correspondence with the source.

In the same vein, the source cannot be considered abstractly. Source domains such as young man or human body may appear to be universal human categories, but in material metaphors they are as specific, historically and culturally situated as the specific pot and the specific village. The source, as such, does not tell you anything in itself, since we just do not know what a young man or a human body implies in contexts where they were created and inscribed in pots or constructed into villages.

The metaphorical and material network of uses and meanings goes beyond the conceptual formula POT IS YOUNG MAN or VILLAGE IS HUMAN BODY. These conceptual formulas are at best provisional helper devices for the anthropologist who is looking for clues. But more often such a formula cannot even be construed: material metaphors can be so embedded and intertwined with numerous cross references that no clear basic conceptual metaphor can be formulated. In Ray's work on the distributed patterns of Igbo inscriptions, for example, there was no such short cut to be found. Material metaphors only emerge *in vivo*, enacted and performed in social practice, or in an elaborative narrative reconstruction by the ethnographic researcher, not in a simple conceptual formula.

Material metaphor as conceptualized in anthropology thus exploits the inherent polysemy of signs and the durability of repeated use and labor, yielding to specific material objects as assemblages of multiple meanings and connections. Sometimes such objects function in

---

47. Christopher Tilley (1999, 2002) has elaborated Ray's insights by reconciling them with Lakoff's conceptual theory of metaphor. The Lakovian claim that metaphors frame and constitute human thought, language, and action is derived from the observation that most metaphors can be traced back as universal image schemas grounded in bodily experiences (Lakoff and Johnson 1999). The suggestion of universality has been criticized severely (see for example Zinken et al. 2003), and Tilley also emphasizes that 'such experiences and images are always mediated through social experiences and thus are culturally variable' (Tilley 2002, 24). Tilley proposes to investigate how human minds with this metaphorical disposition come to produce specific linkages, under historically specific circumstances, with culturally specific material objects, while adhering to the general Lakovian principle: 'To be human is to think through metaphors and express these thoughts through linguistic utterances and objectify them in material forms' (Tilley 2002, 24).

conjunction with explicitly verbalized metaphors, while other times they are silent objectified metaphors. Occasionally, the metaphors are so silent that the metaphorical aspect is seemingly absent. As Ray explains:

> Some objects which are not obviously metaphorical in that they do not involve embodiments or representations of clear symbolic import nevertheless make the kind of communicative statements alluded to above. They may do so by the power of connotation in a practice I would term 'presencing'. This is the remote introduction of individuals or categories of persons into contexts and interactions they are not directly involved in. The means of such remote introduction is the inclusion in such contexts or interactions of objects which connote attributes of persons who habitually use them. (Ray 1987, 67-68)

It is this presencing of actually absent others which makes these material metaphors into so much more than merely conceptual representations; it constitutes them as powerful social organizers. A chain, or better a network of metaphorical and metonymical transformations and invocations is involved, enacted in ritual performance with and by the objects that embody objectifications of self, others, social categories, and environmental living conditions. Material metaphors are thus deeply embedded in social codes, conventions, and attribution, not only, as all metaphors do, to acquire their shared meaning in a cultural speech community, but situated firmly in material social praxis. It is the practical use of the objects in daily life and discourse which invokes the ordering of present and absent social categories, relationships, and interactions.

To summarize this small excursion into post-structuralist anthropology, we have identified specific artifacts which are able to perform active metaphorical assemblage labor in a way that words or concepts can not. Material metaphors not only *signify*, that is, produce mental effects, signifieds, they also *do* things in the world. By being taken up in a network of objects, praxis, and discourse, they assign, produce, and reproduce social relations, social categories, and thereby relations of control and power. Again, as already indicated by Katherine Hayles, material metaphors *matter*, in the double, or better triple sense of the word: they matter as meaningful attribution, they consist of matter as physical-material forms, and they materialize social relations.

Although they emphasize different aspects, the anthropologists and Hayles both evoke material metaphor as a kind of 'scripted objects' (Akrich 1992), that is, material artifacts that are inscribed with specific instructions. They can exist in the form of Hayles' medial interfaces or as Ray's social organizing objects. Before addressing the implications for the analysis of digital-material metaphors, a few questions have to be addressed: the question whether all contemporary material artifacts are (or should be considered) scripted objects, and whether all scripted objects are by definition material metaphors. The next section will address these issues.

4 — CONTEMPORARY SCRIPTED OBJECTS

From the anthropological notion of material metaphor – derived from mythical objects and rituals enacted by isolated African clans – to western globalized network societies may seem to be a long road. Current globalized objects seem to lack the glow of sacred rites, commodified and disposable as they often are. Yet, contemporary Western societies also have artifacts that assemble routine and ritual, symbolic meaning, and social attribution, and not only in the form of Hayles' medial interfaces. Think for instance of ritual-institutional objects such as crowns, country flags, wedding rings, police uniforms, or chairman's hammers. These artifacts are relatively simple, both as object and as readable symbols. They are metaphoric (or symbolic [48]) since they stand for something else, something beyond their instrumental functionality, and as such they matter. By their metaphorical force such objects seem to be able to do things in the world: they arrange and assign subject positions and social categories – citizens, husbands and wives, state office holders, speakers and listeners – by indicating who is sovereign, who is subordinate, who is in charge, who represents the law, who has a monopoly on violence, who will take care of whom, and who may decide who speaks. In addition to these clearly symbolic objects, there are also less institutionalized and seemingly less ritualized objects that function as metaphorical-symbolical organizers. For example, cars are artifacts that stand for freedom of movement, independency, maturity, and autonomy/auto-mobility. Even everyday ordinary objects such as keys, passports, and traffic lights, assign permissions and subject positions, arranging how and where one is supposed and allowed to go, what one is supposed and allowed to do. In fact, all objects such as fences, gates, doors, keys, and locks embody and signify legitimate ways of passing and behaving, by imposing on us their embedded inscriptions and prescriptions (Latour 2004, Van den Berg 2009).

Should we then consider all these scripted objects as material metaphors? What is at stake is whether it is useful to call all significant objects material metaphors. I doubt it. Because if we do so, we may loose sight of the different ways in which objects can order and invoke the social. Let us see what different ways there are to do so, and in what cases a metaphorical force is at work.

Doors, keys, and shavers

Latour (1992) elaborately points out how a door in itself may prescribe the way we use it. Besides the fact that a door in its object-being strongly encourages one to choose *this* entry to a building or room, rather than using the window or breaking through the wall, a door may embody extra scripts for behavior: it may have a lock, enabling only entrance for those who possess a key, or it may have a mechanism that closes the door automatically after someone has entered. In that case, the job of closing the door behind you has been delegated to the artifact. The door is now an object with an extra built-in script to which people have to adjust, by entering with the right

---

48. The difference between symbol and metaphor depends on the theoretical perspective and employed definition, yet the terms are often used interchangeably. Not coincidentally, the authoritative academic journal on metaphor research is called *Metaphor and Symbol* (before 1997 *Metaphor and Symbolic Activity)*. The logo on the cover displays the word 'METAPHOR' in a font size that is 400% of the font size of the words 'AND SYMBOL'. Verily, a logo as Haylesian material metaphor. However, faithful to Peirce's terminology, I define a symbol as having a completely conventional and arbitrary relation to its signified, and a metaphor as having a non-arbitrary associative relation to its object. I realize that the distinction between arbitrary and non-arbitrary can be problematic. Even the arbitrary symbols of the Greek or Latin phonetic alphabet can historically be traced back to a non-arbitrary abbreviated ideograms, such as the letter 'A' representing an oxhead, a symbol for God the creator, and the letter 'B' representing a house (Taylor 1883). What appears to be arbitrary can be a forgotten metaphor, a blackboxed metaphor, hiding its iconic, indexical, and historical associations and connections. To complicate the distinction further, such hidden associations are also the stuff cultural conventions are made of.

force and speed, otherwise the door will smack you in your face. According to Latour (1992, 232), such scripted situations always imply a trade-off. While part of the task has been delegated to a non-human artifact, some new behavior is required for human beings to adjust. Therefore, such built-in scripts discipline people by defining and prescribing appropriate and non-appropriate behavior. In the same way, Latour (2004) analyzed a hotel-room key with a heavy weight attached as an object imposing the imperative 'leave the key at the hotel desk when you go out'. The heavy bulb is a material object that functions as a script, a program to counter the anti-programs enacted by lazy or distracted key users who tend to keep the hotel key with them.

This principle of trade-off between delegation to artifacts and human adjustment is also at work in our daily conduct with more complicated technological devices such as cars, remote controls, shaving devices, mobile phones, and personal computers. All these objects embody in their material design inscriptions and prescriptions for proper use. You do not use the remote control to shave your skin, and you do not use a computer mouse as a remote control.[49] Embedded and embodied scripts, with implicit or explicit inscriptions, are inevitable to regulate the use of complicated artifacts.

However, sometimes the built-in scripts do more than just direct the use of the artifact; sometimes they address, and thereby invoke, specific categories of users, according to divisions by gender, education, or age. For example, Van Oost (2003) showed convincingly how different electric razors made by Philips were not just designed for different kinds of hair on different body parts, but had specific built-in gender scripts. The Ladyshave was designed in pastel colored plastic with smooth curves and as few buttons and screws as possible, and was marketed as a type of cosmetics; the male counterpart, the Philishave, was all black and metal, with lots of buttons, displays, and screws, enabling a do-it-yourself repair in case the thing broke down. The built-in scripts addressed female shavers as 'Barbiefied'[50] and technophobic passive users, while the male shavers were addressed as tech-savvy device managers. Such modes of ideological address – *interpellation,* as Marxist philosopher of ideology Louis Althusser (1969) would call it – do not necessarily succeed in subjecting the subjects thus interpellated, but in any case such gender-scripted objects, embedded in daily practices and routines, do contribute to the social construction of dichotomic sexual difference.

Scripted objects versus material metaphors
Could or should all such scripted objects be called material metaphors? I would argue that this would not be so useful. Neither would it be productive to call all objects that function as a sign, such as traffic lights or advertising billboards, material metaphors. The concept of material metaphor would then cover practically any artifact; it would lose its distinctive analytic and critical value. Hence, the question is, which particular instances of scripted objects could be called material metaphors? And should the term be used to indicate a particular mode of being or does it rather refer to a particular mode of analyzing? I will start with the last question, since it will lead us finally to the first one.

---

49. Except for the former Dutch Prime Minister Kok in February 1998, but he also eventually learned the proper use of a mouse. See http://www.youtube.com/watch?v=30U7TJgJw_A.
50. See also my analysis of the Barbie doll as a material metaphor for both women's emancipation and empowerment, and female enclosure in a pink, non-hackable environment, 'Hacking Barbie in Gendered Computer Culture', in Buikema and Van der Tuin (2009).

The question 'is it a mode of being or a mode of analysis?' touches upon the age-old issue of ontology versus epistemology, with in its slip stream a supposed dichotomy between objectivity versus subjectivity, the object versus the subject. From an ontological perspective, material metaphors would consist of particular pre-established categories of being, while from an epistemological perspective material metaphor would be a heuristic analytical tool that may reveal something that does not show itself immediately on the ontological level. A strictly ontological definition of material metaphor would be completely dependent on the properties and specificity of the object, while a strictly epistemological definition would be dependent on the theoretical-analytical perspective of the researcher, the subject.

However, as several philosophers, especially feminist scholars, have pointed out, issues of ontology and epistemology are inextricably intertwined (Haraway 1988, Hacking 2002, Barad 2003). Therefore, I propose a definition of material metaphor that affirms onto-epistemological dynamics: calling a phenomenon a material metaphor is an onto-epistemological claim, that is, both an ontological claim and a critical epistemological intervention, induced by the analytical/narrative labor it takes to construe the claim. This implies that it is quite possible that phenomena which initially do not seem to comply with the ontological requirements of material metaphor may after all be analyzed as a material metaphor, thereby recursively revealing hidden onto-epistemologies.

I would then propose to use the term material metaphor for specific transference scripts: materially embodied scripts that *import* representations from elsewhere (from outside the domain of object usage) and *export* (transfer, translate, transform) those qualifications into rules of conduct that organize social order and subject positions. Material metaphors, then, are materialized and condensed import-export scripts that constitute gateways between networks of objects, attributions, and people, of cultural practice and social ordering.

This definition in fact fuses the Haylesian and the anthropological perspective on material metaphor. It takes from Hayles the focus on the material-semiotic traffic enabled by medial interfaces, and from anthropology the focus on material objects, social labor, and social organization. While their emphasis is different, both perspectives try to capture material-semiotic exchange and its connections to social discourse and order. Both address the production of surplus meaning, on top of instrumental use and materiality, and on top of symbolic representation and language. Both are more about *processes* than fixed states, more about *presencing* than presence and representation. In other words, scripted objects can be considered as material metaphors when they are marked by imported scripts, and hence go beyond plain instrumental use, and beyond the representation of this use. So the Ladyshave and the Philishave are typical material metaphors – as they import qualifications from elsewhere and transfer them to modes of social address – but not all razors are.

Yet, it is quite possible to find a seemingly non-metaphorical quasi-neutral object (a specific razor, door, key or a child's toy like the Barbie doll) that can be analyzed as a material metaphor. Such an analysis would show which hidden import-export scripts are at work. Latour undertook such an endeavor with the bulbed hotel key and the automatic door, and Van Oost looked at the Ladyshave and the Philishave, and I have analyzed the Barbie doll (Van den Boomen 2009). Hence, a material metaphor is not just an object functioning as a sign (such as a traffic light), neither an object functioning as a metaphor (such as a salt shaker temporarily standing in for a car in a narrative told to table companions). A material metaphor is a social-cultural object that enacts its material design and inscriptions in a special way: it condenses, enforces, enables, inscribes, assigns, and performs social meaning and organization.

Whether an object can be conceived as a material metaphor depends on what it does, on what level of materiality. A red traffic light is a signifying material object, a sign telling you to stop (first level of materiality: the materiality of the sign). Speed bumps on the road and keys are scripted objects – not just telling you to behave in a certain way, but rather enforcing this behavior (second level of materiality: the materiality of the indexical tool). Books, computers, passports, and Ladyshaves are material metaphors – not only telling and enforcing how you should operate the object, but by importing external qualifications also invoking and formatting social categories and arrangements (third level of materiality: the materiality of metaphor and social order). [51] This is achieved by combining design, inscription, and metaphorical traffic, but most of all by enactment, performance, doing. Since the metaphor, the social prescription, and the assignment of subject positions are built-in in the material form, it is hardly a matter of interpretation, reading or decoding – it is a matter of praxis, action and performance, of usage and labor.

Disciplining artifacts and informational objects
It should be noted that this definition of material metaphor as embodied import-export script relies largely on an assumed clear-cut boundary between the domain of 'plain instrumental use' and something beyond or outside this domain. The very idea of import and export assumes such distinct domains. This demarcation is of course problematic, and at least pliable. The distinction may be clear in some cases: a cooking pot can be designed functionally as just a cooking pot, or it can be designed with signs marking it as a young man, implying for instance that it may not be touched by young girls, just as a razor can be designed as a gender-neutral shaving device or as a Ladyshave invoking the category of technophobic women.

But what about the disciplining artifact of the bulbed hotel key? Should the imperative of delivering the key to the reception desk be considered as belonging to the domain of instrumental use or as something extra? And when it comes to complex technological artifacts such as cars, computers, or mobile phones, all of them assembling multitudes of instrumental and organizational scripts, the instrumental can hardly be separated from the metaphorical. This applies even more to informational objects such as passports, contracts, diplomas, bank notes [52], property certificates, staying permits, and other officially or socially authenticated and authenticating scripted objects. These objects, lingering between media-specific interfaces and metaphorical objects, definitely are social-symbolic organizers, sometimes even life determining. They obviously stand metaphorically for something beyond their material being, and they are also more than just signs that could be displayed by any interface. As an assemblage they are inextricably bound to the specific object, its interface, its inscriptions, its signatures, and the material-semiotic network in

---

51. Indeed, material metaphor corresponds to Peircian Thirdness, whereas scripted objects belong to Secondness, and signifying objects to Firstness.
52. In fact, the same hold for coins or any entity that functions as currency. Money, as abstract equivalencing means that enables exchange, has become more and more virtualized: first detached from the represented commodities – an ox, a sheep – and translated into shells, clay, or metal beads, then translated again into paper with inscriptions, then to just inscriptions on your bank account. Yet, it can be considered a material metaphor: an informational scripted object which's metaphorical exchange value over determines its material use value. According McLuhan (1964, 136) money is a metaphor and a medium in its own right, and according to De Kerckhove (1997, 21-25) money may be even the first medium in human history, preceding and evoking the medium of writing as such.

which it is incorporated. They operate as objects within and beyond the realm of signs, they have structural organizing effects in the material world, and they assign specific subject positions and privileges. They are definitely material metaphors, even though – or may be precisely because – they have no instrumentality separate from their metaphoricity. Their metaphoricity coincides completely with their instrumental use.

The same principle seems to be at work in digital informational entities such as desktop icons, files, websites, and application programs, to name just a few of their instantiations. They have no instrumentality outside their metaphoricity, and thus function as material metaphors. However, digital-material metaphors confront us with several problems regarding their ontology and modality, as we will see in the next section.

5 — DIGITAL-MATERIAL METAPHORS

Metaphors in general may take on any material form construed by any medium or modality: textual, visual, auditory, and objectified, plus any multimodal mixture between them. Likewise, a material metaphor can be embodied by any modality – textual (signatures, bank account numbers, books), pictorial (photographs, fingerprints), auditory (national anthems, film music), or as a physical object (door, shaver, book, computer). Material metaphors, hence, are able to materialize in any form, on any scale, in any modality, including the digital modality.

However, the digital modality tend to come with some difficulties since it is in itself hard to pin down. As we have seen digital entities seems to oscillate between several levels of materiality: sign, tool, and icontologized object. As signs, digital entities can be articulated in arbitrary media or modalities (textual, auditory, pictorial, haptic). But once instantiated in a modality they become sign-tools that are definitely non-arbitrary, because of their indexical relation to machine code. On top of that, digital inscriptions enable the further translation into any other modality or format, while retaining their non-arbitrary internal structure.

This kind of digital translation of one format into an other is called transcoding. The technical principle of transcoding can be illustrated with the visual graphics that Windows Media Player shows when playing a music file; the auditive parameters of pitch, loudness and rhythm are translated – proportionally, that is, analogically – into corresponding visual parameters as color, shape, pulse, and movement by transcoding the digital data structure into a visual format. This principle of proportional-analogical retainment of patterns of assigned numbers also implies that digital code can be stored on, copied to, and transmitted by arbitrary carriers – processor chips, hard disks, USB sticks, DVDs, telephone wires, UTP cable, radio frequencies, and so on.

In other words, digital code seems to be both arbitrary and non-arbitrary, and both digital and analogical. What then can be the ontology of digital code, those abstract packages of arbitrarily assigned binary numbers, assembled in non-arbitrary patterns, inscribed on arbitrary carriers, and returned as metaphorical objects? What intricate maneuvers between the arbitrary domain of language and numbers, and the non-arbitrary domain of objects are involved here?

Files, forums, and tweets

First, we have to address the issue whether we can actually consider digitally coded entities actually as *objects*. After all, one might argue that the notions of package and object in this context are 'just metaphors' – a qualification that is usually meant as a dismissal, thrown into a debate in order to cut off any further inference, implication, or responsibility for the articulation. Apart from the fact that I would object that metaphors are rarely 'just metaphors' (that is, innocent figures of speech without further effects) the problem here is more complicated. At stake is the issue to what extent digital entities can be seen as objects. Do they function in the same manner as the pots, canoes, and villages the anthropologists found to be metaphorical objects? Or are they more Haylesian material metaphors, scalable media-specific interfaces, not necessarily taking the form of objects?

At first glance, digital entities do not appear to be objects at all since they have no embodied extension in space, no physical substance, volume, force, or weight – all the attributes that characterize solid (yet degradable) objects in a physical-material world. Digital entities seem to belong solely to the order of representations, of signs, of inscriptions as such, rather than to the order of objects with inscriptions. And yet, digital representations or simulations do have object-like properties, not in the sense of physical substance, but in the sense of being a manipulable modifiable entity, manipulable by humans and by machines – manipulable in a way signs, words, or meanings are not.

We have seen how digital entities can function as end products, as tools, or as machines, tools to produce other end products and tools. These modifiable digital entities are obviously less static and more transformable than solid physical objects. However, precisely because of their modifiability and manipulability they become objects with material qualities. To put it differently, digital entities acquire object-like qualities to the extent that they can be fished out of the digital soup as assemblages that acquire their form and boundaries in metaphors, such as file, forum, blog, tweet, mail, and so on.

As we have observed before, these metaphorically cut-out objects function in two directions: towards human semiotic processing and towards machine processing. As bundled forms for machine processing, they exist as digital-material patterns of indexical inscriptions. By representing parts of these bundled forms on the human-readable interface, they come into existence as metaphorical objects – that is, as material metaphors, embodying metaphorically informed scripts for specific use and manipulation. You can copy a file, talk back on a forum, or send a tweet. And as you do so, you are not just implicitly acknowledging the metaphorical meaning of the signs displayed on your screen, but you are really *doing things* with them. You are transforming and modifying objects, which in turn can be transported, copied, shared, or commodified – as material objects.

The problem with digital materiality is that it conceals its own materiality, that it poses as immaterial. This specific materiality-that-poses-as-if-immaterial has been dubbed *transmateriality* by Mitchel Whitelaw (2008). His notion of transmateriality postulates that the digital is,

> always and inevitably embodied; that concepts like 'data' are functional abstractions for describing the propagation of material patterns through material substrates. But that at the same time these material patterns [...] and the sensations and aesthetics that result are profoundly shaped by data acting *as if it were* symbolic and immaterial. Transmateriality is an attempt to 'ground' the digital without losing sight of its (let's say) generative capacities. (Whitelaw 2008, par. 8)

Hence, while criticizing the ideology of immateriality, the concept of transmateriality simultaneously acknowledges and seeks to give an account of the generated effect of immateriality. Whitelaw's notion of transmateriality thus seems to be precisely the kind of materiality at stake in translations by digital-material metaphors. Yet, I would argue that it is necessary to differentiate between what Whitelaw called 'acting-as-if-immaterial' (indeed, digital-material metaphors do so), and 'acting-as-if-symbolical'. Digital-material metaphors do not act-*as-if*-symbolical; the point is that they *are* also symbolical. Being symbolical does not rule out being material. Digital-material metaphors are, just like other material metaphors, simultaneously symbolical and material. Their ontology as digital entities endows them with an odd mix of qualities: arbitrary and non-arbitrary, attributed and algorithmic, fluid and discrete, language and numbers, analogical and digital. And this is precisely why it is so hard to think them together.

In other words, digital entities are both signs and objects, 'words made flesh', as Florian Cramer (2005) has called them. After all, digital 'words' have to become 'flesh' since digital signifiers – plain binary marks, representing arbitrary assigned numbers – can only signify when clustered and turned into bounded non-arbitrary objects, when objectified and ontologized in human-manipulable and machine-processable things. Only then they can circulate, and get exchanged, modified, assembled, disassembled, reassembled.

Any digitization of information turns it into solidified, ontologized transferable objects and at the same time into free floating signifiers. This yields to strange hybrid entities, previously unimaginable as objects for trade and transference. We already have become familiar with the trade in email addresses by spam entrepreneurs, but who would have imagined a lively trade in informational objects such as consumer profiles, passwords, role-playing characters, or IP addresses of infected zombie computers? This is not digitization as a transformation of pre-existing information into digital forms; this is the production of new informational objects as main products or byproducts of digital praxis, mediated by material metaphors.

To summarize, digital entities become objects when they are objectified by metaphors, enabling programmers or users to intervene in the mode of being of these objects. These digitized objectifications of metaphors function similar to the physical objects conceptualized in anthropology as material metaphors. Yet, we should bear in mind that these two kinds of metaphorical objects differ ontologically. Anthropological material metaphors are primarily physical objects, objects that get designed, crafted, solidified, and socially incorporated as metaphors. Digital-material metaphors come into being from the opposite direction. They are metaphors that get solidified as material objects.

Without metaphor, there are no boundaries, and no digital object. While non-digital material objects can exist without built-in metaphorical power (say, a stone or a table[53]), there are no digital-material objects (or spaces) without a metaphorical form and address. This even holds for seemingly abstract non-metaphorical concepts such as data table, logical address, or command line. These interfacial entities are also already metaphors, imported from other domains in order to construe manipulable material entities in the digital domain, on the edge of language and objects, enabling, in Hayles words, the traffic between symbols and physical artifacts.

Material metaphor analysis

We may conclude that digital-material entities can indeed be taken as material metaphors, both as metaphorical objects in the anthropological sense and as media-specific interfacial assemblages in Hayles' sense. This implies that both approaches are useful for analyzing digital-mate-

---

53. Yet, they may acquire a metaphorical pay-load in specific constellations, such as with a specific stone in a museum or a court table where the judges are seated.

rial metaphors. A combination of the anthropological and the Haylesian approach is probably the best way to conduct digital-material metaphor analysis, though it should be kept in mind that the two approaches have their specific benefits and focus.

The anthropological perspective on material metaphor focuses on the construction, maintenance, and use of objects. Moreover, it foregrounds the incorporation of metaphorical objects in a broader societal praxis, by tracing their contribution to the constitution of social categories and subject positions. This may regard social categories such as class, gender, ethnicity, age, and education, but we can also think of digital-materially invoked social categories such as forum moderators, Facebook friends, blog owners, lurkers, *reaguurders, Redditors* [54], player-characters, legitimate users, spammers, pirates, hackers and so on.

If we return once again to the story of my friend's empty mailbox and analyze this object-and-story-in-one as a material metaphor, we no longer see her only as a puzzled Internet user. Several more subject positions and attributions are 'presenced' (Ray 1987) in the enactment of the material metaphor of that seemingly simple mail problem: working woman, highly educated, working at the office and at home, blending the private realm and work, delegating hardware installation tasks to a hired professional, ISP customer, computer operator, home account owner, work account owner, mail sender, and mail receiver.[55] While not all of these subject positions are represented directly by the material metaphor of the mailbox icon, they are all 'presenced' that is assembled and redistributed in the course of affairs in the praxis evolving around the metaphorical object. In that regard, material metaphors are not only assemblages of objects and metaphors but also of object positions and subject positions.

However, Katherine Hayles' perspective on material metaphor is also needed in the analysis of digital-material metaphorical objects, since her perspective foregrounds the specific role of media and mediation, as object and process, that is, as a dynamic apparatus. What holds for the various material metaphors in so called 'old media' such as books and movies holds all the more for digitally mediated media, usually called 'new media'.

Although 'new media' is a problematic term – indeed, a discourse metaphor in itself, invoking a discourse of the perpetually 'new' (De Vries 2012) and even 'new new' (Levinson 2009) – the term is widely acknowledged and appropriated. The common use of the term refers to everything associated with computable information and communication technology. As vague and imprecise as this description looks, it may be argued that precisely this fuzzy idea of 'everything associated' should be the leading principle of new media studies. Tracking down what associations are implicated and created, what strings are attached and what social-material configurations are construed, should be the aim of this endeavor.[56] Hayles' proposal for Media-Specific Analysis by

---

54. *Reaguurders* is the Dutch word for public commentators used on the Dutch shock-blog GeenStijl (geenstijl.nl) while *Redditors* are contributors to Reddit (reddit.com), a website for user-submitted social news and entertainment.
55. We may even think of digital entities such as IP numbers and data profiles as 'presenced' subject positions, non-human subject positions, invigorated by acts of delegation and the harvesting of representational foot prints. As assigned and assembled digital objects, such material metaphors can certainly backfire on the persons and subject positions represented.
56. Indeed, that is a reformulation of the field of new media studies in terms of a Peircian triad of Firstness (affordances for associations), Secondness (indexical strings attached), and Thirdness (systematic configuration in discourse and social order).

means of excavating material metaphors is one of the more promising ways to do so, as it focuses on the associations induced by symbolic signification and material construction, as well as the conjunctions and traffic in between.

Reconnecting these findings to the issues raised in Chapter 1, we may conclude that considering digital entities as material metaphors provides us with a richer analytical vocabulary than considering them as Peircian signs, Heideggerian tools, or Lakovian conceptual metaphors. The concept of material metaphor seems to be able to integrate these perspectives, and to do much more. It takes the materiality of the sign-tool-metaphor as an integrated object, by considering the metaphorical mechanism, as well as the specific material design, including the icontological, indexical, and symbolical relations involved.

Digital-material metaphors can be said to condense iconicity and indexicality by blending immediate and dynamical objects into one icontologized sign-tool-metaphor object, integrated in a semiotic-material machinery. But precisely because they are condensed assemblages, they can also be disassembled and parsed into their constitutive parts. They can be 'de-icontologized' by digital-material analysis. Mundane, taken-for-granted metaphors such as mailbox, hyperlink, Facebook friend or password are able to fool us by their icontological condensation and routine praxis, but analyzing them as material metaphors can reveal what is depresented: the indexical material connections and their social-semiotic implications.

To deploy a metaphor here, material metaphors are the keys to the black box. The keys are able to close and lock up, but they are also able to open and reveal. They may be used for epistemological reverse engineering:[57] tracking down the subsequent translations, connections, and transferences – this connects to that, this translates that into something else, then it is inscribed and transported to that, and so on. They provide apertures which allow us to peek inside the digital black box.[58] In that sense, material metaphors are epistemological hacking tools. Or to put it more academically, they are heuristic devices for critical deconstruction.

In order to further explore the outlines of a media-specific analysis that is informed by material metaphors, we first have to answer questions such as: what is medium-specificity and what is a medium anyway? The next chapter will address these issues by employing metaphors as keys to the black boxes that we usually call media and mediation.

---

57. Reverse engineering is a deductive method developed in commercial and military research to obtain knowledge about the structure, function, and operation of an artifact. The term is appropriated in hacker circles where it pertains to the methodology by which a closed-source hardware or software object can be opened up: tracking down how output may be derived from input processing, inferring the involved processes, and then reconstructing and rebuilding the construction.

58. The idea of 'aperture' is also one of the classic metaphors of metaphoricity itself (Black 1962, 41).

CHAPTER 3
MEDIATION BY METONYMY AND METAPHOR
HOW MEDIA MULTIPLY AND DISSOLVE

*All media are active metaphors in their power
to translate experiences into new forms.*
(Marshall McLuhan, 1964)

Tracing material metaphors by Media-Specific Analysis is not a matter of following a simple recipe. It is not sufficient to identify something as a metaphor and then map out the ways it is sustained by a material medium. This is especially the case when it comes to digital objects. The first problem we encounter is that the metaphoricity of digital objects can be located on three different levels: on the level of *mediation and medium,* on the level of *representation*, and on the level of *software*.[59] The second problem is that each level opens up different discursive and theoretical fields that in themselves are imbued with competing metaphors and metonyms. In order to unravel these problems, I have distributed these levels over the next three chapters. The present chapter will address the first level: mediation and what we actually call a medium. Chapter 4 will further elaborate on how mediation gets represented as immediacy, and Chapter 5 will address the riddle of software and its metaphors.

The principle of material metaphor as Media-Specific Analysis seems to imply that we know *a priori* what a medium is and that we can subsequently identify the specificities of a particular mediated phenomenon. However, our notions of what a medium is, what it could be or should be, appears to be in itself burdened and buried by metaphors and metonyms. As we will see in this chapter, metaphors of mediation function as discourse metaphors, but they may also be operational as material metaphors.

The first section will address the circulating media metonyms (carrier, production, reproduction, distribution, symbolic forms, modality, setting, and language) and connect these articulations to the concept of discourse metaphors. The subsequent sections flesh out media metaphors of processing (membrane, master, space, ecology), transmission (channel, conduit, tool), and storage (container, inscription), respectively.

---

59. Not coincidentally this is a triad in which Peirce's relational semiotic concepts of Firstness, Secondness, and Thirdness can be recognized in representation (iconic Firstness), software (indexical Secondness), and medium (symbolic-systematic Thirdness), respectively.

1 — WHAT DO WE CALL A MEDIUM?

When we look up the word *medium* in a dictionary, a plethora of meanings meets the eye.[60] References to 'means to accomplish something', in particular 'a means for conveying information' are of course present, but also meanings that come from disciplines such as physics, biology, and art history. These meanings vary from 'liquid solvent', 'space through which waves pass', and 'nutrient solution for cell growth' to 'liquid that carries pigment'.[61] Different as these denotations are, strikingly, in all cases a medium is a transparent or translucent enabler. And while the denotation of 'means for communicating information' seems most apt for our quest here, the connotations of translucency, on the verge of transparency, insistently lurk around the corner.

No wonder we have difficulty in conceiving a medium as material; the ultimate medium is imperceptible and evasive. Even when we take a medium as a 'means for communicating information' – which seems to emphasize apparatus rather than transparency – we encounter multiple meanings. We speak of 'the media' as a general assemblage of all media or of all professionals[62] working in this field, but we also speak of different media, implying medium-specific features and ontologies. But then, what do we mean when we speak of 'the medium of film' as distinguished from other media? Do we mean the celluloid, the cinema, the studio, Hollywood industry, cameras, framing and montage, screen projection, moving images? Or perhaps all of these, in a specific configuration that produces specific subject positions, as maintained in poststructuralist apparatus theory?[63]

In the same way, it is hard to unravel the statement, 'the medium of television deeply changed society'. Does that refer to the device in our living room, to the principle of broadcasting, to the reception setting of couch potatoes, television networks and industrial interests, the impact of live news, the culture of celebrities and soap opera's? Or again, perhaps to all these things together? The same holds for print media: paper can be called a medium, but the same holds for 'writing', 'the printing press', 'the alphabet', or 'the book'. Obviously, in ordinary speech, as

---

60. For example, the lemma 'medium' in the Wiktionary (http://en.wiktionary.org/wiki/medium) reads:
    1. (plural media) The nature of the surrounding environment, e.g. solid, liquid, gas, vacuum, or a specific substance such as a solvent.
    2. (plural media) The material or empty space through which signals, waves or forces pass.
    3. (plural media) A format for communicating or presenting information.
    4. (plural media, microbiology) A nutrient solution for the growth of cells in vitro.
    5. (plural media) The means or channel by which an aim is achieved.
    6. (plural mediums) A liquid base which carries pigment in paint.
    7. (plural mediums, spiritualism) Someone who supposedly conveys information from the spirit world.
    8. (plural mediums) Anything having a measurement intermediate between extremes, such as a garment or container.
    9. (plural mediums) A person whom garments or apparel of intermediate size fit.
61. An interesting intervention in art history is made by my colleague Ann-Sophie Lehmann in her argument that *oil* should be seen as a medium in painting (Bol and Lehmann 2012). Once again this underscores that translucency is decisive for being a medium.
62. Even including non-professionals in the Internet discourse of participatory media, as in *We the Media: Grassroots Journalism by the People, for the People* (Gillmor 2006).
63. As elaborated in the works of Jean-Louis Baudry (1974), Christian Metz (1982), and Laura Mulvey (1989).

well as in media theory, we use the word 'medium' to indicate quite different things, levels, attributes, and assemblages.[64]

The problem multiplies when it comes to *new media*. Of course, the term 'new' is relative and historically bound, as several media scholars have pointed out (Gitelman and Pingree 2003, Chun and Keenan 2005, Gitelman 2006). 'New media' may refer to contemporary digital media, but also to forms of media that were once new, such as the telegraph in the early 19th century or film in the early 20th century. Or even to the Internet in 1995 (which was even then not actually new). Each new medium invoked, at its own historical moment of recognized 'newness', debates on what this new medium would mean for society, social relations, labor divisions, aesthetics, culture, and politics.

But even in the context of new media as referring to digital media, in the sense of electronically computable and programmable, the word medium is ambivalent. Not only because the prefix new has lost its particular meaning of fresh, novel, innovative – similar to New York and New Zealand – but also because the word medium has multiple references in this context too. The Internet may be called a medium, but that surely differs from the notion of media in the piece of software called a media player, not to mention the various electronic and electric devices that are sold at the stores of the European retailer Media Markt, ranging from shavers and coffee machines to computers and mobile phones. In a strictly digital context, medium may pertain to devices (personal computers, web servers, mobile phones, tablets, game consoles), carriers (cables, tape, disks, USB sticks), software entities (operating systems, application programs, databases, websites, apps), or interfacial formats (games, video, tweets). As different as these entities are, they can all be called media depending on the discursive context.[65] In each context

---

64. The problem gets even more complicated when a supposedly clear medium gets collated with another concept, as in the heated debate on the so-called 'Facebook revolution' of February 2011 in Egypt. What is foregrounded by such naming? Revolutions acquire their names according to various metaphorical and metonymical associations, but the metonymical blend with what is conceived as a specific medium, i.e. Twitter or Facebook, apparently provokes huge debates on the alleged determinating power of the medium at stake (Gladwell 2010, Shirky 2011, Morozov 2011, Wellman 2011, Lotan et al. 2011). Did Facebook cause the revolt? Was it the starting point? Can a medium be ascribed that power? Did it contribute at all? How many people were indeed using the medium? The fact that such questions emerge indicates once more that we do not know what a medium is and how it works. While no one would assume that naming a revolution a Carnation Revolution (Portugal 1974), a Velvet Revolution (Czechoslovakia 1989), or a Jasmine Revolution (Tunisia 2011) implies that velvet or specific flowers are the cause or the starting point, but dubbing a revolution after a salient medium apparently does.
65. Even the Internet cannot easily be delineated as a separate medium. Do we mean the infrastructure of cables, routers, and servers? The political economy of providers, regulating institutions, and media conglomerates? The transnational public sphere of global information exchange? The assemblage of protocols and applications, such as SMTP mail and HTTP web? Specific genres and formats, such as blogs and social network sites? Anything goes, so it seems.

a specific part is highlighted that can be called a medium. Apparently, what we call a medium is often a metonym, a specific selection from an assumed larger whole.[66]

Media metonyms

Given that we cannot define *a priori* what a medium is, we can try a detour in order to get an idea of this larger whole by systematizing the metonymical resources. If we take the expression 'X is another medium than Y', and categorize for which phenomena the notion of medium is discursively allowed as a synonym or a legitimate description, then we can distinguish eight main dimensions of media metonyms:

- *Material carriers and storage devices* (clay tablet, papyrus, celluloid, vinyl record, tape, disk, USB stick, radio waves, glass fiber, coax cable);
- *Production apparatuses*[67] (tongue, pen, paper, typewriter, keyboard, paintbrushes, camera, piano, synthesizer, computer, word processor, authors, journalists, photographers);
- *Reproduction and display technologies* (speech, writing, printing, rotation press, film projector, light emanation, computer screen, gramophone, television, xeroxing, tape recording, file copying);
- *Distribution systems* (publishers, book shops, newsboys, cinemas, film distributors, festivals, record companies, telegraph, telephone, broad casting, web servers, computer networks);
- *Symbolic forms and formats* (conversation, song, manuscript, novel, poem, newspaper, telegram, sitcom, live stream, game, flash animation, portal, blog, tweet, file, social network site, app);
- *Modalities of perception* (visual, auditive, tactile, olfactory, gustative, gestural, immersive, telepathic);
- *Social-spatial setting* (physical theater audience, silent reading, dark cinema, living-room television, urban screens, office computing, mobile phoning);
- *Language and protocol* (German, English, 220v, Betamax, VHS, HTML, HTTP, XML, TCP/IP, mp3, PDF, docx).

What can be concluded from such a list? First of all, even when totaled, it does not provide a picture of the notion of medium in general, with all its various aspects and forms included. It just does not add up. The list primarily reveals heterogeneity: how various stable and unstable phenomena can enter the stage under the label 'medium'. And not only the categories themselves are heterogeneous, but also the specific articulations within one category: they can be things, actions, assemblages, processes, people, or attributes.

To increase the complexity even further, each articulation is tied to specific selections from other clusters. Different symbolic forms are inscribed on specific carriers, each of them attached to different production and reproduction technologies. Elements in the category of material carriers implicate technologies of writing or broadcasting, each implicating different modalities of perception, in their turn implicating different social settings and languages, and so on. The categories

---

66. While most of the tropes for media are synecdoches *(pars pro toto,* part that stands in for the whole), I prefer the more encompassing term metonymy, which includes synecdoches, but also toponyms (for example Hollywood for a film genre or production apparatus) and tropes of containment (for example, carriers contain formats and languages, spaces contain display technologies). Metonymy can be defined as shifts along the horizontal syntagmatic axes of a sign system, while metaphor jumps across the vertical paradigmatic axes (Jakobson 1956).
67. In classical Marxist terms, production apparatus as forces of production, that is, means of production (tools, machinery, capital, infrastructure, etc.) plus human labor itself.

are not just overlapping, they are intricately folded and nested into each other, on all levels and scales. Each category can contain other categories, without any order of dominance.[68] It is also important to note that an entity can easily belong to multiple categories. For instance, a 'mailing list' as a medium may refer to the material carrier, the specific symbolic-material form, the specific production apparatus, or the specific distribution apparatus.

However, despite these complications the list seems to function quite unproblematically as a discursive framework for legitimate statements about 'media'. When one wants to argue 'medium A differs from medium B', one can tap from any of these eight categories to make the point. One can compare media within the same category, as in 'a computer is quite another medium than a typewriter' (production device) or 'a computer screen is not a television screen' (display technology). One can also compare between different categories, as in claiming 'a Facebook group is quite another medium than a pamphlet.' Depending on which category is taken as essential for defining a medium, one can claim almost anything about media and how they differ (or not) ontologically.

What we can conclude from this list of media metonyms is that even when we try to frame a medium conceptually as an intricate apparatus instead of a transparent screen the notion of medium dissolves and vaporizes. The metonymical selection may coagulate temporarily picking something out of the media mess, but it rapidly dissolves into a myriad of technological, social, and semiotic associations between and betwixt different levels and categories. Of course, we may determine temporary, working definitions in specific research contexts, but we cannot pin down the definition of 'a medium' once and for all. What we call a medium is historically and semiotically unstable, to say the least. There are no media as such, there are only temporary, unstable configurations we single out and then call them media.[69]

In other words, whenever something is called a medium something has been selected, singled out of an undifferentiated process – which then gets differentiated, recursively. It only takes a short step to reification and icontology from there: taking the specific selection for a general medium ontology, able to account for different media, and thereby retrospectively *making them up* as different media. For instance, it is not hard to imagine that only *after* the introduction of writing, could speech be envisioned as a medium. The medium of speech only emerged in comparison and confrontation with the new medium, as we learn from Plato's *Phaedrus,* with the famous dialogue on the difference between speech and writing regarding memory and wisdom. Speech emerged retrospectively as a process of mediation in which carrier, storage, modality, production, reproduction, symbolic forms and distribution were so firmly united in the human body that there

---

68. The assumption of a possible hierarchical categorization is framed by a specific spatial metaphor that equals the 'space of categorizations' with a physical space that can be filled with containers or boxes. In such a Cartesian 3-D space, a large box may contain a smaller box, but never the other way around. Annemarie Mol, following Michel Serres, proposed an alternative space metaphor that conceives space not as a consisting of boxes but of *sacs*. Sacs can be folded into each other, regardless of their size (Mol 2002, 145). Although this metaphor solves the problem of hierarchy and overlap, it does not account for what is at stake in the media inventory list: large sacs being folded, not in just one smaller sac, but in multiple other sacs both small and large.
69. Some media scholars capture this historically and analytically with the concept of *media dispositif,* 'a concept which links apparatus, the cultural imagination, and constructions of public' (Uricchio 2004, see also Kessler 2006, and Coté 2011). The concept is derived from Foucault, to indicate its genealogical and material-discursive constituents and its relations to knowledge and power.

was no need to differentiate more elements than two or three (presence of the human body as production apparatus, language as communication means, memory as carrier and container). And while currently the eight categories mentioned above seem to cover the available affordances of media practices fairly well from which a medium can be extracted and constructed, it remains to be seen whether this will suffice in the future.

Nonetheless, there are other ways to approach that elusive notion of medium. What if we no longer focus on what media *are* (or are supposed to be), and turn to what media *do?* The German poststructuralist media theorist Friedrich Kittler identified three distinct functions of media: processing, transmission, and storage.[70] Together they constitute, in historically and technologically different configurations, what Kittler calls discourse networks (Kittler 1985). These functions can already be recognized in the fore-mentioned list of media metonyms, but as we will see in the next subsection, when we try to specify more precisely what media do, we leave the field of metonymy, and enter the field of metaphor. Kittler's three functions provide a useful framework to order those media metaphors.

Discourse metaphors of media

Let us begin with the most basic assumption about what media do: they *mediate*. In general discourse (and in practically all languages, see Livingstone 2009), 'mediation' pertains to acts of negotiation, intervention, and alignment between distinct parties or domains. Mediation occurs when conflicting or match-seeking parties (people, institutions) call in a third-party mediator to settle a problem, or to negotiate a match between dating or wedding partners. Media as mediators do the same thing: they connect separate domains – whereby it is assumed that there is a domain of objective reality, separate from the domain of subjective human understanding that has to come to terms with this reality. Media then are conceived as third-party in-betweens, instances that mediate between these two domains. They enable contact with the world by intervening between ourselves and reality.

Yet even with this very basic notion of mediation, it is not clear what media do precisely when they mediate. Evidently, mediation enables something, but any further refinement of the term lets the metaphors march in. As Denis McQuail aptly observed in his classic handbook *Mass Communication Theory* (1994),

> In general, the notion of mediation in the sense of media intervening between ourselves and 'reality' is no more than a metaphor and one which invites the use of other metaphors to characterize the nature of the role played by the media. (McQuail 1994, 65)

McQuail mentions some of these metaphors: MEDIA AS WINDOW, a view on the world, extending human vision; MEDIA AS MIRROR, more or less faithfully reflecting what is happening; MEDIA AS FILTER OR GATEKEEPER, selecting specific parts of reality; MEDIA AS GUIDE OR SIGNPOST, directing ways of seeing and thinking; MEDIA AS FORUM OR PLATFORM for public exchange, and MEDIA AS SCREEN OR BARRIER, presenting a false view that is cut off from reality (ibid., 65-66).

---

70. And here we find another Peircian triad, with storage (an affordance) as Firstness, transmission (connecting two or more points of storage and retrieval) as Secondness, and processing (producing symbols, and thereby social and cultural meaning) as Thirdness.

McQuail does not elaborate on these metaphors, and seems to dismiss them as 'no more than a metaphor' (ibid., 65), suggesting they are innocent and insignificant modes of expression. But metaphors are never innocent. Cases in point are the windows and the mirror metaphor, which profoundly shape media discourses, in particular new media discourses. I will discuss windows and mirrors as metaphors of immediacy more thoroughly in Chapter 4. But the other metaphors McQuail mentions are also not innocent figures of speech. They function as compressed theories, sometimes even as compressed politics. For instance, the MEDIA AS FORUM metaphor implies a normative political stance on the question of how the audience is, could, or should be involved democratically. This metaphor can be seen at work in Stuart Hall's critical coding/decoding paradigm (Hall 1992, 1997). Moreover, metaphors are able to create new epistemological and ontological objects of knowledge and power, especially when they are built-in by design. Again, the still dominant windows metaphor in computing is a case in point. It is the ultimate metaphor of transparent immediacy – as if seen through a window – and its power lies precisely in the implication that the underlying mechanism is none of your business as a user.

Dismissing such metaphors as 'just metaphors', as just figures of speech, ignores their extra-linguistic and extra-cognitive productivity. These metaphors should not be analyzed as merely linguistic entities, but rather as what Michel Foucault has called 'effective statements' (Foucault 1972, 27). According to Foucault, 'effective statements' are articulations that function as statement-events and statement-things in specific discursive formations that form and align objects, subject positions, concepts, and strategies (ibid., 129). To sustain such a system of knowledge, power, and enunciability the effective statements can take the material form of monuments or documents, but, as Foucault argued in his plea for an archaeology of knowledge, these two should, as it were, be 'read' into each other. Just as prehistorical monuments have been read and interpreted as documents by classic archaeologists, modern documents have to be read as monuments by contemporary knowledge archaeologists (ibid., 8). The principle of MONUMENTS AS DOCUMENTS and DOCUMENTS AS MONUMENTS emphasizes a material discursivity that exceeds language in its ordering capacities, and in that regard it is very similar to the notion of material metaphor.

Researchers of scientific discourse and public policies have argued along similar lines proposing the term *discourse metaphors* (Zinken et al. 2008; Nerlich 2012). Discourse metaphors are considered to be key framing devices within a particular discourse. They are condensed statements that tie together narrative clusters of associated conceptual metaphors, assumptions, and legitimations which constitute together a more or less coherent discursive formation that channels behaviour, principles, and policies. A telling example is the discourse metaphor SOCIETY IS A BODY. It evokes metaphorical entailments in popular and political discourse such as, HEALTH IS INTEGRATION, A SOCIETY WITH NON-INTEGRATED PARTS IS SICK, or its critical counterpart, INTEGRATION POLICY IS SOCIAL HYPOCHONDRIA, as fleshed out by the sociologist Willem Schinkel in his analysis of the Dutch discourse and policy on integration and citizenship (Schinkel 2007, 2008). Another example is the metaphor THE NATION IS A FAMILY. Lakoff (2004) detected this discourse metaphor in his analysis of America's two opposing political discourses: the Republican-conservative model of a strict father family, and the Democratic-progressive model of a nurturant parent family.

Discourse metaphors frame and organize shared narratives (be it in the form of public opinion, political agendas, research programs, or world views), but most of all they organize and install standards, rules, norms, and procedures – in short, material-discursive formations of power, truth, and knowledge. They do so by selecting and deciding what is relevant and rational and what is not, by assigning candidates for truth and falsehood, by legitimatizing and favoring certain questions and derivations, by disqualifying or ignoring others, and last, but not least, by producing specific objects of knowledge and subject positions (Foucault 1972, 1982; Hook 2001; Hacking 2002).

Discourse metaphors, in the Foucauldian sense, are obviously no neutral means of expression or operation, but neither do they unambiguously support dominant discourses and the powers that be. They can be mobilized, elaborated, reformulated, and criticized in order to achieve particular goals, as we will see in the next sections of this chapter. These sections address discourse metaphors of media, ordered subsequently by Kittler's three media functions: processing, transmission, and storage.

2 — METAPHORS OF PROCESSING

When it comes to media metaphors of processing four basic discourse metaphors can be discerned: MEDIA AS MEMBRANE, MEDIA AS MASTER, MEDIA AS SPACE, and MEDIA AS ECOLOGY. All of these metaphors are conceptual metaphors as well as discourse metaphors and material metaphors, not only ordering popular discourse, but also material innovations, academic programs, and politics.

Media as membrane

The general idea of media as an enabling in-between already implies a basic conceptual metaphor: MEDIUM AS MEMBRANE, as an in-between entity that conditions modes of transgression. Media are thus conceived as a thin, practically invisible kind of tissue, an organic or artificial boundary mechanism that both separates and connects distinct domains, permeable and impermeable at the same time. But as McQuail already noticed, when we try to figure out how a membrane works precisely – does it let through light, signals, or other stuff? does it filter, direct, or bar things? – we evoke other metaphors, such as window or filter.

However, regardless which metaphor we subsequently choose, the organizing frame of the membrane already limits the field of discourse. Once the principle of a mediating membrane is presupposed and established, the separation between subject and object is secured. The world is assumed to consist of pre-existing objects and pre-existing subjects, and the two interact through a mediating membrane.

Of course, the sharp separation between on the one hand the objective world and on the other hand a sovereign subject that encounters the world, is philosophically contested, to put it mildly.[71] Nevertheless, once the MEDIA AS MEMBRANE metaphor is taken as a starting point in media and communication discourse, a subject-object division is implicated and reinforced, precisely by

---

71. More sophisticated philosophies of subject-object mediation can be distinguished by the location they assign to the membrane. For instance, Descartes, assuming and installing a radical split between subject and object, mind and body, located a tiny membrane in the pineal gland, and Kant's transcendental idealism locates the mediating membrane in the subject's *a priori* categories of time and space. The German philosopher Helmut Plessner (1928) proposed a material-anthropological membrane in his thesis of human eccentric positionality. Unlike plants and animals, human subjects are directed externally to the world and are able to intervene in and reflect on this relation. In this double position – having *and* being a body, being *and* having a membrane – they are, in Plessner's terms, 'naturally artificial' and marked by 'mediated immediacy'.

evoking a third term that mediates between the two. There are subjects and subjectivity (individuals, groups, publics, audiences, perceptions, beliefs, ideologies, politics, social assemblages, in short, culture) vis-à-vis objects and objectivity (materiality, reality, organisms, physical laws, in short, nature). And the two can only meet through a mediating membrane. Subject and object emerge as fundamentally different, with an ontological existence independent from each other, and not as onto-epistemologically produced entities in material-discursive practices of mediation. Yet, the ontological and epistemological status of the mediating membrane remains a riddle – a problem that media studies has been trying to resolve since its very beginning as an academic discipline (Livingstone 2009).

What membrane-derived metaphors have in common is the premise that the membrane may be necessary to perceive the world, but that it actually hinders the subject's access to the real. It is at best a neutral facilitator, but nevertheless a surrogate, as McQuail puts it, 'second-hand' (McQuail 1994, 65). The real thing apparently is immediate access, that well-known utopian figure of immediacy that offers reality as objective and unmediated to an autonomous subject. The impetus is that the mediating membrane should be designed as neutral, invisible and unintrusive as possible, as if it is not there. That is, it mediates, but it should at the same time *demediate* its own existence as membrane in order to mediate the subject into being. Modeling artistry and craft in terms of windows and mirrors is a classic way to do so since the early Renaissance (as we will see in Chapter 4, on the metaphors of immediacy), and in general the screen surface is the perfect candidate for a transparent demediated membrane.

In new media studies the membrane metaphor is explicitly present in the notion of the interface. An interface is by definition a mediating and connecting device, in fact, a medium in a medium, a membrane in a membrane. It connects separate domains, it forms a bridge, a plane of contact that enables, shapes, and constrains access to a machine (Johnson 1997; Cramer 2008). Although we usually think first of screenic human-computer interfaces (either graphical or textual), computer interfaces also consist of specific bridges that link hardware to hardware, hardware to software, and software to software (Cramer 2008). Yet we are not aware of these interfaces as they are rendered invisible over time, by deliberate design. When I bought my first computer and printer in 1986 you not only had to tinker with tiny dip switches in order to get the hardware aligned, but you also had to buy an extra device called 'an interface'. It was a brand-specific connection block that had to be clicked between the computer and the matrix printer.

This kind of alignment labor is currently delegated to simple software settings; in the worst case you have to install so called drivers, but usually it all works 'automagically' by means of plug-and-play software. Indeed, software takes command, as Manovich (2008) argues in his book with that title. While software in itself is saturated with and shaped by metaphors, as will be further explored in Chapter 5, and while interface design is one of the few professional disciplines that explicitly studies metaphors in its curriculum, it is remarkable how persistent the membrane is for thinking about the interface itself.

And it is even more remarkable how easily the membrane interface dissolves into nothing but a surface. We already saw in Chapter 1 how user-input devices like the keyboard and the mouse are easily overlooked as interfaces, and how the screen pushes itself to the fore. Hence, the interface first gets reduced to the user interface – consisting of input devices and feedback devices, positing itself as a membrane between human subject and machinic object – and subsequently the user interface gets narrowed down to that which is displayed on the screen. The ultimate computer interface is a thin screen, a naturalized membrane that smoothly facilitates the flow between subject and object, without cumbersome extra input devices that need specific human acts. Even Steven Johnson, who tries to develop a broad cultural definition of interface and starts out with the promising idea of the medieval cathedral as interface – thus in principle including architecture, labor division, ritual, performance, and authority in the notion of interface – quickly jumps to computer design by desktops and windows (Johnson 2008, 45), and then stays on this screen level for the rest of the book.

Once the notion of interface is captured by the discourse metaphor of the membrane it is hard to get a hold on material media practices, the connected apparatus, and the necessary hands-on acts. There seems to be only one way ahead, both in design and scholarly analysis. The membrane has to become thinner and thinner, until there is nothing left but a screen. And the best screens are completely invisible, only popping up when something needs to be displayed. The idea of invisible screens emerged first as fantasy – the swipes and gestures in popular movies and series such as *Minority Report* or *CSI* that immediately evoke projections of the right images and data on the wall – but today it is increasingly being implemented in consumer devices. We now have keyboards that are nothing but projections in front of a tablet, and screens that are just projections on a touch table or touch wall. No more membranes, no more screens, just surfaces and projections.

Media as master

So far we have seen how the membrane metaphor of media tends to be considered as a neutral facilitator that enables the subject to better perceive the world. However, the membrane also comes in an explicitly non-neutral variant, in which the membrane has become so powerful that it is more aptly covered by the metaphor of MEDIA AS MASTER.[72] This instantiation does not assume an equal alignment of subject and object, beneficial to the autonomous subject, as it projects the center of agency on the membrane itself. Media emerge as powerful master, a hybrid of non-neutral membranes (filter, guard, barrier) condensed into a totalizing force that can be productive and decisive by itself. This determining membrane between humans and the outside world exerts power and authority, either in line with the political and economical powers that be, or autonomously by imposing its own media logic. In any case, it is detrimental for the autonomous subject. The MEDIA AS MASTER metaphor circulates in popular discourse, but also in academic media and communication studies. For example, critical theory in the neo-Marxist tradition of the Frankfurt School conceives mass media primarily as the rude expansion of the capitalist free-market economy that spreads its tentacles deep into telecommunication infrastructures, broadcast networks, and the entertainment industry. This yields to the commodification, fragmentation, and privatization of the public sphere, a colonization of the life world, and to a hegemonic culture industry in which large media corporations channel public debate and eventually the political agenda (Habermas 1989 [1962]). The main tenet is that modern mass media are not just infecting public opinion; the point is that any public or political activity becomes reliant upon the media for its audience or electorate. According to Habermas (1989, 195), this implies a *refeudalization* of politics which poses a serious threat to modern democracy.

---

72. Special thanks to Barry Vacker who suggested this metaphor in his comment on my blog on 12 September 2005 (see http://metamapping.net/blog/?p=38#comment-46). I am also indebted to Irene Costera Meijer who directed me to the debate on mediatization.

Media, thus, are conceived as master – not coincidentally a feudal term – and as manipulator, controlling the minds and consciousness of the people, meanwhile reformatting the definition of politics as such (Anderson et al. 2006). It should be noted that Habermas' analysis of the public sphere is definitely more complicated than just a straightforward take-over by the mass media, notwithstanding his master metaphors. Moreover, Habermas (1996; 2006) updated his diagnosis of the current public sphere by switching from master metaphors to hydraulic tropes such as liquid flows controlled by sluices (see Friedland 2004; Downey et al. 2012).

The mediatization debate
While Habermas has reconsidered his master metaphors, the MEDIA AS MASTER discourse got a new impulse recently in media studies with the debate on what is called *mediatization* (Schulz 2004, Hjarvard 2008b, Lundby 2009). Mediatization, sometimes also called 'mediazation' (Thompson 1995) or just 'mediation' (Silverstone 2005) refers to the late 20th century condition of media-saturated societies. The concept tries to capture the intrusive ubiquity of media and their impact on society by processes of extension, substitution, amalgamation, and accommodation of previously non-mediatized phenomena (Schulz 2004). Though there are different takes on mediatization, I would argue that once the terms 'mediatization' and 'impact' are mobilized the direction and force are already implicated: media overwhelm and usurp society's domains – MEDIA AS MASTER (or MEDIA AS MANIPULATOR, and MEDIA AS MAGIC, in less political terms).

In his classic article 'The Mediatization of Society', Stig Hjarvard takes an institutional stand and diagnoses the current historical situation as one 'in which the media at once have attained autonomy as a social institution and are crucially interwoven with the functioning of other institutions' (Hjarvard 2008b, 110).[73] Mediatization is defined as 'the process whereby society to an increasing degree is submitted to, or becomes dependent on, the media and their logic' (ibid., 113). It refers to a general tendency, but also to specific instantiations, to be distinguished in weak and strong mediatization. The latter pertains to situations of substitution, that is when a given social activity is 'transformed from a non-mediated activity to a mediated form, and in such cases it is rather easy to establish a "before" and an "after" and examine the differences' (ibid., 115). This applies for example to online banking, but Hjarvard argues also to computer games.

The MEDIA AS MASTER metaphor implied in the mediatization thesis, especially the idea of a general 'media logic', has been questioned seriously (Couldry 2008; Lundby 2009; Livingstone 2009). Not only because of the assumption of a monolithic single transformative force, but also because it is hard to separate the assumed media logic from economical logic or technological logic. And indeed, the MEDIA AS MASTER metaphor easily shifts into the equally deterministic metaphors of MEDIA AS MARKET or MEDIA AS MACHINE. Some criticasters therefore dismiss the term mediatization, but it must be acknowledged that this discourse metaphor enables a research agenda for media studies that goes beyond empirical audience studies and representation analysis. It opens up interdisciplinary research objects such as the mediatization of consumption (Jansson 2002), of war (McQuail 2006), of politics (Strömbäck 2008), of theatrical performance (Auslander 2008),

---

73. Notwithstanding Hjarvard's sociological empirical approach it takes a lot of other support metaphors to uphold the notion of mediatization, as illustrated by his work on the mediatization of religion (Hjarvard 2008b) where the author mobilizes the metaphors of media as conduit, media as language, and media as environment to illustrate the process.

of religion (Hjarvard 2008a), of education (Friesen and Hug 2009), and of migrant diasporas (Hepp et al. 2012). These studies show that framing research by the MEDIA AS MASTER metaphor can certainly yield to nuanced and fine-grained analyses. And the great merit is that it focuses attention on issues of power and tacit politics – issues that are easily ignored within a discourse framed by the MEDIA AS MEMBRANE metaphor.

Hjarvard insists that mediatization is a neutral, non-normative concept, since the question whether 'mediatization has positive or negative consequences cannot be determined in general terms' (Hjarvard 2008b, 114). But at the same time the discourse on mediatization is deeply marked by negative terms: submission, dependence, pressure, intrusion, colonization, substitution, and so on. As Schulz puts it, the 'basic assumption of mediatization is that the technological, semiotic and economic characteristics of mass media result in problematic dependencies, constraints and exaggerations' (Schulz 2004, 87).

In a way these negative connotations echo the historically older meaning of the term mediatization, stemming from the German Laws of Mediatization in the early 19th century, when the independent states that were part of the crumbling Holy Roman Empire of the German Nation became 'mediatized' by Napoleon. Mediatization then referred to is the loss of 'imperial immediacy' (German: *Reichsunmittelbarkeit*) that occurred with the annexation of a state by another, whereby the former sovereigns kept their noble titles and some privileges. Habermas used this notion of mediatization when he argued that the uncoupling of system and lifeworld evoked dependency of the latter on the former, resulting in 'the mediatization of the lifeworld by system imperatives' (Habermas 1985, 305). The return of this particular historical etymological meaning is no coincidence: definitions of mediatization as modern master are based on the proposition of annexation and colonization by the media, all too often implying an assumed former state of autonomy and 'imperial immediacy'.

Spaces of media

As mentioned earlier, the notion of mediatization has been heavily criticized, mainly because of the assumed single media logic and the hegemonic annexation perspective, which seems to leave little room for human agency and intervention. Media scholars who criticize the master/mediatization trope mobilize different discourse metaphors in order to make their point. Sonia Livingstone for example pleads for a focus on 'the texture of everyday life' and considers plain mediation a better term than mediatization to capture the intricate interactions between media artifacts, individual appropriation, and social practices (Livingstone 2009, 11). Nick Couldry (2008) also prefers the more open-ended concept of mediation, which, in spite of it vagueness, emphasizes 'the heterogeneity of the transformations to which media give rise across a complex and divided social space rather than a single "media logic" that is simultaneously transforming the whole of social space at once' (Couldry 2008, 375).[74]

Although both scholars seem to fall back on the plain notion of mediation, this is obviously not evoked as a singular membrane. Mediation is metaphorized as a myriad of intricate interactions

---

74. Nonetheless Couldry acknowledges that mediatization can be a useful concept when the claims are specific, aimed to describe the transformation of particular 'social and cultural processes into forms or formats suitable for media representation' (Couldry 2008, 375). Notably, in his latest book *Media, Society, World: Social Theory and Digital Media Practice* (2012), he primarily uses the notion of mediatization.

and exchanges between multiple membranes; membranes within membranes that weave a texture of tools, filters, guides, forums, and spaces in and by which people arrange their daily lives. But the membrane is not the main organizing metaphor here. Most salient in this view is that the mediating membranes are explicitly not conceived as neutral: mediation is seen as marked by struggle and social unevenness regarding the access and the use of media artifacts. This branch of critical media studies assembles itself under several metaphorical headings. In Couldry's work for instance we can discern respectively MEDIA AS SPACE (Couldry and McCarthy 2003), MEDIA AS RITUALS (Couldry 2003), MEDIA AS PRACTICE (Couldry 2004), and MEDIA AS VOICE (Couldry 2010). Heterogeneous as these metaphors may look, they all focus on social-spatial dynamics. Therefore, MEDIA AS SPACE or better SPACES OF MEDIA can be considered the key discourse metaphor here.

What does it mean to frame media dynamics in terms of space? Space is by no means a simple concept. In itself it is actually as evanescent as the notion of medium, since its most striking feature is that it refers to an open void that can be filled and ordered with anything. As a metaphor it seems to be derived from plain, physical space, yet that turns out to be a problematic concept in itself. As Henri Lefebvre noted, the conception of space as supposedly physical and objective is ideologically plagued by two illusions which sound pretty familiar for media scholars: the illusion of transparency (space as luminous, intelligible, as giving action free reign), and the realistic illusion (the appeal to naturalness and substantiality) (Lefebvre 1991, 27-30). Lefebvre argues that physical space, mental space, and social space are inextricably intertwined, and that any notion of space is always a mixture of the perceived, the conceived, and the lived (ibid., 40). Space is always social space. It is produced and can be decoded and read (ibid., 17). Lefebvre proposed the following analytical triad to unravel this social space:

1. spatial practice (perceived, embracing production and reproduction, routine, continuity, cohesion, competence, and performance),
2. representations of space (conceived by scientists, planners and social engineers, identifying what can be perceived, conceived and lived, tied to the mode of production),
3. representational spaces (spaces directly lived through its associated images and symbols, creating inhabitants and users) (ibid., 38-39).[75]

It is not hard to see that Lefebvrian spaces may function as what I called a material metaphor, or Foucault's monuments-documents. Furthermore, Lefebvre's triadic dialectical perspective implies that any notion of space is always already a metaphor, regardless of whether it refers to physical space, mathematical space, geographical space, architectural space, mental space, or textual space. Space is always already metaphorically marked by imported elements from the 'other spaces', perpetually collapsing representations of space into representational spaces and spatial practices, and vice versa.

It is precisely this complex interplay between representation and environment that makes the metaphor of social space – acknowledged as produced *and* contested – so suitable for critical media studies. Media then are not reduced to neutral membranes or controlling masters, but can be located in any form or process that distributes and assembles socio-spatial structures and subject-object relations: MEDIA AS ENVIRONMENT, AS IN-BETWEEN MILIEU (Oosterling 2000, 2003), but

---

75. While it may be tempting to recognize here again an instance of Peircian Firstness, Secondness and Thirdness, this is not appropriate. In Lefebvre's triad, contrary to Peirce's, every instance contains the two others in a dialectical relation.

also MEDIA AS TEXT, AS TOOL, AS VOICE, AS HABIT, AS PRACTICE, AS REPRESENTATION, as these metaphors all implicate specific spatial arrangements and demarcations.

Discourse metaphors based on space can be found in any branch of science, in biology (Haraway 1976), physics (Hayles 1986), and techno-science (Mol and Law 2001), as well as in social sciences and humanities (Silber 1995). And no wonder, space is the ultimate metaphor of order and division, enabling both separation and conjunction. The space metaphor delineates and secures, but it is also extremely flexible and extensible, and therefore able to foster elaborated models and theories. Once departing from a notion of space, a myriad of further spatial entailments can be invoked: fields, boundaries, crossings, dimensions, directions, zones, spheres, passages, blockades, permeability, flows, access, routes, and movements.

Indeed, space is a powerful multipurpose metaphor, useful in any situation that needs division, differentiation, and classification. But it is also a dangerous metaphor, extremely prone to icontology. Illusions of transparency and reality prioritize sharp divisions, supposedly established once and for all by laws of nature that dictate that a thing cannot be in two spaces at the same time. Space is all too often metaphorized and icontologized as a static container, a box, instead of a dynamic working space that produces its own membranes and dimensions.

Virtual and real spaces
Early conceptions of the Internet as a separate, other space are a case in point. The claim of the existence of a completely new space, dubbed cyberspace (Benedikt 1991), hyperspace (Rushkoff 1994) or virtual space (Heim 1994), primarily announced, and heralded, the profound difference with the familiar world of real spaces and things. Cyberspace is first and foremost cast as a space that is different: non-regulated or regulated by other laws, free from the classic material constraints and determinants of bodies, space, and time. Therefore, it enables other things and can be filled with other landscapes and settlements. Borrowed from science-fiction and American Wild West imaginary cyberspace metaphors mark the excitement of new possibilities, propelled by the assumed deep split between the real and the virtual. This split could occur as fundamental and irrefutable precisely because the two domains were conceived as separate spaces rather than different dynamics. Once differences are defined as spatial entities, it is almost impossible to think them back 'into each other' as interrelated processes.

Cyberspace and other spatial metaphors of the Internet (such as the electronic highway) will be further fleshed out in Chapter 6 which is dedicated to network metaphors. For now, in the context of media metaphors, it can be observed that the split between virtual space and real space turned out to be contagious. In the slipstream of this split other things purportedly moved along in the same direction: from the real to the virtual, from the material to the immaterial, from atoms into bits (Negroponte 1995), and from matter to mind (Barlow 1996). While this kind of cyber-transcendental discourse has been criticized right from the start, for instance, as the Californian ideology of cyber-hippie-libertarian entrepreneurship (Barbrook and Cameron 1995), it was pretty persistent in the 1990s, and not only in popular discourse. Traces of it can even be found in Manuel Castells' monumental work on the network society, as far as his analysis is based on the political-ontological split between the 'space of flows' and the 'space of places' (Castells 1996). At that time the supposed split between the real and the virtual was already contested and crumbling down. Scholars in the established academic field of computer-mediated communication, and, in particular, in the new emerging field that studied virtual communities, found much more complex structures. They analyzed virtual communities as cyber-archaeological spatial-material settlements (Jones 1997), hybrid real-virtual technospaces (Mynatt et al.1998; Munt 2001), that could spark of both 'cyber-biographical' and 'geo-biographical' forms of sociality, and their multiple mixtures (Van den Boomen 2000; 2001).

After more than fifteen years of research and development in new media studies, the dichotomy between the real and the virtual is not an issue anymore, at least not as separate spaces.[76] As the Internet moved 'beyond the dazzling light of transcendence' (Graham 2004) and 'slouched into the ordinary' (Herring 2004, Steyaert and De Haan 2007) the idea of a separate cyberspace became obsolete. A much more refined analytical vocabulary could develop, able to account for the burgeoning diversity and multiplicity of digital-social practices that weaved itself into the fabric of daily life (Bakardjieva 2005; Van den Boomen et al. 2009).

This more refined vocabulary did not rule out spatial metaphors. On the contrary. Space turned out to be a very fluid and productive metaphor, gaining relevance as the study of the space formerly known as cyberspace extended outside the field of media and computing into space-oriented disciplines as urban studies, geography, planning, architecture, and transport studies. Some even speak of a spatial turn (Warf and Arias 2008). Especially the mapping metaphor gained ground, from the *Atlas of Cyberspace* (Dodge and Kitchin 2002) – still within the cyberspace metaphor, but already depicting an enormous heterogeneous field of Internet visualizations – to *Else/Where: Mapping New Cartographies of Networks and Territories* (Abrams and Hall 2006) and several other studies that can be labeled digital-performative cartography (Lammes 2008; Verhoeff 2012; Leurs 2012). The shift from space to map, mapping, and map-making may look trivial, but it cannot be stressed enough that the mapping metaphor implies the important double perspective on spatial representation and representational space, by which social space can be analyzed as constructed, performed, and negotiated.

Media ecology

A specific articulation of the MEDIA AS SPACE metaphor or MEDIA AS ENVIRONMENT can be identified in what sails under the flag of media ecology: MEDIA AS ECOLOGICAL SYSTEM. Two strands can be distinguished here. One is the cluster of media studies of the McLuhanist Toronto School, encompassing the works of, of course, Marshall McLuhan, but also Lewis Mumford, Harold Innis, Walter Ong, Jacques Ellul, Neil Postman and Paul Levinson (see for an overview Strate 2004). The other strand can be typified loosely as a critical Deleuzian-Guattarian extension and modification of media theory, exemplified by the work of scholars Matthew Fuller (2005) and Jussi Parikka (2010; 2011).[77]

---

76. The terminology of real and virtual, especially as a dichotomy or as separate spaces, can be situated mainly in late 20th century Internet discourse. After the millennium transition, marked by the dot-com bust and 9/11, the framing of new media praxis changed focus to daily life, surveillance, public sphere, user participation, and social networks. The term virtual world usually refers no longer to online dynamics in general, but to specific platforms that create visual navigation spaces, such as Second Life or World of Warcraft. Only Deleuzian-Lacanian scholars are still grappling with the virtual and the real as such, though not in terms of spaces, but from a broad speculative philosophical approach. See for instance Žižek (2001, 2003), Nusselder (2009) and Massumi (2002).
77. Fuller also includes the media analyses of Katherine Hayles and Friedrich Kittler under his umbrella of media ecology, just as Lev Manovich (2011) subsumes these scholars under 'software studies'.

Media as extension
Orthodox McLuhanist ecology finds its origin in the famous MEDIA AS EXTENSION metaphor. This metaphor in a way combines the previous metaphors: MEDIA AS MEMBRANE, MASTER, AND SPACE, with the proviso that here the membrane is multiple, consisting of integral yet ever extending parts of the human being, reaching out and creating social spaces and galaxies that determine the condition of society and humanity.

McLuhan extended the notion of media so far that it dissolved into any cultural artifact that could be seen as extension of the human body, mind, or ability. Media then can be plows and spades (extensions of the hand and labor), cloths and furniture (extensions of skin and the biological thermostat), cars and bicycles (extensions of legs and motion), books and photography (extension of the eyes), television (extension of eyes and of skin), but also money (extension of labor and exchange) and electricity (extension of the nervous system) (McLuhan 1962; 1964; 1988). McLuhan explored in his inimitable way the whole spectrum of these extensions, claiming that they evolve into historically consecutive master media which define the essence of society, as Tribal, Literate, Print, and the Electronic Era, respectively. The acoustic immersiveness of the speech-driven tribe (extension and dominance of the ear) had, with the emergence of writing and later the printing press, giving way to the contemporary visual linearity of the modern Gutenberg individual (extension and dominance of the eye). And McLuhan did not hesitate to predict a future of a retribalized global village in which electronic media would eventually succeed in activating, integrating, and synthesizing all the human senses, especially the underestimated sense of the skin and the nervous system. This ecology of extensions evolves, according to McLuhan, by what he calls the media tetrad, the four laws of media that each indicate a specific media effect, respectively enhancement (what does the medium enhance?), obsolescence (what does the medium make obsolete?), retrieval (what does it retrieve from the past?), and reversal (what will the medium reverse, flip into when pushed to the extreme?).[78]

The discourse metaphor of MEDIA AS EXTENSIONS OF MAN is at first sight deeply marked by anthropocentrism, but the premise is that those extensions acquire a life of their own, weave themselves into an ecology, an organic system with its own laws. According to the McLuhanist perspective, this extended ecology eventually strikes back at the social and human condition. McLuhan writes: 'All media work us over completely. They are so persuasive in their personal, political, economic, aesthetic, psychological, moral, ethical, and social consequences that they leave no part of us untouched, unaffected, unaltered. The medium is the massage' (McLuhan 1967, 26). MEDIUM AS MASSAGE, an all encompassing massage, in fact shifts the metaphorical frame from MEDIA AS HUMAN EXTENSIONS to MEDIA AS MASTER, tending more to technological determinism than to anthropocentrism – although the jury is still out on this case (see Jeffrey 1989; Strate 2008; Cavell 2002).

Media as rhizomes
The strand of Deleuzian-Guattarian media ecology, though now and then borrowing McLuhan's vocabulary, diverges substantially from McLuhan's principles. It does not ground itself in universal media laws or linear succession; it emphasizes the instability of media systems, the limits and ex-

---

78. See for a creative use of the media tetrad Douglas Rushkoff's *Monopoly Moneys: The Media Environment and the Player's Way Out* (2012), in which the author analyzes the emergence of state-issued money and corporate charters during the Renaissance as a medium.

cess of material energies, and the multiple dimensions and interlacings that can be traced (Fuller 2005). Media are understood as processes embodied as objects, that 'have explicitly become informational as much as physical but without losing any of their materiality' (ibid., 2). Ecology here refers to 'the massive and dynamic interrelation of processes and objects, beings and things, patterns and matter' (ibid.), where objects come into being as settlements of powers, affordances, and interpretations (ibid., 9).

In this strand of media ecology several metaphors are mobilized, not so much specific media metaphors, but broader metaphors of processes. For example, Deleuzian imageries such as the *rhizome* (botanical creeping rootstalks) and *machinic phylum* (a botanic classification, here indicating a perpetual tension between the discrete and the multiplicitous), but also concepts imported from chaos theory (such as *phase space* and *strange attractors*) and from affordance theory (Gibson 1986; Norman 1998).

Deleuzian media ecology seems to be a promising path to unravel new media dynamics because of its principal non-essentialist and material-energetic approach. But it also has its dangers. Deleuzian thinking tends to obscure itself by its abundant proliferation of metaphors, such as *desiring machines, body without organs,* with a strong preference for biological metaphors (*rhizome, becoming molecular, becoming insect*). While there is nothing wrong with mobilizing new metaphors – as they can be very productive – this becomes problematic when they are not acknowledged and theorized as metaphors. Deleuze and Guattari insist again and again that concepts such as *desiring machines* and *molecular unconscious* are certainly not metaphors: 'Something is produced: the effects of a machine, not mere metaphors' (Deleuze and Guattari 1983, 9). The argument is repeated several times: no metaphors, since they are real, have real effects, and are made of matter (ibid., 36, 41, 104, 141, 283).

By articulating a strict dichotomy between metaphor and materiality, the authors seem to adhere to the classical view on metaphors as merely figurative speech. Either something is a metaphor and then it is not material, or something is material and real, and hence not a metaphor.[79] In other words, the authors mobilize metaphors borrowed from biology and evolution without acknowledging the materiality of these metaphors, and what this implies for their own analysis. As Katherine Hayles (2001a) observed in her analysis of evolutionary metaphors in the works of Deleuze and Guattari, their use of these metaphors selectively favors unconstrained dynamism above the material constraints of evolution. She concludes, 'The engine of desire that breaks up subjectivity, organism and signification is not the desire of mutating machines but rather that of the authors' (ibid., 155).

---

79. Yet this only seems to concern their own 'anti-Oedipal' concepts, for the dreaded *Oedipus* itself is acknowledged as a metaphor – and as one with a real material force. Oedipus, the mythical representation the authors seek to abolish, is called a 'universal metaphor' (Deleuze and Guattari 1983, 306) of hegemonic structure that 'attributes a universal metaphoric value to the family at the very moment it has lost its objective literal values' (ibid., 307). Hence, the authors do recognize the material and structuring force of some metaphors, but apparently only when they are part of the hegemonic system. In general, metaphor seems to be situated completely on the hegemonic site, imprisoned in the empire of the signifier: 'For it is this whole constellation of the new alliance – the imperialism of the signifier, the metaphoric or metonymic necessity of the signifieds, *with* the arbitrary of the designations – that ensures the maintenance of the system' (ibid., 219).

We may conclude this section on media metaphors of processing with the observation that many scholars tend to ignore the power of metaphors. At best, metaphors are considered a false image that has to be substituted with the right image. But the right image or the truth is usually just another metaphor. Of course, metaphors can be criticized, and judged as epistemologically or politically wrong, but that is not based on their metaphor-being. The judgment depends on the discursive mobilization of the metaphors and the specific ethics and politics they organize. Regardless of whether metaphors are considered politically right, wrong, or mixed, they produce specific icontologies. Any social theory of media and communication worth its name should account for these semiotic-ideological mechanisms.

Meanwhile, the metaphors of processing I addressed in this section – membrane, master, space, ecology – mainly seem to drag us into more problems of vaporous translucency and imperceptibility. The medium seems to always be that which recedes. As we will see in the next section, on media metaphors of transmission, this seems to be a general tendency.

3 — METAPHORS OF TRANSMISSION

A dismissal of metaphors as 'mere metaphor' not only fails to acknowledge the productivity of the criticized metaphors, but also tends to obliterate the awareness of one's own metaphors. For example, McQuail's insensitivity to metaphors impedes him from noticing his own dominant organizing metaphor: the sender-receiver model. This model, almost inevitable in communication studies, tends to take the medium as a more or less neutral channel – MEDIA AS A RELAY, MEDIA AS TUBE – that does little more than just transporting whatever content from one point to another. McQuail refines and expands the model, for example, by distinguishing four different possible functions of the sender-receiver exchange: transmission, expression, publicity, and reception, each with specific roles and goals for senders and receivers (McQuail 1994, 55). But the underlying metaphorical labor divisions between, on the one hand, senders/receivers as actors, and on the other hand, the medium-as-channel remain untouched and unquestioned.

In this section on metaphors of transmission, I will look into the dominant sending-receiving metaphor, which can be subdivided into MEDIA AS CHANNEL and MEDIA AS CONDUIT. Finally, the metaphor of MEDIA AS TOOL will be addressed as a possibly more dynamic and material alternative.

Media as channel

In a way the MEDIUM AS CHANNEL metaphor is a stripped down version of the processual membrane metaphor. But where the membrane, though usually invisible, still has a flavor of material thickness that invites a further questioning of its internal mechanism, the channel metaphor tends to highlight the immateriality and invisibility of the medium. When a medium is conceived as a channel, a pipeline for transport from point A to point B, it still suggests material infrastructural mechanisms, but the medium easily disappears from sight when the channel goes underground or into the air, as wireless. Notably, what is supposed to get mediated or connected differs in the two metaphors. The membrane mediates between two separate, relatively fixed domains – human consciousness and reality – but the channel seems to be more promiscuous regarding its exchange: it mediates between variable human and non-human senders and receivers.

However, the MEDIUM AS CHANNEL metaphor did not begin its life cycle in discourse as an immaterial abstract conduit of transmission. On the contrary. When Claude Shannon (1948) envisioned and described the transmission model in his paper 'A Mathematical Theory of Communication' – the cradle of what became the science of information and communication – the metaphor was so material and specific that it did not even look like a metaphor. His article proposed the concept of information as a probability function and coined the notion of 'bit' as a contraction of 'binary digit', but most of all it established a general notion of COMMUNICATION AS SENDING along a channel. The transmission model was the perfect material metaphor to address specific engineering issues of telegraph, radio, and telephone technologies: how to transmit a signal through a channel as accurately and efficiently as possible with the least chance of noise and distortion. Shannon illustrated the model with a clear picture (see Figure 2).

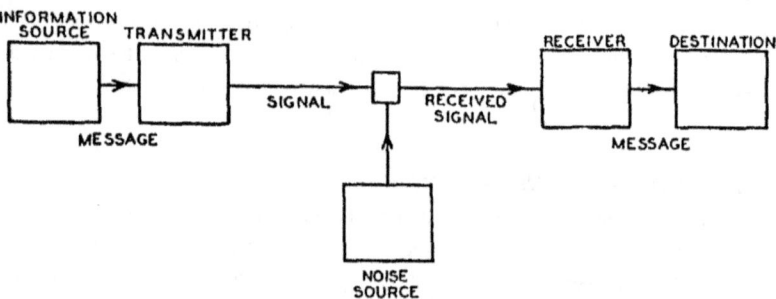

Figure 2. Shannon's 'diagram of a general communication system' (Shannon 1948).

The model consists of the following parts:
— An information source, which produces a message to be communicated to a receiving terminal.
— A transmitter, which encodes the message into signals suitable for transmission over the channel.
— A channel, 'merely the medium used to transmit the signal from transmitter to receiver. It may be a pair of wires, a coaxial cable, a band of radio frequencies, a beam of light, etc.' (Shannon 1948, 7).
— A noise source, which may threaten the integrity of the signal.
— A receiver, which decodes, reconstructs the message from the signal.
— A destination, 'the person (or thing) for whom the message is intended' (ibid., 7).

Saliently, Shannon's model does not identify a separate or overarching instance called the medium. The technological channel was 'merely the medium for transmission', that is, just the infrastructural means for the transportation of signals (wires, radio frequencies). It is also remarkable that in Shannon's initial version of what later came to be known as the sender-receiver model, there is no such thing as a sender. Shannon carefully differentiated the information source from the transmitter, without collapsing them into a general human sender. The same holds for the other end of the chain. The receiver and the destination are also two different things, and the receiver could be human or non-human. And from his engineering perspective that makes sense. Just as it makes sense that information in his model has nothing to do with meaning, interpretation, or intention. As Shannon noted,

> Frequently the messages have *meaning;* that is they refer to or are correlated according to some system with certain physical or conceptual entities. These semantic aspects of communication are irrelevant to the engineering problem. The significant aspect is that the actual message is one *selected from a set* of possible messages. (Shannon 1948, 5)

Indeed, for an engineer it does not matter whether the informational signal constitutes a greeting, a pornographic image, or a list of numbers – his focus is on the material, mechanical and statistical. It was Shannon's co-author Warren Weaver who popularized the mathematical model, and extended it to the socio-cultural realm in their joint book (Shannon and Weaver 1949). Not only did Weaver extend the notion of communication to language, music, art, and the human mind, he also distinguished between technical noise and semantic noise (Helsloot 2002), thus opening the door for further extensions and translations into issues of semantics, meaning and interpretation. However, these extensions were not just Weaver's peculiarity. In the same year Shannon's paper was released, political scientist and communications theorist Harold Laswell published his article 'The Structure and Function of Communication in Society' (Laswell 1948), in which he defined the general communication process as Who (says) What (to) Whom (in) What Channel (with) What Effect. The channel was more or less identical to Shannon's channel, but the chain of apparatuses was absent in order to emphasize communication between humans. In 1948, Lazarsfeld and Merton also published their article 'Mass Communication, Popular Taste and Organized Social Action' which addressed mass-media effects (Lazarsfeld and Merton 1948). Finally, it was communication scholar David Berlo who transformed Shannon's model into the famous and still popular sender-message-channel-receiver model (Berlo 1960). From then on Shannon's careful distinctions were compressed and humanized into one sender, just as the receiver and destination got condensed in a general receiver, and the message and the signal into a general message.

Notably, Shannon's initial model accounted for the three functions Kittler later identified as the main features of media: the relay function of transmitting, the processing function of encoding, decoding and noise reduction, and the storage function as performed by the transmitter, receiver and destination devices. Later popular and academic versions of the model, usually a variant of the sender-message-channel-receiver model, foreground primarily the relay function, at the cost of material processing and storage. And again, when the relay infrastructure becomes invisible (underground, wireless, or otherwise taken for granted and black-boxed), the medium apparatus is easily forgotten.

Here we have a clear example of how a metaphor can travel through discourse. The sender-receiver metaphor, taken metonymically from Shannon's technical model, turned out to be quite adaptable beyond the engineering domain – though not without some translations and transformations. Erase Shannon's mediating transmitter and receiver devices, humanize senders and receivers, coagulate message and signal, shift encoding and decoding into meaning and understanding, and the sender-receiver metaphor can cover human interpersonal communication, as well as technologically mediated communication. With a few updates it could also give an account of mass media,[80] and by adding feedback loops, extra arrows, and hybrids of sender-receivers, such as 'prosumers' (Toffler 1980) and 'produsers' (Bruns 2008), one could even try to capture the dynamics of digital media networks. What happens with these translations and displacements is that the medium becomes footloose. It becomes a floating signifier that may embark on any part of the sender-receiver apparatus. It may indicate a specific element (channel: BROADCAST AS MEDIUM, sender: FILM INDUSTRY AS MEDIUM, receiver: TELEVISION DEVICE AS MEDIUM). It may signify specific instantiations of an element (message:

---

80. Mostly by differentiating between central and decentral senders and receivers, resulting in a matrix of allocation (central sender to many individual receivers, cf. radio), registration (central requests for individual information, cf. census), consultation (individual seekers of centrally stored information, cf. libraries) and conversation (individual senders and individual receivers, cf. speech), representing different combinations of central/decentral senders and central/decentral receivers (Van Dijk 1991, 12-15; McQuail 1994, 56-57).

'a book is another medium than a newspaper', 'a novel is another medium than a philosophical essay'). It may also cover a complete sender-receiver apparatus ('a letter is another medium than a phone call', 'film as medium', 'Internet as medium').

Oddly, in the generalized transmission model, the term medium can mean: the stuff that moves or the mover itself; the stuff that is stored or the storage device itself. But most often the medium is presupposed as the abstract, yes, magic means of *conduit*, accomplishing success without effort (after the engineers have solved the technical problems of noise). The medium then surfaces at most as a contingent wrapping around the message, effacing the involved human labor as well as its own machinery and infrastructure, blotting out that you never can have the message without the wrapping. The more or less material channel is dissolved in an immaterial conduit, and all traces of medium and mediation have disappeared completely. This abstract conduit is profoundly different from Shannon's channel, as will be argued in the next section.

The conduit discourse

The conduit metaphor, as radical dematerialization of the channel metaphor, has far-reaching consequences. Not only in academic disciplines such as communication and media studies, but also for philosophy and vernacular discourse, as metaphor scholars have pointed out. Lakoff and Johnson (1980) analyzed the conduit metaphor as a complex metaphorical assemblage that thoroughly frames our language about language and thought. The assemblage consists of the following conceptual metaphors: IDEAS (or MEANINGS) ARE OBJECTS, LINGUISTIC EXPRESSIONS ARE CONTAINERS, and COMMUNICATION IS SENDING. These metaphorical building blocks generate a coherent discourse in which a 'speaker puts ideas (objects) into words (containers) and sends them (along a conduit) to a hearer who takes the idea/object out of the word/containers' (Lakoff and Johnson 1980, 10).

The authors draw on the work of Michael Reddy (1979), who documented this frame with more than hundred types of expressions in English (these are estimated to account for seventy percent of the expressions used to talk about language). Think of expressions such as: 'She gave you that idea', 'Your reasons came through to me', 'I do not get it', and so on. In this discursive frame message transfer is conceived as the transportation of wrapped stable cargo – indeed, Shannon's technical problems of unstable freight have vanished. While the examples all refer to spoken or written language, it can easily be seen that this frame also holds for other articulations (as well as other languages). Movies, television programs, and websites are supposed to contain ideas that can be sent along to people, who just have to unpack the contingent media wrapping 'to get the idea'.

Reddy also observed that the wrapping is supposed to contain ideas just as human minds are supposed to contain ideas. The conduit frame thus implies and reinforces the idea that thoughts as such are pre-existing within human heads, and are able to flow either disembodied or reified (in words or other representations) through ambient conduits. Eventually they arrive undamaged and unchanged inside other human heads.

According to Reddy, the assumption of *disembodied ideas* can lead to radical conclusions. He writes: 'In the simplest of terms, the conduit metaphor lets human ideas slip out of human brains, so that, once you have recording technologies, you do not need humans any more' (Reddy 1993, 188).[81] The notion of *reified ideas* seems to be more material and embodied, but since the reified

---

81. Here we could recognize the Transhumanist Extropian dream of downloading the human mind. See Moravec (1988) for a believer, and see Hayles (1999) for a thorough critique.

product can be performed by any arbitrary medium without any consequence for the contained ideas, this boils down to the same disembodiment paradigm: 'thoughts and feelings exist independent of any need for living human beings' (ibid., 170). Ideas are considered ready-mades, things inside your head or floating around, ready to get grabbed, wrapped, transported, and unpacked, for every human being under the same conditions.

Lakoff and Johnson pointed out that this metaphor highlights that utterances have meaning in themselves, and hide any dependency on the context. Reddy went further, and argued that this frame imposes a structural bias which sooner or later will lead to frame conflicts, 'even though nothing more than common sense is necessary to devise a different, more accurate framework' (ibid., 165). Indeed, we can easily see that, while our discourse on communication is framed by the seamless conduit metaphor, daily practice is often less smooth, in verbal communication as well as in computerized transferences. When something goes wrong, the frame of the conduit metaphor leaves open only one option: 'blame the speaker for failures. After all, receiving and unwrapping a package is so passive and simple – what can go wrong?' (ibid., 168).

Well, a lot, arguably. Take for example ordinary email, seemingly the ultimate implementation of the sender-receiver model and the conduit metaphor in digital praxis. What is sent is what you get, EMAIL IS TUBE MAIL, just unpack the message with your email client. Until someone sends you an email with a mysterious attachment called 'winmail.dat'. You are unable to open it. Strange enough, when sent to multiple recipients, other email users do not experience any problem. At their site the attachment is displayed with its original file name and extension, and can be unpacked immediately. For them, EMAIL IS TUBE MAIL. Others however, are stuck – they need to open the black box of email transmission, which turns out not to be a seamless tube system, but rather an explosion of Shannon's transmitter and receiver devices. The email network consists of at least four coding/decoding nodes: the sender's email client, the sender's outgoing email server, the recipient's incoming email server, and the recipient's email client, each with its own configuration. Only when both the sender's and recipient's email client are Microsoft's Outlook the network functions as a seamless conduit.

In other words, the conduit is actually Microsoft's proprietary tube, configured with an idiosyncratic format to process and display attachments. When recipients use other email clients they may or may not encounter the winmail.dat problem, depending on what kind of email servers are located along the tube. Some of them translate Microsoft's non-standardized misbehavior into common standards, some do not. Recipients who receive winmail.dat attachments have two options: either obtain a free conversion program or a plug-in that can transcode the winmail.dat file into a decent attachment, or educate Outlook users to send their email in plain text; then the display of attachments follows standard protocols.

It should be clear that the conduit metaphor provides little knowledge about the medium and its black-boxed machinery. It ignores common situations of partially successful communication, of noise, incompatibility, and failure, based as it is on the premise of unproblematic transport by a non-intervening transparent medium.

The toolmakers paradigm

Interestingly, Reddy did not stop at just describing the conduit metaphor and the frame conflicts it induces in daily practices; he also proposed an alternative frame, a narrative he dubbed *the toolmakers paradigm*.[82] Contrary to the conduit metaphor the toolmakers paradigm highlights the transformation and translation processes involved in communicating messages. The toolmakers paradigm is based on quite a different conception of what an idea is. As far as an idea might exist inside someone's head, this is always determined by and dependent on the direct environment of that particular person. Reddy called this 'the postulate of radical subjectivity' (Reddy 1993, 172). You only have tacit knowledge about your own environment, you have no access to other people's environment, and you only know of their very existence indirectly, by cumulative series of inferences, that is, by mediated communication. Reddy provided a picture to illustrate how we should conceive of this situation of compartmentalized subjectivity (see Figure 3).

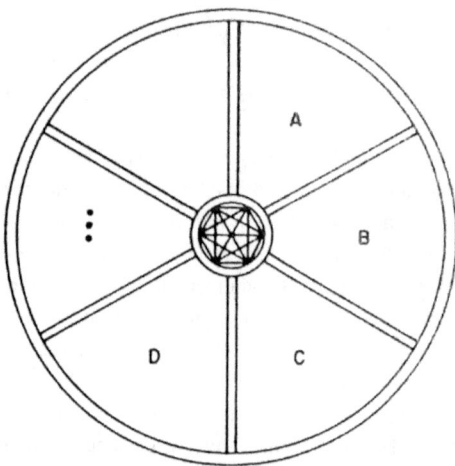

Figure 3. The toolmakers paradigm (from: Reddy 1993 [1979], 172).

The picture displays a kind of a wagon wheel, with spokes as the impermeable walls between isolated individuals. Each is living in its own compartment, where they have to survive with what is at hand. Their respective environments have things in common – say: water, rocks, trees, plants, and the like – yet no two are exactly alike; some have more rocks, some have more trees, some have a river, and so on. At the hub of the wheel there is a kind of machinery which is able to deliver small sheets of paper from one compartment to another. Somehow the people have learned to operate this machine to exchange crude sets of instructions, for example for making tools, shelters, and preparing food. That is the only way to communicate; the radically compartmentalized subjects

---

82. Lakoff and Johnson (1980) and Lakoff (1993) only address Reddy's description of the conduit metaphor, not a word about his toolmaker alternative. This can be explained by their focus on unconscious metaphors, but by ignoring the alternative proposal they also ignore discursive competition between metaphorical frames, i.e. the politics of metaphor. It should also be noted that Reddy does not explain why he speaks of the toolmakers *paradigm* versus the conduit *metaphor*. Both provide discursive frames, both highlight and downplay elements, both are metaphorical assemblages. Reddy seems to imply that metaphors cannot be as accurate as paradigms.

have no way of visiting each others compartment, neither of exchanging samples or pictures of their products and tools.

This model, Reddy suggests, frames more accurately the way daily communication works. Here, ideas can never flow freely and unchanged from one head or context to another since ideas exist as idiosyncratic tools within a particular compartment. And they have to be perpetually adjusted and transformed – both by the writers and the readers – to make them applicable in other domains. In order to exchange such ideas/tools they have to be translated/transcribed onto sheets of paper, and the interpretation of these sheets keeps inducing puzzlement, trial and error, and new adaptations. Here, there is no success without effort. The transformation processes involved, completely depresented in the conduit metaphor, need human effort to take place: cognitive labor (consisting of cumulative series of inferences about another person's mode of existence and environment), tool-making labor (creating your own tools in order to survive in your compartment, and adapting the tools of others), and translation labor (transforming your tools into applicable instructions for others, interpreting the instructions from others into applicable tools for your own environment).

To parse this frame in terms of conceptual metaphors: IDEAS ARE TOOLS, MESSAGES ARE TRANSLATIONS, and COMMUNICATION IS LABOR. In this frame there is no transference without transformation, signification, and interpretation. The ideas/tools change along with their translations. This metaphor explicitly leads to questioning what tools are involved, what they are made of, what inferences can be made of others' environments, and how to transpose instructions into applicable tools. In other words, it raises onto-epistemological questions of how ideas/tools are conceived, externalized, probed, modified, and translated in order to get them transferred to other domains. Sure enough, none of these questions can occur in the frame of the conduit metaphor.

Of course, the toolmakers metaphor also conceals elements. Take for instance that mysterious machinery in the middle. What is it? It may be a medium, or language, or communication as such, but how did it get there? How could such a collectively shared system emerge between people who are not working and living together in shared habitats? The toolmakers paradigm as formulated by Reddy lacks a narrative to explain this part. But, as we have learned from Lakoff and Johnson, there is no metaphor that does not conceal or downplay particular elements. No metaphor can be all-inclusive. This holds for both the toolmakers and the conduit metaphor. Yet, in the latter metaphor the transmission machinery is so taken-for-granted that it does not raise any questions about its mysterious assumptions.

We may conclude that the toolmakers metaphor opens up quite a different discourse than the conduit metaphor. In that sense these metaphors are discourse metaphors, not just conceptual metaphors, as they organize sets of conceptual metaphors in a systematic coherent discourse. In ordinary language we can discern more conceptual metaphors about the ontology of ideas, for instance IDEAS ARE PEOPLE, IDEAS ARE ORGANISMS, IDEAS ARE FOOD, IDEAS ARE COMMODITIES. Some corresponding common expressions – usually not recognized as metaphorical articulations – would be: 'Cognitive psychology is still in its infancy', 'This is a fertile idea', 'I can't swallow that claim', 'He won't buy that'. But none of these conceptual metaphors are connected to other conceptual metaphors in a coherent narrative, as is the case in the conduit and the toolmakers metaphor.

It would be clear that, as a scholar who is after the hidden epistemological productivity of metaphors, I prefer the performative toolmakers metaphor above the quasi-neutral conduit metaphor. The toolmakers metaphor foregrounds dynamic materiality, labor and processing, and as such it seems to provide a material-semiotic frame for the analysis of digital sign-tool-metaphors. And it does so without the pitfall of considering tools as pre-given, neutral means – tools also have to be made and tested in various situations. But even the toolmakers metaphor has a blind spot when it comes to the riddle of the medium, that mysterious hub in the middle.

This seems to be a general feature of media metaphors. In all metaphors of media discussed so far – metaphors of processing as well as metaphors of transmission – the medium keeps lingering on the edge of taken-for-grantedness, disappearance, and imperceptibility. The medium remains a black box, and the best black boxes are those that remain invisible.

There remains one category of media metaphors left to address: metaphors of storage. Would that category imply less evanescent metaphors of media?

4 — METAPHORS OF STORAGE

Metaphors of storage are probably the oldest media metaphors. These metaphors have always been strongly connected to memory. As already documented in Plato's *Phaedrus* (370 BC), Socrates connected the invention of writing to external storage and its detrimental effects on memory. He argued that this discovery would 'create forgetfulness in the learners' souls, because they will not use their memories; they will trust to the external written characters and not remember of themselves.' Socrates feared the substitution of human memory with external storage, and in fact he was right, at least on the level of metaphor. This is observable today with the use of the same word for human memory and computer memory.

Storage and memory are often used as each other's metaphors. And, as Douwe Draaisma (2000) showed in his historical study on the metaphors of memory, a lot of the metaphors employed to indicate memory (and the human mind in general) are metaphors of storage derived from media forms or media devices. For instance, MEMORY AS WAX INSCRIPTIONS, AS MYSTIC WRITING PAD, THE BOOK AS MEMORY, MEMORY AS A BOOK, MEMORY AS PHONOGRAPH, AS CAMERA OBSCURA, AS PHOTOGRAPHIC PLATE, and of course, MEMORY AS COMPUTER and THE COMPUTER AS MEMORY, subdivided in MEMORY AS HARDWARE and MEMORY AS SOFTWARE. When we zoom in on metaphors of media roughly two main categories of storage metaphors can be distinguished: MEDIA AS CONTAINERS and MEDIA AS INSCRIPTIONS.

Media as container

The MEDIA AS CONTAINER metaphor is probably the most frequently used metaphor in popular discourse. The very notion of 'media content' already implies the image of something contained in a container, a delineated enclosed space where stuff can be stored inside, in a kind of box. Most common expressions about media and communication are derived from the container metaphor: books *contain* texts and ideas, a text can be *full of* bullshit, you can get something *out of* a lecture or movie, someone said something *in* a television program but the words were *empty*. Computer interfaces and software are also full of container metaphors: folder, home, trash bin, dialogue box, library, database, package, stack, computer memory, and so on. IBM even patented the 'container metaphor for visualization of complex hierarchical data types', as an alternative for the hierarchical tree metaphor.[83] While the metaphor foregrounds stable storage, the image of a container is scalable and can be reiterated endlessly as boxes in boxes like Matryoshka dolls. Thus, we can find ideas in texts in books in libraries or objects in software commands in files in folders. And

---

83. Patent US 20060080622 A1.

combined with the conduit metaphor content can be moved from container to container: from the human mind into a text into a newspaper article into the television news into a trending topic on Twitter back into newspapers and television.

McLuhan seems to allude to these boxes in boxes in his famous statement, 'The content of writing is speech, just as the written word is the content of print, and print is the content of the telegraph' (McLuhan 1964, 8). But he insisted that media are our environment, and 'environment is process, not container' (McLuhan 1969, 30). As we have seen before in this chapter, Reddy had similar objections to the container metaphor implied in the conduit metaphor.

The container metaphor not only demarcates an enclosed space, it most of all secures and fixates the stuff that resides inside the container. The container promises stability, fixed order, and conservation – so secured we can afford to forget it. This not only affects popular discourse on media and communication, it also has implications for academic discourse, in particular in the field of communication studies.

Communication theorist Klaus Krippendorff listed four entailments of the container metaphor.[84] The first one is 'our *[that is, communications scholars – MvdB]* markedly unequal cultural emphasis on the content of messages that leaves language and communication processes transparent, unreflected and unattended' since these are considered 'mere means for storing and transporting valuable goods' (Krippendorff 1993, 6). Second, it affects the way content is studied and conceived, as the metaphor 'renders communication contents as entities with objective qualities', even thoughts 'become thing-like entities' (ibid.). In other words, the container metaphor reifies and icontologizes the stuff that is supposedly stored in the container while ignoring the materiality of the container itself.

The third implication concerns the earlier mentioned conception of communication as transportation, as getting the contents from here to there, and just unpacking it. The fourth one is, as Krippendorff puts it, 'the acceptance of sharing as logical consequence [and] standard for assessing what "good" communication is. Sharing is presumed to result from exposure to the same messages and explains the cause of common knowledge, subscribing to similar values, or thinking alike' (ibid.). In other words, the formation of social-cultural discourse communities is supposed to emerge from passively receiving the same stable information. Apparently the old behaviorist communication model of the hypodermic needle is still around in the slipstream of the container metaphor. It is assumed that the same content has the same meaning and value for all subjects, who in their turn are conceived as empty buckets where information can be poured in. In that regard, the container metaphor seems to be contagious. It turns every other entity or phenomenon involved into a container where things can be stored orderly and immutable. What this metaphor ignores is that any storage – be it in human memory, papyrus, celluloid, or hard disks – is subject to wear and tear over time, and needs maintenance to keep it more or less in place.

Boxes and clouds
The container metaphor does not only function as a discourse metaphor, especially in the digital domain it can be a fully operational material metaphor. We can recognize the container metaphor

---

84. Krippendorff (1993) distinguishes six major metaphors of communication: container, conduit, control, transmission, war, and dance-ritual. Whereas the last two primarily concern patterns of interpersonal communication, the other four pertain to mediated communication and media. Krippendorff's conduit and transmission metaphor are similar to my accounts of the conduit and the channel; his control metaphor is comparable with what I have dubbed the media as master metaphor.

on the user interface (folders, trash can), but also in Internet business models. Since the late nineties it has been quite a challenge to make money on the Internet, mainly because Internet content and usage is hard to contain or containerize. Internet providers could provide access and application services on a subscriber basis, but what users subsequently did on the Net was largely beyond containment, and hence beyond control and beyond pricing. Content was (and still is) notoriously hard to commodify without specific monopolies. Data traffic could only be controlled loosely by Fair Use Policies, [85] not by proportional pricing based on quantitative expenditure. Due to the technical-historical configuration of the Internet infrastructure combined with the political principle of net neutrality [86] users could not be charged per email, per site visit, or per byte downloaded, unlike the classic business model for electricity, water, or phone calls. Internet access providers could also sell contained storage space for personal homepages, but in the early nineties that was a negligible market.

Hence, business models based on user subscription and advertising were the main models for a long time. In these models the entrepreneur had to contain and keep visitors at their site, a company-controlled container. America Online tried that on a subscription basis – and failed because users finally found their way to the uncontained and unrestrained Internet. Facebook and Google eventually did succeed with the advertising model by extending their controlled container with ever more services and integrations.

However, meanwhile the Internet landscape had changed. With the explosion of corporations going online in the late nineties web hosting (that is, selling online storage space and services to maintain professional websites) became a serious business model. With the advent of ubiquitous broadband and wireless connections, plus the massive adoption of notebooks, digital cameras, and mobile devices that generate ever more data objects, ordinary users also needed more storage space, preferably accessible from any device. Another profitable business model could emerge, independent from existing access and service providers, and chargeable by size and usage: leasing data containers, that is, delineated spaces on online servers where users can store (and usually also share) their files. And this came with an extra bonus for the provider: the ability to data mine the stored content.

Three container metaphors prevail here: THE CONTAINER IS A DRIVE (with brand names such as FreeDrive, Google Drive, OpenDrive, LiveDrive), THE CONTAINER IS A BOX (Box, Dropbox, BoxHost) and THE CONTAINER IS A CLOUD (JustCloud, ownCloud, ZipCloud, iCloud). The drive metaphor, derived from the material storage device on a computer, blends the container metaphor with the inscription metaphor, and hence will be addressed in the next section. Remarkably, the metaphors can be mixed unproblematically, resulting in brand names such as SkyDrive, CloudDrive, BoxDrive, and CloudBox. A cloud can be in a box, [87] and a box can be in the cloud, as Dropbox, one of the most popular free storage services, shows with several images on its site (see Figure 4).

---

85. Fair Use Policy by Internet service providers entails that customers who structurally and significantly use more bandwidth than the average user receive a warning or an adjusted subscription price.
86. Net neutrality is the technical and political principle that Internet service providers and governments should treat all data on the Internet equally, that is no prioritizing, differentiating or charging differentially by user, type of subscription, content, protocol or application.
87. Oracle announced in 2010 the release of its product Exalogic Elastic Cloud, and called it 'a cloud in a box' (Blankema 2010).

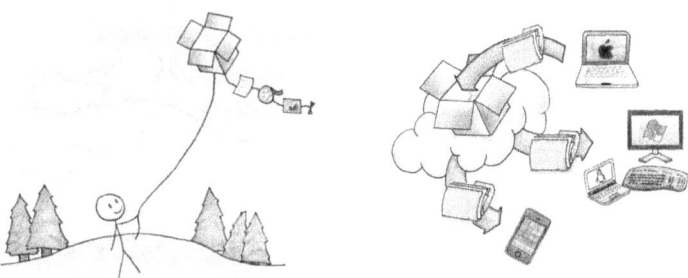

Figure 4. Images from Dropbox.com, illustrating the box in the cloud.

The pictures not only show a box in the cloud, but also something of a connection line or conduit: a kite string, an arrow between the box and local devices. This reminds us somewhat of the tube metaphor, but whereas the tube evokes an image of moving or sending, the default of Dropbox does not even hint at uploading or downloading. Your Dropbox is just a folder on your desktop where you can drag and drop your files; they will synchronize automatically with the parallel Dropbox in the cloud. The box then suggests safety, stability, and standstill, while it is working hard behind the screens: a true black box. Positing the box in the cloud further obscures its processes and transmissions by wrapping the black box in a quasi-transparent haze. The cloud serves as a magic container, processor, and transmitter at once – and we will encounter this powerful material metaphor on several other levels in this study (the level of software, networking, and sociability). For now, we can conclude that the box-cloud metaphor does certainly not provide more insight in the material mechanism of the medium.

The inscription discourse

The other main metaphor of storage is the MEDIA AS INSCRIPTION metaphor. This metaphor foregrounds storage as something that is not contained within a container, but as something that is carved in or inscribed on a surface, either temporarily or more or less persistently. Here, the medium is not a container, but rather an inscription plane.[88] Or better, a media-specific combination of a specific plane, specific inscription marks, and a specific arrangement of these marks on the plane. The metaphor is able to cover with this combination a lot of different media: from wood and stone carvings to cave paintings and hand written papyrus scrolls to typewritten texts and printed books to analog recordings on vinyl and celluloid to digital marks on hard disks and chips. The metaphor seems to be able to account for different modes of durability, mutability, and readability that make up what we can conceive as a medium. Moreover, it also seems to

---

88. Interestingly, the earliest writing artifacts, found in Sumer (4000 BC), were hybrids of inscription and container, and also hybrids of writing, money, and bookkeeping (Mainyu 2012). The artifacts consisted of strings of baked clay tokens with signs carved on them that represented quantities of specific commodities, like sheep. To prevent tinkering with the tokens they were put in a clay pot, that was sealed and then baked. In case of a dispute about the property referred to, the pot could be broken and the tokens recounted. On the outside of the pot number signs and witness seals were carved in, which eventually (3100 BC) became the first written language that could stand on its own, as plain inscription, without a sealed container as a back up.

be able to account for the differential material machineries needed to process and decode the inscriptions on planes as different as celluloid, vinyl, and disks.

In that regard the inscription metaphor goes beyond just storage, as it also implies processing and transmission – almost an encompassing theory of media systems in itself. Perhaps this is why this metaphor has taken more hold in academic discourse than in popular discourse. Cases in point are Friedrich Kittler's notion of *Aufschreibesysteme* (translated as discourse networks,[89] though it actually refers to 'writing-down systems', Kittler 1985), Jacques Derrida's notion of grammatology (the study of written inscriptions as prerequisite for any sign system, Derrida 1998), Bruno Latour's notion of inscription devices, referring to any equipment that 'transforms a material substance into a figure or diagram' (Latour and Woolgar 1997, 51) and Katherine Hayles' media-specific analyses of inscription marks (Hayles 1993b, 2002, 2004).

The inscription metaphor is able to mobilize meticulous analysis and media research programs, but it is too complicated to serve popular discourse or business models. The complications that render the metaphor unsuitable for popular discourse reside in its immanent ambiguities (if there is one thing that popular metaphors seek to eliminate it is ambiguity). The ambiguities of the inscription metaphor pertain to the unresolved tensions of persistence-volatility, engraving-surface writing, and stability-instability. There is no inscription system that can escape these ambiguities, even engravings in stone do not persist forever as stable marks, let alone surface marks on papyrus or celluloid. These ambiguities permeate all types of mediating systems that theoreticians try to cover with elaborated inscription metaphors, from the unconscious and language (Freud's mystic writing pad and Lacan's floating signifier) to photography and film (Barthes' third meaning and Deleuze's image-temps and image-movement).

Flickering signifiers

To complicate things further, when it comes to analyzing the digital with inscription metaphors the ambiguities seem to explode. They multiply on all levels involved: the plane, the marks, the arrangements, and the chain of translations in between those instances. The plane of inscription that conserves digital inscriptions can be practically anything: tape, magnetic or optical disks, silicon chips, flash drives, and radio frequencies, but also paper strips (Turing 1936) or T-shirts (Cramer 2003). Digital marks too can consist of practically anything: electronic polarities, magnetic charges, laser pits, or acoustic signals, and on another level also numbers, symbols, and patterns. All these types of marks can be mobilized to do the digital execution trick when inscribed on the proper plane, according to the proper format, and processed by the proper machinery that is able to translate the marks along multiple coding layers. The varieties on all levels makes it hard to pin down the medium-specificity of digital inscriptions.

Katherine Hayles proposed the notion of *flickering signifier* in order to cover the intricate dynamics of digital inscriptions (Hayles 1999, 30-33). In contrast with Lacan's *floating signifier* (that Hayles considers as print-based and focused on absence and presence as the main dialectics), the flickering signifier operates by pattern and randomness on multiple levels of coding and transcoding. As she explains,

---

89. The notion of discourse networks has the advantage that is foregrounds social and cultural discursive configurations, but it looses the media-specific connotations of the inscription metaphor.

> In informatics, the signifier can no longer be understood as a single marker, for example an ink mark on a page. Rather it exists as a flexible chain of markers bound together by the arbitrary relations specified by the relevant codes. As I write these words on my computer, I see the lights on the video screen, but for the computer, the relevant signifiers are electronic polarities on disks. Intervening between what I see and what the computer reads are the machine code that correlates alphanumeric symbols with binary digits, the compiler language that correlates these symbols with higher-level instructions determining how the symbols are to be manipulated, the processing program that mediates between these instructions and the commands I give the computer, and so forth. A signifier on one level becomes a signified on the next-higher level. (ibid., 31)

In other words, flickering signifiers do not float between lines of inscriptions that make up language; they rather flicker between signifier and signified, on several levels of translation that make up a computer system. They flicker between hard and soft, material and symbolic, persistence and volatility, engraving and surface, pattern and noise, fixation and arbitrariness. The metaphor of flickering also alludes to the flickering CRT computer screens of the nineties, but, while our current screens are definitely more stable for our eyes, the flickering signifiers in digital machineries keep on vibrating.

Again we can see how metaphors of inscription are perfectly apt for theorizing media systems, but not for popular use. The beautiful complexity of the flickering signifier cannot be turned into a meme, brand, or gadget. Inscription metaphors are too complex and too ambiguous to be icontologized into business models, such as the box and the cloud. Even at the level of the user interface, inscription metaphors are non-existent (though maybe the visualization of the process of defragmenting your disk could count as such).

Could it be then that we have the odd situation of a discourse metaphor that is, as one of the few media metaphors, able to account for complex forms of materiality including digital materiality, but does not translate into an operational material metaphor? Well, yes and no. For software developers the inscription metaphor, with all its layers and ambiguities, is a material metaphor that profoundly organizes their daily work: inscribing code, editing, modifying, running it, revising, testing, putting it in a version control system, and so on. But that material metaphor is not supposed to travel outside the programmers' den. After all, the imperative for user-friendly software is precisely to make the large chain of translations invisible for ordinary users.[90]

As mentioned before, the inscription metaphor goes beyond stable storage and preservation. Therefore, it seems particularly apt to capture digital media since here processing, transmission, and storage are even more intertwined than in other media systems. Of course, digital praxis also has its separate metaphors of processing, think of verbs such as to install, subscribe, register, agree, and even like and friend. We can also easily identify distinct metaphors of transmission (being online, send, receive, download, upload) and metaphors of storage (save, copy, delete, move). However, in most digital practices the distinctions between processing, transmission, and storage are blurred. Processing is usually also storing and transmitting; for

---

90. At least when it comes to proprietary, closed software. In contrast, open source software does reveal its source code and its material metaphors of inscription and layering, but also in this case ordinary users do not encounter the material metaphor by just using the software.

example, browsing on the web consists of receiving a copy of the asked-for web page and storing it in a local cache.

In the same vein transmission is always also storing (mail on a mail server, log files at routers and servers) and processing (reading addresses, performing checksums, aggregating data packets, spam filtering). Storage, once it has been done, may exist without processing and transmission, but do not count on that when you store your stuff in the cloud. It will probably get data mined, processed, and transmitted to databases of the cloud provider. As Kittler once remarked on computing: 'with the Universal Discrete Machine, the media system is closed. Media of storage and transmission both dissolve into the simulation of all information machines, simply because it stores, transmits, and calculates in each and every loop of its program' (quoted in Tholen 2002, 664).

We can conclude a few things from our inquiry into media and its metaphors. First, that we cannot define what 'a medium' actually is without mobilizing a metaphor or metonym. There is no medium outside of metaphor. As such, this is no problem. This is what metaphors are for: qualifying in other terms that which has no proper name or definition. However, media metaphors are powerful things. As discourse metaphors they are able to mobilize particular narratives, discourses, and practices, and as material metaphors they are able to organize technical innovations, business models, and professional practices.

Secondly, no matter which metaphor we take, they are always a selection, a partial frame that highlights particular aspects while downplaying others. Again, this is immanent for any metaphor deployment, and no problem as such. However, the prevailing media metaphors in popular and academic discourse – membrane, master, conduit, and container – are selective and skewed in one and the same direction. They tend to obliterate any view on material processes and properties. Those media metaphors that try to capture something of material and social praxis reside predominantly in academic discourse: ecology, space, channel, toolmaker, and inscription. While they open up a rich field of theory and research, they tend to travel less as discourse metaphors and material metaphors.

But the most remarkable conclusion is that in all metaphors that seek to capture that slippery thing we call a medium, the medium as such always seem to escape. The more media multiply in different forms, the more metaphors are mobilized, and the more media dissolve. Apparently, the ultimate medium is invisible. It seems to mediate itself out-of-sight by producing an even more slippery phenomenon: immediacy. The crucial question then is how immediacy evolves or gets produced, in particular in digital praxis. This question will be addressed in the next chapter.

CHAPTER 4
IMMEDIACY BY METAPHOR
HOW MEDIATION BECOMES INVISIBLE

> *The most profound technologies are those that disappear. They weave themselves into the fabric of everyday life until they are indistinguishable from it.*
> (Mark Weiser, 1991)

As we have seen in the previous chapter, whatever metaphor we mobilize, the concept of medium remains extremely multiple and liquid. In digital environments this is even more confusing, since the medium here seems to be both ubiquitously present and absent. While we can manipulate digital entities, we cannot immediately grasp them like other material objects. We need the mediation of a metaphorical interface and machinery running in the background in order to get ahold of these entities. Yet, these mediations are precisely what is depresented by the icontology of digital representational objects. They suggest immediacy, on the verge of the absence of any mediation. How does this come about? What exactly happens when medium, message, and object confluence, icontologize in a metaphorical sign-tool-object, and then seem to disappear all together in an experience of immediacy?

This chapter aims to flesh out how the experience of immediacy is construed and how specific material metaphors contribute to this experience. The first section addresses how media persistently conceals mechanisms of mediation, curiously enough by first becoming a recognized medium and then disappearing. The second section examines how metaphors such as windows and mirrors function as icontological discourse metaphors that not only inform interface design, but also academic media theory. The third section zooms in on the classic new media theory of remediation (Bolter and Grusin 2000), arguing this theory is also imbued by the icontological metaphors of transparent windows and reflecting mirrors. Based on this critique, in the last section some modifications of the theory are proposed that can account for the implicated metaphorical reifications. I will propose to analyze remediation processes as going beyond mirroring prior existing media, since most of all they produce media *a posteriori* – only to blot them out again by demediation.

1 — THE DESIRE FOR IMMEDIACY

Allow me once again to return to the story of my friend's mail problem. She expected her mail to be in her inbox, immediately, just by looking there. In a way, she was far ahead of her time: she enacted the ideal of automatic computing without manual intervention, the ideal of interfaceless processing that makes things happen just by looking, or even more desirable, just by thinking. This ideal has been endlessly predicted, announced, and criticized in various terms – ambient intelligence (Van den Berg 2009), Internet of Things (Van Kranenburg 2008), ubiquitous computing (Greenfield 2006), angelic communication (Peters 1999) – but the imagined interfaceless medium has not yet arrived. Meanwhile, our contemporary computing devices try their utmost to approach this ideal. The advent of touch screens, tablets, and cloud computing exemplify the ongoing trials to do away with buttons and keyboards, but also classic desktop computers with their icons and windows aim at experiences of maximum immediacy.

The idea, or better: the ideal, of immediacy is already evoked by the iconic shortcuts themselves, buttons that make us forget that they are buttons. However, they do not do so on their own account. Immediacy is for a large part produced and sustained by an overall one-click discourse that marks contemporary Internet praxis. This discourse not only proffers conceptual terms as 'immediate access', 'always on', 'one-click shopping', and 'plug & play' – it also provides users with the material-metaphorical buttons of immediacy, such as the indexical icons for 'tweet this', 'like this', or 'share this'.

These articulations do not refer so much to speed and the bridging of time and space, but rather suggest the total defeat of any difference in time and space. They allude to total immediacy, that is, the erasure of reference itself. Reference and referent as one and the same, here and now, immediately. No mediation, indexicality, or translation layers in between; no material, temporal, or spatial obstructions to conquer. These notions reflect the desire and belief in the possibility of ideal communication, that is, of frictionless, unmediated communication, of achievement without effort (De Vries 2012). [91]

At first glance the discourse of the ideal of immediacy seems to be connected to the advent of the 20th century's new digital media, but in fact that is a typical bias of the present. The bias of the present is in itself a recurring historical figure that needs to be demystified over and over again in media studies. For example, contemporary new media studies students tend to think of Multi-User Dungeons (MUDs) from the 1990s as role-playing environments with graphical avatars, as a kind of rough-pixelated World of Warcraft. It is almost unimaginable for them that these MUDs were completely *textual* representations, monochrome online narratives without any graphics.

Beyond the bias of the present, the quest for immediacy turns out to be a persistent theme in media history. It has been analyzed as the motor driving the allegedly progressive sequence of past and present new media, be it the telegraph, film, television, the Internet or mobile phones (Peters 1999; Bolter and Grusin 2000; Chun and Keenan 2005; Gitelman 2006; De Vries 2012). Every time in history when a new medium emerged or was announced, the accompanying claims and promises were similar: the new medium would make up for the mediation fallacies of a previous medium. Retrospectively, the older medium invariably turned out to lack a particular immediacy. The telegraph would improve the mail system by adding speed. Film would improve photography by adding movement. Television would improve cinema with live broadcasts. The Internet would improve mass media by enabling immediate user participation. And the mobile revolution would move the apparatus from your desk to your pocket, proffering availability anytime, anywhere, anyhow. Ever tantalizingly closer to immediacy, yet never reaching it (De Vries 2012).

Tellingly, the claims of alleged media progress always have the same bottom line: immediacy and ease instead of cumbersome mediation and effort. Even pessimistic analyses that assert cultural

---

91. As De Vries (2012) has shown in his discourse analysis of the idea of ideal communication this is in fact a paradoxical desire since the fulfillment of ideal communication would eliminate any need to communicate and to share one's thoughts.

decline caused by the proliferation of new media tap from this ideal. Such analyses criticize new media as demolishing the superior immediacy of real, face-to-face communication (Postman 1993; Borgmann 1999; Dreyfus 2008). In other words, immediacy is all around conceived as the best you can get, the default benchmark by which the merits and demerits of any mediation and communication apparatus can be measured. [92]

Nonetheless, this default of immediacy usually remains unnoticed in daily experience, as it only reveals itself through a contrast. It may emerge as a short pleasant surprise, but most often it pops up in a failure which reveals retrospectively the expectation of immediacy. The fact that my friend expected her mail to be there immediately could only happen because her mail just was *not* there. The thousands of moments a day we could experience as immediacy never occur as such in our minds. It only shows its presence retrospectively when it is gone, in a lapse in a taken-for-granted situation that suddenly appears to be mediated after all. For example, when sound and vision are no longer synchronized in a movie, when subtitles suddenly disappear, or when we notice the delay in a live television interview from the studio. Paradoxically then, immediacy is the imaginary degree zero of any mediation, a lived illusion of absent mediation, deprived of all traditional markers that announce an encounter with media. When it shows itself, the spell is broken. In retrospect, immediacy turns out to be a matter of unnoticed and concealed mediation, revealing itself now in the split into a faltering medium and a stammering message.

Closing the gap

All technologies conceived as media – be it writing, print, telegraph, television, or the Internet – have, in their particular ways, to deal with this lurking onto-epistemological break-up of medium and message. [93] There is always the risk the gap will be revealed, the gap between, on the one hand, the material conditions and enactments of media apparatuses, and on the other hand, the messages – the expressions, representations, simulations, and productions generated by these apparatuses. Our current personal computers grapple with this risk in specific ways. At first sight,

---

92. The perpetual – and never fulfilled – desire for immediacy cannot only be traced in the history of media and communication technology, but has also been indicated as a significant force in the human life form. For example by Helmut Plessner (1928) who formulated three anthropological laws, natural artificiality, mediated immediacy, and the utopian eccentric quest for unmediated immediacy, respectively. From another philosophical perspective, Lacan's rereading of Freud's psychoanalysis comes to a similar conclusion: the subject is split by the entrance into the symbolic order, recursively longing back to an imaginary wholeness, as immediate presence to itself (Nusselder 2009). Also, Derrida's critique of the Western 'metaphysics of presence' – the assumption that foundational knowledge can and should provide unmediated access to reality – can be considered a critique of the ideology of immediacy (Chang 1996).
93. It may be argued that the gap between medium and message is not so much 'onto-epistemological', but plainly 'metaphysical', in the pejorative sense. Indeed, whereas the medium (whatever we call a medium) and the message are ontologically deeply intertwined and interdependent, the metaphysics of the separation between medium and message assumes a preceding *a priori* presence of a message – in the form of meaning, thought, or idea – as a media-independent instance. In short, the infamous conduit metaphor addressed in the previous chapter. However, I would argue that, just as medium and message are inseparable, ontology and metaphysics are. The metaphysics of presence produces powerful ontological (ontologized, reified) objects, and they should be recognized and analyzed as such. Ignoring or disqualifying them as metaphysical (ungrounded, ideational, ideological, just metaphorical) will not undo their onto-epistemological effects – on the contrary.

they just seem to increase the potential gaps by adding ever more stuff between the medium and the message. Ever more extra hardware additions, such as printers, cameras, sticks, hard disks, netbooks, phones, tablets, and players, and ever more software additions: applications, helper applications, drivers, extra toolbars, system tools, dashboards, plug-ins, apps. Yet at the same time these ever extending add-ons [94] diminish the gap by depresenting the material processes involved, rendering them invisible by means of pre-configured system settings, built-in services, pre-installed applications, and automatic updates. The aim is to depresent the increased complexity of hardware and software processes.

The ultimate disappearance of mediation and software labor can be achieved by completely outsourcing system and data management to the so-called cloud. We have encountered the cloud as metaphor of storage in the previous chapter, but as cloudy business models proliferated, the cloud became more than a space for storage. One can also outsource local system management: removing applications and data storage from personally managed hardware devices and move them to centrally managed network servers that deliver software-as-a-service and platforms-as-a-service. But also computers that do not depend on the invisible cloud are configured to automate various processes: get online as soon as the computer starts, get new mail and RSS feeds as soon as the program runs, and check for virus scanner updates daily. And when all this works properly, it may invoke a sense of seamless mediation, on the verge of immediacy.

However, to approach this state a lot of invisible labor has to be deployed.[95] Labor by hardware: transmitting electric current and signals over integrated circuits, wires, and channels, electromechanical processing in CPU's, cooling systems, spinning hard disks, lighting screens. Labor by software: reading instructions, assigning numbers to entities, delineating objects of clustered numbers,

---

94. Analyzed meticulously as 'media extensions' and 'extended platforms' by Tom van de Wetering (2011) in his master thesis on the content management system ExpressionEngine.
95. I adhere to a three-fold definition of labor, derived from Marxism, feminism and physics. Labor in the classic Marxist sense pertains to the living labor by humans and the dead labor conducted by machines and capital. Marxist labor then is that activity that transforms and assembles raw materials into products with use value and/or exchange value, and as such it structurally and historically determines social relations, class divisions, contradictions, and struggles that make up society. Though this idea of labor is usually confined to an analysis of classes and class society in the Marxist framework, I extend this notion of labor as force of production towards the small scale labor that actor-network theorists have dubbed 'overcoming resistance' (Law 1992). That is, the mobilizing labor of persuasion, negotiation, and adjustment performed by heterogeneous human and non-human actors that is needed to keep up the intricate actor-networks that we conceive as blackboxed matters of fact.
Yet there is more to labor than just labor as a force of production and construction. From a feminist perspective, I value labor also as reproductive force. Of course, the figure of the domestic housewife is the classic trope here, but I prefer another figure to illustrate the type of sorting and cleaning labor I have in mind. That type of labor is taken from physics, embodied by the figure of Maxwell's demon. The figure is evoked by James Maxwell in a thought experiment on how to counter the second law of thermodynamics. Maxwell's demon is a hard working creature that rearranges molecules by dividing them into separate basins, altering the state of an entropic system into a new order of potential energy, thus countering local entropy and decay (Hayles 1990). Though Maxwell himself contended that this creature is 'able to do what is impossible for us' (Maxwell 1897), I take this figure as standing for labor in general, that is, any active intervention aimed at rearranging a state of being. This definition of labor accounts not only for the general possibility of counter forces against entropy and decay, but also for the so often misrecognized reproduction labor of housekeeping, cleaning, sorting, and care.

executing algorithms, assigning memory locations, storing inscriptions, rearranging, translating, and, finally, presenting selected output on the interface in human-readable formats and metaphors. Moreover, not to be overlooked, labor by humans – cognitive labor mixed with performative labor, comprised of various acts: installing and configuring, clicking and tapping the right buttons, invoking specific instructions, interpreting signs and symbols, selecting, reading, and writing.

My friend was well aware of the hardware-installation labor that came with a broadband connection at that time in the 1990s. She wisely delegated this to a professional. But she was not prepared for the software-configuration labor. Again, this is not an example of computer illiteracy, but rather demonstrates computer literacy induced by frequent experience. When experienced enough, we tend to forget the joint endeavor of software and our own hands that make computers work. In fact, properly running software urges us to forget this – that is the very reason we have delegated most of the processing labor to imperceptible software processing. The deal is that software should represent on the interface somehow *that* it works, while depresenting *how* it works.[96] Software only reveals something of how it works when it fails. Then we need to open the black box, and consider all the transferences and translations, all the hidden steps and hidden labor in between. After we have corrected the failure, we can forget these indexical transferences, and return to the state of icontological slumber evoked by a properly running computer.

Transparent immediacy

Therefore, we easily get used to handling software as a black box, where only the immediate interfacial output matters. This is the paradigm of so called user-friendliness, aimed at what designers and new media scholars usually call 'transparent immediacy' (Bolter and Grusin 2000). Though this concept is widely accepted as indicating an experience of immediacy elicited by a transparent medium, I want to point out that at its heart it entails a rarely noticed tension.

At stake is the question: what is meant by *transparent?* The notion of transparent (Latin *trans* = through, and *parere* = come in sight, appear) is actually very ambiguous regarding what is made visible and what is made invisible. It may refer to looking through something that is in itself practically *invisible* in order to look at *something else,* which as a result becomes *visible.* Glasses, windows, microscopes, and telescopes fit this definition. But transparent may also mean being able to look through or inside something that thereby becomes *visible itself.* Transparent procedures, transparent policies, and transparent pretenses fall under this second definition. The question then is: which of the two definitions is at stake when we speak of transparent immediacy in media theory?

At first sight, the first definition seems to apply. Transparent immediacy means looking through an invisible thing (a medium) in order to perceive something else. This implies that the notion of transparent immediacy presupposes a specific organizing conceptual metaphor: A MEDIUM IS A TRANSPARENT SCREEN. This metaphor takes the medium to be a visual plane that can be looked through and ignored, like a window or telescope. You can look through the window or telescope to see something of the outside world, and forget the window itself. A transparent medium is an invisible screen that withdraws into imperceptibility and forgetfulness. All attention is drained towards what

---

96. That is, a so called user-friendly interface should provide such reassurance. Yet we are all familiar with those situations of maddening uncertainty when you do not know if your computer is still executing a task or if it is just stuck. Any signal indicating the machine is still at work – a blinking message, an animated icon or a moving time bar, a flickering list of files being copied – would be reassuring on those occasions.

is made available and visible – the image, the representation, maybe a glimpse of reality itself.
The problems with this metaphor have been addressed earlier in Chapter 1. The screen metaphor tends to icontologize digital praxis – that is, it tends to colonize and gobble up all other aspects of mediation into an icontological screen. The same holds for the general concept of transparent immediacy. Paradoxically, then, the concept of transparent immediacy obscures more than it reveals. The screen metaphor denies its own frame and materiality since it focuses on the transparent plane and from there immediately to that what is revealed or represented.

But, as indicated above, transparency is an ambiguous term that locates visibility either outside or inside its own mechanism. The alternative interpretation of transparency would assume a different conceptual metaphor: A MEDIUM IS A BLACK BOX. In that case the visible and the invisible change position. From this perspective, transparency would mean the opposite. It would imply that we are able to *look inside* the medium, thus rendering the inside of the black box visible and raising awareness of the mediating mechanism instead of making it invisible. We may conclude that the meaning of transparency depends on what is considered the organizing metaphor of mediation: a transparent screen or an opaque black box.

Unfortunately, we seem to have little choice in metaphors in our daily encounters with digital media. The problem with our contemporary computing devices is that their design consists of a blend of the two metaphors: they are black boxes posing as transparent screens. They conceal their machinery behind icontologized interfaces that are opaque and thick from the perspective of the apparatus but transparent from the perspective of the screen. Transparent immediacy then appears as an effortless achievement, as if simply looking through a window or at a mirror, while there is a lot of invisible hard work going on by humans, tools, and apparatuses.

To answer the question how and where immediacy is produced, those black boxes wrapped in transparent screens have to be unpacked. Notably, this cannot be achieved by just peeling off and throwing away the wrapping. On the contrary, as will be argued in the next section. In order to unravel its multiple powerful mechanisms, the transparent screen should be taken seriously as a material metaphor in all its different forms: windows, mirrors, and tools.

2 — WINDOWS, MIRRORS, AND TOOLS

While the idea of windows as an organizing metaphor seems to be bound to the age of PCs with Microsoft's graphical user interface, the history of this powerful metaphor is much longer. As is common knowledge among art historians and media scholars, it goes back to Leo Battista Alberti's famous Renaissance window, described in 1435. His treatise on how to paint strictly proportional and perspectival, as if seen through an open window, is widely seen as the historical invention of linear perspective. It marked a new tradition of pictorial representation, but it also introduced a new perspective on knowledge and tools. After the Dark Ages of superstition and religious icontology, the Renaissance perspective invigorated the world with scientific dissection. Alberti's window, as an instructive geometrical device, was firmly inscribed in the burgeoning field of science and technology, and became a metaphor for Enlightenment in general: a new window on the world and new space to be explored.

Virtual windows

Yet, Alberti's window was more than just metaphorical. It literally extended space, by transposing 3-D depth on a 2-D plane, arranged along linear lines of sight. Or may be better, it doubled space, now divided into actual space where the viewer and painter resided and a pictorial space. The latter is not just an imaginary space, but as Anne Friedberg has aptly called it, a virtual space (Friedberg 2006). In her meticulous study *The Virtual Window*, Friedberg genealogically tracks down the transformations in visual representations 'From Alberti to Microsoft', as the subtitle tells. It is important to note that her notion of the virtual is not a synonym for digital or computer-generated, nor does she conceive it as imaginary or as potentiality. For Friedberg, the virtual denotes a type of representation (usually optical) that appears functionally or effectively but not formally of the same materiality as what it represents. The virtual has 'a materiality and a reality but of a different kind, a second-order materiality, liminally immaterial' (ibid., 11).[97] As she explains, 'the virtual in my construction "virtual window" suggests both a metaphoric window and an actual window with a virtual view' (ibid., 12).

Friedberg's knot of the metaphorical, the actual-material, and the virtual covers what I have called a material metaphor. She in fact analyzes Alberti's window as a material metaphor by retrieving its features as an architectural actual object and a practical instructive tool, that is, a geometric technique to enhance the skill of the painter. Friedberg re-materializes Alberti's window in particular by claiming it was not a metaphor of transparency, but a metaphor of framing:

> Alberti used the window predominantly as a metaphor for the frame – the relation of a fixed viewer to a framed view – and not as 'transparent' 'window on the world,' as has been suggested widely by art historians and media theorists. Its frame was to be used to position the viewer in relation to its perspectival construction of space. (ibid., 12)

This is not a minor shift in attention. The metaphor of WINDOW IS A FRAME is almost the inverse of WINDOW IS A GLASS. The frame foregrounds a material cut, a specific practical, instrumental selection, an intervention in a material structure, while the glass foregrounds unhindered sight, transparency, outlook. Friedberg shows with a close reading of Alberti's text how his window first and foremost functioned as a practical device used to help the painter: a material opening in the wall, seen from a single immobile viewpoint, transposed to the rectangle of the painting by first deciding how large a human figure would be on the painting and then inferring lines of sight that are proportional to the human body and that converge into a centric point (ibid., 27). In other words, ALBERTI'S WINDOW IS A DEVICE. It operates as an organizing material metaphor by fixating and immobilizing the viewer and the painter while at the same time evoking the human figure as a standard of measure and as determinant of the centric point (ibid., 27).

The assumed glass transparency of the window was not an issue at all (and besides, though glass making was developed in Italy during the Renaissance, in Alberti's days windows rarely had glass in the frame). Admittedly, Alberti did use the phrase 'transparent and like glass', but as

---

97. Notwithstanding stubborn popular discourse on the virtual as plain illusion, the conception of the virtual as a special configuration of the real has been one of the tenets of new media studies even before its academic establishment (cf. Heim 1994, Levy 1998). The term had already been mobilized in the same vein by philosophers before that (Bergson 1896, Deleuze 1977, Guattari 1995). Remarkably, Peirce already defined the virtual in 1902 in that manner: 'A virtual X [...] is something [...] which has the efficiency (virtus) of an X. This is the proper meaning of the word, but it has been seriously confounded with "potential" which is almost its contrary. For the potential X is of the nature of X, but which is without actual efficiency' (Peirce 1902, 763).

Friedberg convincingly shows, this referred to the transparency of the planar surface of the painting, not to the containment of its rectangular frame (ibid., 29). She insists that ALBERTI'S WINDOW IS A FRAME – to be filled by the painter's geometric and artistic labor – not a transparent view that reveals the outside world.

These observations are not just quibbles about the supposedly original meaning of Alberti's window. Friedberg's genealogical account of the practices and discourses of virtual windows (that is, material-metaphorical windows, mirrors, frames, and screens, ranging from painting and architecture to photography, film, and computers, branching out into philosophical discourse) is primarily an account of metaphorical displacements. Friedberg is well aware of the snake pit of metaphor, and notes, 'The metaphors of windows, mirrors, frames, screens fall into a slippery discursive tumble of synecdoche and displacement' (ibid., 18).

Nonetheless, she found a persistent pattern in the metaphorical displacements, starting with Alberti's window and recurring throughout her study. 'The window has become a metaphor for the screen' (ibid., 12). In other words, WINDOW AS A FRAME has given way to WINDOW AS A SCREEN. The organizing materiality of windows thus gets lost in the ever-returning tendency of shifting into metaphors of transparency. Windows get reduced to invisible screens, over and over again, culminating in the ultimate icontology of contemporary computing windows.

Multiple digital windows

Alberti's window inscribed itself firmly in the vocabulary and praxis of computer interfaces in terms of windows. It started with Douglas Engelbart's first demonstration of a mouse moving over multiple tiled screen planes in 1968 (Myers 1998), dubbed 'viewports' and 'windows' a year later by Alan Kay (Kay 1969), and culminated in Microsoft's 1983 announcement of their cheap answer to Apple's expensive Lisa: the trademarked Windows 'file-operating component' that would become the hegemonic operating system and interface of PCs worldwide. [98]

Friedberg (2006) shows how the upswing of digital computing yielded to the principle of multiple windows (overlapping, tiled, or nested). Multiple windows can be found on the PC screen, but also in film and television (split screens, frames within frames). And indeed, the notion of multiple windows provides a useful metaphor to theorize current phenomena such as the second screen on television and the inextricable knot of nested Web 2.0 services: Twitter and Facebook integrated on Foursquare; Twitter, Foursquare and YouTube embedded in Facebook; Facebook and Twitter nesting themselves into any other web site by the endless multiplication of share and like buttons, and so on. The frames – and hence the machinery and policies behind them – of these nested windows have become invisible, condensed into buttons or seamlessly integrated in the web page (which in itself is by definition a multiple window consisting of headers, footers, text fields, banners, images, movies, and database elements).

Remarkably, Friedberg addresses Microsoft's Windows and its development over the years only in terms of its optical interface and screens, and not as the material architectural framing device it still is, that is, not as an *operating* system. By doing so, she in fact contributes to the ubiquitous tendency to dematerialize the material metaphor of windows.

---

98. Naming the file-operating component 'Windows' (at that time not yet an operating system, just an add-on to MS-DOS) was the idea of Rowland Hanson, a marketing employee at Microsoft, who convinced Bill Gates that this name was far better than Gates' preferred name of 'Interface Manager' (Bellis n.d.).

Revitalized as a material metaphor, the trope of WINDOWS AS OPERATING SYSTEM instead of WINDOWS AS SCREENIC REPRESENTATION, tells us another story than that of an immobile user interacting with multiple screen images (Friedberg 2006) or that of a postmodern user experimenting with multiple identities on multiple screens (Turkle 1995). Windows as a material metaphor reminds us that windows are first and foremost immovable frames that delimit a specific aperture in a wall, which is part of a whole architecture of walls, rooms, doors, and corridors, implicating specific possible and impossible routes of navigation and traversal. An operating system that poses as transparent windows obscures its implied material architecture and denies its users access to backdoors, hidden corridors, underground cellars, and useful tools. Here we recognize the general criticism on Bill Gates' Windows operating system. Some open-source advocates go even further, and suggest that the Windows operating system is not just obscuring its disciplining architecture, but actually building architecture where it is not needed at all. As the famous meme from the Linux community goes: 'In a world without walls and fences who needs Windows and Gates?'

Nevertheless, in new media studies the window metaphor is also predominantly conceived and analyzed as a transparent screen, rarely as a frame or device, as an architectural material metaphor. Even Bolter and Gromala's study *Windows and Mirrors* (2003) – with the promising phrase 'The Myth of Transparency' in its subtitle – does not really deconstruct the myth of transparency as we will see in the next section.

Windows and mirrors

Bolter and Gromala (2003) analyzed digital art and interface design, and arranged their findings in terms of the interplay between metaphorical windows and mirrors. Their main argument is that '[e]very digital artifact oscillates between being transparent and reflective' (ibid., 6). Being transparent is metaphorized in the window, being reflective is metaphorized in the mirror. Again, in line with Friedberg's (2006) observations, the authors' conception of A WINDOW IS A TRANSPARENT SCREEN, is not a material frame. Their notion of the mirror may be more interesting then, precisely because of its suggested dissimilarity to the window.

'Being reflective' is here seen as the main feature of the mirror.[99] The trope of the reflective mirror is also one of the discourse metaphors of mainstream media theory (McQuail 1983, 65). The metaphor MEDIA ARE MIRRORS implies that media (should) reflect reality, truth, and objectivity, with the least distortion as possible. Interestingly, contrary to McQuail's disembodied, quasi-objective mirror, Bolter and Gromala emphasize that the reflective mirror in digital interfaces is not only about objectivity but at least as much about subjectivity and embodiment:

> Digital interfaces are like mirrors in the sense that they reflect the user in context, including her physical surroundings, her immediate working or home environment, and the larger environment defined by her language and culture. (Bolter and Gromala 2003, 27)

---

99. The history of the metaphor of the mirror, especially in film studies, but also in psychoanalytical and feminist discourse, is much richer than can be addressed here. For an elaborate account of feminist cinema and the mirror game between cinema and theory, see Anneke Smelik's study *And the Mirror Cracked: Feminist Cinema and Film Theory* (2001).

Indeed, a mirror is not a window; in the mirror you primarily see yourself, your surroundings and your interventions, not so much the outside world. For Bolter and Gromala, the mirror is explicitly associated with user interaction. In that regard, their trope of the mirror comes close to a tool, a mediating device, a material apparatus, as well as a material metaphor, that organizes not just optical images, but most of all subjects and objects in a particular setting.

This is a promising perspective. If we take the mirror metaphor as a material metaphor, we can identify a lot of specs that are completely contrary to the classic window icontology of immediacy and transparency:

— The mirror is not transparent, its material is necessarily impermeable, consisting of polished metal or of a glass substrate with a layered coating of metals and paint on the backside; it can be a flat plane, but it can also be curved, thereby enabling reflection, but also diffraction and distortion;
— the mirror is not a fixed aperture in a wall, but a movable thing, be it hanging on a wall, attached to a car or as a hand-held device;
— the mirror does not show a framed view on the world *out there;* it shows a virtual, optical image of whatever is *in front of it*;
— the mirror reflects and produces the subject in front of it: it centers the subject by offering it an image of itself, and it decenters the subject by splitting it into a living body and a left-right inversed image of itself — as such it does engage and mobilize the subject instead of immobilizing it.

When we consider these principles, the mirror, conceived as a material metaphor, seems to provide an interesting alternative for the trope of transparent windows. Whereas the classic window hides its materiality and mechanism, thereby producing the myth of transparency and immediacy, the mirror seems to afford looking inside the material and social mechanisms that are involved.

However, Bolter and Gromala's perspective on the mirror remains primarily optical and experiential, at the surface level of the visual interface. The authors conceive digital practice as oscillating between 'looking through' (the transparent window) and 'looking at' (the reflective mirror) – not a word about 'looking inside' or 'looking behind'. Moreover, they seem to imply that the act of looking through the window is the natural default, as they argue:

> There are times, however, when the user should be looking at the interface, not through it, in order to make it function: to activate icons or to choose menu items, for example. At such moments, the interface is no longer a window, but a mirror, reflecting the user and her relationship to the computer. The interface is saying in effect, 'I am a computer application, and you are the user of that application.' No interface can be or should be perfectly transparent, because the interface will break at some time, and the user will have to diagnose the problem. (ibid., 26)

So that is what the authors mean by 'the myth of transparency'. It is not that transparency is a myth, but the fact that designers apparently tend to believe that good interface design should be completely transparent and based on windows metaphors. According to the authors, 'every interface is a mirror as well as a window' (ibid., 26) and designers should focus more on the mirror aspects of the interface, and less on the idea of the transparent window:

> This is a contemporary alternative to transparency: it is the mirror rather than the window – the strategy of reflection, multiplicity, self-awareness in action. [...] Designers should respond

to and appreciate the desire for multiplicity, for making the medium itself an experience to be savored. (ibid., 66)

While this perspective on interface design could lead to conceiving windows and mirrors as helping devices, as instructional material metaphors for interface designers, this is not the path the authors take.

Mirrors or tools

Contrary to their assertion that the mirror in fact tells the user 'I am a computer application' (ibid., 26), Bolter and Gromala explicitly aim to stay away from any notion of tool or device. Their metaphors of windows and mirrors are based on a critique of the notion of tools and appliances: 'For our current culture [...] the term appliance doesn't describe computers very well. Computers don't feel like toasters; they feel much more like books, photograph albums, or television sets. For us today [...] the computer feels like a medium' (ibid., 5). And media 'are not just channels for information, they also provide experiences' (ibid., 12).
The authors illustrate this principle of a medium for experience with several computer art installations. [100] For example *Text Rain,* in which letters are falling down the screen, which can be captured, steered, and manipulated by the projected-reflected body of the viewer/user/participant. *Text Rain* is thus a poem, a video program, and a performance conducted by the user all at once. The work *Wooden Mirror* is based on the same principle. The small wooden blocks react – tic-tic-tic-tic – to the movements of the user, representing a digital-analog virtual image of your body.
In both works of art, the spectator is transformed into a more involved user. And indeed, digital objects such as these installations, but also more mundane artifacts as email programs, Facebook timelines, or phone apps call 'its participants into an active relationship, asking them to perform rather than merely to view' (ibid., 15). The viewing aspect is still present, in the metaphorical forms of mirrors (here quite literally: a video of textual rain mirroring the moving body, or a digitally driven wooden mirror) and windows (here as the quite transparent user interface: just move your body, no instruction for operation needed), but the performative action is permanently interacting with the screen representation.
So far so good, but these observations lead the authors to conclude, 'Today, we do not operate computers; rather, we interact with them' (ibid., 22). Yet it is quite disputable whether this is an either-or issue. Yes, we do interact with our computers, but of course we also operate them. We configure, install, patch, hack, and update our computers. We do not merely experience our computer as a medium, we do things with it as well. As argued before in this study, digital products can take practically any form, but they are always also tools, metaphorical and material tools, sign-tool-objects.
While the tropes of windows and mirrors could be helpful for analyzing the mechanisms by which these sign-tool-objects work, they become counterproductive when they are stripped from their material tool-like affordances. Then both metaphors remain superficial interfacial screen metaphors that produce the myth of immediacy and transparency by hiding all processes of mediation, translation, and organization. Conversely, when these metaphors are taken seriously as ma-

---

100. As shown at the computer graphics exhibition SIGGRAPH 2000 in New Orleans.

terial metaphors, they show something of the mechanisms involved. The window, then, turns out to be a framing device that positions the user as an immobilized subject who can forget about architecture, who just has to peek through the provided aperture in the wall in order to achieve the experience of immediacy.[101] The mirror in its turn is more than a reflective plane, it is a tool in the hands of the user, calling for action, appropriation, and intervention. It may even invite us to check out the tool and its associated machinery, when the mirror-tool as ready-to-hand (evoking looking through and looking at) turns into a tool present-at-hand (evoking looking at and looking inside). For example, our smart phones are better described as hand-held mirrors than as a tiny version of multiple windows. When you look at them, you see yourself, your life, your diary, your contacts, your mail, and your social network. And not to forget, the dozens if not hundreds of various apps that provide you with daily tools, mirroring in their turn the tiniest need that may be satisfied by a bit of information.

Perhaps we can even say that in digital praxis there are no transparent windows, at most there are mirrors disguised as windows – just window dressing. Windows are a metaphor of oblivion and forgetting – forgetting frames, selections, machinery, labor – but we should not forget that to achieve forgetting a lot of labor is involved, that is, design labor, programming labor, patching labor, and user labor.

Bolter and Gromala seem to touch on these issues in the section called 'Making the interface disappear' (ibid., 43-44). It starts promising with the evocation of the metaphor of *wizard-of-ozzing*, a designers' activity that proffers testers the illusion that the whole system is already working while in fact it is not – only the part that has to be tested is up and running. The unfinished features are simulated by programmers 'behind the screen', and this is called wizard-of-ozzing.[102] The authors take this as an apt metaphor for a good user interface, as it lets the user forget what is going on behind the screen. But they miss the main point of the metaphor: it also reminds us that a so-called disappearing interface is not a matter of sliding into a natural state of looking through a transparent window; it always implies the work of an operating wizard, be it a human being or software technology, and usually both. However, the authors do not further elaborate on the labor that made the interface disappear. Instead, they maintain their focus on the magical effect: illusions on the screen, enabled by the metaphors of windows and mirrors, as if by magic and not by material labor.

In order to further unravel the suggestion of immediacy in terms of its material and discourse metaphors, I will examine in the next section the so called remediation thesis as offered by Bolter and Grusin in *Remediation: Understanding New Media* (Bolter and Grusin 2000). While the work by Bolter and Gromala (2003) addressed above explicitly evoked the metaphors of windows and mirrors in interface design, Bolter and Grusin's earlier work *Remediation* already laid out the basic principles of immediacy and mediation, though less explicitly in terms of meta-

---

101. In Windows 8, where the classic windows are transformed into multiple 'tiles', the icontology of transparency and immediacy is even greater since the images displayed by the tiles change, thereby suggesting liveness (for example, after news updates or newly uploaded photographs). See also 'Sense and simplicity' (Van Bart 2013), for a Peircian semiotic analysis of the tiles in Windows 8.
102. The verb is derived from a scene in the movie *The Wizard of Oz*, when Dorothy and her companions accidentally get a glimpse of the phony Wizard at the control panel who is calling up smoke and noise to enhance his image (Bolter and Gromala 2003, 43). It is no coincidence that The Wizards of OS, Wizards of Operating Systems, an open-source advocating community, takes on the same metaphor.

phors. It is important to flesh out the implicit metaphors of this work, since *Remediation* has become a classic landmark in new media studies because of its encompassing and alluring claims on new media in general.

3 — REMEDIATING IMMEDIACY

The subtitle of *Remediation: Understanding New Media* (Bolter and Grusin 2000) not coincidentally alludes to Marshall McLuhan's *Understanding Media* (1964). Bolter and Grusin take up the legacy of McLuhan's famous dictum 'the medium is the message', explicated by the author himself as, 'the "content" of any medium is always another medium. The content of writing is speech, just as the written word is the content of print, and print is the content of the telegraph' (McLuhan 1964, 8). This is where Bolter and Grusin hook up with their concept of remediation, defined as the 'formal logic by which new media refashion prior media forms' (Bolter and Grusin 2000, 273). By 'new media' they refer to all historically new media, not only digital or computational ones. The claim is that all new media refashion, re-purpose, and improve prior media forms, while prior media refashion themselves to answer the challenges of new media (ibid., 15).

Bolter and Grusin argue that processes of remediation always consist of two seemingly contradictory strategies: the strategy of transparent immediacy (making the medium invisible and transparent, suggesting an unmediated experience) and the strategy of hypermediacy (emphasizing the medium, celebrating or even exaggerating its presence). Remediation thus creates an experience of immediacy by borrowing from media so familiar that we just do not see the medium anymore. For example, in the practice of browsing websites or swiping through pictures on a touch screen, we do not see the borrowed medium of paper nor the computer and its implicated network.

Yet the same movement of borrowing from other media can be very explicit and exuberant, thus enacting hypermediacy. For instance, graphical virtual worlds such as World of Warcraft or Second Life borrow modalities and genres from film, theatrical role playing, and video games to evoke a sense of liveness, immersion, and immediacy. The hypermediacy of the textual display of the character's names — never occurring in film or theater — does not spoil the sense of immediacy. On the contrary, this hypermediacy enables you to recognize the other characters, once more enhancing the experience of immediacy. A less spectacular example is ordinary IRC (Internet Relay Chat). This mode of mediation borrows from typographic print, telex, and telegram, but we do not see these prior media shimmering through — we experience the immediate presence of the other. Even when we encounter lags and delays in the chat responses, the experience of immediacy can be maintained. For example by adding a hypermediated meta-message that informs you that 'Mandy is typing…'.

Bolter and Grusin's media theory thus contends that immediacy depends on hypermediacy, and vice versa. Their thesis pertains to all media; all 'old' and once 'new' media refashion themselves by this double logic of remediation. Generic as this may seem, it should be noted that immediacy and hypermediacy are explicitly defined as styles 'of visual representation' (ibid., 272). Notably, this firmly frames the hypothesis of remediation within the screen metaphor. Remediation predominantly takes place on a visual screen that is oscillating between being a window of transparent immediacy and a mirror of reflective hypermediacy. The underlying screen metaphor — or better, metonym, as it takes a particular part of a particular medium, the screen, as standing for any medium — is a strong discourse organizer, but we should keep in mind that all metaphors enable as well as disable particular ways of articulation and thinking. What does the dominant screen metonymy imply for a general media analysis in terms of remediation?

In the next two subsections, I will address two analytical problems in Bolter and Grusin's remediation hypothesis that I consider to be caused by the screen metaphor. The first problem is their emphasis on *states* instead of *processes*. In order to counter this problem, I will propose some modifications in the conceptual vocabulary. The second problem is the implied distinction between pseudo-remediation (which purportedly only remediates the message) and radical remediation (which allegedly reshuffles the whole medium). This problem is harder to tackle, since it inevitably leads us to the question of how to delimit 'a whole medium'.

No remediation without demediation

Whereas the notion of remediation suggests ongoing *processes*, the definition of the two constituting strategies in terms of hypermediacy and immediacy is remarkably static. After all, the words hypermediacy and immediacy refer to *states* – states of mind, states of affairs, states of media-specific configurations – rather than movement, dynamics, and processes. There is no talk of processes of 'hypermediation' or 'immediation'; it is all about hypermediacy and immediacy. In metaphor studies it has been shown how theoretical concepts and categories are often in fact conceptual metaphors (Gluckberg 2008; Johnson 2008). Theoretical concepts frame ways of talking, thinking, and theorizing, by revealing and concealing specific aspects, by invoking certain paths of thought and blocking others. In this case the static categories of immediacy and hypermediacy conceal the very dynamic of remediation processes. The terms obscure the aggregated labor by designers, users, and machinery – the labor that is needed to produce immediacy and hypermediacy as a state of affairs. This implies that immediacy and hypermediacy are the ontoepistemological results of the processes to be explained; they cannot be the explanation themselves as Bolter and Grusin seem to suggest. They are the problem to be solved.

That the authors tend toward this icontological reification is all the more odd, considering the fact that their case studies frequently accentuate how skills and labor are effaced. For instance, when addressing linear perspective in Renaissance painting in terms of remediating a window view, they note:

> The irony is that it was hard work to make the surface disappear in this fashion, and in fact the artist's success at effacing this process, and thereby himself, became for trained viewers a mark of his skill and therefore his presence. (Bolter and Grusin 2000, 25)

This observation is perfectly in line with Friedberg's assertion that Alberti's window is an instructional device, a metaphor of labor and skill. Bolter and Grusin's remark seems to indicate that the combination of hard work, *depresenting* this work (deliberately non-representing and erasing the involved labor), and *representing* the object and the creator in a specific configuration is what is at stake in processes of remediation. The irony then is that the authors, by insisting on ontologized notions of hypermediacy and immediacy, contribute to the onto-epistemological disappearance of the hard work involved.

Arguably, the consistent grammar in terms of hypermediacy and immediacy is not neutral, and not merely a stylistic flaw. It reveals that remediation theory is framed by icontologizing movements. It not only reduces and reifies *processes* into *states* (or things, or places, in any case, stable entities), but on top of that, it subsequently considers these states as constituting elements.[103] This is a reversal and even a reinforcement of the problem that should be accounted for, that is, how icontological immediacy is produced.

Remediation and demediation by metaphor
In order to develop such an account, I propose a reformulation, or better an extension of the concept of remediation. Remediation, defined as the strategy of re-using elements from other media forms, should first and foremost be analyzed as a matter of metaphors. Remediation is underpinned by metaphorical transferences that produce hypermediacy by importing characteristics, allusions, techniques, and scripts from other media domains. Importantly, there is no metaphorical hypermediacy without what I have called icontology, that is, reified iconicity taken as an ontological category. This hypermediated icontology eventually produces a specific kind of immediacy: *immediacy-by-familiarity,* based on exploiting the taken-for-grantedness and familiarity of the re-used media forms. These forms are so familiar and well known that we do not perceive them anymore. For example, postal mail gets blended and erased into 'email'; typing and talking into 'chatting', 'instant messaging', and 'twittering', and so on. The strategy of remediation is thus profoundly informed by interfaces that metaphorize and icontologize the borrowed elements.

Added to this strategy of immediacy by all-too-familiar metaphors, there is a second layer at work that could more aptly be called the strategy of *demediation.* Demediation can be defined as the act of depresenting mediation, that is, depresenting the machinery, the labor, the labor divisions, the task delegations, and most of all, depresenting the icontologizing acts of the first strategical layer. Demediation thereby renders invisible not only the involved material mechanisms, but also the metaphorical mechanisms. Take for example the hidden mechanisms of the storage of mail on a mail server, or the algorithm that ranks the results of a search engine, or the database that aggregates entities marked by the same tag – all instances of material-metaphorical labor made imperceptible for the user.

This second layer enhances and complements the first layer of immediacy-by-familiarity by fusing it with *immediacy-by-erasure,* that is, erasing those parts of the involved media forms and their material processing that would contradict or otherwise spoil the effect of immediacy. They are so well hidden and depresented that we do not perceive them anymore.

In other words, as an extension of Bolter and Grusin's formula 'remediation = immediacy + hypermediacy' (see Figure 5), I add the concept of *icontology* to hypermediacy to indicate that the act of metaphorical borrowing does not just exaggerate other media forms, but also tends to icontologize them (as happened with the mail and the telephone icon in the case of my friend). Furthermore, it is crucial to distinguish two kinds of immediacy, according to their different generating mechanisms. The first mechanism is based on experience and familiarity with other media forms (stored as cultural cognitive resources available for reiteration, transference, and metaphorizing). The second mechanism is based on imperceptibility, that is, the engineered labor of erasure that is conducted by the material apparatus of the medium.

---

103. Katherine Hayles has aptly called this analytical move the illegitimate 'Platonic forehand' that is an onto-epistemological gesture inferred from the legitimate Platonic backhand. Hayles writes: 'The Platonic backhand works by inferring from the world's noisy multiplicity a simplified abstraction. So far so good: this is what theorizing should do. The problem comes when the move circles around to constitute the abstraction as the originary form from which the world's multiplicity derives' (Hayles 1999, 12).

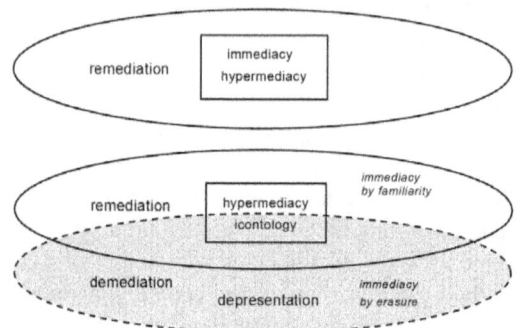

Figure 5. Bolter and Grusin's remediation as a blend of immediacy and hypermediacy vs. remediation as a double process of engineered immediacy.

In this reformulation the involved strategies are *remediation* (surfacing on the interface as blend of hypermediacy and icontology, producing *immediacy-by-familiarity*) and *demediation* (not surfacing but running in the background, producing *immediacy-by-erasure*). Hence, the strategies of remediation and demediation now appear as processes of labor, translation, and transformation – by humans, by metaphors, by machines, by socio-technical circuits – and not in terms of ontologized states.

These are double yet intertwined processes. There is no remediation without demediation, and both strategies are aimed at producing immediacy, the former by familiarity and the latter by erasure. Yet the most interesting process takes place where the two strategies overlap: there where metaphors produce a taken-for-granted icontology. Screen devotees may still be tempted to metaphorize familiarity as a reflecting mirror, and erasure as a transparent window (a gesture that would hark back to Bolter and Grusin's initial model), but that would ignore the black box character, the non-transparency of the re/demediation mechanism involved. Remediated immediacy is not produced by transparent or reflecting screens, but by a socio-technical machinery, a conjuncture of human practice, tacit knowledge, material metaphors, and media machinery.

If we wish to track down how immediacy – as state, as experience, as engineered effect, and as ideology – is produced we need to account for *and* go beyond the screen metaphor and its reifications. Not only *looking through* the screen as if it is a window, not only *looking at* the screen as if it is a mirror, but most of all looking *behind and beyond* the screen that obscures the opaque machinery and its highly productive material-metaphorical networks.

Aggressive remediation

The second problem with Bolter and Grusin's hypothesis pertains to the boundaries of remediation and media. Recall that remediation is defined as the 'formal logic by which new media refashion prior media forms' (Bolter and Grusin 2000, 273). This begs the question: what precisely is a media form? Bolter and Grusin seem to be rather strict on this issue. A movie based on a novel is not considered real remediation, as they note, 'The content has been borrowed, but the medium has not been appropriated or quoted' (ibid., 44). Apparently, remediation comes in gradations, ranging from something that may be called remediation-light to something that marks real, radical remediation. And only the latter is deemed 'a defining characteristic of new media' (ibid., 45). While the authors admit that remediation-light also occurs in new media – 'Much of the World Wide Web also remediates older forms without challenging them' (ibid., 46) – they insist that digital media enable a 'more aggressive remediation [that] throws into relief both the source and the target media' (ibid., 46).

Compelling as these claims sound, being perfectly in line with a general discourse on the radical newness of digital media, they are based on problematic assumptions. To begin with it is assumed that it is possible to separate remediating just the content from remediating the whole medium. In fact, to separate content from medium. This is quite a divergence from McLuhan's principle of 'the medium is the message' that served as inspiration for the remediation thesis. From a McLuhanist perspective, there is no content that is not also a medium. But it is not even necessary to be a McLuhanist to acknowledge that converting content to another medium inevitably changes the content. For example, when one creates a movie based on a novel, the content, the narrative, must also be transformed to enable the translation from the textual medium to the cinematographic medium. And vice versa: the cinematographic modality too has to be adjusted to transfer the specificities of the written story. A first-person voice in a novel can be translated into an auditive voice over, into the image of a person writing, or into subjective camera shots and a montage. Would that not be challenging and appropriating the source and target medium, and thus constitute real remediation?

These adaptations might be considered too small-scale to transform and challenge the medium at large. But then the media question becomes all the more pressing: what scale is large enough to achieve real, radical remediation of the medium at large? And what time span is granted to accomplish this? Creating a movie from a novel does indeed not immediately and completely change the genre of the novel or the cinematographic apparatus, but in the long run of history the narrative feature movie – which can be seen as remediated novel – developed as a dominant genre in cinema (Bordwell and Thompson 2003). Should we then say that somewhere in history the initial pseudo-remediation switched to real remediation?

These problems, stemming from a strict definition of remediation as radical media transformation, cannot be solved easily. Is borrowing a visual representation of a mailbox to create a desktop icon aggressive enough to be called radical remediation? Is the translation of printed high-school yearbooks into Facebook profiles enough to deserve that holy epitaph? Which and how many borrowed parts from other media constitute the threshold for radical remediation? How can this be measured, is there a measure? The list of implicated problems is endless.

Moreover, defining remediation as media transformation imposes a restriction on what can be remediated: apparently only (complete) media – and by implication: nothing but media. Yet Bolter and Grusin also speak about the remediation of reality, the remediation of presence, of bodies, cities, and selves. This would imply that remediation not only pertains to acknowledged media forms, but can be done with anything: shops, banks, churches, friendship, sex, communities – and indeed we can find all these non-media entities remediated on the Internet. Bolter and Grusin seem to acknowledge the fuzzy boundaries of what we consider media and non-media when they stipulate that 'the formal characteristics of media, their "content" and their economic and social functions […] can never be entirely separated; a medium is a hybrid in Latour's sense' (ibid., 67). But then again, when media are considered Latourian hybrids – 'mixtures of 'human subjects, language and the external world of things' (ibid., 57) – it is impossible to insist that radical remediation only pertains to pure media.

All in all, Bolter and Grusin seem to oscillate between two conceptions of remediation. One is very strict: remediation is the fundamental re-purposing of source and target media, implying a clear bounded ontology of different pre-existing media. The other is very broad: remediation is the re-purposing and re-appropriation of anything at hand, anything that can be transferred by or into a medium. The two conflicting conceptions may be reconciled by extending the notion of media so far that it can include anything, even beyond McLuhan's already extended notion of media as extensions of the human body and mind. But Bolter and Grusin keep it short and simple: 'a medium is that which remediates' (ibid., 65). This is a definition that is not only confusingly tautological, but also installs this tautology as the main principle of remediation. It evokes the image of a mirror hall of pre-existing media, perpetually reflecting, refashioning, and remediating each other. This closed mirror hall entails that all possible future media must already be there, as germs, waiting to be awakened and taken up by remediation. But how then can something emerge that is conceived as a 'new' medium?

In our quest for the production mechanism of immediacy in digital praxis, we obviously need a conception of mediation, remediation, and demediation. Probably we also cannot do without a notion of what a medium is, though we have seen in the previous chapter how slippery that notion is. The question then is: what can be saved from remediation theory?

4 — REMEDIATION REVISITED

The principal ungroundable ontology of 'a medium' seems to be bad news for the theory of remediation, as the idea of radical remediation of *a priori* existing media cannot be maintained. Yet it also means good news. Once the term medium is provisionally defined as anything that mediates (transmits, transforms, translates), more candidates can enter the stage of mediation than when this is a restricted privilege of pure, prior existing media. The thesis of remediation as a productive mechanism is still valid, provided that the focus shifts towards the generating mechanisms rather than the reproductive mechanisms of the mirror hall. Remediation then consists of processes of re-appropriation and reconfiguration of anything at hand, by means of anything at hand. Remediation works with whatever can be selected metonymically and reassembled metaphorically. Eventually something transformative may happen with the (re)mediated elements. Or not. Or only partially, limited, local, on a small scale.

Remediation produces media

This enables a focus on an ontology of becoming, in particular the becoming of a new medium — the emergence of a new assemblage that may get ontologized and eventually may get identified as a new medium. This implies that remediation *precedes* media. Media — whatever we excavate metonymically as media — are the result of remediation, not the cause. Remediation produces media, not the other way around. Remediation can be done with recognized prior media forms, with partial elements from media forms, or with hybrids, but also with entities initially not perceived as media at all. In other words, anything can become a medium. That is what remediation does: it turns things into media, it creates media. Only from that perspective, we can argue that digital remediation is indeed a relatively more aggressive remediation, as it creates ever more 'new new media' (Levinson 2009). No wonder we experience an explosion of media and mediatization; anything can be turned into a medium.

Still, it remains questionable whether we should call these proliferating forms 'media' at all. As we have seen in Chapter 3, the notion of medium is extremely polysemous. And while it also refers to mean and tool – concrete equipment at our disposal to perform acts in our environment – its connotation is overdetermined by the ontologized plural form: media as monolithic system of mass broadcasting, which produces passive receivers and viewers. In spite of the work done by media scholars on active and interactive audiences (Hall 1997; Jenkins 1992, 2006; Hermes 2005), showing that no medium is ever passively consumed, the very notion of media in the plural seems to be firmly attached to an ontologized mass apparatus, the MEDIA AS MASTER metaphor we encountered in the previous chapter.

Maybe media is not an adequate concept at all when we try to figure out the onto-epistemological dynamics of digital forms.[104] They may indeed take on recognizable media forms, but their existence and social reach is not exhausted by their medium-being. Digital forms are not merely signs or representations, they are also inherently objects, tools in the hands of the user, material metaphors by which things can be done. But as soon as the sign takes precedence over the tool and the object, the experience of immediacy is established and the medium vanishes into oblivion. In any case, we have to conclude again that a medium is that which multiplies, in order to disappear. All media are generated by remediation. Indeed, this is the inverse of Bolter and Grusin's dictum 'a medium is that which remediates' (ibid., 65). Paradoxically, the authors also describe situations where it was not apparent that a particular thing was a medium at all, until it started remediating other things. The medium thus emerged after remediation, or by remediation. The most prominent example is of course the computer, of which the authors note,

> As long as computers remained expensive and rare [...] their remediating functions were limited. In the 1970s, the first word processors appeared, and in the 1980s the first desktop computer. The computer could then become a medium because it could enter into the social and economic fabric of business culture and remediate the typewriter almost out of existence. (Bolter and Grusin 2000, 66)

It has to be noted that in this small quote computer history as remediation is reduced to the selective metonymy of word processing and desktops. Sure enough, the computer did remediate the typewriter, but also much more than that. The expensive giant computers of the 1960s and 1970s remediated for example also postal mail, card boxes, game boards, file drawers, and calculators, in applications such as CTSS MAIL (1965), Ingres (1973), Microchess (1976), fulist (1987) and VisiCalc (1979). At that time computers were neither 'personal' nor a recognized medium, let alone the common-or-garden device they are today. They came with plain textual interfaces, usually even without something that could be called a screen (punch cards served both as data carrier and as typographical interface). This underscores once more that remediation is not limited to visual rep-

---

104. Framing digital objects as media may even lead to a severe limiting of the objects and processes studied. Though the discipline of new media studies is by definition interdisciplinary, digital objects such as electronic patient dossiers or public transport chip cards easily remain below the media radar, while screen phenomena such as Twitter and YouTube are an easy catch. See also Geert Lovink (2012), who argued that the term media no longer provides critical concepts, and that we have to 'liberate the "digital" from its confinement in general media studies' (ibid., 80). In the chapter 'Media Studies: Diagnostics of a Failed Merger', Lovink proposes a definite disassociation from media studies (theater, film and television studies), including their imports of 'identity-obsessed cultural studies and ethnographic or quantitative social sciences approach' (ibid., 22).

resentations – any object or phenomenon can serve as a conceptual metaphor, and any conceptual metaphor can actuate remediation when incorporated as material metaphor in the apparatus. More remediation resources entered the stage when institutional computers were connected to the early Internet in the 1970s and 1980s. Still within a strictly textual interface, these early so-called internetworked computers remediated postal mail (Mail Box Protocol, since 1971), theater scripts (MUDs, Multi-User Dungeons, since 1975), public debate forums (Usenet, since 1980), telex and conversations (IRC, Internet Relay Chat, since 1988). With the advent of the graphical user interface, remediation was extended to ever more metaphorical and metonymical resources: desktops, offices, magazines, portals, travel agencies, banks, shops, villages, cities. The history of the computer and especially the Internet shows unambiguously that remediation taps from far more resources than only recognizable media forms.

The great merit of this extended conception of remediation – defined as selecting, bending, and blending heterogeneous socio-cultural resources into material metaphors – is that we can analytically break out of the media prison, that alleged mirror hall of prior existing media where no external signal can enter.[105] Admittedly, the mere combination and reconfiguration of prior existing stuff can indeed create new phenomena. The emergence of complexity on a higher level, induced by just combining simple elements that exist on a lower level, is a well known mechanism in systems theory, cybernetics, physics, biology, and software development, and can even be traced in works of literature and art (Taylor 2001; Hayles 1990; 2005). Likely it could also be found in the history of what we call media. Yet, there is no reason why this should be the *only* way to create new forms. Acknowledging the productiveness of recombinations in a closed system does not rule out the possibility of productive combinations with elements from outside the system.

Moreover, as we have seen it is analytically quite problematic to delineate precisely a domain of media as a closed system. Therefore, the media domain can better be seen as a principally open system with permeable boundaries that can be crossed and transgressed anytime. The only thing needed is a mechanism of mediation that can import and export appropriate concepts and objects from other domains. Such a perspective on media enables the detection of the remediation of non-medial things, and brings to the fore material-metaphorical remediations that would otherwise remain unnoticed and undertheorized.

Transmediation beyond media

To summarize, whereas Bolter and Grusin asserted that all media work by remediating other media, I extend and refine their thesis here. Media may remediate, but most of all remediation produces media.[106] From this perspective, the claim that digital media enable a more aggressive remediation is still valid, though not in the sense of throwing 'into relief both the source and the target media' (ibid., 46). Digital remediation throws into relief source and target, period. Sources

---

105. It is no coincidence that I slip into the more acoustically connoted word 'signal' when trying to escape from the visual metaphorical frame of the mirror hall. Western philosophy, and especially new media philosophy, can be accused of having a visual bias, or should we say: deaf ears, for other perceptual modalities.
106. Therefore, media has to be rethought as relations and processes instead of the essentialized origins of processes. Such a reversal is a familiar radical intervention that has been proposed earlier in radical feminism (as the Dutch feminist collective De Bonte Was once put it, 'There are no sexes, there is only sexism') and in anti-reformist Marxism. For example, the Marxist philosopher Louis Althusser asserted in his 'Reply to John Lewis' (1984 [1972]) that class struggle precedes and produces classes, not the other way around.

and targets are not confined to media, neither to display or representation. Digital remediation can be done with any object or phenomenon, from the largest sets of scientific big data to the tiniest acts and trivial questions, anything that can be captured, channeled, and translated into a digital sign-tool-object. I propose to call this *transmediation,* defined as remediation that transgresses and transforms the borders of existing media. Transmediation accounts for the kind of remediation that does not just mirror existing media forms, but that assembles sign-tool-objects by an entangled process of transposing, transferring, and translating cultural material.[107]

The term transmediation is not meant to replace remediation. Remediation, including its dark shadow of demediation, is still a useful term to refer to explicit mobilization of recognized media forms. Those allusions can also be found in digital configurations, in the usage of metaphors such as backward, forward, buttons, files, and mailboxes. Yet, these metaphors, metonymically borrowed from other media (respectively cassette deck, radio, paper, and mail) do more than just provide a metaphorical representation based on familiarity with other media. The point is that they do not just *represent* those objects; they can be operated and handled as such, and in this regard they *are* objects. They are sign-tool-objects informed by material metaphors, and as such they exceed and extend media-induced remediation into a much wider transmediation field.

I am aware of the fact that several other scholars have already proposed a variety of terms to indicate the multiplicity and heterogeneity of current digitally driven mediation processes. Mike Sandbothe (2005) used the notion of *transversality* in order to develop a pragmatic media philosophy about 'transitions in the transitionless' – a concept also resurfacing in the debate on new materialism (Van der Tuin and Dolphijn 2010). Earlier Henk Oosterling (2000; 2003) coined the notion of 'radical medi@crity', to indicate a situation so thoroughly mediated and intermediated that the 'inter' has superseded the medium itself. We may try to hold on to media ontology, but as Oosterling argues, 'The claim that media have a life or existence of their own, can only be made acceptable with a lot of metaphorical displacements' (Oosterling 2000, 10, transl. MvdB). Indeed, and that is why we need a concept such as transmediation that not only covers remediations and intermediations, but also icontology and demediation by metaphors.

Katherine Hayles (2005) has proposed the term intermediation which is very similar to my term transmediation. Distinguishing her term from Bolter and Grusin's remediation, she notes,

> 'Remediation' has the disadvantage of locating the starting point for the cycles in a particular locality and medium, whereas 'intermediation' is more faithful to the spirit of multiple causality

---

107. Note that this definition of transmediation should not be confused with the notion of transmediality as used in the discourse of 'intermediality studies' (Bay-Cheng et al., 2010). In this field the term transmediation pertains to media switch or exchange, for example, the adaptation of a novel into a theater play or a movie. My notion of transmediation resonates more with the notion of intermediality in this field, defined as 'co- or interrelations between media that result in a redefinition of the media, which by impacting upon each other, provoke in turn a resensibilised perception' (Kattenbelt 2010, 35), be it that in my definition of transmediation exceeds media as such – also beyond their interrelations and redefinitions – and that transmediation is first and foremost a material process, not a feature of a work. Maybe needless to say, transmediation is not connected to what in marketing and PR discourse is known as 'crossmediality' or 'transmedial campaigns', pertaining to the simultaneous deployment of several media channels that mutually reinforce each other in order to reach a larger public or different segments of the public with a particular message.

in emphasizing interactions among media. In addition, 'remediation' (thanks to the excellent work Grusin and Bolter have done in positioning the term) now has the specific connotation of applying to immediate/hypermediate strategies. Because the dynamics I want to explore go far beyond this particular cycle, I would rather use the lesser known 'intermediation' [...] I want to expand its denotations to include interactions between systems of representation, particularly language and code, as well as interaction between modes of representation, particularly analog and digital. Perhaps most importantly, 'intermediation' also denotes mediating interfaces connecting humans with the intelligent machines that are our collaborators in making, storing and transmitting informational processes and objects. (Hayles 2005, 33)

By positioning intermediation within what she calls the 'worldviews' of, respectively, speech, writing, and code, Hayles mobilizes the vocabulary of MEDIA AS INSCRIPTION and MEDIA AS LANGUAGE. Tellingly, she also uses the term 'media translation' in order to 'suggest that recreating a text in another medium is so significant that it is analogue to translating from one language to another [...] the analogy with language translation can offer useful insights into the problems and possibilities that haunt media translation' (ibid., 109). This is not surprising, since most of Hayles' work addresses mediation issues of electronic texts and literature. Yet, as she analyzes text and code also as tools and objects, the toolmakers metaphor is also never absent in her work. For Hayles intermediation is always translation and transformation, at work in and between all systems and modes of representation, conceived as interfacial transactions between bodies, texts, and media forms (Hayles 2005, 7). Importantly, Haylesian intermediation implies a non-linear conception of causality, a 'dynamic heterarchy' (ibid., 104) of recursive feedback loops and multiple causalities, which thwarts the dialectics that may be read into the notion of 'inter' as just a mutual interaction between two prior existing phenomena.

While Hayles frequently addresses 'the entanglement of means and metaphor', for example in her analysis of Greg Evan's transhumanist science-fiction work (ibid., 214), she does not explicitly relate intermediation to the concept of material metaphor she proposed in her earlier work (Hayles 2002). Still, I read her notion of intermediation as a theoretical account of the dynamics of heterogeneous transferences, including those enabled by material metaphors. Yet, I prefer to call this transmediation and not intermediation, because of the not-to-be-missed connotations of transference, translation, and transformation beyond interrelated media.

Mediators and intermediaries
Moreover, there is another reason for favoring transmediation above intermediation. Bruno Latour (2005) has pointed out a useful distinction between what he calls intermediaries and mediators:

An *intermediary*, in my vocabulary, is what transports meaning or force without transformation: defining its inputs is enough to define its outputs. For all practical purposes, an intermediary can be taken not only as a black box, but also as a black box counting for one, even if it is internally made of many parts. *Mediators,* on the other hand, cannot be counted as just one; they might count for one, for nothing, for several, or for infinity. Their input is never a good predictor of their output; their specificity has to be taken into account every time. Mediators transform, translate, distort, and modify the meaning or the elements they are supposed to carry. (Latour 2005b, 39)

Note how the distinction between intermediaries and mediators is analogue to the difference between the conduit metaphor and the toolmakers metaphor. Intermediaries do not act or add something, they just transmit along a conduit. Conversely, mediators are significant actors in a network, actors that actually act, by translation and transformation labor. In this vocabulary, intermediation refers to the non-significant work of intermediaries; the term would confusingly lose all transformative and transversal capacities Hayles so ardently supplemented. Much as I am indebted to Hayles' work and terminology, I here comply to Latour's vocabulary, and thus use transmediation instead of Hayles' intermediation.

It should be noted that the classification into mediator and intermediary does not comprise a stable enduring ontology. The distinction provides a vocabulary by which we can describe how an entity – say, a medium – can icontologize (into an intermediary), but also how it can burst open (into a complex network of mediators). Latour illustrates this with a telling example, one that we have encountered before:

> A properly functioning computer could be taken as a good case of a complicated intermediary while a banal conversation may become a terribly complex chain of mediators where passions, opinions, and attitudes bifurcate at every turn. But if it breaks down, a computer may turn into a horrendously complex mediator while a highly sophisticated panel during an academic conference may become a perfectly predictable and uneventful intermediary in rubber stamping a decision made elsewhere. (ibid., 39)

All in all, my notion of transmediation draws upon Hayles' intermediation as well as Latour's differentiation between intermediary and mediator. The material-metaphorical transferences I am after should account for the withdrawal into immediacy and intermediaries, as well as the multiplication of mediators.

Trajectories of digital transmediation

Of course, transmediation does not always follow the same path. Roughly, three main trajectories can be distinguished by which transmediation may unfold. The first one takes explicitly recognized media forms as its starting point. This trajectory complies with classic remediation à la Bolter and Grusin (2000): the refashioning and reappropriation of prior existing media forms. The second trajectory exploits the fuzzy boundaries between media and non-media forms, while the third one taps from non-media raw material, that is social-cultural phenomena that are not considered media forms. Hence, transmediation may tap from media forms and from non-media forms, but also from objects or articulations that cannot easily be classified as media or non-media forms.

Media boundary objects

We might call these objects lingering on the boundaries between media and non-media forms media boundary objects.[108] Examples of these are the ephemeral objects that are located somewhere

---

108. The term media boundary object is partially inspired by Susan Leigh Star's term 'boundary object' (Star 1989; Star 2010). In her work boundary objects are material-semiotic entities 'that allow different groups to work together without consensus' (Star 2010). They are characterized by interpretative flexibility, local appropriation by communities of practice, and a dynamic between ill-structured and tailored uses of the objects, sometimes eventually resulting in standards (Star 2010).

between personal notes and private memory: address lists and phone numbers of friends, to-do lists, shopping lists, wish lists, route maps, favorite things, memos, and so on. Once digitally inscribed and stored, these entities come into being as digital-material objects, indexically linked to specific applications, devices, and databases. Some of these digital-material objects are 'new' in the sense that they had no existence as material inscription before their digital capture. You can have an imaginary list of the names of people you know, or of often used phone numbers, but as long as you did not scribble these things down it does not comprise a material object. Neither does it manifest itself as mediated, let alone as a medium, non-articulated and non-informed as it still is.

Yet as soon as such data are externalized, captured, assembled, and stored digitally, a new object has been created, a digital-material sign-tool-object (which may be experienced as a new media object or even a new medium, but not necessarily). Such objects can be created on the fly, as with the list of conducted calls on your mobile phone, the collection of ever used e-mail addresses automatically aggregated in My Address Book, your browsing history, or the log files that web servers and Internet providers keep of your digital whereabouts. They can also be created on purpose, as with personal route maps derived from Google Maps, book wish lists at Amazon, and bookmarks. By storing these personal reminders as digital inscriptions, they acquire a mediatized ontology and availability not present before. They become digital-material objects, nested in other digital assemblages, ready to be further reiterated, differentiated, transferred, and mined, by yourself, by the public, by governmental surveillance and – not to forget – by commercial exploitation.

Non-medial cultural objects
While these examples of digital inscriptions can be traced back to their analogies in other media domains (usually the domain of writing and print, as with address books, diaries, lists and note pads), the third trajectory of digital transmediation taps from practices of social conduct that are not even remotely considered media practices. Think for instance of friendship, jokes, communities, sex, work, and play. Admittedly, these social practices are always facilitated or even constructed by mediation and communication, but we usually do not consider these phenomena media or material objects. Yet, they can become mediatized, ontologized into digital sign-tool-objects that acquire a productivity and onto-epistemology of their own.

In particular networked computing enables the transmediation and extension of social practices, by cutting out metaphors and metonymies from these practices, and reassembling them as digital sign-tool-objects: Facebook friends, smileys, spam, avatars, profiles, likes, tweets, comments, followers, popularity rankings, and so on. These things are not just concepts, they are objects, digital sign-tool-objects. These objects are generated by trajectories of transmediation that translate, embed, and embody social practices in digital forms. These digital forms in their turn may or may not be derived from other media forms, but that produce new material media objects in any case. It should be noted that the existence of inscribed entities that acquire a onto-epistemology of their own is not unprecedented by other media. Money, passports, and diplomas are good examples of such inscription objects. In fact, all media, old and new, produce media-specific and media-dependent objects: socio-cultural phenomena that are either transformed by media appropriations or that had no presence before particular media produced them. For instance, pornography, pen friends, movie stars, and television celebrities are all entities produced by specific media. Even the historical emergence of nation states has been analyzed as co-constituted by the printing press as enabler of imagined communities based on an imposed shared national language (Anderson 1983).

Hence, media in general are already capable of producing new social-cultural phenomena, as transmediated extensions of social practices that get fused, transformed and incorporated in media-specific entities. Sometimes these phenomena are still clearly recognizable as media-produced (as with pen friends, pornography, television celebrities), sometimes they are so ontologized and culturally embedded that the media-incited trajectory has completely vanished from sight (as with nation-states).

To a certain extent the sign-tool-objects emerging from digital transmediation are of the same order as the above media-generated phenomena, yet the scale, pace, and quantities that mark digital transmediation seem to be unprecedented. The Internet and networked computing in general seem to be able to transmediate everything at hand, regardless of previous media appropriations – everything that can be selected, inserted, enacted, and extended by its apparatus. The proliferation of digital-material objects also seems to be more invasive and radical, in their generative and multiplying capacity, as well as in their entanglement with the social (and economical and political) fabric. In that regard, digital objects are closer to nation states than pen friends: they generate assemblages and environments that may imply societal transformations as large as those that came with the establishment of nation-states.

For that reason, it is questionable whether digital-material transmediated objects should be analyzed as media effects or media objects. While this is a common maneuver, as in the current social media discourse, the objects at stake certainly do not perform the classic media work of communication and representation. Digital sign-tool-objects such as Facebook friends, online communities, or web cam sex are not 'about' or 'like' friendship, community, or sex. These things are not so much *represented* by a medium called the Internet; they are rather *enacted and extended* on the Internet, by taking on specific digital-material forms.

In short, they are more a presencing than a re-presentation. These transmediated enactments may in their turn challenge and transform the social configuration of friendship or community, by recursively questioning them. That is what makes these enactments instances of transmediation beyond media, beyond remediation, and beyond representation.

We can conclude from this chapter that the icontological states of immediacy and transparency are the result of labor and processes of transmediations rather than representational remediations. If we want to capture the outskirts of digital transmediations, the study of digital sign-tool-objects has to break through the screen surface, out of the windows and mirror hall of projected media forms. Only when windows and mirrors are taken seriously as material metaphors can something be revealed of the translations that go beyond representation and remediation.

The next question then is: where do these translations go if they do not halt at the level of representation? Roughly two directions can be distinguished here. One is headed towards society, and involves the transmediation of medial and non-medial cultural objects into digital-material entities that may transform notions of sociability. This will be the subject of the last chapter. The other direction leads to the black boxes of software and machinery, and involves the transcoding of digital code into media and cultural objects. This will be addressed in the next chapter.

CHAPTER 5
CODE RULES
HOW SOFTWARE MATTERS AND METAPHORIZES

> *Mathematics, which most of us see as the most factual of all sciences, constitutes the most colossal metaphor imaginable, and must be judged, esthetically as well as intellectually, in terms of the success of this metaphor.*
> (Norbert Wiener, 1954)

> *Software is, or should be, a notoriously difficult concept. As a set of instructions, it's material status is unstable; indeed, the more you dissect software, the more it falls away.*
> (Wendy Chun, 2004)

The ontology of digital computers is a notoriously hard nut to crack. As a programmable and extendable machine the computer is a virtual all-purpose machine. It runs on software, which is in principle soft and fluid, ever open to adding, modifying, and extending. This precludes any final closure of the digital computer; its basic mode of existence is that of a 'perpetual beta state' (De Mul 2002, 38). In that sense the computer has never left the drawing table, or to say it more accurately, computers are delivered with the drawing table included, in principle ready to be drawn further.
In principle – but not in praxis, as the current chapter on software will show. What exactly is computer code, and what does it actually code: numbers, objects, words, metaphors?
The chapter starts with a short history of software. This is a story of labor and labor division, plus, not to forget, of several metaphorical displacements. The second section addresses the attempts to define the essence of software, organized by their conceptual and discourse metaphors. The last section will address the basic difficulty of software: its paradoxical blend of materiality and assumed immateriality, and the so-called new materialist attempts to come to terms with this paradox.

1 — THE POLITICAL HISTORY OF SOFTWARE
In ordinary computing praxis and popular discourse software is usually taken for granted. Something self-evident that runs invisible on our devices – SOFTWARE AS A BLACK BOX – or as something we see on the screen – SOFTWARE AS INTERFACE. We use it for particular tasks – SOFTWARE AS A TOOL. In that capacity software can be present-at-hand, SOFTWARE AS A THING, as something that has to be purposely obtained, installed, and configured, be it in the commercial version of SOFTWARE AS A COMMODITY that you have to buy, or in the more obscure variant SOFTWARE AS WAREZ, pirated or self-made stuff you can download. But once installed and properly running software is no longer a thing to bother about; it becomes ready-to-hand, transparent on the interface, withdrawn in the black box – SOFTWARE AS VANISHING POINT.

However, the conception of software as black box behind the user interface is by no means an immanent feature of computing. The form and function of artifacts is always designed and constructed, and software is no exception. The assumed transparency of the interface, evoked by the interplay of visibility and invisibility, representation and depresentation, is a matter of labor and politics. Wendy Chun pointed out that this is essentially a politics of forgetting: 'for computers to become transparency machines, the fact that they compute – that they generate text and images rather than merely represent or reproduce what exists elsewhere – must be forgotten' (Chun 2004, 27).

As will be addressed in the following section, the politics of forgetting has been crucial for the emergence of software. The history of software can be described as a political economy of forgotten labor: first by the extraction and separation of software from hardware and human labor, and second, by the separation between programmers and users with the introduction of the graphical user interface.

Commanding girls or computers

Although we usually consider software as inextricably bound to computing machines, software as such did not emerge at the same time as the first working computing hardware. As Wendy Chun describes so thoroughly, in the early days of computing, the 1940s, there was no software – just hardware and human labor (Chun 2004). At that time the hardware consisted of electromechanical (sometimes electronic) machines that could calculate numeric instructions and render the output in human-readable forms, but these machines were not called computers – 'computer' was the name for the associated professionals. Computers were human workers, usually young women with a background in mathematics.[109] They worked as clerical calculators, wielding pencil, paper, and machines. Computing at that time was an intricate, tedious process of human-machine interaction, a form of direct hands-on programming, performed by human cognition and manual labor, aligned with labor delegated to the machine. Chun explains,

> 'Programming' comprised the human task of making connections, setting switches, and inputting values ('direct programming'), as well as the human and machine task of coordinating the various parts of the computer. In 1946 the master programmer for the ENIAC (the first general-purpose electronic digital computer to be designed, built, and successfully used) controlled the sequence of actions needed to solve a problem numerically. The ENIAC was initially rewired for each problem so that, essentially, a new ENIAC was created each time it was used. (Chun 2004, 28)

The ENIAC was a multi-purpose machine, used for military computation, such as artillery firing tables and hydrogen bomb calculations. Setting up a new ENIAC could take three weeks of work for the ENIAC girls. The pressures of hot and cold war urged for efficiency and time saving, and brought on 'automatic programming', based on the principle that the computer could store compu-

---

109. See also Katherine Hayles book title *My Mother Was a Computer* (2005), which refers to the time a computer was a profession, and your working mom could thus be a computer. Yet, Hayles' title is deliberately polysemous, as it also alludes to science fiction and artificial intelligence, as well as to the problematics of subject formation in the age of digitality.

tational instructions in its memory as easily as it could store numerical data. [110] Manual labor could thus be delegated to the machine, which was able to perform the translation labor between symbolic instructions and numerical notations by means of several translation layers of programs designed to operate on or produce other programs (interpreters, assemblers, compilers, and generators).

In other words, when women were computers there was no software; software as such emerged by the extraction, abstraction, displacement, and subsequent forgetting of the labor of women and machines. As Chun remarks, half jokingly: 'One could say that programming became programming and software became software when commands shifted from commanding a "girl" to commanding a machine' (ibid., 33). [111] Programming turned from setting up hardware into writing software, shifting from hands-on numerical labor to problem-oriented writing and data abstraction. It yielded not only to the development of various programming languages, but also to programming as a professional and academic field in its own right, and to different operating systems in order to pre-configure specific hardware assemblages.

Software as (forgotten) labor

These shifts can be recast as a chain of metaphorical condensations and displacements. The word computer shifted from referring to a human worker to a machine, from living labor to dead labor in Marx' terms, thus revealing our contemporary notion of a computer as a reified metaphor of human labor, notably a non-differentiated mix of manual and mental labor. But as the computer became conceptually and materially divided into hardware and software, computation split into a material and a symbolic articulation.

At first glance, this seems to resonate with the split between manual labor and mental labor, but the association with labor in fact disappeared all together. Notions of hardware and software do not evoke images of labor and process; they evoke an imagery of reified, ontologized stuff, with specific characteristics that are qualified by metaphors of hardness and softness: HARDWARE IS HEAVY, THICK, MATERIAL, versus SOFTWARE IS LIGHT, FLUID, IMMATERIAL. Whereas the notion of computer can, with a little effort, be traced back as a metaphor of human labor, the ontologized notions of hardware and software erase all traces of labor and process. Hardware just exists, and software just exists. Moreover, the conception of hardware and software as separate entities not only obfuscates processing, mutual dependencies and perpetual interactions between hardware and software, it also presents itself as a firm mutually exclusive dichotomy. This dichotomy seamlessly ties in with the persistent Cartesian discourse as it re-invokes and reinforces classic dichotomies

---

110. The idea had been around for more than an age. Already in 1837 Charles Babbage conceptualized and designed a programmable computer called the Analytical Engine. Though Babbage never finished the machine, mathematician Ada Lovelace (1815-1852) outlined a working algorithm for the machine in 1843, and is therefore considered the world's first programmer. In 1936, Alan Turing provided the mathematical proof for a universal computing machine in his *On Computable Numbers, with an Application to the Entscheidungsproblem*. Turing's hypothetical machine had an infinite store (memory) that contained both instructions and data. In 1945, John von Neumann formally described the principle of stored-program architecture that came to be known as 'Von Neumann architecture' in his *First Draft of a Report on the EDVAC* (reprinted in 1993).
111. Of course this cannot be interpreted as women's liberation. The crude gendered relations as built-in in the history of computing has been transformed into more sophisticated differential power relations (Van den Boomen 2009). Besides, the computer-girls were sent home after World War II ended.

as body-mind and material-immaterial: HARDWARE AS BODY versus SOFTWARE AS MIND (Minsky 1986). These metaphors not only provide a conceptual scheme to capture the idea of software; they recursively strike back at the conception of the human mind itself: MIND AS SOFTWARE (Lakoff and Johnson 1999; Draaisma 2000; Block 2009).

The implications of the split are not just conceptual and philosophical; they are also profoundly material. The emergence of software as a separate instance implied several other condensations and displacements: the substitution of processes with programs, of women's labor with executable code, of concrete calculations with abstract algorithms, of numerical calculus with symbolic language, of patch cables and switches with preprogrammed configurations, of human operators with operating systems, and of human-machine interaction with automatic execution. In other words, these displacements not only refer to shifts in labor distribution, they also evoked new concepts, objects, and subjects. In Chun's terms: SOFTWARE IS IDEOLOGY. A dangerous ideology, she warns, since 'this abstraction – this drawing away from the specificities of the machine – gives over, in its separation of machine into software and hardware, the act of programming to the machine itself' (ibid., 38).

Software as ideology

Chun's approach to software as ideology draws on Althusser's conceptualization of ideology (Althusser 1971). This Marxist post-structuralist philosopher argued against the usual conception of ideology as a set of false ideas. Althusser contended that ideology has a material existence, and stressed its enactment in daily practices and rituals, aimed at making conditions of existence obvious and self-evident. It does so by interpellating individuals as subjects, that is, assigning and aligning subject positions, such as wage earner, wife, school kid, professional, and so on. Althusser proposed a redefinition of what we term ideology, replacing the common ideational notion (ideology as set of ideas about the real) with the thesis of ideology as 'a "representation" of the imaginary relationship of individuals to their real conditions of existence' (Althusser 1971).[112] This reformulation hints at the ambivalence of the very notion of representation, and most of all, it stresses that in ideological representations *relations* get represented, or better: enacted, instead of providing an immediate representation of the real.

Chun describes software in terms of Althusserian ideological practices that interpellate and produce users:

> Software, or perhaps more precisely OS *[operating systems – mvdb]*, offer us an imaginary relationship to our hardware: they do not represent the motherboard or other electronic devices but rather desktops, files and recycling bins. Without OS there would be no access to hardware – there would be no actions, no practices, no users. Each OS, in its extramedial advertisements, interpellates a 'user': calls it and offers it a name or an image with which to identify [...] You are not, however, aware of software's constant constriction and interpellation (also known as its 'user-friendliness'), unless you find yourself frustrated with its defaults [...] Software produces users, and the term *user,* resonating with 'drug user,' discloses every programmer's dream: to create an addictive product. Users are produced by benign soft-

---

112. A definition that in its threefoldness again resonates a Peircian triad: representation as Firstness, imaginary relations as Secondness, and conditions of existence as Thirdness.

ware interactions, from reassuring sounds that signify that a file has been saved to folder names such as 'my documents' that stress personal computer ownership. Computer programs shamelessly use shifters, pronouns like 'my' and 'you,' that address you, and everyone else, as a subject. (Chun 2006, 21)

In these enactments of ideology the representations-of-relations come in the form of images (files, recycling bins) and pronouns (my, you) – representations that are not coincidentally metaphors; they are metaphorical by necessity. Software cannot be accessed, grasped or manipulated without metaphorical representations, be it as pictorial icons and indexical descriptions on the user interface, or as the symbols and syntax of programming languages. Chun hints at the ideological power of metaphors when she reminds us that we as users in fact know very well that our folders and desktops are not really folders and desktops, but that we treat them as if they were. And that is precisely the ideological moment, as ideology resides in acting, not in knowing. [113]

Yet, Chun's swift shift from software to operating systems, and from operating systems to graphical user interfaces begs the question whether such fast equations are not also effects of ideology, since an operating system is not identical with a graphical user interface. After all, there are still operating systems that are also accessible by a textual command-line interface, such as Unix, Linux, or the old MS-DOS. Would that not imply a difference, a difference in the interpellations of subjects as users?

You are supposed to read, not to write

Florian Cramer argues that this is indeed the case (Cramer 2003, 2008). According to Cramer, the paradigm of the graphical user interface, unleashed to the public in 1984 with the introduction of the Apple Macintosh, created a new division: the separation between programmers and users. As he puts it,

> When Alan Kay developed the first graphical mouse-controlled computer environment at Xerox PARC in the 1970s, the separation between 'usage and 'programming' was for the first time implemented as separation of media. 'Usage' became graphical, 'programming' textual. The gap widened with the commercialization of Kay's ideas through the Apple Macintosh and Microsoft Windows. While Alan Kay's user interface [...] remained fully programmable to the point where users could create their own applications by combining pre-existing and self-written program objects, the Apple Macintosh lacked the programming interface simply for economical and marketing reasons. [The result was an] operating system that gave birth to the 'user', with the message: You are supposed to read, not to write. Through this engineered gap, programming becomes a mystery, a black art, supposedly for the sake of making computing easier. (Cramer 2003, 100)

This split is usually mapped in terms of the graphical versus the textual, but Cramer contends that software is always textual, always a matter of writing. Yet it is a particular kind of writing, in

---

113. Althusser already stressed this with his thesis that ideology is material practice, but the issue is also later elaborated by the Lacanian Marxist Slavoj Žižek (1989) who considers the main principle of ideology to be the disavowal: 'I know but still I do'.

which the tools and the writing, the processor and the processed, are inextricably intertwined, due to the Von Neumann architecture that stores both instruction code and data in the same realm. Remember, a computer is not a coffee machine with a clear ontological difference between the coffee and the button for the coffee.

This implies that any cutting out of access levels for operation, intervention or programming is in principle possible. As Cramer claims, 'The distinction between a "user interface", an "Application Program Interface", and a computer control language is purely arbitrary' (Cramer 2008, 150). There is no ontological necessity for these differentiations: 'To name one computer control language a "programming language," another a "protocol," and yet another a "file format" is merely a convention, a nomenclature indicating different degrees of syntactic restraint built into the very design of a computer control language' (Cramer 2008, 170). In other words, any differentiation in software functions or forms is arbitrary, and therefore a matter of design, convention, and politics – plus ideology, that is, the mechanism that returns the divisions as irrefutable.

Following Roland Barthes' distinction between readerly and writerly texts, Cramer speaks of readerly and writerly software, respectively. Readerly GUI software is software that shelves, stacks, and safeguards meaning, and interpellates a passive reader-user, while writerly command-line software reflects the plurality, openness, and infinity of language, and interpellates a writer-user. Since the writerly modus is the built-in default in the Von Neumann architecture, only extra metaphorical work can turn software into the readerly mode, according to Cramer:

> Since computer software is tools made from writing, processors made from code, the material gap *[between tools and writing - mvdb]* can only be sustained through simulation. To be readerly, popular PC user software creates the illusion of being hardware, visually and tactically disguising itself as solid analog tools. (Cramer 2003, 101)

Cramer's choice of words – 'illusion', 'disguising itself as analog' – reveals a strong condemnation of graphical metaphors. Apparently, 'simulation', 'illusion', and 'analog tools' yield to the corruption of the pure writing that software actually is. Compare this with Cramer's obvious preference for the writerly Unix command line:

> The instantaneous mutual convertibility of text as something processed (i.e. data) and text as a processor (i.e. programs) that is characteristic of all program code is not suppressed in Unix by hiding the code away, but transparently preserved on the level of the user interface. [...] While it is true for all software and all operating systems that the software tool itself is nothing but writing, the elegant simplicity of the Unix command line relies on the idea that programming, instead of becoming a secluded application, is a trivial extension of 'using' the system, simply by writing a sequence of commands into a text file which then can be executed. (Cramer 2003, 102)

Windows and Mac fans might object that only nerdy command-line-literate Unix die-hards would experience programming as a 'trivial extension of use' and 'elegant simplicity', as this assumes extensive knowledge of possible commands and their syntax. However, that would be a matter of learning and getting used to it. After all, we also learned the far less elegant and far more limited simplicity of metaphorical icons, menus, and windows, delegating syntax and control to the black box of the machine.

Corruption by metaphors
More problematic is that Cramer's division into readerly and writerly software seems to be based on an assumed clear-cut split between the figural and the literal, the metaphorical and the non-metaphorical, respectively defined as closed, condensed semantics versus open, recombinable syntax. But such a split is hard to maintain, since even programming languages, with their strict formal logic and syntax, show traces of cultural semantics, in symbolic operators such as 'if', 'then', and 'else', and in commands like 'list', 'move', and 'go to'. Still, Cramer insists that this is all a matter of human attribution:

> The symbols of computer control languages inevitably do have semantic connotations simply because there exist no symbols with which humans would not associate some meaning. But symbols can't denote any semantic statement, that is, they do not express meaning in their own terms; humans metaphorically read meaning into them through associations they make. (Cramer 2008, 169)

The author here implies that metaphors are something extra, something that a reader reads into a text, not something that can be inextricably built-in in the text, or something that emerges from the interaction between the user, the text, and the machine. Metaphors and symbols are thus denied any ability to 'denote semantic statements'.
Yet this is highly debatable. Ordinary writing and speech are a case in point. The use of language is nothing but using arbitrary symbols to denote semantic statements, expressing 'meaning in their own terms', that is, in their own language system, a system of arbitrary relations, sustained by conventions, and shared by a speech community. For software, 'exe.cut[up]able statements' (Cramer 2003), that is SOFTWARE AS WRITING or SOFTWARE AS LANGUAGE, the same principle holds, even though the speech community involved here is a special one: a divided speech community consisting of on the one hand human interpreters and on the other hand machine language interpreters. As different as they are, they both read, write, and execute, in their own terms, in their own language system. And they both contribute to meaning making. It is disputable whether machinic reading and writing already implies meaning (I would argue that is does not), but in any case the meaning-making process is unfinished until some human-readable output is delivered. At that moment meaning evolves, not just by human attribution, but as a reassembled effect of distributed reading, writing, and executing, performed by both humans and machines. Machines do their part, by producing formal and material traces, parts of which are selected and bundled by design for human-readable representation, say, as an email or a menu. That we experience such selected representations of machine states as 'an email' or 'a menu' is not because we just attribute those meanings to arbitrary forms. The point is that these metaphorical forms are not arbitrary. They are substantially in-formed, that is, their form frames their function and causal indexical power, their use, and thereby their meaning.

Software politics
The selections of machine states are translated in a metaphorical form, but while these selections are arbitrary – only constrained by the physical-material affordances of the machine – and while even the choice of metaphor by the designer may be arbitrary, the material-metaphorical form by which they eventually function is not arbitrary, but indexically and metaphorically en-

sured.[114] The associated meaning of the metaphor is mobilized, exploited, and materialized in the design. Once instantiated the use and meaning of these executable metaphors is secured by a chain of necessary causal relations inside the machine. Their specific functionality as readable, writable, and executable objects is thus rendered by their specific metaphorical forms. You can indeed reply to the email, you can indeed make a choice in the menu. You do not just *think* you reply, you *do* so. And it behaves that way, because it is designed that way.

Of course, as a data set these digital-material objects can be transposed into arbitrary other interfacial representations – the email message can be converted into a plain text file, into a screen shot image, into hexadecimal numbers, into sound, or into movement. And even a set of instructions in programming language can be represented in any arbitrary form – printed as text in a book or on a T-shirt, converted into a piano roll, or a painting. But any transposition would also transform its built-in metaphorical functionality, usually not leaving it intact. You cannot reply to the image of the mail, and the T-shirt cannot execute the code. Although one can indeed do things within a command-line operating system that are not afforded in Windows, that does not make Unix email less a built-in material metaphor than the Windows version.

I contend that these interfacial forms are material metaphors, designed material forms that frame, inform, and align specific uses, social practices, and meaning. Indeed, they thrive partly on cultural conventions and arbitrary symbols referring to machine instructions. But the assembled object, its form, design, and functionality, is not arbitrary. That is, not as arbitrary as say, the name of a rose which, according to Shakespeare (and Saussure), 'by any other name would smell as sweet'. Material metaphors are not names; they do things in the world that arbitrary signs cannot do.

That being said, Cramer's insistence on the structural formalism of computer control languages should be taken seriously. It reminds us that we have to be cautious with the easy slippage into assigning autonomous agency to computers, digitality, or software. This dangerous belief in 'automagic' cybernetic intelligence can be found in popular culture and discourse, but it also circulates in academic discourse. For example, in the form of the high expectations of the so-called semantic web. It is a discourse that both idealizes and ontologizes software and digitality, by imputing it with attributions of immateriality (Negroponte 1995; Kelly 1995; Barlow 1996), inherent smartness (cf. De Wilde 2000), and even life (Barabási 2002; Wolfram 2002). An informed understanding and debate about what software actually is and does, is unabatedly urgent, *pace* Kittler's radical statement 'There is no software' (1989). There *is* software, and not just as an ideational-ideological construct; it has a physical, formal, and cultural-political material existence. The same holds for Cramer's adequate diagnosis of the engineered split between users and programmers as induced by the GUI paradigm. The limitations of user control, sustained by an ideological inversion of the notion of transparency – in the GUI paradigm celebrated as hiding the processes behind so-called transparent windows instead of revealing its language-like affordances – cannot be stressed enough. It once again shows that experiences of immediacy are by no means natural; they are generated by engineering, the hard work of humans and machines, and the subsequent obfuscation of this hard work.

---

114. Nevertheless, completely arbitrary choices of metaphor are rare when it comes to software design. Metaphors are imported because of specific associations with specific practical contexts. The choice between, for instance, 'mail' or 'chat' as metaphor for a communication program is not arbitrary, since it implies different technical functionalities. The metaphor of chat implies the affordance of taking turns in a real-time dialogue, whereas the metaphor of mail implies the affordance of sending and receiving asynchronously.

To resume this short expedition into the history of software we may conclude that our current notions of software as black box and as constrained interface is a material effect of the politics and ideology of software, including its metaphorical condensations and displacements. The historical development of software is marked by engineered selectivity, a politics of forgetting that installs software as ideology. First, as Chun showed, by obfuscating the hardwiring of the machine and rendering software as semi-autonomous writerly texts. Then, as Cramer argued, by obfuscating the writerly principles of software by representing it as readerly GUI with metaphorical objects.[115] However, as mentioned before, we should be careful not to demonize metaphors, by imputing them with all the evils of representationalism, icontology, and readerly obfuscation. Metaphors are not inherently bad or good, nor are they neutral. Most of all, they are productive. They are productive as interfacial objects on our screen, but also as discourse metaphors that try to capture the essence of software itself. In the above section we already encountered some of these metaphors (SOFTWARE AS LABOR, AS IDEOLOGY, AS MIND), but several more software metaphors circulate in new media discourse. In the following paragraph, I will sketch the outlines of the debate on the onto-epistemology of software and identify its accompanying metaphors, with Lev Manovich's so-called principles of new media as a springboard.

2 — CODING DIGITS, OBJECTS, AND CONCEPTS

Manovich's work *The Language of New Media* (2001) discussed earlier can be seen as the first attempt to catalog the domain of the digital from a perspective he calls 'digital materialism' (ibid., 10). The book aims to 'scrutinize the principles of computer hardware and software and the operations involved in creating cultural objects on a computer to uncover a new cultural logic at work' (ibid., 10). Though the title suggests a kind of linguistic turn with SOFTWARE AS LANGUAGE as the leading metaphor, this is not the author's main argument. Manovich uses the notion of language merely as an umbrella term to refer to various conventions used by designers and users when creating and operating what he calls new media objects, that is, ontological objects, created by digital computation.

In that regard, Manovich's primary metaphor is rather SOFTWARE AS OBJECTS. According to his definition, new media objects can be of a variety of scales. The web or the Internet as a whole can be considered a new media object, but also a particular video game, a particular web site, a file, a digital image, a layer of a Photoshop image, an icon, or even a pixel. Elaborating this primary metaphor of SOFTWARE AS OBJECTS, Manovich formulates five principles that mark the specificity and affordances of software-generated objects. These principles are, respectively, numerical repre-

---

115. The next step seems to be the ruling out of the significance of the operating system and what is left from user control of 'My Computer' and its hard disk all together, by outsourcing storage, system management, and applications to the cloud. See also the heated thread on the Nettime mailinglist, started by Felix Stalder's 'The return of DRM', on 23 April 2010 (archived online at http://www.nettime.org/Lists-Archives/nettime-l-1004/msg00024.html).

sentation, modularity, automation, variability, and transcoding.[116] As we will see in the following sections, each principle comes with its own metaphors and related issues.

Software as numbers

Manovich's first principle, *numerical representation,* refers to the assignment of numbers *(digits)* to discrete elements, in order to make them available for computation and processing (Manovich 2001, 27). In terms of conceptual metaphors: SOFTWARE IS DIGITAL and DIGITAL IS NUMERICAL. Software is based on the arbitrary yet systematic assignment of numbers to discrete units, and this is what makes those units computable, reiterable, processable, and programmable – that is, available for further translations on various machine and interface levels.

Manovich derives two formal characteristics from this principle: first, that digital objects can be described formally and mathematically, and second, that they are subject to algorithmic manipulation, that is, they are variable and programmable by means of if-then instructions: if number X is larger than Y, then change it into Z, resulting for instance in the removal of red eyes in a photograph, a font change in a text, or a zoomed-in map.

Foundational for Manovich's digital objects then, is the fact that digital objects are all, in the last instance, constructed by numbers, *digits*. Note here that *digits* are plain numbers, the integers humans use for counting separate things. A digit is a countable number.[117] Not coincidentally, digits also means fingers, referring to the first more or less external calculating apparatus human beings used in history. A digit then should not be confused with a binary digit, a *bit*. A bit is a unit of information that can only have one of two values, usually either 0 or 1 – the information unit that the hardware of our contemporary computers work with.

Digital versus analog
While the notion of a digit can be formally defined, this is harder when it comes to the notion of *digital*. The word is rarely used in the strict sense of numerical. In ordinary speech the notion of digital is loosely used as referring to general computer-software-new-media stuff, or more precisely as synonym for *binary* or *electronic* (referring respectively to the numerical system or to the processing mechanism of current computers). But most often it is used as a synonym for *discrete,* referring to separate identifiable elements, usually in contrast with analog as continuous. The issue of how to define the digital is also not settled in new media studies.[118] Can we actually speak of 'digital media'? No, Florian Cramer argues,

> the digital is not a medium, but a type of information; information made up of discrete units (such as numbers) instead of an analog continuum (such as waves). The medium – the car-

---

116. In Manovich's later book, *Software Takes Command* (2013) the terms that describe software have shifted somewhat, but, except for his earlier emphasis on numerical representation, in general they indicate similar principles of modular variability: extendability, remixability, performativity, and hybridity. Saliently, the last feature is addressed mainly in terms of biological metaphors of evolution, species, ecology, and even sexual reproduction (Manovich 2013, 167). Of course, with the caveat that we should not take these metaphors too literally (ibid., 168-169).
117. In Turing's words, a computable number is enumerable (Turing 1936, 230).
118. See for instance the heated debate on mailinglist Nettime about the Digital Humanities Manifesto, archived at http://nettime.org/Lists-Archives/nettime-l-0901/threads.html.

rier – itself is, strictly speaking, always analog: electricity, airwaves, magnetic platters, optical rays, paper. (Cramer 2009, n.p.)

According to this definition, the digital is primarily discrete, and only secondarily enumerable; numbers are just a subset of discrete units: DIGITAL IS DISCRETE. Indeed, digital computation can in principle be done with any finite set of discrete entities: numbers of course, but also arbitrary symbols, or even discretely defined colors or forms – provided that the computing machine is able to read those entities unambiguously. This implies that how we define the notion of digital (numerical? discrete? electronic? programmable?) in fact depends on what we take as 'a computer'. Our current digital computers indeed work with discrete numbers, binary in the last instance, but this is actually contingent.

Moreover, not all computing devices are digital in the sense of discrete. Some are analog, in the sense that they work with continuous values (a slide ruler for example) or forces (water pipes and pumps, or billiard ball movements). An analog computing machine is then an assemblage of continuous and proportional mechanisms, a 'body of physical and geometric "analogies" and their corresponding systems of equations' (Robinson 2008, 22).[119]

However, the distinction between the digital-discrete and the analog-continuous is not without problems. While the distinction may be helpful to differentiate between different mechanisms and different materialities in information processing, it tends to become a rigid dichotomy, in the same vein as the dichotomy between software and hardware. The digital is then not only opposed to the analog as discrete versus continuous, but also as artificial blocks versus relational-proportional correspondences, and as mathematical immateriality versus physical-natural materiality. In such a dichotomy, materiality and relationality tend to be attributed solely to the analog side, leaving the digital as immaterial, abstract, and completely isolated from the analog. It should be clear that this dichotomy is profoundly ideological and delusive. It cannot be stressed enough that in digital praxis the digital and the analog are mutually intertwined, and that both are inherently material and relational. After all, digitality cannot consist of numbers (or symbols) as such, nor of discretion as such – it consists of the systematic conjunction between the two which enables the formation of digital-material objects. In that sense the digital is inherently relational: it creates a relation between an arbitrary number and a cut-out entity. These discrete cut-outs are physically nothing but selections of particular machine states. However, once numbered they can be represented on the interface by any symbol or term, on any scale and of any composite, embedded in nests of representations-of-representations. By definition, the digital

---

119. All computers, whether digital, analog, or human, calculate/compute with variable values and rules (algorithms), regardless of their specific material embodiment. Roughly formulated, digital computers work with discrete values, and analog computers work with continuous values. But actually, whether a computer, or any other calculation machine, is called digital or analog depends on where the decisive difference between the digital and the analog is located: in the value system used for calculations (discrete or continuous; and if numerical: binary or decimal), in the computing mechanism (electronic or mechanical/electromechanical, with as a complicating factor that electronics in its turn is divided in digital electronics, based on discrete voltage levels, and analog electronics, based on continuous ranges of voltage), or in its program control (stored in memory or controlled by patch cables and switches). In any case, our common contemporary computers are manifold digital: discrete-numerical-binary, discrete-electronic, and soft-programmable.

is always embedded in analog mechanisms – on the physical-material level of machinery and medium, but also on the level of material-semiotic translations into human-readable analogies and metaphors.

In that regard the domain of the analog covers more than just physical-proportional relations: it also includes associative relations based on resemblance and resonance. The notion of analog not coincidentally also alludes to the notion of analogy in the Aristotelian sense, that of the trope of proportional equivalence of two relations: A:B is as C:D. In other words, the domain of the analog is both analogous and analogical.

Software as language

Interestingly, the principle of discreteness leads us to the intersection between computation and language. Manovich already remarked that 'all communication requires discrete units' (Manovich 2001, 28). And indeed, any language – be it numerical, alphabetical, or pictorial – consists of discrete units, units that can be recognized, selected, and combined in order to express or signify something. As Roland Barthes put it: 'Language is, as it were, that which divides reality (for instance, the continuous spectrum of the colors is verbally reduced to a series of discontinuous terms)' (Barthes 1968, 64).

From the perspective of discreteness then, numerical language is not fundamentally different from linguistic language; hence, SOFTWARE IS LANGUAGE. The metaphor is based on structural analogies. One can create meaningful things with arbitrary numbers in the same way as one can create meaningful utterances with arbitrary sounds or symbols. To put it in structuralist linguistic terms: software and language both work with a set or chain of discrete arbitrary signifiers that are marked by difference, but that have no meaning in themselves. Both software and language work by selection and combination, whereby meaningless signifiers get attached to conceptual signifieds, compressed into signs. [120] And both evolve into various codified systems, each with its own conventions of vocabulary, syntax, semantics, and spelling, be it in Dutch or in English, or programming languages such as Perl or Java.

However, as with all metaphors, the metaphor SOFTWARE IS LANGUAGE has its limits, even to the point where the metaphor becomes delusive. This point resides in the issue of control and mutability. Language and software are both systems of ordered signifiers that are able to inscribe themselves in durable forms, but when it comes to control software and language diverge. While numerical and linguistic signification are both marked by arbitrary signifiers and arbitrary relations with signifieds, the numerical relation, once implemented in a machine, looses its arbitrariness. In a specific numerical environment (a specific program, routine, or data file), the relation between signifier and signified is formally-materially fixed and subjected to the formal-material laws of the specific code and the hardware it controls or by which it is controlled. This differs dramatically from the linguistic sign, where the relation between signifier and signified remains arbitrary and relatively fixed, as Saussure (1916) already noticed in his claims about the immutability

---

120. The dimensions of combination and selection has been theorized extensively by linguists and semioticians, usually in a two-dimensional scheme with a horizontal and a vertical axis, that have been given several labels: simultaneity and succession (Saussure 1916), syntagmatic and associative relations (Barthes 1968), and metonymical and metaphorical axes (Jakobson and Halle 1956).

and mutability of the sign.[121] In the Saussurean linguistic sign the connection between signifier and signified is secured by convention – no member of a speech community can alter at will the meaning of words.[122] As stable and as immutable as this seems to be, the attachment is not formally or inherently fixated. The boundaries between linguistic signifiers as well as the attached signifieds are far more tolerant for ambivalence, undecidability, and temporal transformation than they are in digital language. Executed digital code just halts or crashes in a case of ambivalence, or it gets stalled in an endless loop. Linguistic code may on such occasions develop into argument, philosophy, or even war, but it certainly does not stop functioning. On the contrary, its very productivity is based on the endless suspension of final signification, as Derrida (1978) argued. Hence, while the assignment of numbers to entities is as arbitrary as the assignment of words to things, once established the numerical relations are inextricably bound to the materiality of the signifier. On that level, digital code is more fixed than linguistic signs.

Coding the signifier

The question then is: what can be considered a signifier when it comes to digital code? Is it the arbitrarily assigned number, or does it reside in the material hardware inscription? In *My Mother Was a Computer* (which, notably, was announced for years with the provisionary title *Coding the Signifier),* Katherine Hayles preferred the latter option: 'Given the importance of the binary base, I suggest that the signifiers be considered as voltages [...] The signifieds are then the interpretations that others layers of code give to these voltages [...] and these interpretations in turn become signifiers for a still higher level interfacing with them' (Hayles 2005, 45). According to Hayles, this accounts for the relative immutability of digital code:

> At the level of binary code, the system can tolerate little if any ambiguity. For any physically embodied system, some noise and, therefore, possible ambiguities are always present. In the

---

121. De Saussure (1916) claimed, in a paragraph dedicated to the 'Immutability and mutability of the sign' that the linguistic sign is arbitrary regarding its relation between the signifier and the signified, immutable regarding its relation to the speech community, and mutable regarding its relation with time: 'The signifier, though to all appearances freely chosen with respect to the idea that it represents, is fixed, not free, with respect to the linguistic community that uses it. The masses have no voice in the matter, and the signifier chosen by language could be replaced by no other. [...] Time, which insures the continuity of language, wields another influence apparently contradictory to the first: the more or less rapid change of linguistic signs. In a certain sense, therefore, we can speak of both the immutability and the mutability of the sign' (Saussure 1916, 70-74).
122. Only Humpty Dumpty, the egg-shaped figure that Alice meets in 'Through the Looking-glass' (Carroll 2010 [1871]), claimed he could manipulate words independent from the conventions in the language-sharing collective:
'When I use a word,' Humpty Dumpty said, in rather a scornful tone, 'it means just what I choose it to mean – neither more or less.'
'The question is,' said Alice, 'whether you can make words mean so many different things.'
'The question is,' said Humpty Dumpty, 'which is to be master – that's all' (ibid., 202).
However, Humpty Dumpty was very aware of the involved labor and costs:
'When I make a word do a lot of work like that,' said Humpty Dumpty, 'I always pay it extra.' [...] 'Ah, you should see 'em come round me on a Saturday night,' Humpty Dumpty went on, wagging his head gravely from side to side, 'for to get their wages, you know' (ibid., 203).

case of digital computers, noise enters the system (among other places) in the voltage trail-off errors discussed earlier, but these are rectified into unambiguous signals of one and zero before they enter the bit stream. As the system builds up levels of programming languages such as compilers, interpreters, scripting languages, and so forth, they develop functionalities that permit increasingly greater ambiguities in the choices permitted or tolerated. (Hayles 2005, 46)

What Hayles sketches here is SOFTWARE AS LAYERS that build up from binary code through several translations into higher level programming languages that are more close and more prone to the dynamics and ambiguities of linguistic code.
Elsewhere she speaks of SOFTWARE AS TOWER OF BABEL (ibid., 110), indicating that the division in different computer control languages, aimed at achieving a unified seamlessly working system, also yields to the confusion of tongues and issues of untranslatability. Overall, the metaphor of layered languages accounts for the formal constraints of digital code as well as its relative flexibility. It acknowledges that code is strictly numerical and formal when close to the machine, and more symbolic and fuzzy when closer to the user interface.
It should be noted that Hayles' tropes of software go beyond the SOFTWARE IS LANGUAGE metaphor. Software is more than language, even though it often represents itself as such. As she remarks, 'Along with the hierarchical nature of code goes a dynamic of concealing and revealing that operates in ways that have no parallel in speech and writing' (ibid., 54). In other words, digital code is immutable and restricted in ways that linguistic code is not, but on other levels digital code is mutable and generative – again in ways that linguistic code is not. For Hayles, software is *performative,* and though this alludes to John Austin's famous speech act theory (1962), she insists that software is material, productive and 'performative in a much stronger sense than that attributed to language' (ibid., 50). [123]
This does not imply that software is inherently performative; it is not an autonomous agent. Assigning such powers to software is ideological in itself. It is the embedding and appropriation in institutions, companies, politics, law, and ordinary habits that make it appear as autonomous. The performativity of software, resulting in meaningful human-readable signs, can only emerge from the joint labor of human interpreters and machinic interpreters – a process that is, as we have seen before, mediated by digital-material metaphors.
In any case, the materiality and systematic fixation of arbitrary numerical representations does not rule out the possibility for human intervention and manipulation. Precisely because the logic of software is, in the last instance, anchored in a formal numerical system, which in its turn is materially anchored to machine states, it enables programmability and object manipulation – to return to Manovich's list: the principles of modularity, automation, and variability.

Software as objects
Manovich's second principle of digitality is dubbed modularity. This feature pertains to the cut-out entities that are represented as objects which can be split, combined, and reassembled

---

[123]. Other scholars have also tried to cover the ambivalent relation of software with language and called software 'executable language' (Cramer 2003; Galloway 2006; Schäfer 2008) and 'digital speech acts', (Poster 2001; Arns 2004, 2005).

into new objects. As modular elements they can be nested in larger-scale objects while still retaining their separate independent identities. Think for instance of the various elements that can be assembled on a single web page: html files, images, videos, sounds, advertising blocks, and database elements such as blog posts, comments, tags, dates, author's names, and so forth. Each element can in principle be accessed and transformed separately, without affecting the overall structure of the object as an assemblage. In its turn, each element consists of an assemblage of smaller independently formatted elements: database tables and data, fonts and characters, colors and forms, layers and pixels. Manovich calls this affordance the 'fractal structure of new media objects' (Manovich 2001, 30), hinting at Mandelbrot's fractal geometry of irregular shapes that expose self-similarity on all scales.

For Manovich, modularity constitutes the plane on which sets of arbitrary numbers get transformed into delineated objects on the user interface: SOFTWARE AS OBJECTS. These objects can be grasped, moved, modified as separate entities, yet they are bound by criteria for success or failure that have been determined before (Evens 2006). So-called object-oriented programming languages work explicitly with such relatively autonomous building blocks. Instead of organizing the code around separate tasks, they divide the code into operative entities in the form of modular objects. Manovich's notion of new media object explicitly alludes to object-oriented programming languages and object-oriented databases (Manovich 2001, 14).[124]

But also in interfaces or languages that are not called object-oriented, the material-metaphoric representation of digital cut-outs as objects is crucial for computer design, praxis, and literacy. As Crutzen and Kotkamp (2008) argue, object orientation has become a general approach, 'a methodology and theory for interpretation, representation, and analysis of worlds of human interaction with which the computer interfaces' (ibid., 201). The authors show that this object-oriented approach is by no means neutral, as it freezes user roles in ready-made objects and defines interaction only on the technical and syntactical level. The approach produces subject positions for users without room for negotiation and doubt regarding the semantic and pragmatic ambiguities that occur in 'being-in-interaction' (see also Kotkamp 2009).

Manovich's principle of modularity returns prominently in all other principles. Clearly, modularity is more than a formal feature since it is constitutive for the author's approach. Which makes it so much more remarkable that he does not specifically address the non-arbitrary, political choices that determine digital objects. Choices and politics reside in the decision of what elements are assembled in the modular object, and by which metaphors the carved-out object will be represented on the interface, thus also determining what is left inaccessible and demediated. Like in object-oriented programming the built-in constraints define and assign insides and outsides, privileges, roles, and access. By approaching these objects as material metaphors and by connecting the technical-indexical features of the objects to their symbolic forms and affordances, such instances of non-neutrality and ideology could be revealed. Moreover, it could also demonstrate that digital entities are not completely covered by the conceptual metaphor SOFTWARE AS OBJECTS, since they hover between the realm of signs and the realm of objects, again on the border of the order of language.

---

124. Interestingly, the metaphor of object-orientation has been extended outside the domain of software design and digital praxis. Harman (2002) proposes an object-oriented philosophy and Latour (2005a) an object-oriented politics.

TRANSCODING THE DIGITAL

Between things and language

The feature of modularity again shows how principles of language and digital computation overlap. As we have seen already in the previous section, digital entities acquire from the domain of language and signs the qualities of difference, iterability, inscription, selection, combination, signification, polysemy, expression, and representation. However, from the domain of objects they also acquire qualities: relative stability, modifiability, resistance, copyability, transferability, and mobility. Precisely the combination of these features generates digital sign-tool-objects that can be analyzed as digital-material metaphors, material-semiotic assemblages of objects and semiotic-ideological interpellations. This holds for icons, commands, and files, but also for Internet entities such as hyperlinks, Facebook accounts, and even more complex assemblages such as The Pirate Bay. [125]

Nonetheless, there are also profound differences between digital and linguistic objects. Contrary to digital objects linguistic objects rarely retain all their qualities after transference or combination. After all, that is precisely the power of conceptual metaphor and semiotic iteration: by transference or insertion into another context particular qualities are selected and embedded in another praxis. On the other hand, transferred digital objects also do not necessarily retain all their qualities after transference into other contexts. Digital transference may imply conversion to another format, and while this does preserve the basic proportional pattern of a data object, it usually does not retain all previous qualities and affordances of the object. These refinements are not just academic or technical nitpicking. The issue whether digital entities should be considered objects or language has deep political and juridical implications. The mainstream software and digital entertainment industry is founded on the principle of objectification and commodification of digital entities. For them, SOFTWARE IS AN OWNABLE OBJECT. As a result, they find themselves in a perpetual battle with copying, downloading, and file-sharing users. These users are frequently accused of having the wrong ethics regarding the property of objects. As the non-skippable opening segment on many DVDs reminds us, 'You wouldn't steal a car, you wouldn't steal a handbag' (Motion Picture Association 2004). However, it can be argued that these users just do not consider digital entities as ownable objects, but as language entities that circulate freely.

---

125. The Pirate Bay (TPB) has been the world's largest BitTorrent indexing and sharing site for years. After the site owners were convicted in 2009 for copyright violations in Sweden, it was announced that the site would be sold to an advertising company for $8.5 million. Although the transaction eventually did not take place, the announcement caused a huge uproar among thousands of users about the betrayal and sell-out of anti-capitalist ideals. The figure of the pirate is in itself already an interesting and ambivalent conceptual metaphor that can be mobilized by copyright prosecutors as a pejorative term and by downloaders and political parties as a positive reappropriation (see also Schäfer 2011, 204, 207). Moreover, the assemblage of Pirate Bay is a perfect example of a material metaphor. As Rasmus Fleischer (2009) put it on the Nettime mailing list, TPB is 'among other things: a domain name, a web site, an ad selling business, a blog, the world's largest bittorrent tracker, a clothing store, three persons, a swarm of users, a symbol.' Fleischer raises interesting questions regarding the objectification of TPB in the light of its possible sell-out: 'We are used to imagine The Pirate Bay as a legendary entity fighting an epic battle, on behalf of the millions of file-sharers. However, it is not exactly a legendary entity that is being sold. It is something different. So what is about to be sold? [...] This assemblage is now being disassembled and reassembled, in one way or another. That means something else than a 'sell-out' of all the parts. All the details of the affair are not clear yet, but to clear up the picture, we should first consider each part for itself, and ask three simple questions: 1) Is it ownable?; 2) Is it sellable?; 3) Is it copyable?'

For them SOFTWARE IS LANGUAGE. The legal and political battles on this issue will probably never be settled, since it is ontologically undecidable whether digital entities are objects or signs. They are both, inextricably intertwined in digital language-objects. This results in objects that are inherently *copyable* (Schäfer 2011, 56) and hence distributable. In that regard, it is actually odd that Manovich does not include this feature in his list of fundamental principles of software.

Software as prescription

Manovich's third principle is what he calls *automation*. This feature is partially derived from the numerical and modularity principle. Since each modular object consists basically of assigned numbers, they can be computed and conditionally manipulated as objects, that is, programmed to perform automated functions. This principle in a way reunites hardware and software; it alludes to CODE AS AUTOMAT, AS MECHANISM, but also to CODE AS PRESCRIPTION that is a blueprint that determines completely the output.[126] According to Manovich, with this principle 'human intentionality can be removed from the creative process, at least in part' (Manovich 2001, 32).

While the metaphor of SOFTWARE AS PRESCRIPTION seems to imply a strictly mechanical functionality, the machine at stake is not an ordinary industrial machine that just delivers products according to a fixed blueprint. Recall, a computer is not a pianola. The point is that the computer and its affordances are not fixed, but variable, precisely because of its programmability.

The *variability* of digital code is Manovich's fourth principle. It pertains to both the mutability of the machine, which can be configured to run various tasks, as well as to the variability and mutability of its data products, which can be delivered, represented, and manipulated differently by different interfaces. Software, then, is inherently variable, modifiable, extendable, updatable, and scalable. It may be a recipe, but in any case a modifiable recipe.

In other words, programmable variable code is that which elevates the machine into a super automat, a 'metamedium' (Kay and Goldberg 1977), highly variable in its configurations, affordances, and end-products.

Software as database

Manovich's main conceptual metaphor to indicate programmability and variability is that of the database, more precisely SOFTWARE AS MEDIA DATABASE. According to Manovich, the Internet 'can be thought of as one huge distributed media database' (Manovich 2001, 35), while in general a 'new media object can be defined as one or more interfaces to a multimedia database' (ibid., 37). On the one hand, the metaphor of the database is a metonym, taking one specific application as standing for computing and software in general. On the other hand, the database metaphor extends the metaphor of the metamedium by evoking the imagery of the totality of collected cultural resources, contained in a huge media database. It covers what Jos de Mul has called *database ontology*, a flexible and dynamic ontology based on persistent storage and software that enables the four basic operations of any computation, the ABCD of Add, Browse, Change, and Destroy (De Mul 2009).

---

126. See Zinken et al. (2008) for an interesting instantiation of the metaphor CODE AS BLUEPRINT in their analysis of the discourse metaphors of DNA and genes. The authors show how DNA is often framed as computer code, whereby computer code is conceived as a strict blueprint that completely determines the outcome.

For Manovich's overall argument about digital culture, the database is an important conceptual and material metaphor. It refers to the digital-material praxis of collecting and storing separate items in a data structure, and retrieving parts of them as linked information by algorithms of selection and combination. But, more importantly, for Manovich it also refers to a general cultural dynamic: 'The computer age brought a new cultural algorithm: reality → media → data → database' (Manovich 2001, 224-225). While this formula describes roughly what digitization is (the translation of mediated representations into digital data objects), and while indeed digitization and databased control is an overall tendency, Manovich's claims go further than that.

According to Manovich, the database is a new cultural form in its own right, and as such it competes and tends to overrule the key cultural form of the narrative as privileged by the novel and cinema (ibid., 218). Although he notes that, 'we should not expect that new media would completely replace narrative with database' (ibid., 229), he positions database and narrative as a dichotomy. In Manovich's words:

> As a cultural form, database represents the world as a list of items and it refuses to order this list. In contrast, a narrative creates a cause-and-effect trajectory of seemingly unordered items (events). Therefore, database and narrative are natural enemies. Competing for the same territory of human culture, each claims an exclusive right to make meaning out of the world. (ibid., 225)

In short, the architecture of the database stands in opposition with the linearity of the classical narrative. Whereas the database is, due to its separation of content and interface, open to perform any query and transformation of its elements, thereby enabling the retrieval of endlessly variable combinations and recombinations, the narrative is closed, firmly held together by its unity of content and interface.

Manovich also claims that databases reverse the relationship between the two classic semiotical axes of language, syntagm (sequence, combination) and paradigm (substitution, selection). In a narrative the paradigmatic axis from which the words are selected is materially absent, implicit, virtual, while the syntagmatic axis is explicit, materially present, articulated in speech or writing. In a database, Manovich argues this relation is reversed: the paradigmatic set is materially present, stored explicitly in the database as lists of alternative terms, while the syntagmatic is immaterial, implicit, and virtual, pertaining to possible outcomes of database operations (Manovich 2001, 230-231).[127]

Despite his quest for digital materialism, Manovich's claims about databases, programmability and variability, comes here eerily close to the ideology of digital wizardry – SOFTWARE AS AUTOMAGIC, the belief in the virtually unrestrained possibilities of digitization and programmability, as proclaimed by overenthusiastic 1995 gurus. Some disclaimers have to be made. The fact that digital entities are inherently programmable, variable, and 'databasable', does not imply that anything is possible or that every intervention costs the same effort. Besides the constraints induced by the material limits of processing power and computer memory, every interface always overrides the

---

127. Katherine Hayles, insisting that narrative and database are 'natural symbionts' instead of 'natural enemies', has criticized Manovich's assumptions regarding databases and its axes. She argues that databases are not paradigmatic in the sense Manovich attributes to them: 'In neither the rows nor columns *[of a database table – MvdB]* does a logic of substitution obtain; the terms are not synonyms or sets of alternative terms but different data values' (Hayles 2012, 180).

default of mutability, thereby limiting and framing what is available for access and intervention. So while mutability is indeed the default setting of the digital, this default mode is never on. It is always already set in a restricted mode.

Software as battlefield

Manovich did not elaborate on the wider social and political implications of the built-in restrictions and prescriptions imposed by software, but other scholars have. For example, lawyer and political activist Lawrence Lessig warns unabatedly against the growing architecture of regulatory control and non-democratic governance enforced by code (Lessig 1999). Such regulation ranges from required identification by digital certificates to the automatic blockade of indecent language in online fora to Digital Rights Management software that prevents copying or other acts considered illegal. Lessig contends, CODE IS LAW. Here code tends to take over legal and political functions which before, for good reasons, were assigned to democratically controlled or at least more transparent institutions. Alexander Galloway takes a similar stance in his analysis of how power and control is effectuated in distributed networks and network societies (Galloway 2004). Galloway argues that this power is exercised and maintained by means of protocol, that is, by software-driven procedures and standards that orchestrate data exchange. For Galloway, CODE IS PROTOCOL, and PROTOCOL IS TECHNO-POLITICAL POWER: built-in control of the behavior of all network nodes, be they computers, interfaces, individuals, or organizations.

Still, no built-in control by software is ever complete. It takes ongoing work, maintenance, and re-adjustment. It has to be sustained by perpetual updates from security patchers and digital rights managers, in their never ending battle with hackers, spammers, virus creators, downloaders, search engine manipulators, and other improper users. These more or less illegitimate trespassers thrive on the same principle of the mutability of software as their prosecutors, and therefore they will always find new apertures – not coincidentally called 'leaks' in a discourse that aspires to immutability and containment.

While this already evokes the image of SOFTWARE AS BATTLEFIELD, the open-source community explicitly takes this metaphor as a leading theme. Here the battle is not about finding apertures in proprietary software or computer systems, but about the economic, juridical, and ethical battle between closed-source software and open-source software. [128] Unlike the mainstream closed-source software industry, open-source developers implement the mutability and copyability of software by default, and grant it as a principal right to its users by providing the mutable source-code along with the executable code. Although the two types of software could exist juxtaposed without any interference, proprietary software manufacturers consider open source a threat to their business model, and fight it with all means available: economical, juridical, political, and symbolic (Van den Boomen and Schäfer 2005). While both sides have adopted the metaphor of software wars, the open-source community is more explicit in its battlefield imagery. For example, in the yearly updates of a detailed war map (see Figure 6, for the 2011 map). The war map de-

---

128. Tellingly, the term 'open source' does not emerge in Manovich' book until the very last page. And even then, it is used as a metaphor for general frictionless automagic availability: 'To use a metaphor from computer culture, new media transforms all culture and cultural theory into an "open source"' (Manovich 2001, 333).

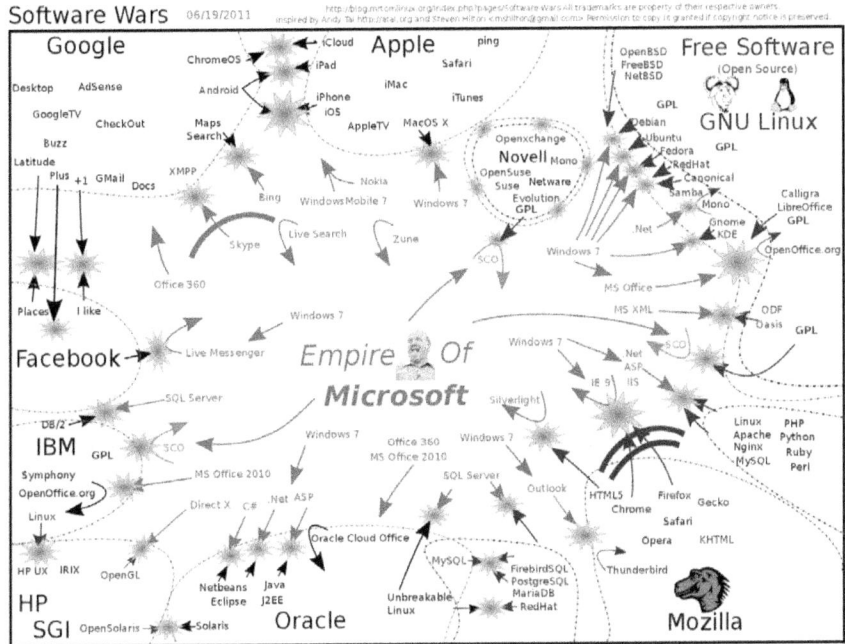

Figure 6. SOFTWARE AS BATTLEFIELD, represented as a war map of the battles between open source and closed source software.

picts closed adversary empires, liberated regions, and some free enclaves inside closed empires. The borders are sparkled with specific conflict zones where juridical and economic battles are still going on between specific software objects. The metaphor of software wars may seem only rhetorical, but it is in fact a powerful discourse metaphor that positions all parties and software objects in terms of good guys and bad guys, friends and enemies.

Software as translator

Manovich's description of the principles of digitality up to this point — numerical representation, modularity, automation, and variability — once again demonstrate that the notion of digital objects is not just a metaphorical attribution which only conceptually exists in the minds of human users. Those objects have a formal and material base in what may be called digital onto-epistemology, sometimes taking the form of a database ontology.

But we have also seen how software itself is imbued with metaphors, not only the metaphors implied in Manovich's principles — SOFTWARE AS NUMBERS, SOFTWARE AS OBJECTS, SOFTWARE AS DATABASE — but also extensions and additions such as SOFTWARE AS LANGUAGE, AS LAW, AS BATTLEFIELD. And precisely because the digital also has language-like and conflictual properties, it cannot be determined completely by Manovich's formal features. Like language, it perpetuates through towers of Babel, marked by polysemy, ambiguity, translation problems, politics, and conflict. These social-semiotic issues are not covered by the seemingly neutral principles of endless variability and programmability that Manovich lays out; often they even run counter to these principles. However, Manovich does not include these wider implications in his description of the formal principles of digitality; he saves the sociocultural entailments for his fifth and last principle, called *transcoding*. Whereas Manovich's first four principles are formal-material features of digitality, his last one refers to the mechanism by which digital materiality gets translated into cultural-symbolic materiality. Not coincidentally this is the only principle that comes as a verb and not as a noun – transcoding is an activity, a process, not an ontological feature.

The term itself is a metaphor, or better a metonym, imported from software praxis. Transcoding is the act of translating a data file into another format, such as converting a Word document into pdf file or a sound file into visual graphs. In Manovich's appropriation the term refers to the process by which the 'computer layer' gets translated into a 'cultural layer' (Manovich 2001, 46), a 'process of "conceptual transfer" from the computer world to culture at large' (ibid., 47). Manovich illustrates this with the two-layered structure of a computer image:

> On the level of representation, it belongs on the side of human culture, automatically entering in dialog with other images [...] But on another level, it is a computer file that consists of a machine-readable header, followed by numbers representing color values of its pixels. On this level it enters into a dialog with other computer files. (ibid., 45)

What we perceive and conceive as a digital image is a transcoded, composite 'blend of human and computer meanings' (ibid., 46), with the two layers inextricably entangled. To use my terms: what we conceive as an icontologized digital image is a composite of iconic-analog, indexical, and symbolic relations. Transcoding seems to be an apt metaphor for the mechanisms by which composite sign-tool-objects acquire their computational, interfacial, and cultural form. The term is able to cover any transposition and translation into any other format or modality, whether from computer code to another computer code, computer code to cultural code, and cultural code to computer code. Accordingly, the metaphor of transcoding enables parsing of the various entanglements of different kinds of code.

The computerization of culture and the culturalization of computing
However, while Manovich admits that the computer layer and the cultural layer mutually influence each other, he insists on a generalized tendency he calls the 'computerization of culture'. This suggests only one-way traffic from computer concepts to cultural concepts:

> In new media lingo, to "transcode" something is to translate it into another format. The computerization of culture gradually accomplishes similar transcoding in relation to all cultural categories and concepts. That is, cultural categories and concepts are substituted, on the level of meaning and/or the language, by new ones that derive from computer's ontology, epistemology and pragmatics. New media thus acts as a forerunner of this more general process of cultural reconceptualization. (ibid., 47)

It is certainly the case that cultural categories and concepts are impregnated with computational forms, meanings, and metaphors, and indeed, we can perceive tendencies of the computerization of culture. The proliferation of the database as a dominant and ever extending cultural form and social organizer is a case in point. For example, the decision of who is a legitimate citizen and who is an illegal non-citizen depends heavily on having the right records in the right databases. But that is not the whole story. Manovich only seems to recognize the influence of the computer layer on the cultural layer, not the other way around. He does not question how and by which transcodings the computer has been divided into hardware and software, turned into a medium, and subsequently into a metamedium. Neither does Manovich acknowledge the cultural tropes that inform and organize how we conceive the computer, its operations, its modalities, its interfaces, its software, and its products. Manovich's clear-cut split between what he describes as the cultural layer and the computer layer is also problematic here as if these were existing separate ontological domains preceding any semiosis.[129] As examples of cultural categories Manovich mentions: the encyclopedia, story and plot, composition and point of view; and as examples of computer categories he discusses concepts such as lists, records, and arrays, process and packet, sorting and matching, function and variable, computer language, data structure and database (ibid., 45-46). However, there is actually no way to decide whether categories such as a record, page, packet, mail, files, servers, and clients belong to the computer or the cultural layer. I would argue that all names and concepts that are used to carve out objects and operations from the digital soup are cultural concepts. They are metaphors, imported from other cultural practices, molded, blended, and incorporated into new objects and new meanings. Eventually, they may get icontologized in their new forms, and subsequently obtain an extra dictionary entry referring to their new meaning in computer discourse, as happened with mail, packet, memory, web, and chat. No new words are needed for new phenomena; combinations and metaphors are language's and culture's efficiency device, affording an inexhaustible source for re-use, re-appropriation, translation, and transcoding.

In other words, the computer layer itself is already infused with cultural tropes and analog representations. It is formed and in-formed by symbols, analogies, and metaphors that afford epistemological and operational access – what I have called digital-material metaphors. They function not so much as bridges between an ontologically separated computer domain and a cultural domain, but rather as tiny connectors between parts of digital code and analog code.

Digital-analog sandwiches
Hence, there is no computer domain that is not already cultural. And there is no digital object that is not also analog. This is not only because physical analog patterns function as metaphors for digital processes, but also because cultural analogies and metaphors format digital objects. Indeed, the notion of analog here has a double meaning. On the one hand, it pertains to analog representations as morphological translations of physical properties into proportional inscriptions. (For example, the grooves in vinyl records as analog captures of sound vibrations or the shades of black and white on photosensitive plates as analog capture of light). On the other hand, it pertains to analogy, the trope of proportional resemblance. Katherine Hayles employs an illustrative metaphor to describe the alignment and the productive interplay between the digital and the analog, each with properties that complement the other:

> Even though scientific instrumentation uses digital technologies for analysis and imaging, some portions of the chain that employ analog representation usually remain, typically at the

---

129. This is comparable to the split that is often made between technology and society which has been criticized by Bruno Latour in *'Technology is society made durable'* (1991).

beginning and the end of the process [...] I will call this digital/analog structure the 'Oreo,' for like the two black biscuits sandwiching a white filling between them, the initial and final analog representations connected with embodied materialities sandwich between them a digital middle where fragmentations and recombinations take place. (Hayles 2005, 207)

In Hayles' metaphor of the Oreo cookie, transcoding consists of the sandwiching of the digital cream between analog biscuit layers, a sandwiching that forms and in-forms both the digital cream and the biscuits. The Oreo structure has no fixed scale and can be found on several levels: a web site is a digital-analog sandwich, but also an email message, a server, an icon, a menu item, a database, or a programming language. The Oreo metaphor indicates that the digital cream cannot be delivered or consumed without the analog cookies holding it together. This implies that every digital concept-object is always already transcoded, always already a material metaphor, packaged in analog tissue, derived from physical proportionality and metaphorical analogy.

In this sense, transcoding is certainly not the straightforward substitution of one type of code with an equivalent other code. This holds even for the seemingly strict instance of converting digital formats. The myth of digital conversion without loss is persistent, yet in any conversion something is lost and something is gained. Properties can disappear (for example, the feature of background transparency when converting a gif image into a jpg image), mutability can diminish or increase. Therefore, even at the level of technical file conversion, transcoding is always a transformation, a change in form and function, and a change in interfacial affordance and social organizing power.

3 — DIGITAL-MATERIAL CODING AND TRANSCODING

Despite my critique of some of Manovich's principles, his list provides a useful framework that at least covers a part of what software actually is and does. It is indeed numerical, object-oriented, programmable and variable, and it does indeed enable transcoding. But most of all – and this seems to be rather undertheorized in Manovich's elaboration – software is relational and material, and therefore, non-neutral, ideological, and political. The following section will explore these issues of materiality and relationality, including the metaphors that are mobilized to indicate these features.

The materiality of software

As odd as it may sound, software is a relatively new issue in new media discourse. In the 1990s, the debates were mainly framed in terms of virtuality and cyberspace metaphors (Heim 1994; Rushkoff 1994; Lévy 1994; Negroponte 1995). At that time, software was rarely addressed, let alone problematized; software was seen AS AUTOMAGIC. Only when software became an ordinary tool in the hands of ordinary users, did it gradually become an issue, especially in the emerging academic discipline of new media studies.

While in popular discourse software still tends to be framed as magic, or at least as immaterial and hence incomprehensible, most new media scholars emphasize that software is material (that is, *if* they actually say something about software, which is still most often not the case). Katherine Hayles was one of the first who focused on this specific materiality (Hayles 1993a), and various others followed (Kittler 1995; Manovich 2001; Fuller 2003; Chun 2004; Galloway 2004; Harris and Taylor 2005; Mackenzie 2006; Kirschenbaum 2008; Schäfer 2011).

Though the notion of SOFTWARE AS MATERIAL seems to be widely acknowledged, the onto-epistemological modus of this digital materiality is still far from clear since it also seems to imply something immaterial. For that reason, some scholars invent neologisms such as 'im/material' (Harris and Taylor 2005) or 'in-material' (Schäfer 2011). But even that does not solve the riddle completely. As Wendy Chun noticed, 'Software is, or should be, a notoriously difficult concept. [...] As a set of instructions, its material status is unstable; indeed, the more you dissect software, the more it falls away' (Chun 2004, 28).

And she is right. Software may be seen as material and performative, but this already implies several levels or modes of materiality. In this study we already encountered:

1. the materiality of arbitrary media-specific signs (programming languages, interface semiotics);
2. the materiality of non-arbitrary physical artifacts (machines, processors, memory, storage devices, hardware interfaces, cables, routers, switches);
3. the materiality of non-arbitrary inscriptions and patterns (executable code, binary code, magnetic poles, voltage states), and
4. the materiality of non-arbitrary digital-material metaphors (objects, tools, places, commands).

Levels 1 and 4 refer to the material semiotics that encapsulate digital processing to make it readable and operational for humans. Levels 2 and 3 remind us that software is inherently attached to hardware, there where it becomes readable and operational for the machine. In short, there are materialities that reside inside the machine and materialities that reside outside the machine.

Inside the machine

All computational hardware is useless without software, and software is useless without the proper hardware. In our contemporary electronic-digital machines constructed on the basis of Von Neumann architecture, computation consists of processual calculations going on in the processor, supported by the *temporary storage* and the retrieval of previous calculations, plus the more *durable storage* of instruction sets and output products. Temporary storage is usually done by inscriptions in random access memory, while durable storage takes the form of inscriptions on a hard disk or another storage device.

As digital humanities scholar Matthew Kirschenbaum (2008) demonstrated in his inquiry into the materiality of digital processing, storage is a largely neglected mechanism in popular digerati manifestos, as well as in academic new media studies. Both discourses tend to focus on interfacial representations, leaving the digits in either an ephemeral realm of supposed mathematical immateriality or in a black box of machinery that remains closed for cultural analysis.

Forensic traces and formal patterns

In order to open up the field of digital storage for further inquiries, Kirschenbaum proposes the insightful distinction between what he calls the forensic and formal materiality of coded inscriptions. *Forensic* inscriptions refer to the physical-material traces that are inscribed or left behind on hard disks: CODE AS TRACES. These traces are arbitrary signifiers that can be made visible with the proper forensic operations and lab apparatuses (revealing for example traces of magnetic poles on a hard disk that have been changed or overwritten with data). This kind of information can be crucial in forensic inquiries and criminal investigations.

However, no specific indexical reference to a particular act or the use of a particular software program can be made from these traces, nor can their code or symbolic meaning be inferred. The traces just show that something has happened (or not). They can only show difference. As

Kirschenbaum puts it, 'forensic materiality rests upon the principle of individualization (basic to modern forensic science and criminalistics), the idea that no two things in the physical world are ever exactly alike' (Kirschenbaum 2008, 10).

Formal inscriptions are also coded inscriptions on hardware, but unlike forensic inscriptions, they form a non-arbitrary pattern, a formal environment for symbol manipulation, from which more information than just difference can be extracted: CODE AS PATTERN. These patterns, or their remnants, can be made visible with dedicated user interfaces, thereby revealing the type of data object and releasing its indexical relation to particular software. In Kirschenbaum's words, formal inscriptions 'will only become visible when the data object is subjected to the appropriate formal processes, which is to say when the appropriate software environment is invoked' (ibid., 13).

It is tempting to equate forensic materiality with hardware and formal materiality with software, but that would be missing the point. Not only, as Kirschenbaum (ibid., 13) notes because the line between hardware and software can be blurred (as for example in firmware and embedded systems with pre-programmed hardware), but also because all data on a computer (stored as well as erased or changed) always leave forensic traces that can be reassembled as patterned data objects when appropriately processed. The difference between forensic and formal materiality is a matter of different interfacing and processing. The interface determines what level of materiality is revealed: forensic traces or formal patterns.

Outside the machine

Besides the forensic and formal there are more levels of materiality that contribute to the dynamic ontology of software. Digital materiality does not only reside in the executed processes and stored data inside the machine, but it also produces traces and patterns outside the machine. It starts with the way computer code comes into being, that is, the labor, translations, and transcodings mobilized in its development. Kirschenbaum sketches vividly the heterogeneous stuff from which software is produced:

> Software is the product of white papers, engineering specs, marketing reports, conversations and collaborations, intuitive insights, professional expertise, venture capital (in other words, money), late nights (in other words, labor) caffeine, and other artificial stimulants. (ibid., 14-15)

And this heterogeneous assembling does not stop after signing, sealing, and delivering executable code. Software developer and philosopher Adrian Mackenzie (2006) puts his finger on SOFTWARE AS RELATION:

> Software is a neighborhood of relations whose contours trace contemporary production, communication and consumption. Code is a multivalent index of the relations running among different classes of entity: originators, prototypes and recipients. These classes might include people, situations, organizations, places, devices, habits and practices. In code and coding, relations are assembled, dismantled, bundled and dispersed within and across contexts. (Mackenzie 2006, 169)

Mackenzie stresses here the necessity of conceiving SOFTWARE AS INDEX: as a thing-sign with multiple material causal relations to things outside itself and outside the machine. Though Mackenzie does not elaborate on this metaphor, the index is an interesting figure in itself, not in the least because of its prominent role in digital praxis. For every website and every webserver directory the starting page is per default called index.html (or index.php, depending on the used scripting language), indicating that a website is in principle a set of pages made accessible by an index, basically a list of links. Even though most websites today are not constructed as HTML pages, but are rather assembled data fragments extracted from databases, the index remains the basic structure here. A database can be seen in general as an index of all its available data, and the same holds for search engines. Contrary to the common idea that a search engine is an application (or company) that 'searches the Internet for you', it does not search the Internet – it just queries its own index. Search engines are indexes, but also indexing machines: they update their index by adding data derived from your acts of searching and by the 'crawling' the web. [130] In the same vein, the sharing and like buttons that sparkle practically all websites today are not only distributed indexes that refer to the respective social media sites, but they also are little indexing machines operated by the clicks of users. In that regard, database ontology is also index ontology: not only a data structure of containment inside the machine, but also a dynamic structure of relations and invitations to things outside the machine.

As Mackenzie noted, these things outside the machine include people, organizations, places, and so on. Put differently, SOFTWARE IS A MEDIATOR, an actor in an actor-network, able to enroll and assemble other actors – human and non-human hardware, software, and wetware. Needless to say, hardware and software are useless without humans – users, operators, manufacturers, developers, engineers, system managers, system architects, and helpdesk professionals. In order to keep this network of hardware, software and wetware, up and running, all actors have to be aligned, doing their visible and invisible work in the work-net, rendering it as a taken-for-granted network-thing.

Yet, there is no way to determine *a priori* what actor – hard, soft or human – is decisive in a particular digital praxis. All actors are inherently intra-networked: inextricably interdependent and mutually co-constructing each other, in an endless leapfrog race of updates, upgrades, and re-indexing. Arguably, these updates not only pertain to hardware and software, but also to humans. By using hardware and software humans also adjust, accommodate, and transform themselves: their cognition and interests, their ways of doing and learning, their ways of communicating and socializing change with the tools they use. Any usage of code, computers, and sign-tool-objects interpellates the user ideologically, and assigns specific subject positions and privileges. [131]

---

130. That search engines send out 'crawlers' and 'spiders' to trace new or updated webpages is of course a misleading metaphor, as Shirley Niemans noted in her master thesis: 'Contrary to what the name suggests, crawlers don't actually travel the Web, but they maintain a long list of URLs that either are indexed already or are known to exist. From this list, the crawler selects a URL that has not been indexed and retrieves the page for analysis (parsing) by the indexing program' (Niemans 2009, 13).
131. A detailed specification of new social categories, subject positions, divisions, and interpellations still has to be documented. The transformation of the subject in the computer age has been theorized thus far in rather general terms, such as the *prosumer* (Toffler 1980) and *produser* (Bruns 2008), stressing the fusion of producer-consumer and producer-user, and the far more sophisticated yet also general metaphor of the *cyborg* (Haraway 1985), which covers the connateness of cybernetics and organic life, humans and machines, nature and culture, science and fiction. More recent analyses of subject transformations point at the perpetual production and reinforcement of the neoliberal subject (Dean 2003; Jarrett 2008) and the loss of collectivity on social network sites (Hui and Halpin 2013). Yet, these studies too, however elaborated, address overall tendencies that supposedly affect all subjects in the same manner.

4 — REPOSITIONING MATERIALITY

Returning to the four levels of materiality of code mentioned at the beginning of this section – the materiality of signs, of physical artifacts, of coded inscriptions, and of digital-material metaphors – we can conclude that even more levels of materiality can be identified in the interactions between these levels. Inside the machine coded inscriptions on physical artifacts produce CODE AS TRACES (forensic materiality) and CODE AS PATTERNS (formal materiality), and outside the machine the intricate semiotics of signs, languages, discourses, coded objects, and material metaphors enrolls and repositions objects and subjects in new contexts – CODE AS INDEX, CODE AS MEDIATOR. Code rules materially and symbolically – not only inside the black box of software and machinery, but also outside the box. Notably, this outside should not be equated with culture and society, leaving the inside of the machine to something called technology, separated from culture. The inside of the machine is as cultural and societal as the outside, and the outside is as technological as the inside. Only their materializations differ, and as we have seen, materiality comes in many forms.

Materiality is not simply physicality or substance. Katherine Hayles describes the aim of her trilogy – inquiries into respectively cybernetic discourse (Hayles 1999), artistic technotexts (Hayles 2002), and the worldviews of speech, writing, and code (Hayles 2005) – as 'repositioning materiality as distinct from physicality' (ibid., 2). Materiality, she asserts, is 'an emergent property created through dynamic interactions between physical characteristics and signifying practices' (ibid., 3). Elsewhere she calls this approach New Materialism. She points out 'the New Materialism I am advocating in this book [...] insists that technologies and texts be understood as mutually interpenetrating and constituting one another' (ibid., 142). This materialism takes materiality as a dynamic process rather than as an ontological state of being, and that is indeed what we need to understand digital-material objects and code.

The returning call for a new materialism
Hayles was not the first to call for a new materialism (cf. Pratt 1922), and probably will also not be the last. The call has to be repeated again and again, especially since the counterforces of essentialism are strong, in cultural praxis as well as in academic analyses. Time and again, critical scholars find traces or even foundational gestures of essentializing closure in the work of their fellow thinkers. This results in the perpetual proclamation of the necessity of a new materialism that is dynamic and politically radical: from Marx' inversion of Hegel and Feuerbach into historical materialism (Marx 1924) to the 1970s structuralist materialism of language and ideology (Coward and Ellis 1977) to Deleuzian and feminist new materialism (Braidotti 2001; Barad 2003; Van der Tuin 2008). Plus not to forget the various branches of digital materialism (Hayles 1999; Manovich 2001; Harris and Taylor 2005; Kirschenbaum 2008; Van den Boomen et al. 2009).

The declaration of a new materialism is always timely. Whether called material semiotics (Law and Mol 1995), transmateriality (Whitelaw 2008), or new materialism (Van der Tuin and Dolphijn 2010), the aim is to formulate an onto-epistemology that is non-essentialist, non-deterministic, non-transcendent, non-Cartesian, non-dichotomic, non-dialectical, non-idealistic, non-representationalist, non-teleological, non-reifying, non-metaphysical, non-reductionist, and non-universalist. Indeed, there are a lot of pitfalls to avoid. And indeed, the contours of new materialisms are usually articulated by rejection and negative terms (some even include 'non-negative' as a prerequisite). Maybe there is no other way than repeating the critiques again and again.

Software as material metaphor

In any case, an inquiry into the riddle of digital praxis and the ontology of software cannot be done without a thorough rethinking of materiality. It cannot be stressed enough that digital praxis is a material praxis, involving several instantiations of material and materiality. The materially stored inscriptions, whether temporary or persistent, [132] correspond, when processed, to conditional changes in the hardware, forensic and formal material transformations that are partially and selectively represented by the user interface, which subsequently interpellates the user as a subject. This implicates not only a materiality of signs, physical apparatuses, social-cultural configurations, and user situatedness (media-specific materialities that are at stake in all media and signifying systems, from speech to print to photography and television), but also a materiality of coded numerical inscriptions that tends to escape semiotics and cultural analysis.

What is more, it also escapes human consciousness. After all, the level of numbers, the level of machine-readable binary code is unreadable for humans. [133] As humans we are just not equipped with a perceptual or cognitive apparatus to read the formal-digital as such, to read patterns of binary numbers, and infer their meaning or effects. Even a translation from binary to decimal numbers will not do; we would even have no clue whether the set of numbers represents an image, a text, or part of a program. We need context and non-numerical symbolic signs to make sense of this digital soup.

Only when translated and bundled into symbolic code (textual or graphic) this code can be made readable, writable, and executable by humans. However, not by humans in general – only those that are properly configured: disciplined and educated humans, with subject positions ranging from professional software engineers to office workers to legitimate members of a community to ordinary users. This is the level where digital-material metaphors intervene as interfacial translators and mediators between machine-readable code and human-readable code. Software cannot function without digital-material metaphors, ranging from menus and icons to Facebook friends and The Pirate Bay. These software-generated sign-tool-objects may import conceptual metaphorical load from any context, but once instantiated as digital object they are profoundly material and powerful. They evoke further translations by enabling the distribution of rights, abilities, and permissions, by configuring and aligning users: their minds, their hands, their goals, their semiotics, their knowledge, their acts, their subject positions.

Software-generated metaphorical objects are material metaphors, but also software as such can be seen as a material metaphor, both in the Haylesian interface-oriented sense (Hayles 2002) and in the anthropological object-oriented sense (Ray 1987). Software typically exemplifies Hayles' material metaphor as it provides a media-specific interface that enables the transference between selected material-physical affordances and symbolic language. Where-

---

132. As Kirschenbaum (2008, 25-27) pointed out, the common-sense idea of the temporality and evanescence of digital storage – 'easily erasable and then gone forever' – is only experienced by ordinary users with a limited interface and apparatus. From the forensic-material perspective every contact always leaves a trace somewhere on the computer, and this causes serious problems for security and intelligence services that sometimes want to erase and destroy data permanently.
133. Admittedly, some trained software programmers are able to check parts of the binary code of a specific program. But they can only do so because this set of zeros and ones is represented by a specific control interface that provides the proper selection and context for interpretation.

as Hayles' perspective on material metaphors primarily focuses on the representational and performative effects on the interface level, the anthropological perspective enables to highlight software as metaphorical object that functions materially as social organizer and sorting mechanism. As we have seen in the historical part of this chapter, the emergence of software as a separate instance engendered historically several social-cultural divisions: between operators and programmers, between men and women, and between writers and readers. It also evoked the 'presencing', the calling into being, of the socio-economical category of software developers.

And of course, the history of SOFTWARE AS SOCIAL SORTING MECHANISM is still going on. The 1990s boom in Silicon Valley (in itself a material metaphor) and the rise of the software industry entailed the emergence of various new social groups: hippie-entrepreneurs, Internet millionaires, digerati, gamers, and new media academics. More recently the unstable materiality of software created new social categories such as hackers, pirates, Wikipedians, Wikileakers, seeders and leechers.[134]

To conclude this chapter it can be argued that software is inextricably connected to and formatted by metaphors and analogies. Firstly, because it needs interfacial translations into digital-material metaphors in order to be read and operated by people. Secondly, because software in itself is a material metaphor, as it embodies symbolic code that is able to do real things in the real world. This code is performative and transformative inside the machine, but most of all outside the machine, where it arranges and distributes objects and subjects. Software may be dissected in its formal and forensic material properties, but it is its ability of translating and transcoding that accounts for its far-reaching power.

Wendy Chun goes even a step further and conceives software as a metaphor for ungraspable mediation, as well as a metaphor for metaphor itself. This because of its 'logic of general substitutability' (Chun 2011, 2). In the introduction to her book, she notes that this diverges from the usual notion of metaphor:

> Software as metaphor for metaphor troubles the usual functioning of metaphor, that is, the clarification of an unknown concept through a known one. For, if software illuminates an unknown, it does so through an unknowable (software). This paradox – this drive to grasp what we do not know through what we do not entirely understand – this book argues, does not undermine but rather grounds software's appeal. (ibid., 2)

I would like to add that the paradox of SOFTWARE AS METAPHOR FOR METAPHOR grounds even more than just software's appeal. It also grounds software as metaphor for material metaphor. And this does not undermine the usual conception of metaphor, it rather extends and enriches it with extra layers of materiality and signification. But as with all metaphors, software reveals and conceals, and it is quite able to conceal both its materiality and its metaphoricity.

---

134. In peer-to-peer file sharing networks *leechers* are users who disconnect from the network after they finished their downloading, thereby contributing barely to the network; *seeders* are users who keep open their file directories for others to download, thereby enriching the network. Interestingly, advanced P2P networks such as BitTorrent use protocols that reward seeders by granting them faster download times.

In order to flesh out how software metaphors travel further outside the machine and get inscribed and incorporated in the social texture, the next chapter will explore some of the most common metaphors that inform these processes. This chapter will look at the tropes of virtual communities, Web 2.0, and social networks in particular. These metaphors will turn out to be more than conceptual or discourse metaphors, firmly connected as they are with the material apparatuses of software and networks.

CHAPTER 6
TRANSCODING THE SOCIAL INTO NETWORKS
HOW THE DIGITAL GETS SOCIALIZED

> *Networks are extremely poor metaphors, since they remain entirely made of nodes and edges to which are often added some conveniently drawn potato-like circles.*
> (Bruno Latour, 2011)

This chapter explores how notions of sociality get transmediated and transcoded into digital dynamics, and vice versa, how digital developments transform and reorganize social configurations. The first section addresses how the material metaphor of the virtual community shifted to Web 2.0 and social network metaphors. Analyzing these tropes as digital-material metaphors reveals the mechanisms of digital-social transcoding as sustained by software-induced icontologies that get aligned with cultural and political-economic forces. The second section delves into the notion of network, which turns out to be deeply informed by metaphors. Three root metaphors will be identified: NETWORK AS INFRASTRUCTURE, AS ORGANISM, and AS GRAPH. It will be argued that classic Internet discourse metaphors, such as the electronic highway and cyberspace, but also current metaphors of social networks and social media tap selectively from these root metaphors, translating into different material configurations and political-ideological implications.

1 — THE VIRTUAL COMMUNITY METAPHOR

Since the 1980s the emergence of online social gatherings have been observed on bulletin board systems and on the early Internet. Howard Rheingold, journalist and lecturer, and one of the first to write about computers as tools for thought and sociality, already coined the term virtual community for this phenomenon in 1987 (Rheingold 1987). Yet it remained largely unnoticed until 1993, when he published his seminal book *The Virtual Community: Homesteading at the Electronic Frontier* (Rheingold 1993). From then on the term became part of the debate about the promises and possibilities of the growth in Internet usage in the 1990s. Though the term virtual community, especially its optimistic if not utopian implications, was contested right from the start (Fernback and Thompson 1995; Turkle 1996; Katz and Aspden 1997), it became appropriated as an established concept to refer to more or less stable collective forms of online sociability in popular culture, as well as in the emerging academic discourse of cyberspace and cyberculture (Jones 1995; 1997; Agre and Schuler 1997; Smith and Kollock 1999).

Public debate and personal relations are key to Rheingold's often-quoted definition of virtual community: 'Virtual communities are social aggregations that emerge from the Net when enough people carry on those public discussions long enough, with sufficient human feeling, to form webs of personal relationships in cyberspace' (Rheingold 1993, 5). These elements – public group debate and personal relations – have remained the core of the virtual community imagery, though the appropriation in scholarly research and popular discourse added some characteristics, in particular the feature of shared space (geographical or virtual) and shared interests. By the end of the millennium a virtual or online community came to be defined as a spatial social aggregation on the Internet, hosting a core of recurrent users who were engaged in ongoing group interaction based on a shared topic (profession, hobby, fandom, politics, parenthood, and so on), or based on a shared virtual place (general chat channels and Usenet groups, cafe, clubhouse, meeting hall). Over time the aggregation may develop shared norms and rules of conduct, especially when shared space and shared interests became inextricably merged, and imagine itself as a community, invoking a sense of belonging and identification (Anderson 1983; Jones 1997; Van den Boomen 2000).

It is important to remember that at that time the Internet was mainly textual, not graphic or otherwise visually enhanced. How did people come to imagine and experience sets of text messages on the screen as a living community? Lev Manovich's distinction between the computer layer and the cultural layer can be helpful in answering this question (Manovich 2001). At the level of the computer we can observe that the community experience is mediated by specific software for public or semi-public communication. In the pre-Web era, the main community-facilitating applications were bulletin boards, mailing lists, Usenet and Internet Relay Chat (IRC).[135] Specific to these applications is, of course, that they enable communication between more than two users, but most important is that their interfaces proffer *collective spaces* where the communication is made visible as group communication. These spaces were clearly bounded and delineated, represented on the monochrome screen as an ordered list of messages. These representations are experienced by users as spaces, virtual spaces, as it was called in the disembodied nomenclature of that time, but nonetheless spaces where you could go to, where you could be and see or meet other people, or at least their traces.

Conceiving a screen representation as a space where you can be is already an instance of translating a computer form into a cultural form, what Manovich (2001) would call transcoding, yet more translations are needed to secure a sense of sociality and collectivity. At the second level, the cultural level, the mobilization of a strong metaphor enabled this sense of sociality: the metaphor of community. Indeed, this is a metaphor, although we barely recognize it as such, used as we are by now to the notion of an online community. Rheingold's additional terms of 'homestead-

---

135. Usenet, developed in 1979, is a forum-like client-server plain text system with its own NNTP protocol (Network News Transfer Protocol) consisting of thousands of so-called newsgroups that could be created on any topic imaginable. In some categories, specific voting procedures are needed to implement a new newsgroup or subgroup, but in the so-called alt category no procedure was required, anyone could create a new group in this hierarchy. It lead to group names such as alt.parenting.twins-triplets, alt.women.supremacy, alt.buddha.short.fat.guy, alt.tasteless.jokes, among others. Usenet still exists today even though as a public debate sphere it gave way to web forums and social network sites. Web-based archiving of Usenet groups and posts has been done by Deja News since 1995. Google acquired this database in 2001, and called it Google Groups.

Internet Relay Chat (IRC), created in 1988, is a client-server plain text system that affords synchronous message exchange over so-called channels. Channels are not pre-given, but made on the fly. When someone opens a channel and gives it a name, it is publicly available. When the last user logs out, the channel is gone.

ing' and 'electronic frontier' were more easily recognized (and criticized) as metaphors. Maybe that is also the reason these terms did not get so intricately and permanently blended with online sociality as did the concept of community. The strongest metaphors are those who conceal their metaphoricity and become icontologized as a thing in itself.

However, this was not achieved without struggle and negotiation. Especially to detach the concept of community from its primary associations with physical or geographical space and attach it to virtual space can be considered hard metaphorical work. For example the work done by Quentin Jones, who elaborated on the metaphor of cyber archaeology and introduced the concepts of virtual settlement and virtual cultural artifacts as quantifiable and qualifiable indicators of online community formation (Jones 1997).

The implication of a specific space can be considered foundational for the success of the metaphor of virtual community, as it connects the spatial interface ordering to spatial social experiences. The metaphor of community enforces and reinforces the sense of place and the sense of social gathering; it frames and models the digital assemblage into a social collective. This cannot be done by software alone; something social does not emerge automatically from something digital – a lot of mediation and transmediation work has to be done. And metaphors, conceptual and material, play a dominant role in this process.

Community as village

What kind of metaphor then is the metaphor of the virtual community? Let us first try the conceptual approach. Recall, the conceptual theory of metaphor assumes that the metaphorical concept is imported from a source domain, and transferred to the target domain, where it conceptually highlights and downplays specific qualifies of the target (Lakoff and Johnson 1980). The transference work can be tracked down by parsing the metaphorical concept into the different domains and associations, and mapping their correspondences.

This is not difficult for the metaphor of community. The virtual community metaphor is derived from the source domain of a pre-modern village: COMMUNITY AS VILLAGE. [136] Whether historically correct or not, the source domain of the village is associated with characteristics such as: clear borders, rigid demarcations of insiders and outsiders, clear subject positions, an almost self-sufficient economy, a homogeneous morality, and strong social cohesion. Everyone knew each other by face, by name and by status. The village was a place for living and work, but also leisure, celebrations, and funerals. Most of these features can be mapped without problems onto the target domain of virtual communities: spatial borders, identification of insiders and outsiders, status recognition based on longevity and quality of contributions (positive: helpful, interesting, well written, authoritative – or negative: big mouth, querulant, egocentric, sloppy writing, insulting). In a textual virtual community you may not know others by face (unless you also knew them 'in real life', as it was called then), but you could know them by (nick)name and status. And as Rheingold (1993) already showed in his case study of The Well, the famous San Francisco based online community, virtual communities were places for work and leisure, wise types and idiots, fun and sorrow. Of course, not all features of the imagined village could be transferred to the target

---

136. The more or less nostalgic notion of community as village has been present in the discourse of modernity and the loss of community since the very first contours of modernity emerged. See for example the work of sociologist Ferdinand Tönnies, *Community and Society* (Tönnies 1887).

domain (economic self-sufficiency for instance), [137] and features such as homogeneous morality and social cohesion turned out to be wishful thinking (Dibbell 1993; Van den Boomen 2000). The transference of a pre-modern notion of community to online configurations has been criticized because of its historical inaccuracy, its romanticism, its nostalgia, and its utopian projections, nonetheless the conceptual metaphor of virtual community became a common trope to indicate the emerging social praxis on the Internet. We should not forget that in the 1990s the community metaphor served a particular discourse intervention: to bring to the fore the communicative and social bonding capacities of computer-mediated communication. That was against the grain of common belief, for at that time computers were still conceived as cold calculation machines, at best only serving communities of computer nerds and geeks.

Community discourse
In that regard the conceptual metaphor of the virtual community was right from the start also a discourse metaphor. It became associated with debates on the erosion of offline communities, citizen's participation, and bottom-up democracy. Rheingold already referred to the work of Jürgen Habermas (1962) and Ray Oldenburg (1989) on the demise of the public sphere and public spaces in the modern era. It raised the question whether online communities could revitalize offline communities and public engagement (Doheny-Farina 1996; Wellman and Gulia 1999; Hampton 2002).

While the debates were often naive and utopian, the discourse not only produced documents but also monuments, to put it in Foucauldian terms (Foucault 1972). It led to various local initiatives in the so-called community network movement (Schuler 1994). Some of them took on names that up-scaled the village imaginary to the more contemporary dynamic of a city, also because most projects were initially geographically bound to a specific city, as for example Netville in Toronto (Hampton and Wellman 1999), the Digital City in Amsterdam (Van den Boomen 1995; Lovink 2009), and the International City in Berlin. Many of these initiatives were quite successful for a couple of years, including the Digital City in the Netherlands, in large part because they provided free or cheap Internet access for ordinary people before that became a huge commercial market. However, it soon became clear that online community building and maintenance was as hard as offline community building, and when commercial Internet access providers finally emerged on the scene (some also free in the beginning, just to collect a large user base), most of these idealistic initiatives disappeared into oblivion.

After the euphoric pioneering era, the utopian dreams of online community building as a motor for local offline democracy and political engagement faded away. What remained was a notion of online community as a neutral association between a virtual space and a group of recurring users: COMMUNITY AS SPATIAL GROUPING. Yet, this ideological neutrality did not weaken the metaphor; on the contrary, it established the concept even stronger as a discourse metaphor, now for a much wider public than nerds, techno-hippies, and leftish activists. Moreover, the metaphor of community did not only survive the demise of political utopian promises, it was able to successfully attach itself to the next wave of utopian promises. It turned out to be perfectly compatible with business

---

137. Though several online community initiatives tried to achieve economic autonomy, independent from corporate business and state funding, this usually did not succeed. See for example the history of the Dutch Digital City (Rustema 2001; Van den Besselaar and Deckers 2005; Lovink 2009).

models and marketing concepts (Hagel and Armstrong 1997). The dot-com hype that developed at the end of the 1990s was in many respects also a dot-community hype: online communities and community portals became big business. Earning money with Internet content was still notoriously difficult, but providing web spaces where people could build their own content turned out to be a viable business model. It was based on providing free community space and free tools for users (web-based software to create web forums, guest books, chat rooms, archives, and later blogs), while the revenues came from targeted advertising.

Some of the largest community organizers managed to survive the dot-com crash in 2001, including Yahoo! and GeoCities[138] and so did the community metaphor itself. It still had its appeal, not only as an accepted business and marketing model, but also as an organizing principle and self-description of various counter movements, such as anti-globalization groups and open-source software developers.

Hence, the metaphorical concept of community, whether or not with implied utopian connotations of social change, still functioned (and functions) as a discourse metaphor that organizes and aligns online social gathering, debate and personal relationships. Enabled and formatted by specific software that regulates space boundaries (usually in the format of the page as aggregation of exchanges), it also functions as a material metaphor. It binds software, interface, page-space, and a group of users into a specific configuration that is both metaphorical and material: it orchestrates social conduct and assigns subject positions in the social ranking order that emerges from ongoing collective debate.

Yet, the term online community has lost its specific materiality in many cases. Any trace of communication between any random group of users is easily called a community today. Any virtual space for customer's complaints is proudly announced as 'our community', any webforum, any collection of interlinking blogs can be featured as a community – by PR departments, marketeers, and consultants (e.g. Smith 2009), but also by journalists, academics (e.g. Kaplan and Haenlein 2010), moderators, developers and users. This easy equation of COMMUNITY AS ANY INTERACTION is rarely embodied in an organizing material metaphor that validates and substantiates an online gathering as a community. The concept of community (with in it slipstream sloppy notions of public space and public sphere) has in these cases shifted into a conceptual and discourse metaphor that primarily serves consumerist ideology and communicative-capitalist interests (Dean 2003). Meanwhile, a new utopian wave hit the Internet after 2004, and competing metaphors of social gathering showed up: Web 2.0, social networks, and social media.

2 — THE WEB 2.0 METAPHOR

In 2004, after the publisher O'Reilly organized some conferences on the next generation of web software and services, and dubbed it Web 2.0, this name became a sticky buzzword (O'Reilly

---

138. GeoCities, founded in 1994, was a web portal to build communities by organizing users in cities. These cities could refer to real cities, but could also function as metaphorical names for specific topics and interests, such as SiliconValley for computer-related content and Hollywood for movie fans. In 1990, Yahoo! acquired GeoCities. Tellingly, Yahoo! soon left behind the collective geo metaphors in favor of the personal names of users, thereby moving toward a social network organization instead of communities. However, Yahoo! GeoCities proved incapable of catching up with the rise of social network sites like MySpace and later Facebook. Since 2009, the service is available only in Japan.

2005; Anderson 2010; Allen 2013). The idea of Web 2.0 functioned as a vital conceptual and discourse metaphor right from the start. And indeed, it is an interesting and versatile metaphor, not in the least because its source domain is the domain of software development itself. As a conceptual metaphor the imagery of '2.0' is imported from the field of software releases, and examining this source domain will reveal some of its peculiarities.

Web 2.0 as software upgrade

A version 2.0 of a software package is supposed to be a fundamental upgrade of version 1.x, not just a minor update with some patches, since it would then be called version 1.1, 1.2 and so on. The message is that version 2.0 compared to 1.x is fundamentally innovative and new; WEB 2.0 AS MAJOR UPGRADE. The release of such an upgrade is usually accompanied with a strong urge to install this version, for security reasons or because earlier versions will not be supported anymore. The metaphor also suggests an integral package, and though software releases need not necessarily be commercial, the metaphor of WEB 2.0 AS SOFTWARE IN A BOX certainly has a connotation of branding, marketing, and business models.

It is a strong metaphor, though of course a lot can be said against it. It can be argued that the Web is not an integral software package from the shelves released to paying customers. The Web is not, and never will be, a finished product, it is an assemblage of linked entities in permanent beta status. At the same time, the commodification aspect of the metaphor is certainly something not to be missed; it might not take the form of a packet from the shelve, but there are several other ways to commodify software usage.

Most intriguing about the Web 2.0 metaphor is that it focuses on software as such. This is rare for conceptual and discourse metaphors in digital praxis; most of them deliberately lead our attention away from software by substituting it with other terms in order to obliterate any trace of design, materiality, and politics. However, this one foregrounds it, by explicitly claiming a fundamental change in software design and features. O'Reilly (2005) highlighted the following software specs for Web 2.0:

1. The web as platform: a linked system of web services instead of stand-alone sites and pages; device-independent software; permalinks and feeds that work across sites.
2. Harnessing collective intelligence: aggregating and recombining user-added content and user-added data (posts, comments, reviews, tags, ordered products, views, any trace).
3. The importance of data and databases: storing, retrieving, searching, and recombining core data on location, identity, calendars, and product identifiers.
4. Light-weight programming without software release cycles: scripting languages 'as the duct tape of the Internet', designed for rich user experiences by immediate interaction (without having to reload the page), designed for flexibility, hackability, and remixability.

In short, the main upgrade of web software resides in the use of interactive scripts and databases that together generate the formerly relatively static HTML pages as dynamic, sometimes even personalized, reassemblages. Web 2.0 software aggregates and generates webpages from database entries, each fragment ready to be reassembled again, enabling endless nested recombinations and remediations: WEB 2.0 IS DATABASED, not page based, WEB 2.0 IS SCRIPTED, software processing rather than rendering a layout, and WEB 2.0 IS FRAGMENTING AND RECOMBINING, changing pages perpetually. In fact this shows how the metaphor of the web *page,* imported from the domain of print and books, is retiring. There was a time that scholars and digerati thought that computers would undermine the linearity of print by introducing hypertext and hyperlinks (Barrett

1991; Landow 1994). But with the wisdom of hindsight, we can now see how the web before 2.0 implied its own linearity, aligned by more or less stable pages. Web 2.0 shows that the age of the page is over, that there are other forms of software-enabled space construction, crisscross assembled on the fly, generated by data remediations and transmediations, not by page metaphors. When looked at from this software perspective, Web 2.0 seems to be more about data entities interacting with each other, than about users interacting with each other; more about information than communication. But of course, there is communication on Web 2.0. You can find others, you can communicate with them, by chatting, by commenting on a blog, a Wikipedia entry, or a social network profile, and by posting a video, a photo, or a tweet. Communication is ubiquitous, and all types of communication can be integrated and assembled on a reassembled webpage – chat, Twitter, forums, blogs, writing walls, time lines. Which brings us to the next level of the metaphor of Web 2.0: the discourse of sharing and linking.

Web 2.0 as sharing and linking

While the Web 2.0 debate was initially about a new generation of web software and business models, it soon developed into a discourse that heralded a new Internet culture. This new culture is indicated by a couple of recurring keywords: participatory culture, collective intelligence, sharing, user-generated content, and the wisdom of the crowds. Typical web services for this type of sharing discourse are Flickr and Pinterest (sharing photo's and pictures), YouTube and Vimeo (sharing movies), Delicious (formerly Del.icio.us, sharing bookmarks), MySpace and Facebook (sharing friends and interests), Wikipedia (sharing knowledge), Blogger and LiveJournal (sharing diaries, links, and essays), and Twitter, Tumbler and Weibo (sharing short messages). In short, WEB 2.0 IS SHARING: sharing stuff, or just sharing, with no object at all (Johns 2012).

Saliently, this sharing is not just publicizing in the sense of delivering a self sufficient product, as was the case in what became retrospectively called Web 1.0, where the aim was to keep visitors stuck to a bordered website. Sharing on Web 2.0 is about making things public as semi-autonomous entities in a collective linking system, as already indicated by the software paradigms: WEB 2.0 IS LINKING. This linking system, afforded by specific algorithms, is provided as an infrastructure by the overarching website, but the acts of linking and tagging are up to the users. They create their own connections to other entities and formulate their own keywords (tags) to categorize their stuff. And, again adhering to the software paradigm, these acts are not necessarily confined to the providing website. Web 2.0 services in principle encourage linking and connecting to other sites and applications, and sometimes also the free implementation of third-party applications on the platform. [139] Unlike the contained and static earlier web, Web 2.0 works across websites and uses the WEB AS PLATFORM for linking, distributing, and producing content, that is, for archiving, accumulation, and construction, as Schäfer (2011) calls it.

In these discourse metaphors of sharing, Web 2.0 is all about user participation, or better yet, it is all about YOU. In 2006, TIME magazine announced on its cover that the Person of the Year was

---

139. Facebook especially has a policy of enrolling third-party app developers, but with constraints, as can be illustrated with the history of the Web 2.0 Suicide Machine. This was an app created by political net artists based at WORM in Rotterdam. The service enables users of Facebook, MySpace, LinkedIn and Twitter to commit social network suicide by automatically removing private content and listed friends, contacts, and followers/followed relationships (without deleting their accounts). In 2010, Facebook sent a legal cease and desist letter that demanded the withdrawal of the service from Facebook.

YOU: 'Yes, you. You control the information age. Welcome to your world.' Web 2.0 was celebrated as 'a massive social experiment', 'an opportunity to build a new kind of international understanding, not politician to politician, great man to great man, but citizen to citizen, person to person' (Grossman 2006).

This massive sharing seems to imply the final victory of the idea of community building. The web has finally been turned into a common ground where people collectively share their stuff and thoughts. And it is massive indeed: a far larger proportion of Internet users are active on Web 2.0 sites than in the online communities of the nineties. It has even been dubbed 'digital maoism' (Lanier 2006), though this was not meant to be complementary. But despite the rhetoric of massive participation and collectivity the individualized YOU is the main actor in Web 2.0 discourse. It is you who is giving away your digital content, your comments, your tags, your reviews, your votes, your lists, your status updates, your new friends, your bookmarks, your data. And this YOU is the target of the business models of Web 2.0.

Web 2.0 as harnessing and harvesting

We should not forget that the subtitle of O'Reilly's foundational article read: 'Design Patterns and Business Models for the Next Generation of Software' (O'Reilly 2005). It is about software and design for business models, not for social change, democracy, or community building. Tellingly, O'Reilly defined as one of the main features of Web 2.0 'harnessing collective intelligence' (ibid.) – WEB 2.0 IS HARNESSING. As Tiziana Terranova pointed out in her keynote lecture at the ICA [140] conference in 2007, in O'Reilly's text on Web 2.0 the term 'harnessing' is mentioned several times. This is quite an anomaly in a discourse on user control and freedom. Harnessing suggests quite the opposite: disciplining, taming, domesticating, saddling. The concept is taken from the domain of work horses and horse power, which invokes the question: who is the work horse and who is in power? Somehow the metaphor of harnessing collective intelligence achieves to blend domestication and exploitation with personal freedom and control.

Several scholars critically analyzed Web 2.0 and its user-generated content ideology in terms of unpaid and immaterial labor by users (Terranova 2000; Scholz 2008; Schäfer 2011). Harnessing then is not just about disciplining, it is also about harvesting, that is, harvesting data value. What appears on the interface and in discourse as the freedom of user-generated content, boils down to user-generated data for a money making machine.

3 — RECOUNTING THE WEB

This does not imply that the metaphor of Web 2.0 is just a capitalist smoke curtain. As with all metaphors, it reveals and conceals. Any sticky metaphor of digital dynamics should be taken seriously, as they articulate particular access to the digital. Taking a metaphor seriously also means taking it literally, including its implications. Doing so with the Web 2.0 metaphor already lead us to some software implications but there is more in this metaphor. It also opens up a discourse concerning previous and future versions of the web, counted and recounted by numbers, and recounted by narratives (Allen 2013; Barassi and Treré 2012; Pillegi et al. 2012).

---

140. The International Communications Association (CA) organizes large yearly conferences, where thousands of communication scholars meet.,

A notion of Web 2.0 recursively evokes a notion of Web 1.0, the earlier version of the web. The earliest version of the web was outlined by Tim Berners-Lee in 1989 (Berners-Lee 2000), computer scientist at the Swiss CERN (Conseil Européen pour la Recherche Nucléaire), as a design for an easy to use information management system for researchers. In 1990, the feature of hyperlinks was added, and in 1991 Berners-Lee posted his proposal in the Usenet group alt. hypertext (Long 2007). The World Wide Web, as it was called then, was set loose on the Internet. And since it was an open protocol, it was up for grabs.

Since the mid-1990s, the web was implemented as an application for information display, a graphical alternative for the textual menu-based Gopher system. It was, as most Internet applications, a so-called client-server application, consisting of dedicated webservers that provided content which could be viewed (actually: copied) by a user's client program, a webbrowser. Three features were essential: it used its own protocol (HTTP, Hyper Text Transfer Protocol) to transfer files, it used a standardized mark-up language to display information (HTML, HyperText Markup Language), and it used hyperlinks: standardized unique pointers that refer to web resources by means of URLs (or URIs, Uniform Resource Locators or Identifiers). A web woven of linked pages emerged as a new extensible information platform. New was the multi-media aspect: the HTML-assemblage of text, graphics, and images, delivered as one integral page. The components constituting the page usually resided on one webserver, but could also be assembled from multiple dispersed servers. Relatively new was the easy hyperlinking to other web documents.

Compared to the monochrome plain texts of the pre-web Internet, it looked pretty dynamic and new. Yet, Web 1.0 pages mainly supported reading and clicking: WEB 1.0 IS INFORMATION DISPLAY. Some basic interaction, such as sending mail, ordering products, or leaving a message in a guest book, was possible by filling in simple forms that were sent to the web server via CGI (Common Gateway Interface) scripts, but dynamic interaction and communication was reserved to non-web Internet applications such as e-mail, Usenet and IRC. Moreover, despite the 1995 web discourse that 'now everyone can be a publisher' websites had to be maintained by skilled webmasters who had extensive knowledge about HTML, FTP (File Transfer Protocol) and server configurations. WEB 1.0 IS MASTER CONTROL.

Web 1.1: Scripting the web

A few things changed in the mid-1990s with the advent of more sophisticated scripts. We could call this moment Web 1.1 to stay within the software release metaphor. It is not a fundamental upgrade, but surely an update towards more dynamic webpages by introducing more elaborate scripts. Scripts are small routine programs that can perform actions on data components. They consist of executable source code in their own language (Perl, PHP, JavaScript, among others) and function on the web as an extra software layer between webbrowsers and servers.

These web scripts finally enabled user interactivity on a web page. Scripts were developed for polls, quizzes, advertising banners, site search, database queries, and member's access rights. For each function a separate set of scripts could be developed, thereby transforming these functions into distinct visible and operable data objects, that is, into sign-tool-objects, into digital-material metaphors. Hence, WEB 1.1. IS INTERACTION, with the proviso that INTERACTION IS A FUNCTION and A FUNCTION IS AN OBJECT. Particularly engaging were the scripts that simulated communication applications such as Usenet and IRC, resulting in material metaphors such as webforums and webchatrooms. As conceptual metaphors we can add: WEB 1.1 IS COMMUNICATION, COMMUNICATION IS A FUNCTION and A FUNCTION IS AN OBJECT.

Most of these scripts work with a database running in the background – a new actor on the web. Design merged with programming. The implementation of scripts was still in the hands of the webmasters – they now also had to manage databases and scripts – but from then on webpages could be both an information and a communication platform. The scripted Web introduced dynamics. Pages could now be transformed by user input: by adding user content, or by retrieving and assembling a personalized page from a database. At this point, the web could really take off. And it did.

On Web 1.1 virtual communities could emerge, since group communication and public debate were now possible, as a scripted function, as an object, as a virtual space, as a digital-material metaphor. This created a boom of community portals on the web, including new business models to exploit it. Yet, what made these webcommunities less dynamic than for instance Usenet groups, was the fact that group communication remained internal, object-bound and space-bound, within the borders of the webpage. Where mailing lists and Usenet groups afforded crossposting messages to other lists and groups, thereby merging and extending the debates onto wider networks, webcommunity discussions were confined to their specific forum or chatroom. Hyperlinking of course was possible, but these links were at that time one-way information pointers, not two-way connections and communication channels.

Web 1.2: Extending the hyperlink

Web interactivity got a new boost with the emergence of blogging software. This type of software consists of a bundle of elaborate scripts that together constitute a light-weight content management system for websites. At first sight this is just another set of scripts for a particular function that generates new digital-material objects, but blogging software implied a set of new features that would eventually transform the web into a platform. Let us call this stage Web 1.2: an update of the scripted web, with new features and affordances, but not yet what later would be called Web 2.0.

Blog software, developed as a tool for updating web sites with new content, led to the unfolding of weblogs as a digital sign-tool-object: a relatively new web genre, or better, a new type of website. A blog can be defined as a website that materially and metaphorically takes on the form of a diary or logbook. It uses the format of a page that is built up by separate entries, so-called blog posts, thereby merging the logbook metaphor with the mail and bulletin board metaphor. Each post is stamped by date, and each has its own URL in its title. The pre-formatted design enables ordinary users to maintain a webpage from a user-friendly dashboard without the need to master FTP and HTML. A blog can be maintained by one person, the blogowner, or by a group of blogowners. It can also be a collective blog, when both comments and main entries can be submitted by ordinary users. What makes a blog more than an information platform is that every separate entry can in principle function as a webforum, initiating its own debates on the topic by allowing comments from readers.

Blogging software consists of a set of scripts and a database. The scripts can be managed and adjusted by a webmaster/blogowner who runs its own webserver, but soon the software was also proffered in the form of a web service, such as LiveJournal and Blogger. Here, users only need their webbrowser and an account to set up a blog. Now indeed 'everyone could be a publisher', and millions did so. In 2004, 8 million American adults (7%) had created a blog, 32 million (27%) read blogs, and 12% had posted comments on blogs (Rainie 2005). The user-friendliness of the interface – for blog owners as well as blog readers – contributed significantly to the popularization of blogs and the so-called blogosphere, inciting again a revival of the debate about the Internet as a public sphere (Poell 2009).

Yet, the importance of blogs for the development of the web should also be located at a deeper digital-material level: data fragmentation and reassemblage. The point is that data objects on a blogpage can be reassembled from the database on the fly in various ways: by subsequent date, by monthly archives, by author, by full text search words, by blogowner-defined categories, by user ratings, or by whatever is implemented as an object in the database. Any user is able to reassemble the display of blog data, just by clicking on a link. While in Web 1.1 clicking on a URL just brought you to the referred to document or site, in Web 1.2 hyperlinks do much more: they process database entries. They split pages into pieces, pieces that function as distinct digital-material objects that can be further processed due to their publicly available URL, a so-called permalink. Therefore, posts from different blogs can be aggregated and reassembled as searchable directories, as RSS [141] feeds, and as topically organized blog communities.

In that regard, blog software meant an update of the hyperlink, by extending its functions. While Web 1.0 hyperlinks usually referred to a complete webpage or to a specific point on that page, bloglinks can refer to separate data entities and to scripts that can be executed. Permalinks refer to separate posts and comments and enable targeted referencing and processing, both within and between sites. The bloglinks called trackbacks even function as two-way hyperlinks that enable crossposting and cross-debates between blogs. [142]

In other words, blog software combined three things: cutting up webpages into separate data objects, storing and processing these in databases, and extending the functionality of the hyperlink. The combination enabled several ways of recombining and reassembling data objects beyond the borders of the blog or website. WEB 1.2 IS CUTTING UP AND REASSEMBLING, a relatively new web dynamics evoked by the connection to databases. The HTML page itself is no longer a confined fixed unity, a textual file that resides on a server in a directory, but consists of heterogeneous data fragments, which can be addressed and processed separately.

These principles of cutting up the page and extending the hyperlink, boosted by the blog wave of Web 1.2, afforded the further integration of functions and the development of several other types of web assemblages, in particular social network services (SNSs) such as MySpace, Facebook, and LinkedIn. The announcement of Web 2.0 then marked the final upgrade of Web 1.2 into a radically different web: a web of data objects rather than pages, a web assembled by databases, and a web with 'algorithmized hyperlinks', as Anne Helmond (2013) calls them. Hyperlinks have been extended in their functionalities. They are no longer just referrers and navigational devices, but also processors of database calls. Sometimes even the act of clicking is no longer required, as is the case with the infamous Facebook Like button. It is enough just to visit a webpage with a Like button to get tracked and added to Facebook's database of web traffic and browser behavior (Roosendaal 2010).

---

141. RSS (originally Rich Site Summary, usually called Real Simple Syndication) is a format for simple text display of separate web entities. It enables the fast scanning of headlines and new blog posts from multiple sites without having to visit them.
142. A trackback consists of a notification appearing on your blog that another blog has referred to an entry of yours. The notification consists of a short summary and a link to the referring blog entry. This allows for conversations spanning several blogs that readers can easily follow.

Decentered spaces and socialities

The algorithmization of the web, focused on sharing and linking, may primarily be aimed at tracking and targeting possible consumers, but this does not foreclose the formation of new types of social organization and bonding. Not coincidentally the Web 2.0 metaphor has shifted the last couple of years into a discourse on so-called social media. Though a lot can be alleged against the rhetoric of the social (all media are social; social is not a synonym for harmony and peace), new forms of sociality have unmistakably emerged as a result of the algorithmized web. Patterns and clusters emerge, patterns of popularity, ranking, and quality, of topics and issues, of hypes and memes, of wisdom perhaps (Surowiecki 2004), and also patterns and clusters of groups, of personal networks (Wellman 2001), and of issue networks (Marres 2006).

The conceptual and discourse metaphors that emphasize the social dynamics of Web 2.0 – participatory culture, social sharing, community building, collective intelligence – are also material metaphors, built-in by software, interfaces, and protocols. There is not just the imperative or invitation to share, link, and participate: users do actually act accordingly. Material metaphors such as friending, following, sharing, rating, liking, writing on walls or timelines do indeed enroll users into new forms of sociability and connectivity, and assign and create new subject and object positions: Facebook friends, LinkedIn contacts, A-list blogs, trending topics, Twitter followers, Twitter stars, and so on. [143] As media scholar José van Dijck puts it in her analysis of social media platforms: 'Connectivity has become the material and metaphorical wiring of our culture, a culture in which technologies shape and are shaped not only by economic and legal frames, but also by users and content' (Van Dijck 2013, 142).

As could be expected, the social dynamics of Web 2.0 also tends to get subsumed under the notion of community. Indeed, a blog or Facebook page may assemble a core group of recurring participants that negotiate group norms and develop personal relations, thereby constituting a virtual community in the classic Rheingoldian sense: page-bound, debate-bound, and group-bound. Such communities may even become a major social actor of public resistance, as happened with the famous Facebook group 'We are all Khaled Said' during the early days of the Arab Spring in Egypt. [144] However, as we have seen, the reconfigured algorithmic web predominantly supersedes page-bound organization. Many new media scholars for that reason take hyperlink relations rather than page-bound debates as community indicators (Park 2004; Efimova 2005). These scholars infer and identify new types of communities based on hyperlink analyses, but whether these forms of new sociability also evoke a sense of community for its users remains an open question. At the same time, in popular social media discourse the term community is loosely used for any circle of friends and any public sharing of opinion or content. This is what Schäfer (2011) describes as the 'rhetoric of community': 'claiming that users belong to a community [...] and] claiming mediated communication equals publishing' (Schäfer 2011, 37). Van Dijck also warns, 'Terms such as "community" and "communality" have become inflated notions as more networks

---

143. Actually, it is hard to decide whether these social media data entities embody subject positions or object positions. As digital-material sign-tool-object-metaphors they somehow seem to compress subjects and objects.
144. The very name of the group may be illustrative for a new type of political organizing formatted by the model of personal social networks: not framed by topic, issue, ideology, or enemy, but centered around the name of a person that comes to embody the collective that affirms 'we are all that person, and what happened to him may happen to us if we do not resist'.

of strangers start calling every invitee a friend and every clicker a follower' (Van Dijck 2013, 147). Though it can be objected that online as well as offline communities may very well exist of strangers, indeed a few things have changed regarding the community metaphor. It has to be acknowledged that social media transforms notions, as well as practices of sociality and community. To be sure, the constituting elements of the material metaphor of the virtual community metaphor have been transformed profoundly with the rise of SNSs. This pertains, respectively, to sense of place, sustained debate, and the software that aligns place and debate. First, there is no common collective place of gathering provided by the interface – instead there are millions of vaporous micro-spaces with ever shifting permeable borders, millions of floating personal MySpaces, MyFaces, and MyFollowers. These micro-spaces are not isolated, they are connected in multiple ways by multiple types of hyperlinks, and there is definitely social dynamics and power at stake, but their forms are no longer sustained by the material metaphor of the virtual community.

Second, there is no ongoing debate between a recurrent group of users – instead there are thousands of coming and going micro-exchanges between ever shifting participants. Admittedly, users form what Rheingold called 'webs of personal relations'. These relations are even the main organizing material metaphor for social network sites; they are made explicit in friends lists and numerous apps that make them more available and addressable than ever before. But though personal relations are required to generate and sustain a virtual community, not every set of personal relations implies a community with a collective ground or practice. While the 1990s discourse on virtual communities was framed as COMMUNITY IS COLLECTIVITY, the current social media discourse is framed as COMMUNITY IS CONNECTIVITY. This is not just a conceptual shift; the interfaces and algorithms of SNSs have practically and materially translated collectivity into connectivity.

In that regard, the scripted and databased Web 2.0 technologies are radically decentering technologies. They decenter virtual spaces, pages, communities, and subjects, by cutting up everything into fine-grained data objects and patterns.

Hence, the age of the page seems to be over. We are now in the age of the hyperlink, the algorithm, and the database. At the same time, the page, as delivered on our screen, is still the only means of access we have to the software we work with. As users we can see, or at least infer, the data remediations, as long as they show themselves on the page interface of our webbrowser. But we do not see the further reading and writing that goes on behind the page, we do not see what is collected in databases, what they process and reassemble, and how they may be connected to other databases. This is where the material harnessing and harvesting takes place. There is a hidden dataweb at work simultaneously behind the public Web 2.0, reassembling and remediating data, and also constructing digital objects that are able to do things in the world. The digital-social assemblages thus constructed might be more remediating and transmediating our lives and thoughts than the metaphorized objects we see on our screen. We are often not even aware that something is going on inside the networks of servers, databases, and data centers. Networks seems to be as inaccessible for human knowledge as software is. Yet they are key to the emergence of new social configurations as well as to the harnessing of the social. In order to flesh this out, the next section will explore the concept of network itself.

4 — NETWORK METAPHORS

Since sociologists Jan van Dijk (1991) and Manuel Castells (1996) analyzed our current society in terms of the network society, the idea that *technological* networks are able to frame and organize *social* networks has become common knowledge. The concept of social networks already existed in psychology and sociology since the 1930s, but only recently the notion invaded everyday discourse. The most prominent Web 2.0 applications, such as Facebook and Twitter, are usually called social networks (though it would be more correct to speak of social network *sites*). The appropriation of the term social network also alludes to the general 20th century tendency towards light-weight networked communities (Van den Boomen 2000; Wellman 2001; Duyvendak and Hurenkamp 2004), indicating a further deterritorialization of formerly place-bound communities, first offline, now also online.

However, the notion of network itself is not without problems. To begin with there are several kinds of networks. Jan van Dijk distinguishes six types of networks:

1. physical networks (ecosystems, river networks);
2. organic networks (blood circulation, nervous system);
3. neuronal networks (neuronal connections, brain functions);
4. social networks (relations between people, groups, organizations);
5. technological networks (roads, railways, telecom networks, computer networks);
6. media networks (systems of senders, receivers, and representations)

(Van Dijk 2006 [1991], 25).

Issues of digital praxis and sociability should undoubtedly be located somewhere in the last three types, but even these distinctions do not seem to fit. For example, when we consider a Facebook profile, we cannot easily answer the question whether this is a social network (of people and their connections), a technological network (of hardware devices and their connections), or a media network (of devices, messages, and representations). Moreover, the technological network seems to refer only to hardware devices and physical connections, while computer networks can also consist of protocological networks, that is, networks built by software and protocols, implying that one hardware computer network can be configured as various protocological networks, if necessary, even concurrently layered.[145]

One might argue that a digital-material assemblage such as a Facebook profile embodies all these kinds of networks simultaneously, as a sophisticated nested construction, but even then the concept of network as an umbrella term remains problematic. We then ignore that the implicated network aspect of a social network is fundamentally different from the network aspect of a technological or protocological network. Connecting people is not the same as connecting computers, no matter how strong the Internet seems to have achieved the blurring of these phenomena by compressing everything into an overarching network frame.

Besides, the word network is used for completely different subsections or selections of a larger network. A single Facebook profile with its list of friends can be considered a social network, a collection of Facebook members who joined a thematic Facebook page can also be called a social network, and the complete Facebook site is also referred to as a social network. Not to mention the fact that any Facebook application constitutes another social-technical-protocological-media network, and that all Facebook data traffic is based on several protocological networks, such as the HTTP-network of the web and the TCP/IP-network of the underlying Internet. All these networks are ontologically different networks, not just as different elements or subsets

---

145. One hardware machine can be configured as multiple network servers by assigning computing resources to different protocols, a principle called *virtualization* in computer engineering.

from one set, but as completely different sets that are based on completely different laws and dynamics. In other words, the concept of network is not only scalable, but it is also highly variable just like software itself. How many networks can the Internet contain or imply? Unmeasurable, undecidable.

Of course, we might say, the Internet *is* a network, a network of connected computers, routers, switches and the like. To be more precise, a hardware network running on software and multi-layered protocols. And of course, the Web is also a network, of webservers, domain names, and sites, running by web protocols. Or, from another perspective, the web is a network of HTML pages and data fragments connected by hyperlinks. Or, on another level, the web is a network of visitors who favor some sites with more traffic than others. Or, at yet another level, the web is a network of clustered communities, connected by hyperlinks, issues and debates. Or, at yet another level, it is a social network of people connected by strong or weak ties. Indeed, the Internet is 'a network of networks' (Krol 1992; Berners-Lee 2000), but reiterating and nesting an abstract term does not clarify its meaning.

The telegraph and the nervous system

Hence, the notion of network is a slippery signifier, a fuzzy frame which can be used to capture and isolate any kind of connected cluster, at any scale. It has fully the appearance of a metaphor. Can we discern patterns in the deployment of this metaphor? What kind of imageries, materialities, and translations can be made visible by tracing network metaphors?

In her study *Networking with Bodies and Machines in the 19th Century*, Laura Otis (2001) shows how the network metaphor can be traced back to two 19th century source domains: respectively the telegraph and the nerve system. They both indicate networks of transmission and they have been intertwined right from the start, as scientists and engineers borrowed metaphors from each other's discourse to direct ideas and research. Yet, if we parse the metaphors into their constituting elements, we see that they stand for two profoundly different kinds of networks in several respects: constructed vs. organic, cultural vs. natural, infrastructure vs. dynamic processes, homogeneous vs. heterogeneous, and hard vs. fluid.

The telegraph network is a constructed infrastructure, consisting of homogeneous equal nodes connected by hard wires enabling point-to-point transmission. The NETWORK AS TELEGRAPH metaphor thus pertains to infrastructural networks: roads, pipes, and channels that enable transportation, be it of cars, gas, electricity, or signals. These networks consist of channels or conduits between homogeneous nodes. They are controlled by the basic physical architecture, sustained by externally imposed standards, rules, and protocols.

The second model, the nerve system, is not an empty infrastructure waiting for traffic. The NETWORK AS NERVOUS SYSTEM is far more complex; it is organic and dynamic, consisting of heterogeneous elements (neurons, axons, receptors, glia, neurotransmitters, electrochemical signals) that perform heterogeneous and distributed processes of transmission, translation, and feedback. Traffic, structure, and connections are not pre-given: they emerge and co-evolve over time. Nodes and connections can be distributed as well as concentrated (brain, spinal chord), together mediating between mind, body, and the external world. Here, control is not externally enforced: the nervous network develops by growth, adaptation, and self-organization.

These two metaphors can be considered the two basic root metaphors of networks, one standing for infrastructure and the other standing for organic emergence. Both types of metaphor arguably can function as conceptual metaphors that frame our notions of contemporary digital network praxis. For instance, Facebook can be seen as a telegraph infrastructure of servers, clients, and databases, but also as a complex organic nerve system of play, work, business models, and social interaction. This seems to imply that those metaphors can be used arbitrarily, but since each of them mobilizes specific features and qualities the choice is never neutral. For example, when Facebook is represented as a hardware infrastructure any sight on immaterial labor by users gets lost. In other words, these metaphors can also function as discourse metaphors that format and channel specific issues.

The two root metaphors can also be identified as organizers that shape and channel public and academic discourse on network technology. Analyses of the network society usually stay within the frame of infrastructure (Van Dijk 1991; Castells 1996), but sometimes the nerve system is also mobilized. For instance, Van Dijk added a chapter called 'Networks: The Nervous System of Society' in the revised edition of *The Network Society* (Van Dijk 2006). Yet, the two root metaphors are basically antagonistic. Tellingly, the two opposing discourse metaphors that accompanied the advent of the Internet in the 1990s – the electronic highway and cyberspace – bear the traces of the telegraph and the nerve metaphor, as will be argued in the following sections.

The electronic highway
During the mid-1990s Internet technology surfaced from the rather hidden world of military organizations and science foundations into the broad daylight of popular imagery. The main trope to indicate what this would mean for society at large was the metaphor of THE INTERNET AS ELECTRONIC HIGHWAY. It referred to an infrastructure that enabled traffic, analog with the root network metaphor of the telegraph: a connected system of wires or other channels that affords traffic of signals between homogeneous or homogenized local stations. [146] Typically, the very notion of electronic (usually abbreviated, as in email, e-commerce, e-learning and e-democracy), also refers to the network as infrastructure for traffic: the adjective electronic qualifies types of circuits and transmission (unlike the now more common adjective *digital*, which refers to a type of information).

The most influential mobilization of the highway metaphor for the Internet stems from US politics. According to the High Performance Computing Act of 1991 the country needed to turn the early Internet into a so-called National Information Infrastructure (NII), which Vice President Al Gore popularized as the information highway. His metaphor was based on an analogy with the American interstate highway system, more particularly its important economic function: THE ELECTRONIC HIGHWAY IS PROSPERITY. As Gore put it in his famous speech in 1993:

> It used to be that nations were more or less successful in their competition with other nations depending upon the kind of transportation infrastructure they had. Nations with deep water ports did better than nations unable to exploit the technology of ocean transportation. After World War II, when tens of millions of American families bought automobiles, we found our network of two-lane highways completely inadequate. We built a network of interstate highways. And that contributed enormously to our economic dominance around the world.

---

146. Traces of the telegraph are also recognizable in the then current use of the prefix 'tele', as in telecommuting, teleworking, teledemocracy, teleportation, telecommunication, telematics, and telecottage. Different from older tele notions, such as telegram, telephone, telescope and television, these usages referred specifically to *electronic* acting over distance.

Today, commerce rolls not just on asphalt highways but along information highways. And tens of millions of American families and businesses now use computers and find that the 2-lane information pathways built for telephone service are no longer adequate. (Gore 1993)

The analogy went further than just an imagery to make Americans feel as familiar with computing as they were with driving their cars on the highways. It also implied an all-American business plan: 'unlike the interstates, the information highways will be built, paid for and funded by the private sector' (ibid.). Private innovation would be stimulated by the removal of judicial and legislative restrictions in the field of telecommunication, while some government funding and regulation would ensure an open system with a 'public right of way' (ibid.). This tension between public and private interests, explicitly formulated by Al Gore, would remain inherent in any evocation of the electronic highway metaphor thereafter.

Though today we usually associate the highway metaphor with the Internet, in particular with the Internet-to-come of the 1990s, the hardware infrastructure the metaphor refers to has shifted over time. Al Gore was not the first who used the metaphor. In the 1970s, the highway metaphor referred to an extension of cable television towards an interactive, two-way system; in the 1980s the metaphor was appropriated by libraries and education institutes advocating nation-wide access to vast amounts of institutionally cataloged information and knowledge (Flichy 2001). In the early 1990s the metaphor had an industrial branch in 'cable-phone mania', pertaining to the huge mergers between telephone and cable companies, and a social-political branch in the form of a design dream of a nation-wide fiber-optic network serving every household in civil society. Gradually, the metaphor became associated with the forecasted convergence of television, telephone, and computers, until it finally became linked to the infrastructure now commonly known as the Internet (ibid.).

The electronic highway metaphor has been extensively researched (Rohrer 1997; Gozzi 1999; Flichy 2001). Most analyses point at the political and regulatory framing the metaphor implies, and criticize the frame as either too much regulation, centralization and bureaucratic control (Dyson et al., 1994), or as too much deregulation, a mere justification for liberalization policies (Flichy 2001). In any case, the conceptual metaphor of the highway persistently raises questions about regulation, control, and politics – THE ELECTRONIC HIGHWAY IS POLITICS. This is evoked by the extended analogy with roads and traffic: should there be road taxing, license plates, driver licenses, traffic signs, and police patrol on the electronic highway? While the metaphor seems dead as a discourse metaphor, it is remarkable how it gets awakened every time when issues arise regarding Internet politics and regulation, as for instance in the debate on so-called Net-neutrality (Weiss 2006).

In a way, the highway metaphor also functioned as a material metaphor that channeled design, usage, and social order according to its road map. There have been material and economic consequences from the NII policies and deregulations, and the highway metaphor certainly evoked a distribution of subject positions (of builders, providers, users-as-drivers, and governmental institutes) and a reordering of public and private space on the Internet. Moreover, it made the idea of the Internet tangible by its imagery of materials and embodiment. THE ELECTRONIC HIGHWAY IS MATTER and USERS ARE DRIVERS, seated in a car, hands at the steering wheel, in control, racing fast to prosperity, across the familiar space of urban middle-class America with gas stations, motels, and shopping malls. However, it can also be argued that nowhere the highway metaphor has been incorporated as a taken-for-granted sign-tool-object that orchestrates Internet usage. Internet users do not 'drive on the electronic highway' in the same digital-material sense as they 'send email' or 'poke a Facebook friend'.

In any case, the metaphor of the electronic highway is or was a strong conceptual metaphor, as well as a strong discourse metaphor. Though limited in its focus on infrastructure, the metaphor evokes important political questions. Whenever the metaphor of the highway is mobilized it channels the debate towards issues regarding construction, labor divisions, funding, governmental regulation, and public-private antagonism – all issues that should be raised in a society that considers itself a network society.

Cyberspace imagery

Concurrent with the highway trope the metaphor of cyberspace emerged to indicate the nature of the Internet. While the electronic highway clearly referred to the existing infrastructure that had to be expanded, the cyberspace metaphor was ambiguous about the implied technology. The metaphor referred speculatively to future technologies as virtual reality, but technology or infrastructure was not the main target. The main target was the new virtual space that was opened up by these technologies (Benedikt 1991). This cyberspace was explicitly not the familiar trimmed space along the electronic highway; it stood for the wild anarchistic opposite of domesticated space. CYBERSPACE IS ADVENTURE, unexplored areas, endless possibilities, no restrictions, no borders. Here, USERS ARE EXPLORERS. In cyberspace you are not seated in a car, you can roam disembodied through a magic space that develops and grows organically according to its own internal dynamics. A space like the brain, or better like the mind itself. CYBERSPACE IS MIND – a radicalized version of the nerve system metaphor.

The notion of cyberspace has been imported from the postmodern science-fiction genre of cyberpunk, a genre that featured high tech virtual reality and the low life of space cowboys and hackers that plug in to cyberspace by cranial jacks. By jacking in you leave your body behind and you enter the mind-boggling space of cyberspace. As William Gibson's much quoted description of cyberspace in his novel *Neuromancer* reads:

> Cyberspace. A consensual hallucination experienced daily by billions of legitimate operators, in every nation by children being taught mathematical concepts... A graphic representation of data abstracted from the banks of every computer in the human system. Unthinkable complexity. Lines of light ranged in the nonspace of the mind, clusters and constellations of data. Like city lights, receding... (Gibson 1984, 69) [147]

The quote alludes to a firmly controlled system with legitimate operators, good children, and megacorporations, but the cyberpunk protagonists preferably explore the dark illegal sides of cyberspace. As Sally Wyatt observed, Gibson's cyberspace is simultaneously framed as an ordered matrix and as chaotic city life, and therefore allows for multiple and ambiguous interpretations (Wyatt 2004, 250).

---

147. It is rarely noticed that this description does not come from the omniscient narrator of the story of *Neuromancer*. It is a quote from a voice-over in a kids show on television that Case, the protagonist, happened to have activated. In that regard, Gibsonian cyberspace is double fiction, nested as a fictitious quote in a fictitious story.

However, the appropriation of cyberspace in popular culture and discourse, as celebrated in the hip technophilic magazine *Wired*, did not allow for much ambiguity. Here, cyberspace was represented as an inherently free space to explore. Remarkably, the same holds for the academic discourse on cyberspace in the early 1990s.[148] As Michael Benedikt puts it in his description of cyberspace: CYBERSPACE IS FREEDOM OF MOVEMENT (Benedikt 1991, 126). The author stipulates,

> [I]n patently unreal and artificial realities such as cyberspace, the principles of ordinary space and time, can, in principle (!), be violated with impunity. After all, the ancient worlds of magic, myth, and legend to which cyberspace is heir, as well as the modern worlds of fantasy fiction, movies, and cartoons, are replete with violations of the logic of everyday space and time: disappearances, underworlds, […] wormholes, scale inversions, and so on. And after all, why have cyberspace if we cannot (apparently) bend nature's rules here? (ibid., 128)

Bending nature's rules – CYBERSPACE IS MAGIC. However, taken into account how the Internet looked at that time – textual, monochrome, command-line based – cyberspace fantasies can be seen as a visionary prelude to the later development of online game worlds such as World of Warcraft. It was not all hallucination. Moreover, the cyberspace metaphor, including its assumption of disembodiment, has also been deployed as a political metaphor. For instance in John Perry Barlow's famous *Declaration of the Independence of Cyberspace*, an act of resistance against the Telecommunications Reform Act of 1996. Barlow declared,

> Governments of the Industrial World, you weary giants of flesh and steel, I come from Cyberspace, the new home of Mind. On behalf of the future, I ask you of the past to leave us alone. You are not welcome among us. You have no sovereignty where we gather. […]
> Cyberspace does not lie within your borders. Do not think that you can build it, as though it were a public construction project. You cannot. It is an act of nature and it grows itself through our collective actions. […]
> Ours is a world that is both everywhere and nowhere, but it is not where bodies live. […] Your legal concepts of property, expression, identity, movement, and context do not apply to us. They are all based on matter, and there is no matter here. (Barlow 1996)

Just as with the metaphor of the electronic highway, the cyberspace trope functioned as a strong conceptual and discourse metaphor in which expectations, strategies, and political claims could be articulated. The two metaphors implied opposing positions on Internet regulation issues, but apart from some explicit confrontations, they primarily organized their own discourse and public. The electronic highway appealed mostly to policy makers, telecom corporations, and consultants, whereas cyberspace was the domain of academics, hip journalists, geeks, activists, and new economy entrepreneurs. The cyberspace ideology undoubtedly led to new digital-material objects

---

148. Notably, the assumption of disembodiment in cyberspace discourse has been criticized right from the start (Stone 1991; Featherstone and Burrows 1996; Cherry and Weise 1996), but somehow these voices remained marginal in overall cyberspace discourse.

and innovations (one can think of games, net art, public encryption software, P2P file sharing services), but again it is debatable whether cyberspace also functions as a material metaphor that is inextricably ingrained in hardware or software.

After the bust of the dot-com bubble, the clash between the highway and cyberspace faded away. Both terms currently seem pretty out-of date, even though they still pop-up now and then. However, the prefix cyber did survive. Ironically, it often refers to authoritative policing politics: cyber security, cyber patrol, cyber attacks, and cyber war.

The metaphors of the electronic highway and cyberspace were typically time-bound metaphors that accompanied new exciting things to come. Two decades later the Internet has become a familiar common-or-garden tool for millions, a tool or medium that needs no overarching framing metaphors anymore. Of course there is still (or again) excitement for the next big things to come: augmented reality, Internet of things, semantic web, more big data, more cloud computing. But there is no metaphor battle anymore. The two 19th century network metaphors, the telegraph and the nerve system, whether or not translated into highways or cyberspace, seem to have merged peacefully into what we know now as the Internet: a constructed and controlled infrastructure, as well as an evolving and self-organizing system.

However, it still takes metaphorical labor and other translations to capture both construction and self-organization, in the popular mind as well as in science. As we will see in the next section on network science and network theory, even the notion of network itself has become a metaphor.

The network graph

As the Internet evolved into a complex system of economic, political, cultural, and social actors that create ever expanding sign-tool-objects by which ever more domains of human life get organized, the notion of network became a familiar term. The Internet is known as a technological network, accessible by computers, phones, and tablets. And everyone with a Facebook or LinkedIn account also knows what a social network is: that organized list of friends or contacts on the screen. Our notion of what a network is, is fundamentally formatted by our Internet praxis. Yet, as familiar as the term is, it is at the same time extremely abstract. It does not refer to something specific; it indicates a vague structure of interconnectedness. In daily discourse this usually suffices; in contemporary network science the definition is more detailed, but just as abstract. A network is a structure that consists of *nodes* (points, network elements, also called vertices) and their *links* (relations, connections, paths, ties, also called edges) (Barabási 2002, 11).

This abstract notion of networks has a history in science that amply precedes the Internet, and even the telegraph. It can be traced back to Leonhard Euler's 1736 paper, in which he solved a particular mathematical puzzle: can one cross the seven bridges of Königsberg and never cross the same one twice? Euler translated the problem into what later came to be called a *graph,* an abstract mathematical model consisting of nodes (the four land areas divided by the river) and links (the seven bridges). He proved with this model that the answer to the bridge puzzle was 'no', that this was caused by the properties of the graph, and that the model could be generalized to all problems that could be translated into a graph (ibid.,10). Euler's work was the starting point of what came to be called *graph theory* in the 19th century, a rich methodology and vocabulary that found applications in topology, chemistry, physics, biology, sociology, engineering, computer science, and linguistics.

Notably, despite the term graph, a graph is a non-graphical non-visual mathematical abstraction. Of course it can be represented in a *graph drawing* that depicts nodes and links by dots and lines – the now so familiar *network diagram*. However, a picture of a graph is not a graph. The map is not the territory. This is not a network (Figure 7).

By applying graph theory and statistical methods various different network types could be distinguished and studied, such as small-world networks, random networks and scale-free networks.[149] Network science became a field in its own right by the end of the 20th century, when the methodologies to extract networks from data sets proliferated due to computational tools such as data mining and information visualization. Practically any phenomenon that can be translated into a relation between nodes can be an object of study in this field: animals that eat each other, social support by neighbors, Internet traffic between routers, cells that process enzymes, actors playing together in movies, hyperlinks that get clicked, scientists or bloggers quoting each other, Tweets that get retweeted, and so on.

The distinct specialism called *social network analysis* (SNA) needs special attention. SNA evolved when graph theory fused with the work of social scientists that were mapping interpersonal and group relations. Sociologists have been using the concept of 'social networks' since early 20th century to describe clustered relationships between members of social systems. Social networks consist of people, gathered at any scale: neighborhoods, birthday parties, corporations, families, activist groups, friends circles, and so on. SNA takes a principally different approach than classic social sciences which seek explanations for the dynamics of social networks in terms of, for instance, group processes, human needs, or specific attributes of members. SNA adheres to the basic principle of network theory: explanation lies in the graph, not in individual attributes or characteristics of the nodes (Wellman and Marin 2011). Less strict are SNA researchers when it comes to what counts as nodes and links in a social network. Nodes can be people, but also other 'socially-relevant nodes' (ibid.) such as journal articles, hyperlinks, blogs, Tweets, Facebook likes, and so on. Not unlikely, this extension of what may count as a node in SNA is induced by the availability of data mining software and the plethora of socially interesting data objects on the Internet. Hyperlinks are considered socially significant actors, and can be taken up in SNA as indicators of authority, academic performance, political affiliations, public debates, communities in blogs, and international flows of information (De Mayer 2012).

As might be expected, SNA also found its way to Internet business. Google's superior algorithms for determining the order of search results by probable relevance rely heavily on the network principle of links above content. The same can be said of its general business model of targeted advertising as enabled by data aggregation and analysis throughout its numerous services (Gmail, YouTube, Blogger, Google+, Maps, Docs, and so on). And Facebook, while certainly not the first service that afforded online bookkeeping of individual personal networks,[150] can be seen as the ultimate digital-material fusion of SNS and SNA. It invites all of us to translate our personal social network into their digital sign-tool-objects, in order to share our data not only with our own social network, but most of all to share it with Facebook's SNA database, not coincidentally called

---

149. A *small-world network* is a network that enables a relatively short path from any node A to distant node B via in-between nodes that are extremely highly connected, so-called hubs. A *random network* is characterized by a normal distribution of the amount of links over nodes, unlike a *scale-free network* that has a skewed, so-called power-law distribution, where a few nodes get the large majority of links.

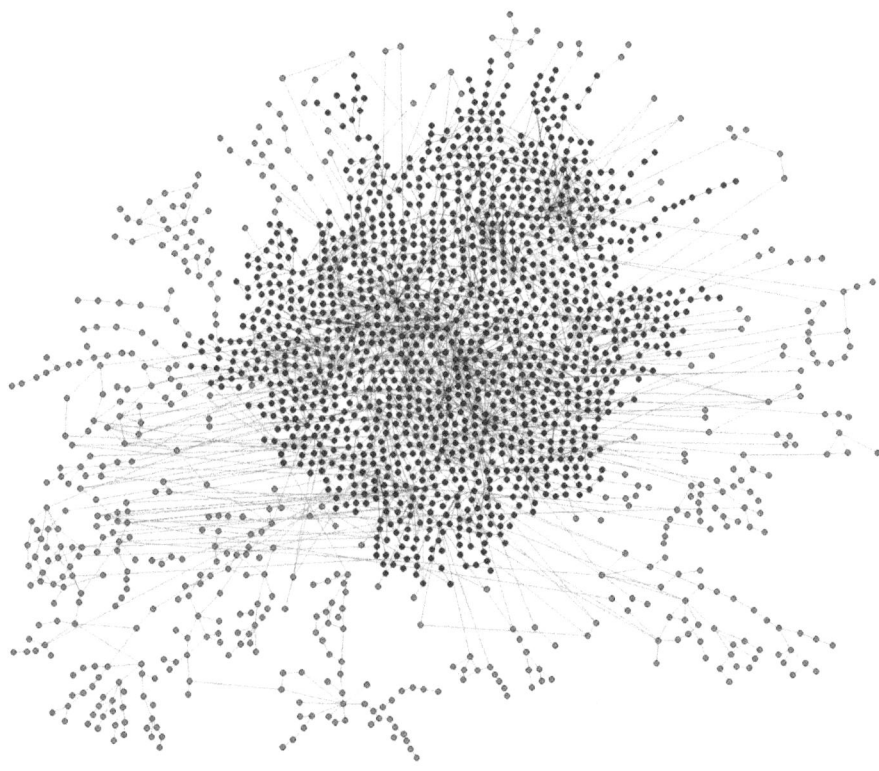

Figure 7. Network diagram: this is not a network.

the *social graph*.[151] Facebook turned out to be so successful that it soon became a synonym for social network. This metaphorical displacement is also mobilized in the movie about Facebook entitled *The Social Network* (Fincher 2010). The title refers to the company and its product, but, as the movie plot strongly suggests, it refers actually most of all to the lack of stable and warm personal relationships of its founder Mark Zuckerberg.

---

150. Founded in 1995, Classmates.com, was, as the name tells, a site that re-united old classmates and can be considered the first SNS. Founded in 1997, SixDegrees.com was the first SNS that aimed to collect personal social networks, explicitly inspired by the network-theoretical notion of 'six degrees of separation', that is, the theory that it takes at maximum six steps through other people's personal social networks to connect any two individuals. Since 2000 hundreds of SNSs have flourished, of which MySpace, founded in 2003, was by far the largest, until Facebook, founded in 2004 took over that position in 2009.
151. The term *social graph* became popularized when Facebook introduced its platform for third-party Facebook app developers in 2007. The platform offered a set of APIs (Application Programming Interfaces) that enabled developers and their software products to access Facebook's data set. The introduction of the platform was announced as the opening up of the social graph of Facebook (Farber 2007), but soon the term became extended and used to indicate the totality of all Internet users and their relations.

Indeed, in this network discourse there no trace left of any notion of electronic highway or cyberspace; the notion of network seems to stand on its own feet. However, to stay with the metaphor, it tends to change shoes every time we try to track its footprints: from mathematical graph to visual diagram, from mathematics to the social, from the social to the hyperlink, from the social network to the personal network to the SNS, back again to the graph that now takes the form of a database. In any case, the network graph is no longer an abstraction that primarily circulated in mathematical and scientific discourse, and the social network is no longer merely a concept in sociology discourse. By several translations, the two terms have been merged, split, and recombined, circling around what may be identified as a third root metaphor for network: NETWORK AS DIAGRAM, AS MAP, with as its hidden shadow NETWORK AS DATABASE. This metaphor, a visualization of the abstract graph, a picture of dots and lines, renders an image and a tool for a wider public than only mathematicians. As a conceptual metaphor it makes the abstract network tangible, traceable and manageable, and as a discourse metaphor it is able to organize scientific research as well as commercial data mining. Moreover, it is a powerful material metaphor that is integrated in software products, that feeds business models, and reorganizes thoroughly the texture of the daily lives of millions.

Notably, this metaphor might well be the most dangerous metaphor of the addressed network metaphors, in spite of its neutral appearance. Or better, precisely because of its neutral, seemingly objective appearance. The diagram suggests scientific truth and authority, and because it does not even look like a metaphor, it stirs no public debate. Admittedly, there is some scholarly criticism of SNA and link analysis that points at the danger of quantitative reification and the importance of qualitative interpretation (Thelwall 2006; De Maeyer 2013), even also in terms of metaphor (Knox et al., 2006). But there is no public debate comparable with that on the electronic highway and cyberspace, no discourse about the implicated politics, economics, and control. Diagram control is practically invisible, as it consists of the collection and processing of data. Control is in the hands of the diagram designer who defines, selects, and decides what counts as nodes and as measured relation. The designer may be a human being or an algorithm, but in any case the translation labor remains invisible, beyond the reach and control of those who are affected. In other words, as with all metaphors, the network diagram tends to ontologize and reify. The model, a constructed reduction, becomes easily equated with the phenomenon itself. The map becomes the territory. We live in networks and no one is in control – that is the message.

5 — THIS IS NOT A NETWORK

But as Latour reminds us that '[m]aps have always been platforms of calculation interfaces' (Latour et al. 2010, 582). He also insists that a network is an artifact of research, an aftereffect. In his words,

> the network does not designate a thing out there that would have roughly the shape of interconnected points, much like a telephone, a freeway, or a sewage 'network'. It is nothing more than *an indicator of the quality of a text* about the topics at hand. (Latour 2005b, 129)

Hence, A NETWORK IS A TEXT, a written account. Latour refers here to so-called actor-network analyses, which give an account of how actors assemble a more or less stable fact from various translations. Arguably, this also holds for the discourse and material metaphors described in the previous sections. Therefore, this last section will address what actor-network theory (ANT) can mean for the analysis of digital-material metaphors.

So the claim is that any network, be it cyberspace, a social network, or a SNS, does not pre-exist as an entity before it gets described, translated, assembled, and metaphorized. It takes labor. And, in the case of software-driven networks, it also takes transcoding labor that translates the digital into the analog and vice versa.

As mentioned before, transcoding is a verb. It refers to the multiple acts deployed by digital-material metaphors: importing, exporting, splitting, assembling, associating, mobilizing, streamlining, bridging, dividing, selecting, demarcating, framing, assigning, representing, and depresenting. Saliently, all these acts are movements: transports and transferences that are simultaneously transformations and translations. Even in cases of the plain transportation of data objects, such as images or music files, several interventions by transcoding devices are necessary: properly configured screens and loudspeakers, operating systems that know how to handle instructions, programs that render files correctly, network protocols that orchestrate transmission, error checking, and correcting. These devices are all continuously transcoding digital data into digital-analog objects and vice versa. Only some of these devices reveal in their name something of their procedural transcoding mechanism. For instance, a *modem* (modulator-demodulator), a device that translates analog audio signals into digital beeps, and back again, or a *codec* (compressor-decompressor or coder-decoder), a software program that encodes a video data stream for transmission or storage, and decodes it for playback or editing.

Yet most hardware and software devices hide their transmission and transcoding in icontologized metaphors, thereby hiding their network labor. In that regard it is remarkable that none of Manovich's five principles of digitality accounts for transport and mobility. Every act in digital praxis involves data transport, on various scales: on the micro scale of electronic circuits and analog mechanisms inside a machine, on the meso scale of transfer to peripherals as mouse, keyboard, screen, and printers, and on the macro scale of networks of geographically and physically distributed servers and routers. Such travels can only be possible because of another crucial feature of digital code: its mobility, better, its *immutable mobility,* as Latour has called it (Latour and Woolgar 1979; Latour 1990).

Immutable mobiles
The concept of the 'immutable mobile' refers to the translation of 'material substance into a figure or diagram' (Latour and Woolgar 1997, 51). The inscription devices that register traces of these translations produce objects such as maps, diagrams, record tables, and data lists. These informational objects are transportable, yet have to remain stable during their travels to other locations. As Latour put it, they 'have the properties of being mobile but also immutable, presentable, readable and combinable with one another' (Latour 1990, 6). Immutable mobiles contribute to the building of actor-networks by their ability to circulate and enroll actors at distant locations. A geographical map is a good example of an immutable mobile. Territories cannot be moved or carried around the world, but they can be translated into maps that can travel instead, as a substitute of the territory. The map is not only an iconic and indexical sign, referring to the territory; it enables acting at distance as it discloses the territory for action, be it a holiday trip, warfare, border patrol, or colonization. Indeed, what I would call a material metaphor. While moving to other locations the map can be compared with other inscription registrations, and can be recombined, adjusted, and transformed into new objects. The same holds for scientific data lists generated in laboratories,

obtained by the translation of rat's or people's behavior into inscriptions that can be transported and distributed, thereby mobilizing scientists, public debates, political decisions, pharmaceutical investments or other interventions and translations.

The immutability of these mobiles is a prerequisite of their ability to travel and to arrive with the inscriptions intact. If they would change, degenerate, or extinguish while underway there would no point in their mobility and travel. Yet there is a trade-off between mobility and immutability: inscriptions in stone are more durable than those on paper, but clearly less mobile. And while paper is more prone to wear and tear, modification, and counterfeit, it is also more cuttable and re-combinable, which increases its mobilizing mobility. Latour claims that 'the best of these mobiles had to do with written, numbered or optically consistent paper surfaces' (Latour 1990, 20), but perhaps the utter best mobiles are those that consist of digital code.

The mobility of digital code resides in physical-material inscriptions that can in principle travel to other locations without losing their coded pattern during travel. Digital code, in whatever format, is a perfect immutable mobile, able to circulate and spread its inscriptions at any scale and on any carrier through various infrastructural networks.

However, it is important to stress that the immutability and preservation of traveling digital code does not come naturally, by default, without effort. Contrary to popular belief bits are not flawless – bits can mutate while underway. They are prone to tiny errors, yielding to tiny perturbations that, when reaching a threshold, may render the bit stream useless, unreadable, non-executable, unable to enroll any action or actor. As Matthew Kirschenbaum noticed,

> computers are not flawless. Errors typically occur at the juncture between analog and digital states, such as when a drive's magnetoresistive head assigns a binary symbolic value to the voltage differentials it has registered or when an e-mail message is reconstituted from independent data packets moving across the TCP/IP layer of the Internet. All forms of modern digital technology incorporate hyper-redundant error-checking routines that serve to sustain an illusion of immateriality by detecting error and correcting it, reviving the quality of the signal, like old-fashioned telegraph relays. (Kirschenbaum 2008, 12)

Hence, to assure the immutable mobility of digital code, perpetual repair labor is needed.

Net-works, work-nets, and mobility

When it comes to the mobility of digital objects, its should also be noted that mobility in actor-network theory is not confined to infrastructural or technological networks. An actor-network does not resemble a telegraph network, nor does it resemble a self-evolving organ like the brain or the nervous system. It does not look like a network at all, it has the appearance of a matter of fact, a black box that is taken-for-granted. It is a 'work-net' rather than a net-work. As Latour puts it, '*Work*-nets could allow one to see the labor that goes on in laying down *net*-works: the first as an active mediator, the second as a stabilized set of intermediaries' (Latour 2005b,132). And even such a settled black boxed net-work need not necessarily be a technological network – a functioning car or computer can be described as a net-work, but also a highway system or the Internet. In other words, we have to distinguish analytically between technological-infrastructural *networks,* reified and blackboxed *net-works,* and tracked down *work-nets.*

Therefore, we can distinguish two kinds of digital mobility. First, as referring to the transport over dedicated pathways between nodes of a laid-down infrastructural network such as the Internet, a household PC network, or a mobile cell net. The second kind of mobility refers to the mobilization of various actors that hold together a settled net-work as a matter of fact, such as a functioning computer, your web browser, or Google's search engine. The silent mobility and mobilization at work in those frozen net-works can be revealed after a breakdown, either a mechanical breakdown, as when the car, the computer or Google stops functioning, or after an analytical breakdown, consisting of the tracing of translations and documenting the work-net involved.

When figuring out what digital praxis implies, we should take into account that computer networks, and the Internet in particular, accommodate mobility as well as mobilization. The Internet is both a network (infrastructure), a net-work (blackboxed matter of fact) and a work-net (ongoing translation, transcoding, and mobilization). The three instances of networking are inextricably intertwined, but they should not be confused. The infrastructural network of the Internet is quite different from the culturally conceived Internet as net-work (be it as electronic highway, cyberspace, Web 2.0, or social graph), and also from what can analytically be traced as work-net. The Internet as work-net is even able to mobilize actors that are not infrastructurally connected, such as the indigenous peasants of the Zapatista movement in Mexico during the 1990s (Castells 1997; Cleaver 1998).

Nonetheless, it is important to keep an eye on the Internet as a technical infrastructure that accommodates transport mobility. Self-evident as this may look, it cannot be stressed enough that the Internet came into being because of this plain mobility – the simple transport of digital data as immutable mobiles. Despite the haunting myth that the Internet was created to survive a nuclear attack, it was implemented for efficiency reasons: using computer resources on systems at distance (Abbate 2000; Castells 2001). The principle of blind data transport is still the main principle of the Internet (though under enduring pressure). However, the plain material existence of hardware devices, wires, and channels is not enough to ensure data traffic. Both the immutability and the mobility of the transported data has to be ascertained, and this is done by network protocols.

Control by protocol

The infrastructural mobility of the Internet is regulated by the TCP/IP (Transmission Control Protocol/Internet Protocol) suite. As its combined name already indicates, it consists of a set of protocols that accommodate the transmission of data objects (TCP) over connected internetworks (IP). [152] It is an open protocol that provides end-to-end connectivity and regulates transmission, but also other translations that are needed to reach a particular Internet address. TCP/IP manages the transmission process by slicing data objects into small packets (packet switching), and transporting these packets towards the nearest available IP node. If necessary TCP/IP distributes the packages over different routes. TCP also performs error checks and corrections on the packets, and finally reassembles the data packets into a functional whole at the destination node. On top of these basic transmission protocols, every application (email, file transfer, chat, web browsing) has its own protocol encapsulated within this basic transport layer, in order to process, maintain, and reassemble their own modular entities. In short, network mobility is controlled by protocol, not by the hardware network infrastructure.

---

152. TCP is part of the transport layer of the Internet architecture, IP is part of the internet layer (uncapitalized). This layer is responsible for the formation of so-called *internetworks* through gateways. Gateways connect independent networks of different protocols, thus making them available for IP traffic. In that regard, the Internet is a network of networks, or better, a network of internetworks unified by the TCP/IP protocol.

As new media scholar Alexander Galloway (2004) has pointed out, these protocols are simultaneously technological and political. Protocol historically referred to diplomatic agreements within a specific system of conventions. They specified rules of conduct and proper behavior that were documented and sealed. In the context of networked computing, protocols serve the same function now as standards that 'govern how specific *technologies* are agreed to, adopted, implemented, and ultimately used by people around the world' (Galloway 2004, 7). Galloway considers network protocols as political 'management style' for what Deleuze (1992) has called the society of control. This new type of society is characterized by a databased cutting up of formerly molded entities, as Deleuze noted,

> The numerical language of control is made of codes that mark access to information, or reject it. We no longer find ourselves dealing with the mass/individual pair. Individuals have become 'dividuals,' and masses [have become], samples, data, markets, or 'banks.' (Deleuze 1992, 5)

In opposition to the common misconceptions of networks, and especially the Internet, as being inherently decentralized, democratic, and out of control, Galloway argues that there is no network without protocol and, hence, control. However, protocol is not necessarily univocal. Galloway suggests that there is a fundamental tension between two opposed protocological machines (Galloway 2004, 8): one of autonomous locales with distributed peer-to-peer relations (with TCP/IP as the ultimate case) and one of centralized rigid hierarchies (with the Domain Name System protocol as the ultimate case).

One might think that these two protocols serve as metaphors for similar tensions between autonomy and hierarchy in the society of control, and maybe they could even be analyzed as material metaphors that generate such tensions. But that is out of the question. According to Eugene Thacker in his foreword to Galloway's book, the concept of protocol is meant to demonstrate the nonmetaphorical quality of networks: 'Understanding networks not as metaphors, but as materialized and materializing media, is an important step toward diversifying and complexifying our understanding of power relationships in control societies' (Thacker, in Galloway 2004, xv).

As I hope to have shown throughout this study, the material and the metaphorical are not mutually exclusive categories. It is indeed necessary to understand networks (and protocols) in their material form, but any choice for a particular material form (infrastructure, hardware innovation, tiering, growth, data streams, protocol, and so on) is inherently also a metaphor or metonym. And, especially when the aim is to flesh out the protocological formatting of the society of control, a lot more metaphors will be encountered underway. Control protocols do not translate directly into control societies. That takes a much longer chain of enrollments, translations, mobilizations, and transcodings.

Network protocols are transcoding mechanisms. They translate digital code into cultural code and vice versa, thereby rendering and mobilizing various digital-material metaphors (think of gateways, peers, packets, and addresses). Thinking in terms of transcoding by and into digital-material metaphors forces us to think of networks as a verb, as work-nets that take labor, by digital-material metaphors among others. The questions to be asked of digital-material metaphors are questions about the work going in the net: what is mobilized from which setting? what is captured in inscriptions? what is translated into what, by which protocol, by which actors? what is lost, what is gained? what gets represented and remediated? what gets depresented and demediated? what gets ontologized and blackboxed, what gets opened up for further translations?

what labor gets obfuscated or substituted, what new labor and subject interpellations can be identified?

The concepts of transcoding and digital-material metaphors enable researchers to evade two pitfalls that can be considered the Scylla and Charybdis of new media studies. The first one is *'screen essentialism'* (Kirschenbaum 2008, 27) which is a narrow focus on visual representations and interface effects that ignores the material base in inscription, storage, and mobility. The second pitfall could be called *network essentialism*, and this tendency comes in three variations. First, 'seeing only one kind of network': an exclusive focus on either technological networks (of artifacts) or social networks (of people), while there are so many mixtures and other network types simultaneously at work. Secondly, the variant of 'seeing networks everywhere': translating anything into network diagrams and attributing inherent network laws to anything that can be translated into a set of nodes and relations.

Thirdly, and in fact the most common pitfall, 'seeing no network at all': taking blackboxed and metaphorized forms for granted, without tracing the work-nets that uphold them. Apparently self-evident facts or forms, that do not look like networks at all, can be traced as real working networks, work-nets. Work-nets work hard to assemble and align various actors and to maintain their performance as coherent self-evident things or phenomena. As we have seen throughout this study, they often condensate into metaphors. Metaphors are work-nets.

CONCLUSIONS
A MANIFESTO FOR HACKING METAPHORS
HOW METAPHORS MATTER IN DIGITAL PRAXIS

> *True interaction with technical systems involves creative use*
> *and abuse outside the box, metaphorization, writing and rewriting,*
> *configuring, disconfiguring, erasing.*
> (Florian Cramer, 2005)

Throughout this study I have followed the trail of metaphors in order to investigate how they format digital and cultural praxis. I divided this general question into three subquestions:
1. Which digital-material transcodings and material-semiotic translations can be traced if we follow metaphors as actors?
2. How do such transcodings and translations get stabilized as taken-for-granted, as naturalized matters of facts?
3. Which further translations are attached to those transcoding metaphors, that is, which ideologies, narratives, and discourses are sustained (or suppressed)?

In order to answer these questions I mapped a route through what I consider the main issues involved in digital praxis: interface (Chapter 1), materiality (Chapter 2), media (Chapter 3), immediacy (Chapter 4), software (Chapter 5) and sociability (Chapter 6).

It was clear from the start that the metaphors that were examined and the material-semiotic networks in which they partake are wildly heterogeneous, as each chapter demonstrates by its varied cases and discourses. Nevertheless, some general findings can be carved out. I will present them in the form of a manifesto.

The genre of the manifesto has a longstanding history in new media discourse (see for example Haraway 1995, Barlow 1996, Van den Boomen 2001, Wark 2004). The manifesto is usually a bold cultural-political declaration that articulates an urgent perspective and aims to mobilize others into action or a change of mind. This also holds for the present 'Manifesto for hacking metaphors', though its focus is also academic and theoretical. It aims to sketch the outlines of the field of research I explored in this study: the wild adventurous lands at the intersection of metaphor analysis, material semiotics, and new media studies.

The first part of the manifesto serves to clear the terrain. A series of statements are made concerning metaphors in general, focusing in particular on what they are not. The second part consists of a methodological call to analyze the material-semiotic performativity of digital-material metaphors. The third part addresses how digital matters of fact come about by the transcoding labor of metaphors, ordered by the themes of the previous chapters.

1 — WHAT METAPHORS ARE NOT

Metaphors are never just metaphorical

Metaphors are never 'just a metaphor', without any implications beyond the intentions of the speaker. Wider implications are part and parcel of the dynamics of metaphor, independent of human intentions or whatever meaning is presupposed.

Metaphors do not transfer meaning
In fact, metaphors do not transfer meaning at all, contrary to the common conception of metaphor. This common idea implies a very limited idea of both metaphor and meaning. Seeing metaphor as the transfer of meaning reduces metaphor to a neutral vehicle, and reduces meaning to a ready-made package to be transported. But meaning does not precede metaphor, it is the other way around. Metaphors generate meaning. If we have to use a metaphor for metaphor: metaphor is a meaning-making machine, not a mechanical meaning-transferring vehicle.

Metaphors are not figural
To tackle another common idea of metaphor: metaphor is also not figurative meaning, conceived as opposed to literal, original meaning. Phenomena do not have an intrinsic, natural meaning; meaning is always produced in social and cultural translations and iterations. The distinction between the literal and the figurative is a cultural after-effect, with a hidden dominance of the literal, the supposedly 'real', 'true', 'proper' origin.
Nevertheless, metaphors should be taken seriously – that is, literally. Not as a metaphysical original truth, but as a productive and performative material-semiotic device that articulates meaning by usage (Davidson 1978). Metaphors mobilize experiences and associations, and create meaning by selecting and assembling from these resources – literally.

Metaphors are not neutral
Metaphors are neither good nor bad, but least of all are they neutral. All metaphors reify, unify, and homogenize, and at the same time they connect, multiply, and differentiate. All metaphors ontologize and liquefy.
Metaphors are by definition double mechanisms in themselves. They are marked by simultaneous contraction and expansion. They enable the condensation, contraction, and ontologizing of elements collected from different cultural-semantic domains, and they also enable transfer and expansion into not yet associated domains. They are able to squeeze a relation into a unified thing, and conversely they are able to create a relation between separate things. They are able to freeze, and they are able to set in motion.
Deceiving as metaphorical freezing may sometimes be, it is a highly convenient and efficient mechanism. It enables us to deal with the complexities of the world we live in, without being overwhelmed by the intricate constructions that keep things going, and without needing to invent in each case new words and concepts for new phenomena and things.

Metaphor is not limited to language and thought
Though most illustrations of metaphor are taken from speech and language, metaphors are not limited to this modality. Metaphors can take the form of words, images, sounds, smells, gestures,

objects, acts, movements, and any combination of these modes. Any modality, mode, or medium is able to carry out metaphorical transfer.

Digital computer technology is extremely marked by metaphors. Here, metaphors nestle themselves not only in the representations of the technology and the discourse on its use and functions, but also in the technological objects themselves: the very thingness of digital objects consists of metaphors made material and operational. Such digital-material metaphors go beyond mere representation and language. They act as signs and metaphors, but also as things and procedures. The effects and implications of such sign-tool-object-metaphors are discursive and non-discursive, yet by all means material, embodied, and medium-specifically inscribed.

2 — TRACING DIGITAL-MATERIAL METAPHORS

Go beyond conceptual metaphors

According to the dominant conceptual theory of metaphor, metaphors frame the way we think, talk and act (Lakoff and Johnson 1980). This theory thus acknowledges that metaphors can have material consequences, but metaphor as such remains completely semantic and cognitive, captured in the human mind. For this reason, the conceptual theory of metaphor cannot account for the executive and material productivity of metaphors, in particular in digital praxis.

Shift to sign-tool-objects

In order to investigate digital praxis, the notion of metaphor should be extended beyond the notion of conceptual metaphors. What we need is a shift from sign to sign-tool-object: a shift from iconicity to indexicality (Peirce 1967), and from conceptual metaphoricity to material metaphoricity (Hayles 2002). Such an analysis not only accounts for the sign part (conceptual, cognitive, semantic, semiotic, discursive), but also for the tool and object part (operational, organizational, material), and most of all, for the affordances of further translations into wider social praxis and discourse.

Material metaphors matter

The notion of material metaphor elevates the operational reach of metaphor beyond language and cognition towards material and social configurations.

Material metaphors can be defined as embodied metaphors (sign-tool-objects) that connect and coalesce symbolic concepts with technological artifacts. Interface metaphors such as page, windows, or hyperlink are material metaphors. They embody material affordances and constraints, as well as a specific connection to the digital back office, which' configuration affords and assigns different subject positions such as developers, maintainers, and users.

Discourse metaphors matter

The notion of discourse metaphor elevates the operational reach of metaphor beyond language and cognition towards organized discursive formations. Discourse metaphors can be conceptual metaphors (electronic highway, cyberspace) that frame broad social discourses, but in digital praxis they are often also material metaphors directly connected to technological artifacts (email, virtual community, Web 2.0, Facebook friend). In any case, discourse metaphors organize social-political discourse, not merely as language and documents, but rather as monuments regulating power, authority, institutional embeddedness, and the assignment of subject positions (Foucault 1972).

Material metaphors transfer, translate, and transform
Material metaphors and discourse metaphors perform transference labor on several levels. First, transference as translation from one code or mode (linguistic, semiotic, cultural, analog, digital) to another code. Second, this implicates the political-representational mobilization of other actors. And last, but not least, transference in the sense of labor and generation: the transformation of raw material into something else, be it symbolic, material, or hybrid, as is the case with digital-material metaphors.

Metaphorical transfer = translation + transformation + generation. Metaphors work by isolating a specific part of a perceived or conceived unity (semantic or situational) and transferring/translating this cut-off slice to another context, thereby reformatting that context and generating meaning. Metaphor is partiality, iterability and recombinability in action. Cut, copy, paste, remix.

Material metaphors are actors
Again, material and discourse metaphors generate more than mere conceptual meaning. They generate material-semiotic conditions for further translations. They are actors (mediators, translators) in actor-networks (Latour 2005b). Like conceptual metaphors they associate, blend, format, highlight, and obscure on the conceptual level. But as material metaphors they also equalize, substitute, essentialize, and ontologize at the level of material organization. And as discourse metaphors they differentiate, qualify, and legitimate particular social, cultural or political orders.

Use material metaphors as keys to the black box
Material metaphors are the keys to the black boxes of software and machinery. They are able to close and conceal, but also able to open up the black box and reveal its insides. They can be used for epistemological reverse engineering. That is, tracking down the subsequent translations and transferences: this connects to that, this translates that into something else, then it is transported to that, and so on. A material metaphor is an epistemological hacking tool, enabling us to hack the black boxes of code and machinery by reverse engineering.
In other words, material metaphors not only assemble associations, experiences, and acts, and not only perform the necessary indexical labor of translations between hardware, code, and events, but they also provide analytical apertures in the various digital-material black boxes, enabling us to peek inside their construction and attachments.

Follow the trails of metaphors
Reverse engineering digital-material metaphors is a matter of following trails, and describing what exactly happens on the trail by means of trail-bound questioning. The trails to follow are threefold.
First, there is the trail of metaphorical icontology and transference. What does the metaphor foreground and amplify – literally, materially, and discursively – and what does it nullify and ignore? What does this mean for user control, knowledge, qualification, disqualification, possible and impossible subject positions?
Second, there is the trail of software-driven indexicality, pointing towards and inwards the machine and the wider networks. What software commands are attached to specific user acts, how are these assembled in specific interfaces, practices, and back offices, and how do these practices in their turn get metaphorized and icontologized?

Third, there is the trail of the cultural connection to broader discourses and social transcoding. How do interfaces, digital-material metaphors, and discourse metaphors enroll and enact each other? How do they organize social order by assigning social positions and privileges? Are there possibilities for disembedding and discontinuity?

3 — HACKING DIGITAL MATTERS OF FACT

Hack the icontology of interfacial immediacy

User interfaces are built around various metaphors of one-click immediacy: icons, menu options, hyperlinks, like buttons, share buttons. Though these clickable or tappable interface metaphors certainly contribute to user-friendliness and wider adoption of digital devices, they also withhold user control and knowledge about the system. They are sign-tool-objects that hide their tool-being. Their clickability is based on indexical connections to the machinery of hardware, software, and protocols, but this indexicality is superseded by icontology: the seductive iconicity of metaphorical objects that ontologize iconic representations into taken-for-granted icon-objects.

Hack the screen metaphors of transparency
The screen – as hardware interface and as projection plane – is the most imperialist interface metaphor of contemporary digital devices. The screen not only colonizes and subdues other interfacial devices such as keyboard, mouse, and wires, it also reduces digital and social praxis to visual representations on a transparent plane. Representation has lost its body, due to icontologizing metaphors such as windows and mirrors that accentuate surface and reflection. Yet, the reverse engineering of those metaphors as material metaphors can lay bare their material embeddedness and retrieve something of the receded embodiment, skills, translations, and labor at stake.

Hack mediation beyond media
Media-specific analysis is a hard endeavor since we actually do not know what a medium is. The very notion of medium is a floating signifier, able to embark on any contingent, metonymical or metaphorical ship that passes by. In popular discourse metonyms prevail: medium as carrier, as production tool, as display, as distribution system, as modality, or as language. In media theory the notion of medium is often marked by metaphors of functionality: media as membrane, channel, container, or master, and more recently, as space and ecology. At stake is the issue whether media should be conceived as ontologized things or rather as process enablers, that is, as marked by the disembodied conduit metaphor or by the embodied toolmaker's paradigm (Reddy 1993).

Hack beyond new media
Material-semiotic transferences and translations seem to disappear the moment we talk about them in terms of media. It does not help much to call them new media or social media or to mobilize extra characteristics such as interactivity, as long as interactivity is seen as a feature of an ontologized medium, and not as acts, or flows of events that have to be performed by multiple actors: hardware, software, humans, standards, protocols, institutions, laws, money,

and metaphors. No matter how much dynamics we include in our definition of digital media, the very concept of medium tends to mobilize a focus on signs, signals, and representation, rather than on tools and acts by users and machines.

There are no media anymore – instead there are perpetual transmediations and translations of life and labor, including the metaphorical transferences that delivers them as icontologized executables.

Hack remediation beyond media
While interfaces often remediate (Bolter and Grusin 1999) and metaphorize recognizable media forms such as print (document, page, browse), film (forward, zoom, pause), television (life streams, YouTube), and theater (role playing games), there is a growing domain of digital-material metaphors that are are not derived from media formats. Metaphors such as virtual community, Web 2.0, Facebook friend, following, phishing, and liking all tap from other resources. They translate and transform conventions, acts, habits, and desires into digital-material entities that subsequently become mediatized and 'app-etized'.

The concept of transmediation is proposed to indicate translation processes of remediation and demediation that go beyond ontologized media forms. The ongoing proliferation of transmediations and the increased mobility of inscription devices results in ever more material-semiotic, digital-analog, and techno-social blends.

Hack software ideology and its metaphors

Computer code is usually conceived as artificial or executable language, but that is already a metaphor. Compared to human language computer code is more rigid (due to its indexical connection to machine code) and constrained (by icontologized interfacial representation), which easily flips over the metaphor of software as language into software as a thing. Yet, at the same time software is more mutable and mobile than things and human language, as it allows in principle user intervention, multiplication, and modification.

The political economy of software can be described as a history of erasing and forgetting labor (labor by women, and other humans, by hardware, by design, by software, and by metaphors). Thereby, the historical split between hardware and software, and between programmers and users, becomes naturalized. Software functions as Althusserian ideology (Chun 2006), a digital-material ideological apparatus that not only configures machines but also subjects with specific prescriptions and proscriptions.

Hack digital immateriality
The collocation in terms of digital-material does not refer to a contradictory blend of a supposed digital immateriality on the one hand and a physical materiality on the other hand. The digital is not immaterial, it is always in-material (Schäfer 2011), both formally and forensically (Kirschenbaum 2008). The formal materiality of digital entities can be described by five principles: numerical representation, modulation, automation, variation, and transcoding (Manovich 2001).

Transcoding implies any traffic and translation between the computational and the cultural, including those between the digital and the analog, resulting in new inscriptions and digital-material objects. Digital-material transcoding draws its productivity on the material-semiotic entanglement of physical affordances, procedural labor (by humans and machines), and material-metaphorical coding.

Hack the digital-analog dichotomy
Human-readable digital objects are always already composites of the digital and the analog. They are digital-analog Oreo cookies (Hayles 2005), packages of numerical representations sandwiched between analog representations. The notion of analog has a double meaning: it refers to the proportional translation of a physical phenomenon onto an inscription device (for example light patterns captured on a photograph), but also to translations by means of semantic analogies and metaphors.

Digital-material metaphors are constructed by analog transferences of both kinds. They acquire their form as sign-tool-objects by analog-metaphorical import from other semantic domains, but they are also analog in the sense of proportional containment so that when transferred over distance or converted into another format they preserve their proportional patterns.

Hack network metaphors
Just like concepts such as media and software, the notion of network is imbued with metaphors. Three root metaphors prevail here: the telegraph (network as technical infrastructure enabling transport), the nervous system (network as dynamic self-organizing organ), and the graph (network as diagram representing relations between nodes).

In new media discourse the metaphors of electronic highway and cyberspace are typical examples of respectively the infrastructural and the organic network metaphor. While these metaphors primarily seem to be discourse metaphors that mobilize different narratives of space, they are to some extent also material metaphors that organize and regulate digital space in different ways, thereby implicating different political orders.

Hack the network graph
Currently the most prominent – and probably the most dangerous – network metaphor is that of the graph, with the social network site as its glorious instantiation. The diagram of the graph became a representational instrument that enables the translation of a two-dimensional data spreadsheet into a suggestive three-dimensional visualization of relations, patterns, and clusters. But as all representational forms, it is prone to representationalism and icontology, easily yielding to the misleading equation of map and network. Nonetheless, misleading equations can be strong material metaphors. As a material metaphor the network graph not only informs and organizes relatively new academic fields such as social network analysis and digital humanities, but most of all it can be translated into successful business models, such as Google's and Facebook's.

Hack the metaphors of sociality
Metaphors of sociability and social organization have been present since the early days of the Internet, and even before that. The global village is a case in point (McLuhan 1962), but the village metaphor really gained ground as a material metaphor in the 1990s with the advent of virtual communities (Rheingold 1993). Firmly connected to the software affordances of that time – articulated by the page metaphor as a structural and social space organizer – the metaphor of the virtual community embodied a new form of sociability.

When the material metaphor of the page dissolved into dynamic aggregations of data fragments, the material metaphors of Web 2.0 and social graphs superseded the virtual community. Online sociability was no longer framed as collective, but rather as connective. It marked the rise of networked individualism (Wellman 2001), performed on social network sites and other user-generated content sites, later loosely assembled under the label social media.

Hack social media and the cloud
While there are definitely forms of sociability going on in social media, the metaphor of social media overemphasizes both the social and the media – as if these notions are explanations of current digital praxis instead of what has to be explained.

The metaphor of social media, strongly connected to the metaphor of the cloud, is a prime example of a material metaphor that successfully obscures its own materiality while creating robust matters of fact. Unlike the Web 2.0 metaphor it ignores and mystifies the role of software design and business models. Instead, it proffers a cloudy image of ownerless machines in the sky, maintained by angels, freely available for human social use. Clouds may be even harder to hack than black boxes – let it be a challenge for new media reverse engineers.

REFERENCES

Abbate, Janet. 2000. *Inventing the Internet*. Cambridge: MIT Press.
Abrams, Janet, and Peter Hall, ed. 2006. *Else/Where: Mapping - New Cartographies of Networks and Territories*. 1st ed. University of Minnesota Design Institute.
Agre, Philip E., and Douglas Schuler. 1997. *Reinventing Technology, Rediscovering Community: Critical Explorations of Computing as a Social Practice*. Greenwich: Ablex.
Akrich, Madeleine. 1992. 'The De-Scription of Technical Objects'. In *Shaping Technology/Building Society: Studies in Socio-Technical Change*, edited by Wiebe E. Bijker and John Law, 205-24. Cambridge: MIT Press.
Allen, Matthew. 2013. 'What Was Web 2.0? Versions as the Dominant Mode of Internet History'. *New Media & Society* 15 (2): 260-75.
Althusser, Louis. 1971 [1969]. 'Ideology and Ideological State Apparatuses (Notes towards an Investigation)'. In *Lenin and Philosophy and Other Essays*. New York: Monthly Review Press.
Althusser, Louis. 1984 [1972]. 'Reply to John Lewis'. In *Essays on Ideology*, 61-139. London: Verso.
Anderson, Benedict. 1983. *Imagined Communities: Reflections on the Origin and Spread of Nationalism*. London: Verso.
Anderson, Chris. 2010. 'The Web Is Dead? A Debate'. *Wired Online* 18 (9). http://www.wired.com/magazine/2010/08/ff_webrip_debate/.
Anderson, Jon, Jodi Dean, and Geert Lovink. 2006. *Reformatting Politics: Information Technology and Global Civil Society*. New York: Routledge.
Aristotle. 1996 [328 BC]. *Poetics*. London: Penguin Books.
Arns, Inke. 2004. 'Read_me, Run_me, Execute_me: Software and Its Discontents, or: It's the Performativity of Code, Stupid!' In *Read_Me: Software Art & Cultures*, edited by Olga Goriunova and Alexei Shulgin, 176-193. Arhus: Digital Aesthetics Research Center.
Arns, Inke. 2005. 'Code as Performative Speech Act'. *Artnodes* (4). http://www.uoc.edu/artnodes/espai/eng/art/arns0505.pdf.
Auslander, Philip. 2008. *Liveness: Performance in a Mediatized Culture*. London: Taylor & Francis.
Austin, John Langshaw. 1962. *How to Do Things with Words*. Cambridge: Harvard University Press.
Bakardjieva, Maria. 2005. *Internet Society: The Internet in Everyday Life*. London: Sage.
Barabási, Albert-László. 2002. *Linked: The New Science of Networks*. Cambridge: Perseus.
Barad, Karen. 2003. 'Posthumanist Performativity: Toward an Understanding of How Matter Comes to Matter'. *Signs: Journal of Women in Culture & Society* 28 (3): 801-831.
Barassi, Veronica, and Emiliano Treré. 2012. 'Does Web 3.0 Come after Web 2.0? Deconstructing Theoretical Assumptions through Practice'. *New Media & Society* 14 (7): 1-17.
Barbosa, Simone D. J., and Clarisse Sieckenius de Souza. 2000. 'Extending Software through Metaphors and Metonymies'. In *Proceedings of the 5th International Conference on Intelligent User Interfaces*, 13-20. New Orleans: ACM Press.
Barbrook, Richard, and Andy Cameron. 1995. 'The Californian Ideology'. *Mute* 1 (3). http://www.alamut.com/subj/ideologies/pessimism/califIdeo_I.html.
Barlow, John Perry. 1996. 'A Declaration of the Independence of Cyberspace'. http://homes.eff.org/~barlow/Declaration-Final.html.
Barrett, Edward, ed. 1991. *The Society of Text: Hypertext, Hypermedia and the Social Construction of Information*. Cambridge: MIT Press.
Bart, van, Adraan. 2013. 'Sense and Simplicity'. *New Media Studies Magazine* Digital Visual Culture 2 (7). http://www.newmediastudies.nl/magazine/sense-and-simplicity.
Barthes, Roland. 1968. *Elements of Semiology*. New York: Hill and Wang.
Barthes, Roland. 1977. *Image-Music-Text*. London: Fontana.

Baudry, Jean-Louis, and Alan Williams. 1974. 'Ideological Effects of the Basic Cinematographic Apparatus'. *Film Quarterly* 28 (2): 39-47.

Bay-Cheng, Sarah, Chiel Kattenbelt, Andrew Lavender, and Robin Nelson, ed. 2010. *Mapping Intermediality in Performance*. Amsterdam: Amsterdam University Press.

Bellis, Mary. n.d. 'The Unusual History of Microsoft Windows'. *About.com Inventors*. http://inventors.about.com/od/mstartinventions/a/Windows.htm.

Benedikt, Michael. 1991. *Cyberspace: First Steps*. Cambridge: MIT Press.

Berg, van den, Bibi. 2009. *The Situated Self: Identity in a World of Ambient Intelligence*. Rotterdam: PhD thesis Erasmus University.

Bergson, Henri. 1990 [1896]. *Matter and Memory*. New York: Zone Books.

Berlo, David Kenneth. 1960. *The Process of Communication: An Introduction to Theory and Practice*. New York: Holt, Rinehart & Winston.

Berners-Lee, Tim. 2000. *Weaving the Web: The Original Design and Ultimate Destiny of the World Wide Web*. New York: Harper Paperbacks.

Besselaar, Peter van den, and Dennis Beckers. 2005. 'The Life and Death of the Great Amsterdam Digital City'. In *Digital Cities III: Information Technologies for Social Capital: Cross-Cultural Perspectives*, edited by Peter van den Besselaar and Satoshi Koizumi, 66-96. Berlin: Springer.

Bijker, Wiebe E., and John Law. 1992. *Shaping Technology/Building Society: Studies in Socio-Technical Change*. Cambridge: MIT Press.

Black, Max. 1962. *Models and Metaphors: Studies in Language and Philosophy*. Ithaca: Cornell University Press.

Blankema, Freek. 2010. 'Oracle lanceert "cloud in een doos"'. *Automatisering Gids* (38) (September 24): 4.

Block, Ned. 2010. 'The Mind as the Software of the Brain'. In *Science Fiction and Philosophy: From Time Travel to Superintelligence*, edited by Susan Schneider, 126-170. Chichester: Wiley-Blackwell.

Blood, Rebecca. 2000. 'Weblogs: A History And Perspective'. *Rebecca's Pocket*. September 7. http://www.rebeccablood.net/essays/weblog_history.html.

Bol, Marjolijn, and Ann-Sophie Lehmann. 2012. 'Painting Skin and Water: Towards a Material Iconography of Translucent Motifs in Early Netherlandish Painting'. In *Rogier van der Weyden in Context*, edited by Lorne Campbell, Jan van der Stock, Catherine Reynolds, and Lieve Watteeuw, 215-228. Understanding and Technology in Painting 17. Leuven: Peeters.

Bolter, Jay David, and Diane Gromala. 2003. *Windows and Mirrors: Interaction Design, Digital Art, and the Myth of Transparency*. Cambridge: MIT Press.

Bolter, Jay David, and Richard Grusin. 2000 [1999]. *Remediation: Understanding New Media*. Cambridge: MIT Press.

Boomen, van den, Marianne, and Mirko Tobias Schäfer. 2005. 'Will the Revolution Be Open-Sourced? How Open Source Travels through Society'. In *How Open Is the Future? Economic, Social and Cultural Scenarios Inspired by Free*, edited by Jan Cornelis and Marleen Wynants, 31-67. Brussels: VUB University Press.

Boomen, van den, Marianne, Joost Raessens, Ann-Sophie Lehmann, Sybille Lammes, and Mirko Tobias Schäfer, ed. 2009. *Digital Material: Tracing New Media in Everyday Life and Technology*. Amsterdam: Amsterdam University Press.

Boomen, van den, Marianne. 1994. 'Annie, Get Your Email! Virtuele avant-garde in cyberspace'. *Lust & Gratie* 11 (44): 75-86.

Boomen, van den, Marianne. 1995. *Internet ABC voor vrouwen: Een inleiidng voor datadames en modemmeiden*. Amsterdam: Instituut voor Publiek en Politiek.

Boomen, van den, Marianne. 2000. *Leven op het Net: De sociale betekenis van virtuele gemeenschappen*. Amsterdam: Instituut voor Publiek en Politiek.

Boomen, van den, Marianne. 2001a. 'Cybermanifesten zonder body'. *Lover* 28 (1). http://boom.home.xs4all.nl/artikel/nieuw/art_lover_manifesten.html.

Boomen, van den, Marianne. 2001b. 'Utopia in Cyberspace: Virtual Communities and Social Reality'. In *Contemporary Utopia Struggles: Communities between Modernism and Postmodernism*, edited by Saskia Poldervaart, Harrie Jansen, and Beatrice Kesler, 31-43. Amsterdam: Aksant Academic Publishers.

Boomen, van den, Marianne. 2006. 'Metaphors in Computer Advertising'. *Meta BlogNote*. October 10. http://

metamapping.net/blog/?p=83.
Boomen, van den, Marianne. 2007. 'What Is Web 2.0?' In *Cultuur 2.0*, edited by Bart Groen, 6-7. Amsterdam: Virtueel Platform. http://metamapping.net/blog/?p=85.
Boomen, van den, Marianne. 2009. 'Hacking Barbie in Gendered Computer Culture'. In *Doing Gender in Media, Art and Culture*, edited by Rosemarie Buikema and Iris van der Tuin, 193-206. New York: Routledge.
Bordwell, David, and Kristin Thompson. 2003. *Film History: An Introduction*. New York: McGraw-Hill.
Borgmann, Albert. 1999. *Holding On to Reality: The Nature of Information at the Turn of the Millennium*. Chicago: University Of Chicago Press.
Boyd, Danah M., and Nicole B. Ellison. 2007. 'Social Network Sites: Definition, History, and Scholarship'. *Journal of Computer-Mediated Communication* 13 (1): 210-230.
Braidotti, Rosi. 2001. 'Toward a New Nomadism: Feminist Deleuzian Tracks; Or, Metaphysics and Metabolism'. In *Deleuze and Guattari: Critical Assessments of Leading Philosophers*, edited by Gary Genosko, 1414-1439. London: Routledge.
Braidotti, Rosi. 2012. *Nomadic Theory: The Portable Rosi Braidotti*. New York: Columbia University Press.
Brown, Bill. 2001. 'Thing Theory'. *Critical Inquiry* 28 (1): 1-22.
Bruckman, Amy, and Mitchel Resnick. 1995. 'The MediaMOO Project Constructionism and Professional Community'. *Convergence: The International Journal of Research into New Media Technologies* 1 (1): 94-109.
Bruns, Axel. 2008. *Blogs, Wikipedia, Second Life, and Beyond: From Production to Produsage*. New York: Peter Lang.
Callon, Michel. 1986. 'Some Elements of a Sociology of Translation: The Domestication of the Scallops and St Brieuac Fishermen'. In *Power, Action and Belief*, edited by John Law, 196-223. London: Routledge.
Carroll, Lewis. 1995 [1871]. *Alice's Adventures in Wonderland and Through the Looking-Glass*. Gutenberg Project. http://www.jus.uio.no/sisu/alices_adventures_in_wonderland_and_through_the_looking_glass.lewis_carroll/landscape.a5.pdf.
Cassell, Justine, and Henry Jenkins, ed. 1998. *From Barbie to Mortal Kombat: Gender and Computer Games*. Cambridge: MIT Press.
Castells, Manuel. 1996. *The Rise of the Networksociety*. Vol. 1. The Information Age: Economy, Society and Culture. Malden: Blackwell Publishers.
Castells, Manuel. 1997. *The Power of Identity*. Vol. 2.The Information Age: Economy, Society and Culture. Malden: Blackwell Publishers.
Castells, Manuel. 2001. *The Internet Galaxy: Reflections on the Internet, Business and Society*. Oxford: Oxford University Press.
Catledge, Lara D., and James E. Pitkow. 1995. 'Characterizing Browsing Strategies in the World-Wide Web'. *Computer Networks and ISDN Systems* 27 (6): 1065-1073.
Cavell, Richard. 2002. *McLuhan in Space: A Cultural Geography*. Toronto: University of Toronto Press.
Certeau, de, Michel. 1984. *The Practice of Everyday Life*. Berkeley: University of California Press.
Chang, Briankle G. 1996. *Deconstructing Communication: Representation, Subject, and Economies of Exchange*. Minneapolis: University of Minnesota Press.
Cherny, Lynn, and Elizabeth Reba Weise, ed. 1996. *Wired Women: Gender and New Realities in Cyberspace*. Seattle: Seal Press.
Chisholm, Richard M. 1985. 'New Metaphors for Understanding the New Machines'. In *Proceedings of the 4th Annual International Conference on Systems Documentation*, 88-96. Ithaca: ACM Press.
Chun, Wendy Hui Kyong, and Thomas W. Keenan. 2005. *New Media, Old Media: A History and Theory Reader*. London: Routledge.
Chun, Wendy Hui Kyong. 2004. 'On Software, or the Persistence of Visual Knowledge'. *Grey Room* 18: 26-51.
Chun, Wendy Hui Kyong. 2006. *Control and Freedom: Power and Paranoia in the Age of Fiber Optics*. Cambridge: MIT Press.
Chun, Wendy Hui Kyong. 2011. *Programmed Visions: Software and Memory*. Cambridge: MIT Press.
Cilliers, Paul. 1998. *Complexity and Postmodernism: Understanding Complex Systems*. London: Routledge.
Cleaver Jr, Harry M. 1998. 'The Zapatista Effect: The Internet and the Rise of an Alternative Political Fabric'. *Journal of International Affairs* 51 (2): 621-622.

Coté, Mark. 2011. 'What Is a Media Dispositif? Compositions With Bifo'. *Journal of Communication Inquiry* 35 (4) (October 1): 378-386.
Couldry, Nick 2012. *Media, Society, World: Social Theory and Digital Media Practice*. London: Polity.
Couldry, Nick, and Anna McCarthy. 2003. *Mediaspace: Place, Scale and Culture in a Media Age*. London: Routledge.
Couldry, Nick. 2003. *Media Rituals: A Critical Approach*. London: Routledge.
Couldry, Nick. 2004. 'Theorising Media as Practice'. *Social Semiotics* 14 (2): 115-132.
Couldry, Nick. 2008. 'Mediatization or Mediation? Alternative Understandings of the Emergent Space of Digital Storytelling'. *New Media & Society* 10 (3): 373-391.
Couldry, Nick. 2010. *Why Voice Matters: Culture and Politics after Neoliberalism*. London: Sage.
Coward, Rosalind, and John Ellis. 1977. *Language and Materialism: Developments in Semiology and the Theory of the Subject*. Boston: Routledge & Kegan Paul.
Coyne, Richard. 1995. *Designing Information Technology in the Postmoden Age: From Method to Metaphor*. Cambridge: MIT Press.
Cramer, Florian. 2003. 'Exe.cut[up]able Statements: The Insistence of Code'. In *Code: The Language of Our Time*, edited by Christine Schöpf and Gerfried Stocker. Osterfildern-Ruit: Hatje Cantz.
Cramer, Florian. 2005. *Words Made Flesh: Code, Culture, Imagination*. Rotterdam: Piet Zwart Institute. http://cramer.pleintekst.nl/00-recent/words_made_flesh/html/words_made_flesh.html.
Cramer, Florian. 2008. 'Interface'. In *Software Studies: A Lexicon*, edited by Matthew Fuller, 149-153. Cambridge: MIT Press.
Cramer, Florian. 2009. 'Re: <nettime> Digital Humanities Manifesto'. *Nettime Mailinglist*. http://nettime.org/Lists-Archives/nettime-l-0901/msg00026.html.
Crutzen, Cecile, and Erna Kotkamp. 2008. 'Object Orientation'. In *Software Studies: A Lexicon*, edited by Matthew Fuller, 200-206. Cambridge: MIT Press.
Danielewski, Mark Z. 2000. *House of Leaves*. New York: Pantheon.
Dant, Tim. 2005. *Materiality and Society*. Maidenhead: Open University Press.
Davidson, Donald. 1978. 'What Metaphors Mean'. *Critical Inquiry* 5 (1): 31-47.
Dean, Jodi. 2003. 'Why the Net Is Not a Public Sphere'. *Constellations* 10 (1): 95-112.
Deleuze, Gilles, and Claire Parnet. 2002 [1977]. 'The Actual and the Virtual'. In *Dialogues II*, 148-52. New York: Columbia University Press.
Deleuze, Gilles, and Felix Guattari. 1983. *Anti-Oedipus: Capitalism and Schizophrenia*. Minneapolis: University of Minnesota Press.
Deleuze, Gilles, and Felix Guattari. 1987. *A Thousand Plateaus*. Minneapolis: University of Minnesota Press.
Deleuze, Gilles. 1992. 'Postscript on the Societies of Control'. *October* 59 (1): 3-7.
Derrida, Jacques. 1974. 'White Mythology: Metaphor in the Text of Philosophy'. *New Literary History* 6 (1): 5-74.
Derrida, Jacques. 1978. *Writing and Difference*. London: Routledge.
Derrida, Jacques. 1998 [1976]. *Of Grammatology*. Baltimore: Johns Hopkins University Press.
Dibbell, Julian. 1993. 'Rape in Cyberspace or How an Evil Clown, a Haitian Trickster Spirit, Two Wizards, and a Cast of Dozens Turned a Database into a Society, A'. *The Village Voice*, December 23.
Dijck, José van. 2013. 'Facebook and the Engineering of Connectivity: A Multi-Layered Approach to Social Media Platforms'. *Convergence: The International Journal of Research into New Media Technologies* 19 (2): 141-55.
Dijk, van, Jan. 1991. *De netwerkmaatschappij: Sociale aspecten van nieuwe media*. Houten: Bohn Stafleu Van Loghum.
Dijk, van, Jan. 2006. *The Network Society: Social Aspects of New Media*. London: Sage.
Doane, M. A. 2007. 'The Indexical and the Concept of Medium Specificity'. *Differences: A Journal of Feminist Cultural Studies* 18 (1): 128-152.
Dodge, Martin, and Rob Kitchin. 2002. *Atlas of Cyberspace*. London: Addison-Wesley.
Doheny-Farina, Stephen. 1996. *The Wired Neighborhood*. New Haven: Yale University Press.
Dourish, Paul. 2004. *Where the Action Is: The Foundations of Embodied Interaction*. Cambridge: MIT Press.
Downey, John, Mike Stephens, and Jan Flaherty. 2012. 'The "sluice-Gate" Public Sphere and the National DNA Database in the UK'. *Media, Culture & Society* 34 (4): 439-456.

Draaisma, Douwe. 2000. *Metaphors of Memory: A History of Ideas about the Mind*. Cambridge: Cambridge University Press.
Dreyfus, Hubert L. 2008. *On the Internet*. London: Routledge.
Duyvendak, Jan-Willem, and Menno Hurenkamp, ed. 2004. *Kiezen voor de kudde: Lichte gemeenschappen en de nieuwe meerderheid*. Amsterdam: Van Gennep.
Dyson, Esther, George Giilder, George Keyworth, and Alvin Toffler. 1994. 'Cyberspace and the American Dream: A Magna Carta for the Knowledge Age (Release 1.2, August 22, 1994)'. *The Information Society* 12 (3): 295-308.
Efimova, Lilia, and Stephanie Hendrick. 2005. 'In Search for a Virtual Settlement: An Exploration of Weblog Community Boundaries' presented at the 2nd International Conference on Communities and Technologies, June, Milano, Italy. https://doc.telin.nl/dsweb/Get/Document-46041/weblog_community_boundaries.pdf.
Egan, Greg. 1994. *Permutation City*. New York: HarperPrism.
Eskelinen, Markku. 2001. 'Towards Computer Game Studies'. *Digital Creativity* 12 (3): 175-183.
Evens, Aden. 2006. 'Object-Oriented Ontology, or Programming's Creative Fold'. *Angelaki* 11 (1): 89-96.
Farber, Dan. 2007. 'Facebook's Zuckerberg Uncorks the Social Graph'. *ZDNet*. http://www.zdnet.com/blog/btl/facebooks-zuckerberg-uncorks-the-social-graph/5156.
Fauconnier, Gilles, and Mark Turner. 2003. *The Way We Think: Conceptual Blending And The Mind's Hidden Complexities*. New York: Basic Books.
Featherstone, Mike, and Roger Burrows, ed. 1996. *Cyberspace/Cyberbodies/Cyberpunk: Cultures of Technological Embodiment*. London: Sage.
Fernback, Jan, and Brad Thompson. 1995. 'Virtual Communities: Abort, Retry, Failure?' Paper presented at Annual meeting of the International Communication Association. Albuquerque, New Mexico. http://www.rheingold.com/texts/techpolitix/VCcivil.html.
Fincher, David. 2010. *The Social Network*.
Fleischer, Rasmus. 2009. 'The Schizo-Politics of The Pirate Bay, Inc.' *Nettime Mailinglist*. http://nettime.org/Lists-Archives/nettime-l-0907/msg00000.html.
Flichy, Patrice. 2007 [2001]. *The Internet Imaginaire*. Cambrdige: MIT Press.
Forceville, Charles. 2008. 'Metaphor in Pictures and Multimodal Representations'. In *The Cambridge Handbook of Metaphor and Thought*, edited by Raymond Gibbs, 462-482. Cambridge: Cambridge University Press.
Foucault, Michel. 1971. 'The Order of Discourse (The Discourse on Language)'. *Social Science Information* 10 (2): 7-30.
Foucault, Michel. 1972 [1969]. *The Archaeology of Knowledge*. London: Tavistock.
Foucault, Michel. 1982. 'The Subject and Power'. *Critical Inquiry* 8 (4): 777-795.
Foucault, Michel. 1989 [1966]. *The Order of Things: An Archaeology of the Human Sciences*. London: Routledge.
Friedberg, Anne. 2006. *The Virtual Window: From Alberti to Microsoft*. Cambridge: MIT Press.
Friedland, Lewis A., Hernando Rojas, and Thomas Hove. 2004. 'The Networked Public Sphere'. *Javnost - The Public* 13 (4): 5-26.
Friesen, Norm, and Theo Hug. 2009. 'The Mediatic Turn: Exploring Concepts for Media Pedagogy'. In *Mediatization: Concept, Changes, Consequences*, edited by Knut Lundby, 63-83. New York: Peter Lang.
Fuller, Matthew. 2003. *Behind the Blip: Essays on Software Culture*. New York: Autonomedia.
Fuller, Matthew. 2005. *Media Ecologies: Materialist Energies in Art and Technoculture*. Cambridge: MIT Press.
Fuller, Matthew. 2008. *Software Studies: A Lexicon*. Cambridge: MIT Press.
Gallaugher, John M., and Charles E. Downing. 2000. 'Portal Combat: An Empirical Study of Competition in the Web Portal Industry'. *Journal of Information Technology Management* 11 (1-2): 13-24.
Galloway, Alexander R. 2004. *Protocol: How Control Exists After Decentralization*. Cambridge: MIT Press.
Galloway, Alexander R., and Eugene Thacker. 2007. *The Exploit: A Theory of Networks*. Minneapolis: University of Minnesota Press.
Gibson, James J. 1986. *The Ecological Approach to Visual Perception*. Hillsdale: Lawrence Erlbaum.
Gibson, William. 1984. *Neuromancer*. London: Grafton.

Gillmor, Dan. 2006. *We the Media: Grassroots Journalism by the People, for the People.* Sebastopol: O'Reilly Media.
Gitelman, Lisa, and Geoffrey Pingree, ed. 2003. *New Media, 1740-1915.* Cambridge: MIT Press.
Gitelman, Lisa. 2006. *Always Already New Media, History, and the Data of Culture.* Cambridge: MIT Press.
Gladwell, Malcolm. 2010. 'Small Change: Why the Revolution Will Not Be Tweeted'. *The New Yorker*, October 4.
Glucksberg, Sam. 2008. 'How Metaphors Create Categories - Quickly'. In *The Cambridge Handbook of Metaphor and Thought*, edited by Raymond W. Gibbs, 67-83. Cambridge: Cambridge University Press.
Goggin, Gerard. 2010. *Global Mobile Media.* London: Taylor & Francis.
Goossens, Louis. 1990. 'Metaphtonymy: The Interaction of Metaphor and Metonymy in Figurative Expressions for Linguistic Action'. *Cognitive Linguistics* (1): 323-340.
Gore, Al. 1993. 'Remarks by the National Information Infrastructure'. Speech at the National Press Club, December 21, 1993. http://www.ibiblio.org/nii/goremarks.html.
Gozzi, Raymond. 1999. *The Power of Metaphor in the Age of Electronic Media.* Cresskill: Hampton Press.
Graham, Stephen. 2004. 'Beyond the "Dazzling Light": From Dreams of Transcendence to the "Remediation" of Urban Life – A Research Manifesto'. *New Media & Society* 6 (1): 16-25.
Greenfield, Adam. 2006. *Everyware: The Dawning Age of Ubiquitous Computing.* San Francisco: New Riders.
Grossman, Lev. 2006. 'You – Yes, You – Are TIME's Person of the Year'. *Time*, December 25.
Guattari, Félix. 1995. *Chaosmosis.* Bloomington: Indiana University Press.
Gunkel, David J. 2003. 'What's the Matter with Books?' *Configurations* 11 (3): 277-303.
Gunning, Tom. 2007. 'Moving Away from the Index: Cinema and the Impression of Reality'. *Differences: A Journal of Feminist Cultural Studies* 18 (1): 29-52.
Gutenplan, Samuel. 2005. *Objects of Metaphor.* Oxford: Claridon Press.
Habermas, Jürgen. 1985. *The Theory of Communicative Action, Volume 2: Lifeworld and System: A Critique of Functionalist Reason.* Boston: Beacon Press.
Habermas, Jürgen. 1989 [1962]. *The Structural Transformation of the Public Sphere: An Inquiry into a Category of Bourgeois Society.* Cambridge: MIT Press.
Habermas, Jürgen. 1996. *Between Facts and Norms: Contributions to a Discourse Theory of Law and Democracy.* Cambridge: MIT Press.
Habermas, Jürgen. 2006. 'Political Communication in Media Society: Does Democracy Still Enjoy an Epistemic Dimension?' *Communication Theory* 16 (4): 411-426.
Hacking, Ian. 2002. *Historical Ontology.* Cambridge: Harvard University Press.
Hagel, John, and Arthur Armstrong. 1997. *Net Gain: Expanding Markets Through Virtual Communities.* Boston: Harvard Business School Press.
Hall, Stuart. 1991. 'Encoding/decoding'. In *Culture, Media, Language: Working Papers in Cultural Studies, 1972-79*, 128-138. New York: Routledge.
Hall, Stuart. 1997. *Representation: Cultural Representations and Signifying Practices.* London: Sage.
Hampton, Keith N., and Barry Wellman. 1999. 'Netville Online and Offline Observing and Surveying a Wired Suburb'. *American Behavioral Scientist* 43 (3): 475-492.
Hampton, Keith. 2002. 'Place-Based and IT Mediated 'Community''. *Planning Theory & Practice* 3 (2): 228-231.
Haraway, Donna. 1976. *Crystals, Fabrics and Fields: Metaphors of Organicism in Twentieth-Century Developmental Biology.* New Haven: Yale University Press.
Haraway, Donna. 1985. 'A Manifesto for Cyborgs: Science, Technology, and Socialist Feminism in the 1980s'. *Socialist Review* 15 (80): 65-108.
Haraway, Donna. 1988. 'Situated Knowledges: The Science Question in Feminism and the Privilege of Partial Perspective'. *Feminist Studies* 14 (3): 575-599.
Haraway, Donna. 1991. *Simians, Cyborgs, and Women: The Reinvention of Nature.* London: Routledge.
Harman, Graham. 2002. *Tool-Being: Heidegger and the Metaphysics of Objects.* Chicago: Open Court Publishing.
Harman, Graham. 2005. *Guerrilla Metaphysics: Phenomenology and the Carpentry of Things.* Chicago: Open Court Publishing.
Harris, Jan, and Paul Taylor. 2005. *Digital Matters: The Theory and Culture of the Matrix.* London: Routledge.

Hauben, Michael. 1993. 'The Social Forces behind the Development of Usenet News'. *The Amateur Computerist* 5 (2): 13-21.
Hayles, N. Katherine. 1986. *The Cosmic Web: Scientific Field Models and Literary Strategies in the 20th Century*. Ithaca: Cornell University Press.
Hayles, N. Katherine. 1990. *Chaos Bound: Orderly Disorder in Contemporary Literature and Science*. Ithaca: Cornell University Press.
Hayles, N. Katherine. 1993a. 'The Materiality of Informatics'. *Configurations* 1 (1): 147-170.
Hayles, N. Katherine. 1993b. 'Virtual Bodies and Flickering Signifiers'. *October* (66): 69-91.
Hayles, N. Katherine. 1999. *How We Became Posthuman: Virtual Bodies in Cybernetics, Literature and Informatics*. Chicago: University of Chicago Press.
Hayles, N. Katherine. 2001a. 'Desiring Agency: Limiting Metaphors and Enabling Constraints in Dawkins and Deleuze/Guattari'. *SubStance* 30 (1): 144-159.
Hayles, N. Katherine. 2001b. 'Metaphoric Networks in Lexia to Perplexia'. *Digital Creativity* 12 (3): 133-139.
Hayles, N. Katherine. 2002. *Writing Machines*. Cambridge: MIT Press.
Hayles, N. Katherine. 2004a. 'N. Katherine Hayles Responds in Turn: Riposte to: Metaphoric Networks in Lexia to Perplexia'. *Electronic Book Review*. http://www.electronicbookreview.com/thread/firstperson/materialmetaphor.
Hayles, N. Katherine. 2004b. 'Print Is Flat, Code Is Deep: The Importance of Media-Specific Analysis'. *Poetics Today* 25 (1): 67-90.
Hayles, N. Katherine. 2005. *My Mother Was a Computer: Digital Subjects and Literary Texts*. Chicago: University of Chicago Press.
Hayles, N. Katherine. 2012. *How We Think: Digital Media and Contemporary Technogenesis*. Chicago: University of Chicago Press.
Heidegger, Martin. 1979 [1927]. *Sein Und Zeit*. Tübingen: Max Niemeyer Verlag.
Heim, Michael. 1994. *The Metaphysics of Virtual Reality*. Oxford: Oxford University Press.
Helmond, Anne. 2013. 'The Algorithmization of the Hyperlink'. *Computational Culture* 3 (3). http://computationalculture.net/article/the-algorithmization-of-the-hyperlink.
Helsloot, Niels. 2002. *Afstand en ruis: Conceptuele grondslagen van de informatie- en communicatietechnologie*. Rotterdam: Seminar Filosofie van de ICT.
Hepp, Andreas, Cigdem Bozdag, and Laura Suna. 2012. 'Mediatized Migrants: Media Cultures and Communicative Networking in the Diaspora'. In *Migrations, Diaspora, and Information Technology in Global Societies*, 172-188. London: Routledge.
Hermes, Joke. 2005. *Re-Reading Popular Culture*. London: Blackwell.
Herring, Susan C. 2004. 'Slouching Toward the Ordinary: Current Trends in Computer-Mediated Communication'. *New Media & Society* 6 (1) (January 2): 26-36.
Herring, Susan C., Lois Ann Scheidt, Sabrina Bonus, and Elijah Wright. 2004. 'Bridging the Gap: A Genre Analysis of Weblogs'. In *Proceedings of the 37th Annual Hawaii International Conference on System Sciences*, 1-11.
Hjarvard, Stig. 2008a. 'The Mediatization of Religion: A Theory of the Media as Agents of Religious Change'. *Northern Lights: Film and Media Studies Yearbook* 6 (1): 9-26.
Hjarvard, Stig. 2008b. 'The Mediatization of Society: A Theory of the Media as Agents of Social and Cultural Change'. *Nordicom Review* 29 (2): 105-134.
Hodder, Ian, ed. 1987. *The Archaeology of Contextual Meanings*. Cambridge: Cambridge University Press.
Hodge, Robert Ian Vere, and Gunther R. Kress. 1988. *Social Semiotics*. Ithaca: Cornell University Press.
Hook, Derek. 2001. 'Discourse, Knowledge, Materiality, History Foucault and Discourse Analysis'. *Theory & Psychology* 11 (4): 521-547.
Hui, Yuk, and Harry Halpin. 2013. 'Collective Individuation: The Future of the Social Web'. In *Unlike Us Reader: Social Media Monopolies and Their Alternatives*, edited by Geert Lovink and Miriam Rasch, 103-116. Amsterdam: Institute of Network Cultures.
Jakobson, Roman, and Morris Halle. 1971 [1956]. *Fundamentals of Language*. Den Haag: Walter de Gruyter.
Jansson, André. 2002. 'The Mediatization of Consumption: Towards an Analytical Framework of Image Culture'. *Journal of Consumer Culture* 2 (1): 5-31.

Jarrett, Kylie. 2008. 'Interactivity Is Evil! A Critical Investigation of Web 2.0'. *First Monday* 13 (3). http://firstmonday.org/htbin/cgiwrap/bin/ojs/index.php/fm/article/viewArticle/2140/1947.

Jeffrey, Liss. 1989. 'The Heat and the Light: Towards a Reassessment of the Contribution of H. Marshall McLuhan'. *Canadian Journal of Communication* 14 (4).

Jenkins, Henry. 1992. *Textual Poachers: Television Fans and Participatory Culture*. London: Routledge.

Jenkins, Henry. 2006. *Convergence Culture: Where Old and New Media Collide*. New York: New York University Press.

John, Nicholas A. 2013. 'Sharing and Web 2.0: The Emergence of a Keyword'. *New Media & Society* 15 (2): 167-82.

Johnson, Mark. 2008. 'Philosophy's Debt to Metaphor'. In *The Cambridge Handbook of Metaphor and Thought*, edited by Raymond W. Gibbs, 39-52. Cambridge: Cambridge University Press.

Johnson, Steven. 1997. *Interface Culture: How New Technology Transforms the Way We Create and Communicate*. New York: Basic Books.

Jones, Quentin. 1997. 'Virtual-Communities, Virtual Settlements & Cyber-Archaeology: A Theoretical Outline'. *Journal of Computer-Mediated Communication* 3 (3).

Jones, Steven G., ed. 1995. *CyberSociety: Computer-Mediated Communication and Community*. London: Sage.

Jones, Steven G., ed. 1997. *Virtual Culture: Identity and Communication in Cybersociety*. London: Sage.

Kaplan, Andreas M., and Michael Haenlein. 2010. 'Users of the World, Unite! The Challenges and Opportunities of Social Media'. *Business Horizons* 53 (1): 59-68.

Kaptelinin, Victor, and Mary Czerwinski. 2007. *Beyond the Desktop Metaphor: Designing Integrated Digital Work Environments*. Cambridge: MIT Press.

Kattenbelt, Chiel. 2010. 'Intermediality in Performance and as a Mode of Performativity'. In *Mapping Intermediality in Performance*, edited by Sarah Bay-Cheng, Chiel Kattenbelt, Andrew Lavender, and Robin Nelson, 29-37. Amsterdam: Amsterdam University Press.

Katz, James E., and Mark Aakhus. 2002. *Perpetual Contact: Mobile Communication, Private Talk, Public Performance*. Cambridge: Cambridge University Press.

Katz, James E., and Philip Aspden. 1997. 'A Nation of Strangers?' *Communications of the ACM* 40 (12): 81-86.

Kay, Alan Curtis. 1969. *The Reactive Engine*. Salt Lake City: Doctoral thesis University of Utah.

Kay, Alan, and Adele Goldberg. 1977. 'Personal Dynamic Media'. *Computer* 10 (3): 31-41.

Kelly, Kevin. 1995. *Out of Control: The New Biology of Machines, Social Systems, & the Economic World*. Reading: Addison-Wesley.

Kerckhove, de, Derrick. 1997. *The Skin of Culture: Investigating the New Electronic Reality*. London: Kogan Page Publishers.

Kessler, Frank. 2006. 'Notes on Dispositif'. http://www.let.uu.nl/~Frank.Kessler/personal/notes%20on%20dispositif.PDF.

Kessler, Frank. 2009. 'What You Get Is What You See: Digital Images and the Claim of the Real'. In *Digital Material*, edited by Marianne van den Boomen, Sybille Lammes, Ann-Sophie Lehmann, Joost Raessens, and Mirko Tobias Schäfer, 187-198. Amsterdam: Amsterdam University Press.

Kirschenbaum, Matthew G. 2008. *Mechanisms: New Media and the Forensic Imagination*. Cambridge: MIT Press.

Kittler, Friedrich. 1990 [1985]. *Discourse Networks, 1800/1900*. Stanford: Stanford University Press.

Kittler, Friedrich. 1995. 'There Is No Software'. *Ctheory* 10 (18). http://www.ctheory.net/articles.aspx?id=74.

Kittler, Friedrich. 1997 [1986]. *Gramophone Film Typewriter*. Stanford: Stanford University Press.

Kittler, Friedrich. 1997. *Literature, Media, Information Systems: Essays*. Edited by John Johnston. Amsterdam: Overseas Publishers Association/G+B Arts.

Knox, Hannah, Mike Savage, and Penny Harvey. 2006. 'Social Networks and the Study of Relations: Networks as Method, Metaphor and Form'. *Economy and Society* 35 (1): 113-40.

Kotkamp, Erna. 2009. 'Digital Objects in E-Learning Environments: The Case of WebCT'. In *Digital Material: Tracing New Media in Everyday Life and Technology*, edited by Marianne van den Boomen, Sybille Lammes, Ann-Sophie Lehmann, Joost Raessens, and Mirko Tobias Schäfer, 65-77. Amsterdam: Amster-

dam University Press.
Kranenburg, Rob van. 2008. *The Internet of Things: A Critique of Ambient Technology and the All-Seeing Network of Rfid*. Amsterdam: Institute of Network Cultures.
Kress, Gunther. 2013. *Multimodality: A Social Semiotic Approach to Contemporary Communication*. London: Routledge.
Krippendorff, Klaus. 1993. 'Major Metaphors of Communication and Some Constructivist Reflections on Their Use'. *Cybernetics and Human Knowing* 2 (1): 3-25.
Krol, Ed. 1992. *The Whole Internet User's Guide and Catalog*. Sebastopol: O'Reilly.
Lacan, Jacques. 1977. *Écrits*. London: Routledge.
Lakoff, George, and Mark Johnson. 1980. *Metaphors We Live By*. Chicago: University of Chicago Press.
Lakoff, George, and Mark Johnson. 1999. *Philosophy in the Flesh: The Embodied Mind and Its Challenge to Western Thought*. New York: Basic Books.
Lakoff, George. 1987. *Women, Fire and Dangerous Things: What Categories Reveal about the Mind*. Chicago: University of Chicago Press.
Lakoff, George. 1993. 'The Contemporary Theory of Metaphor'. In *Metaphor and Thought*, edited by Andrew Ortony, 202-251. Cambridge: Cambridge University Press.
Lakoff, George. 2004. *Don't Think of an Elephant! Know Your Values and Frame the Debate: The Essential Guide for Progressives*. White River Junction: Chelsea Green.
Lammes, Sybille. 2008. 'Playing the World: Computer Games, Cartography and Spatial Stories'. *Aether: The Journal of Media Geography* 3: 84-96.
Landow, George P., ed. 1994. *Hyper/text/theory*. Baltimore: Johns Hopkins University Press.
Lanier, Jaron. 2006. 'Digital Maoism: The Hazards of the New Online Collectivism'. *The Edge*. http://www.edge.org/conversation/digital-maoism-the-hazards-of-the-new-online-collectivism
Lasswell, Harold D. 1948. 'The Structure and Function of Communication in Society'. In *The Communication of Ideas*, edited by Lyman Bryson. New York: Harper and Brothers.
Latour, Bruno, Eduardo Camacho-Hübner, and Valerie November. 2010. 'Entering a Risky Territory: Space in the Age of Digital Navigation'. *Environment and Planning D: Society and Space* 28: 581-99.
Latour, Bruno. 1986. 'Visualization and Cognition: Thinking with Eyes and Hands'. *Knowledge and Society* 6: 1-40.
Latour, Bruno. 1987. *Science in Action: How to Follow Scientists and Engineers through Society*. Cambridge: Harvard university press.
Latour, Bruno. 1991. 'Technology Is Society Made Durable'. In *A Sociology of Monsters: Essays on Power, Technology, and Domination*, edited by John Law, 103-131. London: Routledge.
Latour, Bruno. 1992. 'Where Are the Missing Masses? The Sociology of a Few Mundane Artifacts'. In *Shaping Technology/building Society: Studies in Sociotechnical Change*, edited by Wiebe E. Bijker and John Law, 225-258. Cambridge: MIT Press.
Latour, Bruno. 1996. 'On Actor-Network Theory'. *Soziale Welt* 47 (4): 369-381.
Latour, Bruno. 1999. 'On Recalling ANT'. In *Actor Network Theory and after*, edited by John Law and John Hassard, 15-25. Oxford: Blackwell.
Latour, Bruno. 2004. 'The Berlin Key or How to Do Words with Things'. In *Material Culture: Critical Concepts in the Social Sciences*, edited by Victor Buchli, 327-337. London: Routledge.
Latour, Bruno. 2005a. 'From Realpolitik to Dingpolitik: Or How to Make Things Public'. In *Making Things Public: Atmospheres of Democracy*, edited by Bruno Latour and Peter Weibel, 4-31. Cambridge: MIT Press.
Latour, Bruno. 2005b. *Reassembling the Social: An Introduction to Actor-Network-Theory*. Oxford: Oxford University Press.
Latour, Bruno. 2011. 'Networks, Societies, Spheres: Reflections of an Actor-Network Theorist'. *International Journal of Communication* 5 (2011): 796-810.
Law, John, and Annemarie Mol. 1995. 'Notes on Materiality and Sociality'. *Sociological Review* 43 (2): 274-294.
Law, John, and Annemarie Mol. 2008. 'The Actor-Enacted: Cumbrian Sheep in 2001'. In *Material Agency*, edited by Carl Knappett and Lambros Malafouris, 57-77. New York: Springer.

Law, John. 1992. 'Notes on the Theory of the Actor-Network: Ordering, Strategy, and Heterogeneity'. *Systems Practice* 5 (4): 379-393.

Law, John. 2009. 'Actor Network Theory and Material Semiotics'. In *The New Blackwell Companion to Social Theory*, edited by Bryan S. Turner, 141-158. Oxford: Blackwell.

Lawley, James, and Penny Tompkins. 2000. *Metaphors in Mind: Transformation through Symbolic Modeling*. London: Developing Company Press.

Lazarsfeld, Paul F., and Robert K. Merton. 2004 [1948]. 'Mass Communication, Popular Taste and Organized Social Action'. In *American Social Thought: Key Texts, 1919-1968*, edited by John Durham Peters and Peter Simonson, 230-241. Lanham: Rowman & Littlefield.

Lefebvre, Henri. 1991. *The Production of Space*. Malden: Blackwell.

Lessig, Lawrence. 1999. *Code and Other Laws of Cyberspace*. New York: Basic Books/Perseus.

Leuf, Bo, and Ward Cunningham. 2001. *The Wiki Way: Collaboration and Sharing on the Internet: Quick Collaboration on the Web*. Reading: Addison-Wesley.

Leurs, Koen. 2012. *Digital Passages. Moroccan-Dutch Youths Performing Diaspora, Gender and Youth Cultural Identities across Digital Space*. Utrecht: PhD thesis Utrecht University.

Lévi-Strauss, Claude. 1963 [1958]. *Structural Anthropology*. New York: Basic Books.

Lévi-Strauss, Claude. 1987. *Introduction to the Work of Marcel Mauss*. London: Routledge. [1950].

Levinson, Paul. 2009. *New New Media*. New York: Allyn & Bacon.

Lévy, Pierre. 1994. *L'intelligence collective: Pour une anthropologie du cyberspace*. Paris: La Découverte.

Lévy, Pierre. 1998. *Becoming Virtual: Reality in the Digital Age*. New York: Basic Books.

Livingstone, Sonia. 2009. 'On the Mediation of Everything: ICA Presidential Address 2008'. *Journal of Communication* 59 (1): 1-18.

Lotan, Gilad, Erhardt Graeff, Mike Ananny, Devin Gaffney, Ian Pearce, and Danah Boyd. 2011. 'The Revolutions Were Tweeted: Information Flows during the 2011 Tunisian and Egyptian Revolutions'. *International Journal of Communication* 5: 1375-1405.

Lovink, Geert. 2009. *Dynamics of Critical Internet Culture (1994-2001)*. Amsterdam: Institute of Network Cultures.

Lovink, Geert. 2012. *Networks Without a Cause: A Critique of Social Media*. London: Polity.

Lundby, Knut. 2009. *Mediatization: Concept, Changes, Consequences*. New York: Peter Lang.

Mackenzie, Adrian. 2005. 'The Performativity of Code: Software and Cultures of Circulation'. *Theory Culture Society* 22 (1): 71-92.

Mackenzie, Adrian. 2006. *Cutting Code: Software And Sociality*. New York: Peter Lang.

Maeyer, Juliette De. 2013. 'Towards a Hyperlinked Society: A Critical Review of Link Studies'. *New Media & Society* 15 (5): 737-51.

Mainyu, Eldon A., ed. 2012. *History of Writing Ancient Numbers*. Saarbrücken: Aud Publishing.

Manovich, Lev. 2001. *The Language of New Media*. Cambridge: MIT Press.

Manovich, Lev. 2013. *Software Takes Command*. New York: Bloomsbury Academic.

Marres, Noortje. 2006. 'Net-Work Is Format Work: Issue Networks and the Sites of Civil Society Politics'. In *Reformatting Politics: Information Technology and Global Civil Society*, edited by Jon Anderson, Jodi Dean, and Geert Lovink, 3-17. New York: Routledge.

Marty, Robert. 1997. '76 Definitions of the Sign by C.S. Peirce'. http://www.cspeirce.com/rsources/76DEFS/76defs.htm.

Marx, Karl. 1998 [1924]. 'Theses on Feuerbach'. In *The German Ideology: Including Theses on Feuerbach and Introduction to The Critique of Political Economy*, by Friedrich Engels and Karl Marx, 569-573. Amherst: Prometheus Books.

Massumi, Brian. 1998. 'Sensing the Virtual, Building the Insensible'. *Architectural Design* 68 (5-6): 16-25.

Massumi, Brian. 2002. *Parables for the Virtual: Movement, Affect, Sensation*. Durham: Duke University Press.

Maxwell, James Clerk. 1897. *Theory of Heat*. London: Longmans, Green & Company.

McLuhan, Marshall, and Eric McLuhan. 1988. *Laws of Media: The New Science*. Toronto: University of Toronto Press.

McLuhan, Marshall, and Quentin Fiore. 1967. *The Medium Is the Massage: An Inventory of Effects*. New

York: Bantam.
McLuhan, Marshall. 1962. *The Gutenberg Galaxy: The Making of Typographic Man*. London: Routledge.
McLuhan, Marshall. 1964. *Understanding Media: The Extensions of Man*. Cambridge: MIT Press.
McLuhan, Marshall. 1969. *Counterblast*. Toronto: McClelland & Stewart.
McQuail, Denis. 1994. *Mass Communication Theory: An Introduction*. London: Sage.
McQuail, Denis. 2006. 'On the Mediatization of War'. *International Communication Gazette* 68 (2): 107.
Metz, Christian. 1982. *The Imaginary Signifier: Psychoanalysis and the Cinema*. Bloomington: Indiana University Press.
Minsky, Marvin Lee. 1986. *The Society of Mind*. New York: Simon & Schuster.
Mol, Annemarie, and John Law. 2001. 'Situating Technoscience: An Inquiry into Spatialities'. *Society and Space* 19: 609-621.
Mol, Annemarie. 2002. *The Body Multiple: Ontology in Medical Practice*. Durham: Duke University Press.
Moravec, Hans. 1988. *Mind Children*. Cambridge: Cambridge University Press.
Morozov, Evgeny. 2011. *Net Delusion: The Dark Side of Internet Freedom*. New York: PublicAffairs.
Motion Picture Association. 2004. 'Piracy, It's a Crime'. http://www.youtube.com/watch?v=HmZm8vNHBSU.
Mul, de, Jos, ed. 2002. *Filosofie in cyberspace: Reflecties op de informatie- en communicatietechnologie*. Kampen: Klement.
Mul, de, Jos. 2009. 'The Work of Art in the Age of Digital Recombination'. In *Digital Material: Tracing New Media in Everyday Life and Technology*, edited by Marianne van den Boomen, Joost Raessens, Ann-Sophie Lehmann, Sybille Lammes, and Mirko Tobias Schäfer, 95-106. Amsterdam: Amsterdam University Press.
Mulvey, Laura. 2009 [1989]. *Visual and Other Pleasures*. New York: Palgrave Macmillan.
Munt, Sally R., ed. 2001. *Technospaces: Inside the New Media*. London: Continuum.
Murthy, Dhiraj. 2013. *Twitter: Social Communication in the Twitter Age*. Cambridge: Polity.
Myers, Brad A. 1998. 'A Brief History of Human-Computer Interaction Technology'. *Interactions* 5 (2): 44-54.
Mynatt, Elizabeth D., Vicki L. O'Day, Annette Adler, and Mizuko Ito. 1998. 'Network Communities: Something Old, Something New, Something Borrowed'. *Computer Supported Cooperative Work* 7 (1-2): 123-156.
Neale, Dennis C., and John M. Carroll. 1997. 'The Role of Metaphors in User Interface Design'. In *Handbook of Human-Computer Interaction*, edited by Martin G. Helander, Thomas K. Landauer, and Prasad V. Prabhu, 441-462. Amsterdam: Elsevier Science.
Negroponte, Nicholas. 1995. *Being Digital*. New York: Knopf.
Nerlich, Brigitte. 2012. 'The Role of Metaphor Scenarios in Disease Management Discourses: Foot and Mouth Disease and Avian Influenza'. In *Windows to the Mind: Metaphor, Metonymy and Conceptual Blending*, edited by Hans-Jörg Schmid and Sandra Handl. Berlin: De Gruyter Mouton.
Niemans, Shirley. 2009. *Define: Web Search, Semantic Dreams in the Age of the Engine*. Utrecht: Master thesis Utrecht University.
Nietzsche, Friedrich. 1977 [1873]. *On Truth and Lie in an Extra-Moral Sense*. Vol. 42. The Portable Nietzsche. London: Penguin Books.
Norman, Donald A. 1998. *The Design of Everyday Things*. Cambridge: MIT Press.
Nusselder, André. 2009. *Interface Fantasy: A Lacanian Cyborg Ontology*. Cambridge: MIT Press.
O'Reilly, Tim. 2005. 'What Is Web 2.0: Design Patterns and Business Models for the Next Generation of Software'. *O'Reilly Net*. http://www.oreillynet.com/pub/a/oreilly/tim/news/2005/09/30/what-is-web-20.html.
Oldenburg, Ray. 1989. *The Great Good Place: Cafés, Coffee Shops, Community Centers, Beauty Parlors, General Stores, Bars, Hangouts, and How They Get You through the Day*. New York: Paragon House.
Oost, van, Ellen. 2003. 'Materialized Gender: How Shavers Configure the Users' Femininity and Masculinity'. In *How Users Matter: The Co-Construction of Users and Technologies*, edited by Nelly Oudshoorn and Trevor Pinch, 193-208. Cambridge: MIT Press.
Oosterling, Henk. 2000. *Radicale middelmatigheid*. Amsterdam: Boom.
Oosterling, Henk. 2003. 'Sens(a)ble Intermediality and Interesse: Towards an Ontology of the In-Between'. *Intermédialités* (1): 29-46.
Otis, Laura. 2001. *Networking: Communicating with Bodies and Machines in the Nineteenth Century*. Ann

Arbor: University of Michigan Press.

Parikka, Jussi. 2010. *Insect Media: An Archaeology of Animals and Technology.* Minneapolis: University of Minnesota Press.

Parikka, Jussi. 2011. 'Media Ecologies and Imaginary Media: Transversal Expansions, Contractions, and Foldings'. *Fibreculture Journal* (17). http://seventeen.fibreculturejournal.org/fcj-116-media-ecologies-and-imaginary-media-transversal-expansions-contractions-and-foldings/.

Park, Han Woo. 2003. 'Hyperlink Network Analysis: A New Method for the Study of Social Structure on the Web'. *Connections* 25 (1): 49-61.

Peirce, Charles Sanders. 1902. 'Virtual'. In *Dictionary of Philosophy and Psychology*, edited by James Mark Baldwin. New York: Macmillan.

Peirce, Charles Sanders. 1931a [1888]. 'A Guess at the Riddle'. In *Collected Papers of Charles Sanders Peirce*, edited by Charles Hartshorne, Paul Weiss, and Arthur W. Burks. Vol. 1. Cambridge: Harvard University Press.

Peirce, Charles Sanders. 1931b. *Collected Papers of Charles Sanders Peirce*. Edited by Charles Hartshorne, Paul Weiss, and Arthur W. Burks. Vol. 1. 8 vols. Cambridge: Harvard University Press. [1931-1958].

Peirce, Charles Sanders. 1958 [1888]. 'A Letter to Lady Welby'. In *Collected Papers of Charles Sanders Peirce*, edited by Charles Hartshorne, Paul Weiss, and Arthur W. Burks. Vol. 8. Cambridge: Harvard University Press.

Peirce, Charles Sanders. 1981 [1873]. 'Of Logic as a Study of Signs'. In *Writings of Charles S. Peirce*, edited by Peirce Edition Project. Vol. 3.82. Bloomington: Indiana University Press.

Peirce, Charles Sanders. 1998. 'A Letter to William James'. In *The Essential Peirce: Selected Philosophical Writings*, edited by Peirce Edition Project. Vol. 2.498. Bloomington: Indiana University Press. [1909].

Peters, John Durham. 1999. *Speaking into the Air: A History of the Idea of Communication.* Chicago: University of Chicago Press.

Pileggi, Salvatore F., Carlos Fernandez-Llatas, and Vicente Traver. 2012. 'When the Social Meets the Semantic: Social Semantic Web or Web 2.5'. *Future Internet* 4 (3): 852-64.

Plessner, Helmut. 1928. *Die Stufen Des Organischen Und Der Mensch.* Berlin: De Gruyter.

Poell, Thomas. 2009. 'Conceptualizing Forums and Blogs as Public Sphere'. In *Digital Material: Tracing New Media in Everyday Life and Technology*, edited by Marianne van den Boomen, Sybille Lammes, Ann-Sophie Lehmann, Joost Raessens, and Mirko Tobias Schäfer, 239-51. Amsterdam: Amsterdam University Press.

Poster, Mark. 2001. *What's the Matter with the Internet.* Minneapolis: University of Minnesota Press.

Postman, Neil. 1993. *Technopoly: The Surrender of Culture to Technology.* New York: Vintage.

Pratt, James Bissett. 1922. 'The New Materialism'. *The Journal of Philosophy* 19 (13): 337-351.

Preucel, Robert W. 2006. *Archaeological Semiotics.* Chichester: Wiley-Blackwell.

Rainie, Lee. 2005. 'The State of Blogging'. Washington: Pew Internet & American Life Project. http://www.pewinternet.org/~/media//Files/Reports/2005/PIP_blogging_data.pdf.pdf.

Rammert, Werner. 1999. 'Relations That Constitute Technology and Media That Make a Difference: Toward a Social Pragmatic Theory of Technicization'. *Society for Philosophy and Technology* 4 (3).

Ray, Keith. 1987. 'Material Metaphor, Social Interaction and Historical Reconstructions: Exploring Patterns of Association and Symbolism in the Igbo-Ukwu Corpus'. In *The Archaeology of Contextual Meaning*, edited by Ian Hodder, 66-77. Cambridge: Cambridge University Press.

Reddy, Michael J. 1993 [1979]. 'The Conduit Metaphor: A Case of Frame Conflict in Our Language about Language'. In *Metaphor and Thought*, edited by Andrew Ortony, 164-201. Cambridge: Cambridge University Press.

Reid, Elizabeth. 1991. *Electropolis: Communication and Community on Internet Relay Chat.* Melbourne: PhD thesis University of Melbourne. http://www.irchelp.org/irchelp/communication-research/academic/academic-reid-e-electropolis-1991.html.

Rheingold, Howard. 1987. 'Virtual Communities: Exchanging Ideas through Computer Bulletin Boards'. *Whole Earth Review* 3 (Winter): 78-81.

Rheingold, Howard. 1993. *The Virtual Community: Homesteading on the Electronic Frontier.* Reading: Addison-Wesley.

Rice, Jesse. 2009. *The Church of Facebook: How the Hyperconnected Are Redefining Community*. Colorado Springs: David C. Cook.

Richards, Ivor Armstrong. 1936. *The Philosophy of Rhetoric*. New York: Oxford University Press.

Ricoeur, Paul. 1975. *The Rule of Metaphor: The Creation of Meaning in Language*. New York: Routledge.

Robinson, Derek. 2008. 'Analog'. In *Software Studies: A Lexicon*, edited by Matthew Fuller. Cambridge: MIT Press.

Rohrer, Tim. 1997. 'Conceptual Blending on the Information Highway: How Metaphorical Inferences Work'. In *Discourse and Perspective in Cognitive Linguistics*, edited by Wolf-Andreas Liebert, Gisela Redeker, and Linda R. Waugh, 185-205. Amsterdam: John Benjamins.

Roosendaal, Arnold. 2010. 'Facebook Tracks and Traces Everyone: Like This!' SSRN Scholarly Paper ID 1717563. Rochester: Social Science Research Network.

Rushkoff, Douglas. 1994. *Cyberia: Life in the Trenches of Hyperspace*. San Francisco: Harper.

Rushkoff, Douglas. 2012. *Monopoly Moneys: The Media Environment of Corporatism and the Player's Way out*. Utrecht: PhD thesis Utrecht University.

Rustema, Reinder. 2001. *The Rise and Fall of DDS: Evaluating the Ambitions of Amsterdam's Digital City*. Amsterdam: Doctoral thesis University of Amsterdam. http://reinder.rustema.nl/dds/rise_and_fall_dds.html.

Saffer, Dan. 2005. *The Role of Metaphor in Interaction Design*. Pittsburgh: Master thesis Carnegie Mellon University. http://www.odannyboy.com/portfolio/thesis/saffer_thesis_paper.pdf.

Sandbothe, Mike. 2005. *Pragmatic Media Philosophy: Foundations of a New Discipline in the Internet Age*. http://www.sandbothe.net/pmp.pdf.

Saussure, de, Ferdinand. 1983 [1916]. *Course in General Linguistics*. Edited by Charles Bally and Albert Sechehaye. La Salle: Open Court Publishing.

Schäfer, Mirko Tobias. 2011. *Bastard Culture! User Participation and the Extension of Cultural Industries*. Amsterdam: Amsterdam University Press.

Schinkel, Willem. 2007. *Denken in een tijd van sociale hypochondrie: Aanzet tot een theorie voorbij de maatschappij*. Kampen: Klement.

Schinkel, Willem. 2008. 'Schaf het integratiebeleid af'. *Tijdschrift voor Sociale Vraagstukken*, (4): 8-11.

Scholz, Trebor. 2008. 'Market Ideology and the Myths of "web 2.0"'. *First Monday* 13 (3). http://firstmonday.org/ojs/index.php/fm/article/viewArticle/2138/1945.

Schuler, Doug. 1994. 'Community Networks: Building a New Participatory Medium'. *Communications of the ACM* 37 (1): 38-51.

Schulz, Winfried. 2004. 'Reconstructing Mediatization as an Analytical Concept'. *European Journal of Communication* 19 (1): 87-101.

Shannon, Claude E. 1948. 'A Mathematical Theory of Communication'. *The Bell System Technical Journal* 27 (July, October): 373-423, 623-656.

Shannon, Claude E., and Warren Weaver. 1949. *The Mathematical Theory of Communication*. Urbana: University of Illinois Press.

Shirky, Clay. 2011. 'The Political Power of Social Media: Technology, the Public Sphere, and Political Change'. *Foreign Affairs* 90 (1): 28-41.

Silber, Ilana Friedrich. 1995. 'Space, Fields, Boundaries: The Rise of Spatial Metaphors in Contemporary Sociological Theory'. *Social Research* 62 (2): 323-355.

Silverstone, Roger. 2005. 'The Sociology of Mediation and Communication'. In *The Sage Handbook of Sociology*, edited by Craig J. Calhoun, Chris Rojek, and Bryan S. Turner, 188-207. London: Sage.

Smelik, Anneke Margriet. 2001. *And the Mirror Cracked. Feminist Cinema and Film Theory*. Houndmills: Palgrave.

Smith, Marc A., and Peter Kollock, ed. 1999. *Communities in Cyberspace*. London: Routledge.

Smith, Tom. 2009. 'The Social Media Revolution'. *International Journal of Market Research* 51 (4): 559-61.

Stalder, Felix. 2010. 'The Return of DRM'. *Nettime*. http://www.nettime.org/Lists-Archives/nettime-l-1004/msg00024.html.

Star, Susan Leigh. 1989. 'The Structure of Ill-Structured Solutions: Boundary Objects and Heterogeneous Distributed Problem Solving'. *Distributed Artificial Intelligence* 2: 37-54.

Star, Susan Leigh. 2010. 'This Is Not a Boundary Object: Reflections on the Origin of a Concept'. *Science,*

Technology & Human Values 35 (5): 601-617.

Steyaert, Jan, and Jos de Haan, ed. 2007. *Jaarboek ICT en samenleving 2007: Gewoon digitaal*. Amsterdam: Boom.

Stone, Allucquere Rosanne. 1991. 'Will the Real Body Please Stand up? Boundary Stories about Virtual Cultures'. In *Cyberspace: First Steps*, edited by Michael Benedikt, 81-118. Cambridge: MIT Press.

Stoter, Michiel. 2009. 'Here Goes Nothing: How Control Vanished into Everywhere'. *Journal of Network Theory* 4 (1). http://www.networktheory.nl/2009/gardens-of-control/26/here-goes-nothing-%e2%80%93-how-control-vanished-into-everywhere.html.

Strate, Lance. 2004. 'A Media Ecology Review'. *Communication Research Trends* 23 (2): 23-28.

Strömbäck, Jesper. 2008. 'Four Phases of Mediatization: An Analysis of the Mediatization of Politics'. *The International Journal of Press/Politics* 13 (3): 228-246.

Suchman, Lucy. 1987. *Plans and Situated Actions: The Problem of Human-Machine Communication*. Cambridge university press.

Suchman, Lucy. 2006. *Human-Machine Reconfigurations: Plans and Situated Actions*. Cambridge: Cambridge University Press.

Surowiecki, James. 2004. *The Wisdom of Crowds: Why the Many Are Smarter Than the Few and How Collective Wisdom Shapes Business, Economies, Societies and Nations*. New York: Doubleday.

Taylor, Isaac. 2009 [1883]. *The Alphabet: An Account of the Origin and Development of Letters*. Charleston: BiblioBazaar.

Taylor, Mark C. 2001. *The Moment of Complexity: Emerging Network Culture*. Chicago: University of Chicago Press.

Terranova, Tiziana. 2000. 'Free Labor: Producing Culture for the Digital Economy'. *Social Text* 18 (2): 33-58.

Thelwall, Mike. 2006. 'Interpreting Social Science Link Analysis Research: A Theoretical Framework'. *Journal of the American Society for Information Science and Technology* 57 (1): 60-68.

Tholen, Georg Christoph. 2002. 'Media Metaphorology: Irritations in the Epistemic Field of Media Studies'. *The South Atlantic Quarterly* 101 (3): 659-673.

Thompson, John B. 1995. *The Media and Modernity: A Social Theory of the Media*. Cambridge: Polity Press.

Tilley, Christopher, Webb Keane, Susanne Kuechler, Mike Rowlands, and Patricia Spyer, ed. 2006. *Handbook of Material Culture*. London: Sage.

Tilley, Christopher. 1991. *Material Culture and Text*. London: Taylor & Francis.

Tilley, Christopher. 1999. *Metaphor and Material Culture*. Oxford: Blackwell Publishers.

Tilley, Christopher. 2002. 'Metaphor, Materiality and Interpretation'. In *The Material Culture Reader*, edited by Victor Buchli. Oxford: Berg Publishers.

Toffler, Alvin. 1980. *The Third Wave*. New York: Bantam Books.

Tönnies, Ferdinand. 1957 [1887]. *Community and Society*. East Lansing: Michigan State University Press.

Trend, David. 2001. *Reading Digital Culture*. Malden: Blackwell.

Tuin, Iris van der, and Rick Dolphijn. 2010. 'The Transversality of New Materialism'. *Women: A Cultural Review* 21 (2): 153-171.

Tuin, Iris van der. 2008. *Third Wave Materialism: New Feminist Epistemologies and the Generation of European Women's Studies*. Utrecht: PhD thesis Utrecht University.

Turing, Alan. 1936. 'On Computable Numbers, with an Application to the Entscheidungsproblem'. *Proceedings of the London Mathematical Society* 42: 230-265.

Turkle, Sherry. 1995. *Life on the Screen: Identity in the Age of the Internet*. New York: Simon & Schuster.

Turkle, Sherry. 1996. 'Virtuality and Its Discontents: Searching for Community in Cyberspace'. *The American Prospect* 24 (Winter): 50-57.

Turkle, Sherry. 2007. *Evocative Objects: Things We Think With*. Cambridge: MIT Press.

Uricchio, William. 2004. 'Historicizing Media in Transition'. In *Rethinking Media Change: The Aesthetics of Transition*, edited by David Thorburn and Henry Jenkins, 23-38. Cambridge: MIT Press.

Valenduc, Gérard, Patricia Vendramin, Caroline Guffens, Anna M. Ponzellini, Adele Lebano, Laurence d' Ouville, Isabelle Collet, Ina Wagner, Andrea Birbaumer, and Marianne Tolar. 2004. *Widening Women's Work in Information and Communication Technology*. Brussels: European Commission. http://www.ftu-namur.org/fichiers/D12-print.pdf.

Verhoeff, Nanna. 2012. *Mobile Screens: The Visual Regime of Navigation*. Amsterdam: Amsterdam University Press.

Vries, de, Imar. 2012. *Tantalisingly Close: An Archaeology of Communication Desires in Discourses of Mobile Wireless Media*. Amsterdam: Amsterdam University Press.

Warf, Barney, and Santa Arias, ed. 2008. *The Spatial Turn: Interdisciplinary Perspectives*. London: Routledge.

Wark, McKenzie. 2004. *A Hacker Manifesto*. Cambridge: Harvard University Press.

Weaver, Warren. 1955. 'The New Tower'. In *Machine Translation of Languages*, edited by William N. Locke and A. Donald Booth, v-vii. Cambridge: MIT Press.

Weele, van der, Cor, and Marianne van den Boomen. 2008. 'How to Do Things with Metaphor?' *Configurations* 16 (1): 1-10.

Weiser, Mark. 1991. 'The Computer for the 21st Century'. *Scientific American* 265 (3): 94-104.

Weiss, Aaron. 2006. 'Net Neutrality? There's Nothing Neutral About It'. *netWorker* 10 (2): 18-25.

Wellman, Barry, and Alexandra Marin. 2011. 'Social Network Analysis: An Introduction'. In *The Sage Handbook of Social Network Analysis*, edited by Peter Carrington and John Scott, 11-25. London: Sage.

Wellman, Barry, and Milena Gulia. 1999. 'Net Surfers Don't Ride Alone: Virtual Communities as Communities'. In *Communities in Cyberspace*, edited by Marc A. Smith and Peter Kollock, 167-194. London: Routledge.

Wellman, Barry. 2001. 'Physical Place and Cyberplace: The Rise of Personalized Networking'. *Journal of Urban and Regional Research* 25 (2): 227-252.

Wetering, van de, Tom. 2011. *This Extends ExpressionEngine: Hoe een alledaags script uitgroeide tot een complexe software-industrie*. Utrecht: Master thesis Universiteit Utrecht.

Whitelaw, Mitchell. 2008. 'Notes on Transmateriality'. *The Teeming Void*. http://teemingvoid.blogspot.com/2008/03/notes-on-transmateriality.html.

Wiener, Norbert. 1988 [1954]. *Human Use of Human Beings: Cybernetics and Society*. Cambridge: Da Capo Press.

Wilde, Rein de. 2000. *De voorspellers: Een kritiek op de toekomstindustrie*. Amsterdam: De Balie.

Winograd, Terry, and Fernando Flores, ed. 1985. *Understanding Computers and Cognition*. Norwood: Ablex.

Wolfram, Stephen. 2002. *A New Kind of Science*. Champaign: Wolfram Media.

Woolgar, Steve, and Bruno Latour. 1979. *Laboratory Life: The Social Construction of Scientific Facts*. London: Sage.

Wormeli, Rick. 2009. *Metaphors & Analogies: Power Tools for Teaching Any Subject*. Portland: Stenhouse.

Wyatt, Sally. 2004. 'Danger! Metaphors at Work in Economics, Geophysiology, and the Internet'. *Science Technology Human Values* 29 (2): 242-261.

Wynn, Eleanor, and James E. Katz. 1997. 'Hyperbole over Cyberspace: Self-Presentation and Social Boundaries in Internet Home Pages and Discourse'. *The Information Society* 13 (4): 297-327.

Zhuo, Xiaolin, Barry Wellman, and Justine Yu. 2011. 'Egypt: The First Internet Revolt?' *Peace Magazine* 27 (3): 6-10.

Zinken, Jörg, Iina Hellsten, and Brigitte Nerlich. 2003. 'What Is Cultural about Conceptual Metaphors?' *International Journal of Communication* 13 (1-2).

Zinken, Jörg, Iina Hellsten, and Brigitte Nerlich. 2008. 'Discourse Metaphors'. In *Body, Language and Mind: Sociocultural Situatedness*, 363-86. Berlin: Mouton de Gruyter.

Žižek , Slavoj. 1989. *The Sublime Object of Ideology*. New York: Verso.

Žižek , Slavoj. 2001. 'From Virtual Reality to the Virtualization of Reality'. In *Reading Digital Culture*, edited by David Trend, 17-22. Malden: Blackwell.

Žižek , Slavoj. 2003. *Organs without Bodies: Deleuze and Consequences*. New York: Routledge.

SAMENVATTING

INLEIDING: METAFOOR, BETEKENIS EN CODE

Het gebruik van digitale en genetwerkte media is tegenwoordig onderdeel van het dagelijkse bestaan. We mailen, we chatten, we zoeken, we voegen vrienden toe aan ons sociale netwerk, we zetten fotoalbums online – allemaal gewone, vanzelfsprekende gewone handelingen. We realiseren ons echter nauwelijks dat deze benamingen stuk voor stuk metaforische concepten zijn, dat wil zeggen, termen ontleend aan andere domeinen dan het domein van digitale code. Metaforen zijn hier noodzakelijk aangezien wij mensen geen directe toegang hebben tot het digitale als zodanig, dat immers bestaat uit binaire getallen die alleen voor machines leesbaar zijn. Alleen een vertaling in metaforen, in digitaal-symbolische objecten, maakt dit domein leesbaar en hanteerbaar voor ons.

Dit roept urgente vragen op over hoe deze vertaling tussen digitale code en culturele code plaatsvindt, welke metaforen daarvoor worden ingezet en hoe dit niet alleen ons computergebruik maar ook bredere maatschappelijke vertogen rond ICT en digitalisering vormgeeft.

In deze studie zal ik deze vertaalslagen analyseren met behulp van Lev Manovich' concept 'transcoderen' (de vertaalslag van het digitale naar het culturele) en het actor-netwerktheoretische concept 'translatie' (vertaalslag tussen heterogene actoren).

Digitale praxis, oftewel de omgang met digitaal-symbolische entiteiten, stelt ons voor een onto-epistemologisch raadsel: deze entiteiten zijn noch puur objecten, noch puur symbolische vormen, noch puur digitale patronen. Het zijn hybriden van berekeningen, algoritmen en taal die door machines en mensen verwerkt worden. Hoe komen zulke samenstellingen van rekenen en taal, van algoritmen en vertogen, van computercode en culturele codes tot stand? En hoe faciliteren (of blokkeren) specifieke metaforen deze processen?

Metaforen behoren traditioneel tot het domein van de retorica, taalkunde en literatuurwetenschap. Primair worden ze bestudeerd als dragers van betekenis, niet als materiële vertalingen die ingebed zijn in een breder materieel netwerk, en al helemaal niet als digitaal-materiële transcoderingen. Aangezien deze studie zich begeeft op het weinig verkende gebied tussen *new media studies*, metafoor-analyse en actor-netwerk theorie, is de ontwikkelde methodologie noodzakelijk eclectisch, en soms wel en soms niet trouw aan de uitgangspunten van deze drie academische velden.

Het best is de methodologie te omschrijven als materiële semiotiek. Daartoe put ik uit het vocabulaire van de pragmatische semiotiek van Charles Sanders Peirce – in het bijzonder zijn notie van indexicaliteit – en uit het vocabulaire van Katherine Hayles, in het bijzonder haar concept van de materiële metafoor. Met behulp van deze begrippen kunnen semiotische vertaalslagen gevolgd worden die verder reiken dan het domein van de taal en de representaties, opdat zichtbaar wordt wat zij materieel bewerkstelligen en ordenen.

Concreet gaat het in deze studie om de volgende onderzoeksvragen:
1. Welke digitaal-materiële transcoderingen en materieel-semiotische translaties zijn te traceren als we het spoor volgen van metaforen als actoren?
2. Op welke wijze worden zulke transcoderingen en translaties gefixeerd en genaturaliseerd tot stabiele en vanzelfsprekende entiteiten?

3. Welke verdere translaties worden in gang gezet door de vigerende metaforen: welke ideologieën, verhalen en vertogen worden mogelijk gemaakt en bestendigd, welke worden uitgesloten of onderdrukt?
Het corpus van metaforen is in deze studie beperkt tot de meest gebruikelijke en gebruikte metaforen op het gebied van nieuwe media, zoals dat te onderscheiden is in enerzijds de dagelijkse gebruikerspraktijk en anderzijds het academische vertoog over nieuwe media.

HOOFDSTUK 1: INDEXICALE ICONEN ALS INTERFACE
Hoe onze mailbox ons kan misleiden

Omgaan met een computer vinden we over het algemeen gemakkelijk en vanzelfsprekend. Maar wat gebeurt er nu eigenlijk als we dat doen? Dit hoofdstuk laat zien hoe het beeldscherm en alle behulpzame iconen daarop ons niet alleen helpen maar ook misleiden, omdat ze onzichtbaar maken hoe de machinerie van hardware en software werkt.

Beeldschermen zijn interfaces, grensovergangen waar het verkeer tussen twee systemen plaatsvindt, in dit geval tussen mensen en computers. Computers zijn speciale machines. Ze produceren niet simpelweg output in de vorm van een product, zoals een koffieautomaat of een pianola, ze leveren tevens het gereedschap om output te creëren, te modificeren, en om geheel andere producten te maken (alsof de pianola film gaat vertonen). Computerproducten kunnen bovendien bestaan uit gereedschap (softwareprogramma's) waarmee nieuwe producten, gereedschappen en machines te maken zijn. Die producten, gereedschappen en machineprocessen bestaan in laatste instantie allemaal uit digitale code, nullen en enen. Alleen via de visuele interface verschijnt die code afgebakend, gedifferentieerd in hanteerbare producten en gereedschap. Digitale code is daar vertaald in metaforische iconen, commando's en menuopties. Maar zoals alle metaforen geven ze een beperkt beeld van de toegang en mogelijke omgang met de computer. Het beeldscherm zelf, een visueel beeld ontleend aan de wereld van de film, is de dominante metafoor voor zowel computergebruik als de computercultuur in bredere zin. Zowel in materiële als in metaforische zin slokt het beeldscherm alle andere elementen van de gebruikersinterface in zich op: toetsenbord en muis – werktuigen voor menselijk handelingsvermogen – verdwijnen letterlijk en figuurlijk uit het zicht.

Ook het werk dat binnen in de computer plaatsvindt wordt onzichtbaar gemaakt, en wel door de aard van de iconen op het scherm. De mailboxicoon suggereert bijvoorbeeld een onmiddellijke toegang tot de mail, en doet ons vergeten dat een klik erop in feite een complex machineproces in werking zet, dat pas na een keten van machine- en netwerkhandelingen resulteert in het binnenkomen van mail in de inbox. Dat is precies de functie van computericonen: in naam van gebruikersvriendelijkheid vertalen ze complexe processen in een enkelvoudig beeld van een ding (mailbox) of plaats (inbox). Met andere woorden: ze verdichten tot wat we kunnen noemen icoon-ontologie, *icontology,* waarin geldt: beeld = ding = resultaat.

Om de werking van computericonen beter te begrijpen is het semiotische vocabulaire van C.S. Peirce verhelderend. Hij onderscheidt drie soorten tekens op basis van hun relatie tot hun object: iconen, op basis van gelijkenis; indexen, op basis van een causale relatie of fysieke nabijheid; en symbolen, die een arbitraire relatie hebben met dat waar ze naar verwijzen. Volgens deze indeling is een computericoon als de mailbox zowel iconisch (metaforische gelijkenis met gewone post in de brievenbus) als indexicaal (verwijzend naar de causale keten die in werking moet worden gezet om de mail op te halen en te kunnen lezen). Maar de indexicale werking wordt overschaduwd door de icontologie. Dat is niet onschuldig: voor zover machineprocessen een *black box* blijven zijn we er aan overgeleverd, en worden we afhankelijk van mensen die ze wel begrijpen, of denken te begrijpen.

De dominante metafoortheorie van het moment – de conceptuele theorie van Lakoff en Johnson – is slechts beperkt bruikbaar om computericonen en andere digitale metaforische objecten te kunnen analyseren, omdat zij alleen aandacht heeft voor de overdracht van het ene conceptuele domein naar het andere en niet voor de overdracht van conceptuele naar materiële domeinen en terug. Om aan de indexicale werking van digitale metaforen recht te doen hebben we een meer materialistische metafoortheorie nodig.

HOOFDSTUK 2: MATERIËLE METAFOREN
Hoe objecten sociale orde creëren

De materialiteit van digitale entiteiten is te lokaliseren op verschillende niveaus. Ten eerste is er de medium-specifieke materialiteit van het *teken*, los van waar dat naar verwijst (de verschillende materialiteiten van woorden, afbeeldingen, geluid, beweging); ten tweede is er de indexicale materialiteit van het *werktuig* (refererend aan de materiële werkzaamheid van software-instructies); en ten derde is er de ingebouwde symbolische materialiteit van het *metaforische object* (de verdichting tot een gecomprimeerd teken-werktuig-object dat de andere materialiteiten in zich bergt en er een specifieke niet-arbitraire vorm aan geeft).

Katherine Hayles gebruikt het begrip materiële metafoor in haar medium-specifieke analyses van digitaal-literaire werken en andere *computer art*-installaties. Bij materiële metaforen, stelt ze, is het associatieverkeer niet beperkt tot woorden of symbolen, maar vindt er vooral verkeer plaats tussen woorden of symbolen en fysieke artefacten. Materiële metaforen zijn actieve mediators die mediëren tussen woorden en een specifieke selectie uit de fysieke materiële wereld.

Digitale materiële metaforen importeren beelden en handelingen uit tal van domeinen: andere media (webpagina's, Word-documenten, afspelen, beantwoorden, verzenden); architectuur (home, window, exit); dagelijkse objecten (menu, knop, map); beroepen of rollen (server, client, host); of publieke ruimten (forum, community). Zulke metaforen vergemakkelijken het gebruik van digitale objecten maar hun icontologie kan zowel de metafoor als het object aan het zicht onttrekken. Vaak zien we immers wel een object (een blog, mail, zoekmachine), maar niet de metaforen die het mede zijn specifieke vorm geven; of we zien wel de metafoor (browsen, portal, community) maar niet de objecteigenschappen die de metafoor schragen.

In de antropologie werd het begrip materiële metafoor gemunt om het te kunnen hebben over objecten die gelijktijdig als symbool en als handelingsvoorwerp functioneren (bijvoorbeeld een kookpot die een jonge man voorstelt). Bij materiële metaforen zijn de symbolische en praktische werking onlosmakelijk met elkaar verbonden (zo mag bijvoorbeeld een maagd niet met zo'n kookpot koken). Zo'n object belichaamt sociale relaties en organiseert ze. De betekenis van zo'n materiële metafoor is niet te achterhalen middels een algemene conceptuele metafoor-analyse maar alleen door het praktische gebruik te observeren.

Veel objecten in moderne praktijken bevatten een handelingsscript, zoals deuren (ga hier naar binnen/buiten) of roze scheerapparaten met weinig knopjes (gebruik dit als je vrouw bent). Zulke objecten zijn materiële metaforen wanneer ze beelden van elders importeren (bijvoorbeeld een voorstelling van 'vrouw') en deze exporteren en inbouwen in een specifiek ontwerp dat subjectposities toewijst (een cosmetisch apparaat met weinig knopjes adresseert vrouwen als technofobe wezens).

Digitale objecten zijn per definitie materiële metaforen; hun werktuigelijkheid toont zich pas in de metaforische uitsnede. Maar waar de antropologie objecten (zoals de kookpot) als *ook* metaforisch kon identificeren, geldt voor digitale objecten dat het primair metaforen zijn, die *ook* een materiële vorm hebben gekregen.

Door digitale objecten als materiële metaforen te analyseren wordt het mogelijk bloot te leggen welke ideeën, ideologie en interpellaties erin zijn ingebakken en hoe die mee vorm geven aan de sociale praktijken die digitale objecten op hun beurt mogelijk maken. Het begrip 'materiële metafoor' is dan ook een heuristisch instrument om de black box van computers, netwerken en digitale code open te maken. Of, anders gezegd, het valt te gebruiken om deze black boxen epistemologisch te hacken.

HOOFDSTUK 3: MEDIATIE DOOR METONYMIE EN METAFOOR
Hoe media zich vermenigvuldigen en oplossen

Medium-specifieke analyse veronderstelt dat we op voorhand weten wat een medium is, maar elke bepaling daarvan blijkt doordrenkt met metaforen en metonymieën. Dit hoofdstuk behandelt vigerende mediametonymieën en -metaforen en beoordeelt ze op hun vermogen om de materialiteit van media te conceptualiseren. Tevens worden ze onderzocht op hun eventuele werking als vertoogmetaforen. Vertoogmetaforen organiseren gedeelde verhalen die de vorm kunnen aannemen van publieke opinie, politiek agenda's, onderzoeksprogramma's of wereldbeelden. Ze verbinden een min of meer coherent cluster van conceptuele metaforen, aannames en legitimaties tot een discursieve formatie die bestaat uit, in de woorden van Foucault, 'monument/documenten' die gedrag, principes en beleid aansturen en subjectposities genereren.

Als we een lijst maken van gebruikelijke definities van wat een medium *is* komen we tot acht metonymieën, die telkens een deel belichten: media als drager of opslagcontainer, als productie-apparaat, als reproductieapparaat, als distributiesysteem, als format of genre, als waarnemings-modaliteit, als sociale setting, en als taal. Zo'n lijst maakt duidelijk dat het concept medium in elke context anders kan worden uitgesneden en voortdurend wordt uitgebreid met nieuwe kwalificaties zo gauw er een nieuw medium wordt gesignaleerd. Maar een alomvattende definitie van wat een medium is, is er niet uit te halen.

Een andere benadering bestaat eruit te kijken naar wat media worden verondersteld te *doen*. Drie functies kunnen daarbij worden onderscheiden: verwerking, transmissie en opslag. Iedere functie kent verschillende conceptuele metaforen, die soms ook werken als vertoogmetaforen. *Verwerkingsmetaforen* typeren media als membraan, als heerser, als ruimte, of als ecologie. Al deze conceptuele metaforen fungeren tevens als vertoogmetaforen voor onderzoeksagenda's, en sommige ook als materiële metaforen die worden ingebouwd in technologische innovaties. De membraanmetafoor bijvoorbeeld, die ervan uitgaat dat media een dun doorlaatbaar vlies vormen tussen ons en de wereld, vindt zijn vertaling in technologiewedloop naar steeds dunnere beeldschermen, met als ultieme innovatie schermloze projectie. De heersermetafoor leidde in mediastudies tot zowel botte veroordelingen van mediamacht als tot genuanceerd onderzoek naar mediatisering, machtsrelaties, medialogica en onzichtbare politiek.

Transmissiemetaforen nemen de vorm aan van media als kanaal, als geleiding, en als gereedschapscreatie. In Shannon's (1948) ingenieursversie van de kanaalmetafoor is het kanaal duidelijk een materieel gegeven, maar de vertalingen naar een algemener zender-ontvanger-model maakten daar al gauw een immateriële geleiding van waarin het medium oplost in onzichtbaarheid. Media verschijnen dan als magische overbrengers van ongeschonden boodschappen van mensenhoofd naar mensenhoofd. Het gereedschapsmakersparadigma van Reddy (1993) stelt daar tegenover dat het overbrengen van boodschappen per definitie transformatie en vertalings-processen impliceren, juist omdat zender en ontvangers in verschillende materiële omstandig-heden leven. Maar deze metafoor fungeert nergens als vertoogmetafoor of materiële metafoor.

Opslagmetaforen ten slotte kennen twee varianten: media als container en de inscriptiemetafoor. De containermetafoor is de meest gebruikte, in combinatie met media-inhoud die ergens in kan worden bewaard, als in een doos. De metafoor suggereert stabiliteit, orde en houdbaarheid, en fungeert zowel als vertoogmetafoor in mediaonderzoek alsmede als productieve materiële me-tafoor voor businessmodellen voor dataopslag in de 'cloud'. Materieel als dit businessmodel is, de metafoor van de cloud miskent alle materialiteit door haar te versluieren achter een luchtige onschuldige wolk.

Inscriptiemetaforen van opslag vormen het tegendeel van containermetaforen. Opslag gaat hier niet in een doos, maar wordt ingekerfd in materie, en is daardoor ook niet stabiel en bestendig. De inscriptiemetafoor omvat bovendien niet alleen opslag maar ook bewerking en overdacht. Als vertoogmetafoor mobiliseert zij interessant mediafilosofisch onderzoek, maar voor populair gebruik of businessmodellen is zij te complex.

Zonder metonymieën en metaforen kunnen we niet duidelijk maken wat media zijn. Mediameta-foren zijn krachtig. Als vertoogmetaforen mobiliseren ze specifieke verhalen, vertogen en prak-tijken. Als materiële metaforen organiseren ze technische innovatie, businessmodellen en pro-fessionele praktijken. Alle vigerende en dominante metaforen vertekenen echter naar dezelfde richting: ze neigen ernaar materiële processen en eigenschappen in de werking van de media uit te wissen. Hoe meer media we hebben, hoe meer metaforen ontstaan waarin de media zelf oplossen en verdwijnen. Het ultieme medium is onzichtbaar.

HOOFDSTUK 4: ONMIDDELLIJKHEID VIA METAFOREN
Hoe mediatie onzichtbaar wordt gemaakt

Materiële metaforen benadrukken niet per definitie hun eigen materialiteit. Ze kunnen zelfs de ideologie van de immateriële onmiddellijkheid belichamen door de bereikbaarheid van een onver-vulbaar verlangen te suggereren. In de materiële metaforen die deze ervaring van onmiddellijk-heid beschrijven en materialiseren lijkt het complexe conglomeraat van teken-gereedschap-ob-ject weer op te lossen en te verdwijnen. Neem bijvoorbeeld wederom de cloudmetafoor. Waar de bewerkelijkheid en het gereedschapskarakter van digitale objecten zich duidelijk voordoet aan de pc-gebruiker die frequent software patcht en bestanden synchroniseert op verschillende appa-raten, neemt de wolk deze processen in zich op. Updates en synchronisaties vinden automatisch plaats; alle onderhoudsarbeid aan software en hardware is aan het oog onttrokken. Daarmee poogt de metafoor de paradox op te lossen tussen de belofte van ongemedieerde ervaring en het werk dat nodig is om deze ervaring te produceren.

Er zijn twee materiële metaforen die het verlangen naar onmiddellijkheid al lang voor de komst van nieuwe media belichaamden: het venster en de spiegel, verbonden aan de visuele erva-ring van transparantie dan wel reflectie. Het venster (window) is door Apple en later Microsoft neergezet als vanzelfsprekende standaard voor de gebruikersinterface en nog steeds verschij-nen nieuwe media als een aaneenschakeling van vensters en als vensters in vensters. Naast de belofte van het erdoorheen kijken is er ook de materialiteit van een venster, die een afgebakende opening in een starre architectuur laat zien. Daarmee wordt de windowsmetafoor er een van framing en beperking in plaats van doorzichtig uitzicht.

De andere grote metafoor, de spiegel, heeft het potentieel om letterlijk en figuurlijk te reflecteren op de gebruiker, haar handelingen en omgeving. Maar in het inmiddels klassieke mediatheoretische concept *remediatie* van Bolter en Grusin fungeren het venster en de spiegel slechts als twee visuele interface-opties: of we kijken *door* de interface (venster) of we kijken *er tegen aan* (spiegel). Die metaforen corresponderen met de theoretische begrippen *immediacy* (venster op de wereld, er doorheen kijken, geen medium zien) en *hypermediacy* (spiegel van andere media, er tegenaan kijken, het medium waarnemen). Deze twee mechanismen, zo stellen Bolter en Grusin, wisselen elkaar voortdurend af in alle media en worden in nieuwe media steeds gereproduceerd. Noch het venster noch de spiegel worden ingezet om *in* of *achter* het medium te kijken; transparantie en reflectie creëren slechts een zichzelf reproducerend spiegelpaleis.

Om de rol van dit soort materiële en vertoogmetaforen te kunnen verklaren dient het concept van remediatie aangepast te worden. Remediatie is geen gesloten proces, maar gaat altijd gepaard met zijn schaduw, *demediatie:* het uitvlakken van mediatieprocessen en metaforen. Maar vooral is remediatie niet het gevolg van bestaande media die elkaar weerspiegelen; remediatie genereert nieuwe media, met name in digitale vorm. Remediatie is beter te zien als transmediatie, aangezien media ook buiten het mediavaatje tappen om zichzelf te vernieuwen. Transmediatie creëert media door fenomenen die voorheen niet als medium functioneerden in digitale objecten te vertalen, zoals bureaubladen, boodschappenlijstjes en spelletjes, maar ook sociale praktijken als gemeenschapsvorming, seks of vriendschap.

HOOFDSTUK 5: DE REGELS VAN DE CODE
Hoe software metaforiseert

Software, als een van de basiskenmerken van digitale media, is eveneens onderhevig aan paradoxen van transparantie en zichtbaarheid, vanzelfsprekendheid en raadselachtigheid, materialiteit en immaterialiteit. Software verschijnt voor gebruikers als gereedschap maar ook als black box en verdwijnpunt, terwijl het voor softwareproducenten verschijnt als verhandelbaar object.

De geschiedenis van programmeerbare rekenmachines laat zien hoe politiek-historische verschuivingen leiden tot wat software nu is. De eerste programmeerbare machines kenden geen aparte softwareprogramma's. De machines werden aangestuurd door meestal vrouwelijke professionals genaamd 'computers' die de hardware en switches omzetten om een bepaalde taak te laten uitoefenen. Software is dan nog menselijke arbeid, vrouwenarbeid. Dat verandert als die arbeid gedelegeerd blijkt te kunnen worden aan dezelfde machine door de instructies voor hardwareomzetting van te voren uit te schrijven, en ze in te voeren in de machine die ze vervolgens uitvoert. Programmeren verschuift van hardware manipuleren naar software schrijven. Software als taal is een materiële metafoor die nieuwe arbeidsdelingen, subjectposities en objecten in het leven roept: programmeurs en gebruikers, schrijvers en lezers, softwarepakketten, besturingssystemen, en grafische interfaces.

De software-als-taal metafoor blijft echter ambivalent. Anders dan taal is software niet arbitrair en genereert het manipuleerbare objecten die werkelijk iets doen in de wereld. Bovendien bestaat software als taal uit een toren van Babel van verschillende vertaalslagen en lagen. De laagste laag zit het dichtst op de machine en bestaat uit patronen van nullen en enen die corresponderen met lage en hogere voltagewaarden in elektronische schakelingen. Deze laag tolereert weinig tot geen ambiguïteit, anders dan de bovenliggende lagen van machinetaal en programmeurstalen, uitmondend in de hoogste laag van de symbolisch-metaforische gebruikersinterface, met oplopende tolerantie voor semiotische ambivalentie en spraakverwarring.

Daarmee is ook gegeven dat het digitale noodzakelijkerwijs verpakt is in analoge lagen; analoog niet alleen in de betekenis van proportioneel equivalent of als continuüm aan waarden, maar ook als semiotische analogie en metafoor.

Software is niet te vatten zonder metaforen, maar welke metafoor wordt ingezet is niet neutraal. Wie software ziet als strikt determinerend voorschrift heeft weliswaar oog voor de materiële basis maar kan niet de inherente modificeerbaarheid van software verklaren of tegenhouden. Dat kan ook grote politiek-juridische gevolgen hebben als softwaremetaforen worden ingezet als vertoogmetaforen. De strijd tussen open-source software en closed-source software is in feite een strijd tussen software-als-taal (publiek bezit, te gebruiken en te veranderen door eenieder) en software-als-ding (als onvervreemdbaar bezit, beschermd door patenten en intellectuele eigendom).

De eigenaardige zich als immaterieel voordoende materialiteit van software genereert verschillende materiële metaforen, en dus verschillende software, verdienmodellen en softwarepolitiek. Maar bovenal is software zelf de ultieme belichaming van een materiële metafoor die symbolische betekenis verbindt met daadwerkelijke ingrepen in de fysieke en sociale wereld.

HOOFDSTUK 6: DE TRANSCODERING VAN SOCIALE NETWERKEN
Hoe het digitale gesocialiseerd raakt

Vanaf de allereerste computernetwerken is er gesignaleerd dat er sociale aggregaties ontstaan door computergemedieerde communicatie. Om dat te omschrijven zijn er historisch verschillende metaforen ingezet. In de begintijd van het toen nog tekstuele Internet was dat de metafoor van de virtuele gemeenschap, ontleend aan het beeld van een besloten dorp. Die metafoor functioneerde als metaforisch concept om te benadrukken dat computers meer waren dan kille rekenmachines, en als vertoogmetafoor in een publiek en academisch debat over het internet als redmiddel voor de moderne teloorgang van sociale cohesie en gemeenschapsbanden. Ook was dat als materiële metafoor ingebouwd in de software die het collectief weergaf als een ruimte, een tekstpagina waarop de communicatie tussen de leden bij elkaar gehouden werd.

Dat veranderde met de opkomst van de Web 2.0 metafoor, die eveneens zowel een vertoog als relatief nieuwe materiële softwarepraktijken initieerde. Web 2.0 refereert primair aan software als pakket met een fundamentele update (met name de koppeling van het web met databases), inclusief de nieuwe verdienmodellen die dat oplevert. Niettemin werd het een metafoor voor nieuwe vormen van online sociabiliteit, een gedistribueerde participatiecultuur gebaseerd op *sharing*, *linking*, en *liking*. Connectiviteit komt in de plaats van collectiviteit, datafragmenten in de plaats van ruimtelijke stabiele pagina's, sociale netwerken met het individu als centrum in de plaats van virtuele gemeenschappen met de groep als centrum.

Ook de metaforisering van het concept netwerk c.q. het internet veranderde. Waar voorheen conceptuele en vertoogmetaforen gebaseerd op infrastructuur (de elektronische snelweg) dan wel gebaseerd op organische zelforganisatie (cyberspace) de overhand hadden, werd, naarmate internetgebruik inburgerde, de notie van netwerk steeds alomvattender. In alles was een netwerkpatroon te ontwaren: het internet als netwerk van servers, routers en gateways, of als een netwerk van commerciële providers, of als een netwerk van websites verbonden door hyperlinks.

Offline gemeenschappen waren te zien als netwerken van persoonlijke sociale netwerken, en ook online gemeenschappen veranderden softwarematig in sociale netwerksites, een zeer lucratieve materiële metafoor zoals blijkt uit het succes van MySpace en later Facebook.

Het netwerk als *graph*, oorspronkelijk een wiskundige abstractie om mogelijke patronen van een set elementen en hun onderlinge links te berekenen, is toegeëigend door onderzoeksgebieden variërend van scheikunde, biologie en topologie tot linguïstiek, sociologie en economie. In het vertoog van wat intussen heet *network science* en *social network analysis* is elk fenomeen dat kan worden ontleed in termen van knopen *(nodes)* en één welgedefinieerde relatie een netwerk, in de regel weergegeven als een *diagram,* een kaart van punten en lijnen, die in een oogopslag clusters, hubs en marginale nodes tonen. Een kaart is niet het gebied, maar in combinatie met computerhulpmiddelen als databases, big data analyse en datavisualisering, is het netwerkdiagram een krachtige materiële metafoor geworden die op veel plekken kan worden waargemaakt, berekend en gevisualiseerd.

CONCLUSIE: EEN MANIFEST VOOR HET HACKEN VAN METAFOREN
Hoe metaforen ertoe doen in digitale praktijken

In deze studie heb ik metaforen getraceerd om na te gaan hoe ze vorm helpen geven aan digitale praktijken. Het ging me erom transcoderingen en vertalingen zichtbaar te maken, na te gaan wat zij vanzelfsprekend doen lijken en welke ideologieën ze versterken dan wel verzwakken. Ik wil eindigen met een manifest: een tekst die weliswaar academisch en theoretisch is, maar ook mobiliserend. Een manifest voor het hacken van metaforen.

Wat metaforen niet zijn.
Metaforen verplaatsen geen betekenissen (ze genereren betekenissen). Metaforen zijn niet figuurlijk (ze mobiliseren ervaringen, hebben letterlijke effecten). Metaforen zijn niet neutraal (ze verbinden, verdelen, relateren, simplificeren). Metaforen zijn niet louter een kwestie van taal en denken (ze zitten ook vervat in technieken en objecten).

Traceer digitale materiële metaforen.
De dominante metafoortheorie leert dat conceptuele metaforen vorm geven aan de manier waarop we denken en spreken, maar gaat voorbij aan de materiële productiviteit van metaforen, cruciaal voor digitale handelingspraktijken.

Materiële metaforen bemiddelen tussen concepten en materiële praktijken. Ze maken sommige dingen en gebeurtenissen mogelijk en andere onmogelijk. Dat geldt ook voor digitale materiële metaforen: interfacemetaforen (pagina, windows, hyperlinks) en vertoogmetaforen die discursieve formaties organiseren (elektronische snelweg, cyberspace). Materiële metaforen hebben politieke effecten en genereren subjectposities.

Metaforen vertalen de ene code in de andere (talig, cultureel, analoog, digitaal). Een metaforische verplaatsing = vertaling + verandering + schepping. Metaforen halen stukjes en beetjes werkelijkheid uit elkaar en plakken die elders, anders, weer vast. Knip, kopieer, plak, meng.

Metaforen zijn als de sleutel van de black box van machinerie en software. Ze maken het mogelijk om zaken af te sluiten maar ook om de doos open te maken en te onthullen wat erin zit. Een materiële metafoor is een epistemologisch instrument dat het mogelijk maakt om digitale code te hacken. Materiële metaforen analyseren is *reverse engineering*.

Daarbij komt het aan op het volgen van de sporen: het spoor van de iconen en wat ze vergroten, verkleinen en verbergen (welke gevolgen heeft dat voor de macht, onmacht en subjectposities van gebruikers?); het spoor van de softwarecoderingen en wat ze doen en laten (welke gebruikerstaken zitten er aan vast, welke verborgen praktijken?); het spoor van de verbindingen met vertogen, ideologieën en privileges (hoe wordt dat gereguleerd en in stand gehouden? wat valt hier te ontregelen?).

Hack digitale vanzelfsprekendheden.
Hack de ogenschijnlijke doorzichtigheid van de schermmetafoor. Schermen verdringen andere interfaces en suggereren dat alles draait om wat je ziet.
Hack het idee dat enkel media mediëren, of dat enkel nieuwe media dat doen. Er zijn veel meer mediaties en transmediaties in het spel.
Hack nieuwe media, breek er doorheen, treed buiten het mediavertoog. Computers veranderen en vertalen ook sociale en materiële praktijken die niet als medium worden gezien.
Hack remediaties, want computers remediëren weliswaar andere media (drukwerk, film, televisie, theater) maar ze vertalen en transformeren ook gewoonten, handelingen en verlangens die media te buiten gaan.

Hack software en netwerkideologieën.
Software lijkt een taal, maar het is ook een ideologie ingeschreven in apparaten.
Hack de veronderstelde digitale immaterialiteit. Het gaat bij digitale materiële metaforen niet alleen om immateriële code maar om hun materiële productie.
Hack de dichotomie tussen digitaal en analoog. Digitale objecten zijn samengesteld uit digitale en analoge componenten in een keten van vertalingen.
Hack netwerkmetaforen. Netwerken nemen verschillende vormen aan, die telkens iets anders impliceren voor de werkelijkheid van het internet.
Hack de graph – die, hoe mooi en driedimensionaal ook, suggereert dat de kaart staat voor wat hij representeert.
Hack metaforen van sociale binding – zowel collectiviteit als connectiviteit zijn zelden eenduidig, maar wel altijd normatief.
Hack sociale media, die sociabiliteit en media benadrukken en materialiteit en mediaties verbergen.
Hack de cloud – die het beeld oproept van een wolkig systeem zonder eigenaren, onderhouden door engelen. De cloud is nog moeilijker te hacken dan zwarte dozen – een uitdaging voor de omgekeerde ingenieurs van nieuwe media.

(Met dank aan Joke Hermes, Ann-Sophie Lehmann, Annemarie Mol, Ben Smit, Garjan Sterk, en Cor van der Weele.)

CURRICULUM VITAE

Marianne van den Boomen studied psychology in Utrecht and political sciences in Amsterdam. For twenty years she has worked as editor, journalist, and web designer; from 1990 to 2000 mainly for the weekly opinion magazine De Groene Amsterdammer. She was involved in the development of the early Dutch Digital City (1994), and published several articles and books on internet culture including *Internet ABC voor vrouwen* (1995) and *Leven op het Net: De sociale betekenis van virtuele gemeenschappen* (2000). Since 2003 she works as a lecturer-researcher at the Department of Media and Culture Studies (Utrecht University), where she teaches BA and MA courses in the program New Media and Digital Culture.